Gender and Seriality

Screen Serialities

Series editors: Claire Perkins and Constantine Verevis

Series advisory board: Kim Akass, Glen Creeber, Shane Denson, Jennifer Forrest, Jonathan Gray, Julie Grossman, Daniel Herbert, Carolyn Jess-Cooke, Frank Kelleter, Amanda Ann Klein, Kathleen Loock, Jason Mittell, Sean O'Sullivan, Barton Palmer, Alisa Perren, Dana Polan, Iain Robert Smith, Shannon Wells-Lassagne, Linda Williams

Screen Serialities provides a forum for introducing, analysing and theorising a broad spectrum of serial screen formats – including franchises, series, serials, sequels and remakes.

Over and above individual texts that happen to be serialised, the book series takes a guiding focus on seriality as an aesthetic and industrial principle that has shaped the narrative logic, socio-cultural function and economic identity of screen texts across more than a century of cinema, television and 'new' media.

Titles in this series include:

Film Reboots
Edited by Daniel Herbert and Constantine Verevis

Reanimated: The Contemporary American Horror Remake
By Laura Mee

Gender and Seriality: Practices and Politics of Contemporary US Television
By Maria Sulimma

Gender and Seriality

Practices and Politics of Contemporary
US Television

Maria Sulimma

Edinburgh University Press is one of the leading university presses in the UK. We publish academic books and journals in our selected subject areas across the humanities and social sciences, combining cutting-edge scholarship with high editorial and production values to produce academic works of lasting importance. For more information visit our website: edinburghuniversitypress.com

© Maria Sulimma, 2020, 2022

Edinburgh University Press Ltd
The Tun – Holyrood Road, 12(2f) Jackson's Entry, Edinburgh EH8 8PJ

First published in hardback by Edinburgh University Press 2020

Typeset in 11/13 Ehrhardt MT by
IDSUK (DataConnection) Ltd

A CIP record for this book is available from the British Library

ISBN 978 1 4744 7395 8 (hardback)
ISBN 978 1 4744 7396 5 (paperback)
ISBN 978 1 4744 7396 5 (webready PDF)
ISBN 978 1 4744 7398 9 (epub)

The right of Maria Sulimma to be identified as the author of this work has been asserted in accordance with the Copyright, Designs and Patents Act 1988, and the Copyright and Related Rights Regulations 2003 (SI No. 2498).

Contents

List of Figures vi
Acknowledgements ix
    Introduction: Serial Genders, Gendered Serialities 1

Part I Serial TV Criticism and *Girls*

1 The Thinkpiece Seriality of *Girls* 25
2 Carousel: Gendering through Controversy 47
3 Navigating Discourses of Universality and Specificity: The (Feminist) Voice of a Generation? 68

Part II Television Audience Engagement and *How to Get Away with Murder*

4 The Looped Seriality of *How to Get Away with Murder* 91
5 Outward Spiral: Gendering through Recognisability 113
6 Evoking Discourses of Progressivism, Social Activism, and Identity Politics: Such an Important Episode! 134

Part III Television Authorship and *The Walking Dead*

7 The Paratext Seriality of *The Walking Dead* 153
8 Palimpsest: Gendering through Accountability 175
9 Neoliberalising Discourses of Serialised Survivalism: You Make It . . . Until You Don't 195
    Conclusion: Archiving Snapshots 215

Bibliography 225
Index 244

Figures

1.1	No *Sex and the City* family dinners: rare instances of all female characters appearing together in one scene	33
1.2	'I hate you!': Shoshanna reacts with anger to Marnie's confession of her affair with Shoshanna's ex-boyfriend Ray	37
1.3	The 'erotic' photo shoot breaks with the fetishisation of Hannah's body by, for example, prominently placing photographer Ray within the camera frame	43
2.1	Shoshanna admires Marnie as the apparent embodiment of her aspirations	53
2.2	Contrasting female and male intimacy in the 'bathroom scenes' of 'Pilot' (1.1) and 'I Saw You' (3.11)	62
2.3	Transparent masculinity: Ray's final appearance concludes with a kiss on a carousel	66
3.1	*Girls*'s last season did not deviate from its previous textual practices, which also meant that the portrayal of Hannah's parenting a baby of colour was fraught with ambiguity and omissions	75
3.2	A self-absorbed Hannah cannot get enough of her bright red coloured drink, which evokes vampiric associations of the 'unruly woman' as a parasite	78
4.1	Tableau staging in a 'client shot' and promotional poster from the second season. This distinctive display characterises by contrast, highlights the cast's diversity, and positions the characters as jury-detectives	99

4.2	By dramatically comparing being shot to the attempt to follow the show's complex timeframe, this meme adopts *Murder*'s melodramatic mode	104
4.3	Leading ladies Kerry Washington, Ellen Pompeo, and Viola Davis share red wine and popcorn (with one another and with their viewers) in this #TGIT advertisement from September 2017	108
5.1	In contrast with the prisoner's uniform of her client Rebecca, Annalise's outfit negotiates the pressures placed on black professional femininity within the racialised and gendered space of the courtroom	117
5.2	Annalise kisses Eve goodbye on her porch. Some black female viewers found Annalise's willingness to wear a turban in front of her love interest to be an indicator of their strong connection	124
5.3	Annalise arranges for Eve to defend Nate. Viewers were as torn as the character herself over whom they wanted Annalise to pursue a relationship with	130
6.1	Annalise comforts her friend and client Jill before the transphobic behaviour of the authorities requires her to adapt her defence strategy	138
6.2	In a rare scene of collaboration (4.4 'Was She Ever Good at Her Job?'), Annalise joins the defence team of fellow lawyer Tegan and her former intern Michaela to defend their client Soraya	143
7.1	Top to bottom: first-season showrunner Frank Darabont with comic book writer Robert Kirkman; *Talking Dead* appearance by Kirkman, Laurie Holden (Andrea), and showrunner Glen Mazzara (1.13); Kirkman, showrunner Scott M. Gimple, Jeffrey Dean Morgan (Negan), and Norman Reedus (Daryl) (*Talking Dead* 5.16)	159
7.2	Villain Negan's speech implies authorial self-reflection and reveals him to be a stand-in for Robert Kirkman (#100)	166
8.1	Michonne equipped with her katana and zombie escorts/pets in the comic book and television show	178
8.2	The brief appearance of Daryl's 'fanboys' Patrick and Zack in the fourth season amuses Carol and allowed the show to reflect on the idealisation of its most popular character	185

8.3	Her selfless and gruesome death – a caesarean performed with a pocketknife – aspires to redeem the most disliked character Lori (3.4 'Killer Within')	193
9.1	Screenshots from the first episode (1.1 'Days Gone By') illustrate the comparison between Rick, Morgan, and the female zombies they set out to kill	197
9.2	*Talking Dead*'s sequence 'Survival Tips' featuring Matt Mogk (2.14); the 'Survival Kit' of AMC's online shop	201
9.3	Survival essentials worth risking your life for: colourful cat decorations	208

Acknowledgements

Most of this book was written in the Staatsbibliothek West in Berlin, one of the greatest libraries I know. I owe thanks to the librarians, cafeteria workers, and the security staff at the Stabi. There are many other people without whom *Gender and Seriality* would not have been possible. I am grateful for the academic community surrounding me, my biological and chosen families. A very special thanks to:

My editors, Claire Perkins and Constantine Verevis, as well as Richard Strachan and everyone else at Edinburgh University Press. I am proud to be a part of the Screen Serialities book series and look forward to the future scholarship it will publish.

My advisor, Frank Kelleter, who has been as central to this project's conception as to the final book. Frank is an incredible mentor who takes his students seriously as scholars right from the start and engages in our work as if we were his peers. Thank you for being a role model for what a university professor should be, a critical thinker but also an empathetic intellectual, for trusting in my capabilities from early on, as well as for all your sound (and fast) advice when I was freaking out about issues small or large.

My second advisor, Katja Kanzler, whose own sophisticated writing on television and gender I greatly admire. It is due to Katja's support, pragmatism, and expertise that this project became manageable and did not proliferate into a confusing mess like the serial materials I investigate.

Kathleen Loock, Emily Petermann, and Abby Fagan, for reading and commenting on the entire manuscript. Your unfaltering support, diligence, and knowledge carried me through the writing process – and made this a much more compelling read. Emily was my first office mate and formed my writing and teaching immensely (how did you never make fun of me for all the things I did not know?!?). In a weak moment, Kathleen told me she'd hunt me down if I ever dropped out of writing my dissertation. I believe she would have. Kathleen's confidence in my work has been an important driving force over the past years. And Abby helped me elegantly smooth out so many last-minute kinks with her own calm, warm demeanour. I can't imagine ever writing without you again.

Some of the most intelligent people I know, who read parts of this book: Rieke Jordan, Bettina Soller, Anne Nassauer, Marleen Knipping, Alexander Starre, Sophie Spieler, and Lisanna Wiele. I am grateful beyond words for the support, friendship, and inspiration you bring to my professional and personal life. I love the ways your minds work and look forward to continuing to learn from you.

Robyn Warhol (and Sean O'Sullivan, and Jared Gardner), who generously hosted me during a research stay at OSU's Project Narrative, and Amanda Lotz who did the same in the Department of Communication Studies at the University of Michigan. I cherish the conversations with you and your colleagues, all of which helped me figure out this book more clearly.

The members of the two research groups that were instrumental to this book and my scholarly profile.

The Popular Seriality Research Unit at the Freie Universität Berlin, of which I was a member during its second funding period. Among them especially: Regina Bendix, Ilka Brasch, Felix Brinker, Shane Denson, Fabian Grumbrecht, Christine Hämmerling, Christian Hißnauer, Frank Kelleter, Nathalie Knöhr, Britta Lesniak, Kathleen Loock, Ruth Mayer, Christina Meyer, Stefan Scherer, Bettina Soller, Daniel Stein, Claudia Stockinger, Andreas Sudmann, Babette B. Tischleder, and Lisanna Wiele. Also, to our fellows Julia Leyda, Robyn Warhol, Constantine Verevis, Sean O'Sullivan, John Durham Peters, William Uricchio, Rita Felski, and most of all, Jason Mittell. I am grateful for the intellectual home that the research unit offered for my thinking, and all of you played no small part in establishing this special place.

The brand-new research group 'City Scripts/Scripts for Postindustrial, Urban Futures: American Models, Transatlantic Interventions' based at the American Studies Departments of the three Ruhr Universities for dangling a carrot/post-doctoral research position in front of me so that I could finish this project. But also for your willingness to let me think about gender, seriality, and television a little bit more before committing fully to Urban Literary and Cultural Studies. It is a pleasure to work and think with Barbara Buchenau, Jens Martin Gurr, Juliane Borosch, Christine Cangemi, Florian Deckers, Stefan Dierkes, Kornelia Freitag, Walter Grünzweig, Randi Gunzenhäuser, Elisabeth Haefs, Chris Katzenberg, Johannes Maria Krickl, Josef Raab, Hanna Rodewald, Julia Sattler, Michael Wala, and Katharina Wood.

ACKNOWLEDGEMENTS xi

Those inspiring colleagues with whom I had the pleasure of working and have not already mentioned. At the English Department in Göttingen: Susanne Hamscha, Madita Oeming, Birte Otten, Diana Rosenhagen, and Stephanie Sommerfeld. At the John-F.-Kennedy-Institute in Berlin: Martin Lüthe, Regina Wenzel, Karl Imdahl, Maxi Albrecht, Annelot Prins, Talel Ben Jemia, Sören Schoppmeier, and Boris Vormann. And at the Department of Anglophone Studies in Essen: Elena Furlanetto, Dietmar Meinel, Florian Freitag, and Zohra Hassan-Pieper.

Anyone who heard me speak about these topics at colloquiums, conferences, or work dinners, all your suggestions and encouragement helped bring this into being. The academe can be a beautiful but also frustrating and self-deprecating space, yet, I could never have asked for a more supportive and brilliant group of colleagues, collaborators, and mentors to work with, talk to and be inspired by. Every single one of you are the reason that I continue on this path. Institutions are nothing, people are everything.

My friends Janna, Ina, Anisza, Anne, Zehra, Olga, Ilaria, Laura, and Rabea. For sharing my enthusiasm for television, watching and talking TV with me. For knowing when to forward me memes, but also when to stop my shop talk and take me out for a walk.

My parents, Karin and Bernhard, my siblings Linda and Alex, Dorothea, Sabine, Günter, and my other aunts and uncles, Sara and the Souzas, Selma, Maren, and the cousins . . . I continue to be amazed at the beauty that emerges when we are all together.

And Jonas. Last and First and Always. Because this one could also not have been done without you. Thank you for embarking on this journey with me, for believing in me, for making sure I stay healthy and happy and remember there is a life outside of academia. And I am so glad it is with you. Can we get a cat now that this is published?

My baby loves me, I'm so happy.
Happy makes me a modern girl.
Took my money and bought a TV,
TV brings me closer to the world.

– Sleater Kinney, 'Modern Girl' (2005)

Introduction: Serial Genders, Gendered Serialities

Television is one of popular culture's most visible and viable sites and brings with it distinct formations of gender. Media historian Amy Villarejo finds television to be 'one of the – if not *the* most – gendered and sexualized repetition apparatuses of modern technoscience, *the* modern implantation of gendered and sexualized social time' (2014: 7). Like its object of inquiry, television studies is interested in the ways that popular culture is gendered, racialised, and classed. The discipline often struggles with approaches that view the genders of fictional characters as static, rather than consider the diverse processes with which audiovisual media introduce continuously shifting gender performances. Serial storytelling, in particular, offers such complex negotiations of identity that the 'results' of televisual gender performances cannot be approached as separate from the processes that produce them.

With this book, I seek to develop a practice-focused approach to gender and seriality in television narratives. By practice-focused, I simultaneously mean the practices through which television narratives generate gender, the viewer practices these narratives inspire, as well as the ways television narratives themselves can be considered an accumulation of practices. As my case studies will illustrate, when it comes to gender and serial television, these different procedures are intrinsically connected. By bringing the disciplines of gender studies and media studies into dialogue about seriality, *Gender and Seriality* seeks not only to examine the cultural work of gender as a serial phenomenon that is continually renegotiated in television texts, but also to analyse how gendered formations of characters, genres, audiences, and authorship impact the seriality of television shows. It offers the mostly media studies and cultural studies-based research on seriality an intersectional understanding of gender as serial, and suggests to gender studies and feminist theory a possibility to rethink the dilemma of identity via seriality studies' conception of series, networks, and agency.

The book's double inquiry – by what processes does seriality produce gendered identities and which kinds of gender are performed and prioritised? – brings together two conceptions of seriality: the seriality of television shows and the seriality of gendered identity performance. Altogether, this book understands gender to be a serial collective of multiple practices located within a media text, its production and reception. This collective is intersectional and discursively produced. As a consequence, the book is necessarily interdisciplinary and draws on several theoretical frameworks of seriality. While its strongest ties are with feminist media studies, TV studies, and gender studies, it can also easily be linked to conversations situated more generally within media and communication studies, political science, sociology, as well as cultural studies. Lastly, it finds an accommodating space in the discipline of American studies, which especially in its transatlantic form can pride itself on housing interdisciplinary scholarship.

My work draws on an understanding of gender as discursively produced through the intermingling of cultural artefacts' different characteristics, as well as their processes of production and reception. I contest both conceptions of gender as either a biological fact mirrored in fictional universes and as consciously enacted by individuals. Instead, this study aims to develop an analytical approach to gender as exceeding textual boundaries in that it is discursively produced and continuously managed. My work connects with what is often called the performative turn of gender studies, according to which gender performances are the result of subjects' interactions with their surroundings (Butler 2008; contributions in Bell 1999; see Hemmings 2011: 105–10). While television series are not subjects, I examine gender performances as interactions of different processes and agencies. To trace the intricate connections within the discursive complex 'gender and television', I ask what kind of gender is established in which contexts and, in particular, how gender performances are stabilised and destabilised in the course of the show – quite literally, how gender is being serialised. Aside from initial characterisations, it is by means of comparison, correction, or blatant negation that gender performances repeat and develop. As such, characters' gender performances are never stable, and they also shape the gendered discourses of genre, authorship, and audience that interact with the shows themselves.

One of the core premises of feminist media studies is that popular culture picks up current political issues in order to interrogate them. Thus, popular culture becomes a battleground – or maybe more apt: a test field – not only for targeting underrepresentation and problematic stereotypes, but also to address current socio-political controversies. This book observes how television narratives comment on, engage with, and trigger viewer discussions of political and social issues. Its approach to feminist cultural analysis follows in the footsteps of feminist critics and feminist media studies. It is motivated by an understanding of feminism as a 'building project', which Sara Ahmed formulates with political urgency and eloquence:

> if our texts are worlds, they need to be made out of feminist materials. Feminist theory is world making. This is why we need to resist positioning feminist theory as simply or only a tool, in the sense of something that can be used in theory, only then to be put down or put away. It should not be possible to do feminist theory without being a feminist, which requires an active and ongoing commitment to live one's life in a feminist way. (Ahmed 2017: 14)

My study understands gender by means of a critical intersectional approach. As a result, 'gender' can never *only* refer to gendered identity layers; rather, any gendered meaning or identity is always also configured by ethnic and racial affiliations, sexual orientation, class belonging, age, and constructions of ablebodiedness or 'disability' (Crenshaw 1989; Bowleg 2008). Long practised by black female activists, the notion of intersectionality is attributed to legal scholar Kimberlé Crenshaw. Current scholarship still draws on Crenshaw's foundational conception of identity as never an 'either/or proposition' (Crenshaw 1991: 1242) but, instead, as an overlap of different systems; for example, the overlap of racism and sexism in the lives of women of colour. Despite its impressive track record within academia, as a methodological design intersectionality risks various pitfalls. There is an 'et cetera' dilemma when scholars list ever more identity categories as relevant to their intersectional framework but are unable to address these categories' combined impact. Lisa Bowleg describes the problem of 'additive assumption' as a contradiction that arises when scholars translate the concept into their methodological approaches: 'the additive (e.g., Black + Lesbian + Woman) versus intersectional (e.g., Black Lesbian Woman) assumption inherent in measurement and qualitative and quantitative data analyses contradicts the central tenet of intersectionality' (2008: 312). Throughout my study, gender should be construed as shorthand for intersectional performances of complex identities, particularly in regard to race, sexual orientation, class, and physical or mental impairments that may be culturally or socially framed as 'disability'.

In line with feminist methodology such as Sandra Harding's 'standpoint epistemology' (2009) or Donna Haraway's 'situated knowledge' (1988), such intersectional aspirations may be limited by my own positioning. In line with these feminist traditions, I acknowledge my situatedness as a white, middle-class, bisexual, able-bodied, cis-female researcher of German nationality with an academic background in both social science and the humanities, hence a subject position vested with various forms of social, cultural, and economic privilege. The reference to such an epistemology of situatedness should serve not to justify how this study overlooks other subject positions but to challenge my work to treat subject positions with care and attention to their specific intersectional locations and affordances.

This project owes much to my interactions with the vibrant, international, and interdisciplinary community of scholars that has assembled around a research group called 'Popular Seriality: Aesthetics and Practice'.[1] It draws on the shared framework of seriality and popular culture developed throughout the group's different projects. The loose network of this research group came to understand its work as opening up a distinct field of seriality studies, to which this study contributes through its decided focus on gender and seriality. I engage with the work of these seriality scholars and seek to extend it toward serial performances of gender as well as feminist media studies' conceptions of postfeminism within a highly complex and contradictory media culture. This project also derives its definition of popular culture from the shared framework of the research unit. The term 'popular culture' describes a dynamic, expansive field of aesthetic, social, and technological practices that began to develop in the mid-nineteenth century (Kelleter 2012: 17; 2017: 9). This field is characterised by commercial orientation, wide distribution via modern technological practices, and a broad appeal focusing on mass audiences. Further, it is within serialised popular culture that new narrative formats, roles, and practices of authorship and audiences emerge. For example, despite their promotion of singular authorship, most current popular cultural artefacts are produced collaboratively.

This book explores gender and seriality in three television shows, which I understand to be relevant discursive knots of a broader discussion about gender and US-American serial television. Each case study is an intricate example of commercialised engagement with continued systems of sexism and racism in US-American culture – and Western cultures more generally. These shows are *Girls* (HBO, 2012–17), *How to Get Away with Murder* (ABC, 2014–), and *The Walking Dead* (AMC, 2010–). They reflect the different industrial backgrounds of US-American television: *Girls* is a premium cable series, *How to Get Away with Murder* is a network show, and *The Walking Dead* runs on a basic cable channel.[2] Further, the respective similarities and differences between these shows constitute their combined appeal for my study. All three series are multi-protagonist, yet, among their large casts, certain characters are privileged as particular focal points and, thus, reflect their ideal gender identities. This similarity allows me to shift my attention between a comparison of 'preferred', ideal genders with 'subordinated' gender performances in *Girls*, to an interrogation of different layers of one specific character in *How to Get Away with Murder*, and an exploration of beloved, popular characters in contrast with 'disliked', marginalised characters in *The Walking Dead*. All three shows are genre hybrids (the dramedy *Girls*, the melodrama/legal drama/crime series *How to Get Away with Murder*, the horror/melodrama *The Walking Dead*) that, consequently, combine a variety of genre-specific practices, cultural types, and intertextual references particular to certain genres. These references become the foundation for specific forms of serial gendering, and the ways in which a show evokes them indicates its approach to serial storytelling and gender.

All three shows were developed in the wake of their networks' prior successes and did so through stark variations of an earlier success formula: through *Girls*, HBO sought to extend its 'Quality TV' brand by introducing a millennial, female-centric show that referenced its earlier *Sex and the City* (1998–2004). *How to Get Away with Murder* is produced by media sensation Shonda Rhimes's company Shondaland and airs in ABC's scheduling block TGIT (short for 'Thank God It's Thursday') together with *Scandal* (ABC, 2012–18) and *Grey's Anatomy* (ABC, 2005–). AMC tailored *The Walking Dead* to supplement its horror film library and as a follow-up to its 'first' original series, *Mad Men* (2007–15). Additionally, the show adapts and continues a long-running comic series by Image Comics published from 2003 to 2019. In some ways, these shows can be thought of as continuing the commercial success stories with a twist. *How to Get Away with Murder* and *The Walking Dead* have each successfully generated strong fandoms and dedicated viewers. Moreover, while *Girls* failed to find a broad viewership, the show excelled at positioning itself within cultural conversations. Of the three, *Girls* is the show most frequently considered by scholarship, whereas academic engagements with *How to Get Away with Murder* are almost non-existent.

Through these shows, this study covers a time span from 2010 (when *The Walking Dead* premiered) to 2018 (when *How to Get Away with Murder* concluded its fourth season). Scholars often hesitate to engage with ongoing narratives because a new instalment could render prior readings obsolete. The fear of dated analysis is compounded by the lengthy time spans of academic publishing. From a seriality studies and gender studies perspective, however, the overlap of analysis and continuation of the research object should instead be considered an opportunity. Because my research on and writing about these shows has overlapped with their original airing, I have never been tempted to reduce their complex serial storytelling and processes of gendering to a static conception.

To focus my analysis, each part (comprised of three chapters) investigates one specific facet of the larger discourse of gender and seriality for the respective television show. This focus allows me to trace different modes of serial interactions between cultural artefact, audience, and industry. These modes can be referred to as authorial, critical, and conversational: in Part I, I explore the critical mode, that is the 'critical sphere' of academia, journalism, and recapping for *Girls*; in Part II, the conversational mode of fan interactions on social media for *How to Get Away with Murder*; and, in Part III, processes of authorship and authorisation for *The Walking Dead*. However, the chapters of each part never aspire to present this aspect as the sole source of gendered performance.

The book is structured as follows: Chapters 1, 4, and 7 investigate the specific kind of serial storytelling of the show in question, its gendered serialities. To do so, these chapters trace textual characteristics such as temporality, genre, setting, or camera perspective as constitutive of a show's serial storytelling. Chapters 2, 5, and 8 ask which processes of gendering are set in motion through this serial storytelling. They develop analytical figures to explore which gendered identities are formed, organised, and prioritised. The analytical figures proposed as models for serial genders are all concerned with fluidity and movement: the carousel, the spiral, the palimpsest. The figures serve to disentangle the specific discourses that comprise what we may call the identity of a show, illustrate which role intertextual references to other cultural artefacts play in serial gendering, and organise the responses television may mobilise, whether critical, conversational, or authorial. Lastly, Chapters 3, 6, and 9 place the respective show within a broader socio-political discourse. They investigate in what cultural conversations these series participate through their forms of gendered serial storytelling and serialised management of gendered identities. Although derived from specific shows, the terminology this book develops can be applied in the analysis of popular cultural artefacts with similar serial storytelling, and hence similar practices of gendering *of* and *through* characters, plots, and genres, as well as production personnel, audiences, and critics.

To reiterate, I define gender as a serial and discursively produced, intersectional entanglement of different practices and agencies in the interaction of text, production, and reception. Accordingly, this book relies on a mixture of different methods. I provide readings of the different television series, the discursive practices surrounding them, and their various paratextual manifestations. To acquire an understanding of these discourses, the book relies on discourse analysis, as well as qualitative content analysis.[3] To analyse the serial genders of serialised television, it is indispensable to consider the cultural artefacts alongside their reception practices as well as the promotional strategies of the industry. Thus, gender performances are never restricted to the cultural artefact itself, but they extend beyond the development of characters, depictions of settings, bodies of actors, themes of storytelling, and so on. They are located in authorised paratexts, such as interviews with author figures and actors, spin-offs, or making-ofs, as well as non-authorised cultural sites such as online viewer conversations on social media, fan fiction, recaps, and TV criticism.

As any project on seriality and mass-culture can attest, issues of selection pose a dilemma: where to end with a text that, despite being obsessed with an elusive ideal of closure, is designed to continue endlessly? Similarly, on a more abstract level, which gestures and aspects matter in a gender performance that soaks through so much of our lives, let alone the cultural products we consume and surround ourselves with? To counter such dilemmas of selection and prioritisation, this book explores particular characters, scenes, and themes as exceptional, as standing out from the serial flow. These aspects thereby highlight the very nature of this flow, an understanding which applies both to the seriality of television as well as the seriality of identity performance.

SERIALITY IN GENDER STUDIES

Rather than develop a one-size-fits-all model for my subsequent case studies, this Introduction develops a theoretical framework that guides my analysis. This section traces the trajectory of different theoretical accounts within feminist theory, gender studies, and queer theory that – despite apparent disparity – harmonise with respect to their understanding of gender as a serial process.[4] The notion of serial identity performance runs as a strong undercurrent through the vibrant, interdisciplinary, and multi-methodological fields of gender studies, feminist theory, and queer studies. Seriality allows such theories to approach gender as a cultural and social construction continuously enacted and inscribed in bodies through processes of reiteration, repetition, and normalisation. However, explicit considerations of a serial enactment of gender are surprisingly scarce. Even though most research in gender studies would agree that seriality is the foundation of gender performance, only rarely do scholars spell out its apparent function. When research does focus on gender's serial dimensions, it is pursued on theoretical grounds, never embedded in popular culture's serial dynamics of storytelling, production, and reception.

A poststructuralist emphasis on the discursive construction of realities, as well as sociological attention to the discursive powers of social interactions, both influence the canonical work of gender studies introduced in the following. Our route begins with the feminist historical materialism that political theorist Iris Marion Young became known for: her notion of 'gender as a series'. Part of her 'pragmatic theorizing' (1994: 718), Young proposes that we view gender as a serial collective in order to counter the dilemma feminist theory and activism faces when understanding gender as an identity category.[5] Despite objecting to Jean-Paul Sartre's misogyny, Young adopts his differentiation between 'group' and 'series' in the *Critique of Dialectical Reason* (1976). Although group members are self-conscious and aware of their collective and its purpose or goals, the social collective of the series is composed by unaware individuals 'unified passively by the objects around which their actions are oriented or by the objectified results of the material effects of the actions of the others' (Young 1994: 724). As a deciding factor of alignment in serial collectives, Young calls such relationships with objects and materialised histories 'practico-inert' (725). She explains that these objects are 'practical' because they manifest as 'the result of human action', and 'inert' because they establish 'constraints on and resistances to action' (725). As a serial collective, gender is constituted by a variety of such practico-inert relationships with activities, locations, and items. Young lists different examples, such as pronouns, verbal routines, habits, gestures, rituals, verbal or visual representations, social and cultural spaces, clothes, cosmetics, tools, furniture, and bodily practices (729–30). However, she specifies that these examples are not 'defining attributes of individuals but are material social facts that each individual must relate to and deal with' (730–1). This distinction is relevant for bodily manifestations, such as the capacity to menstruate or bear children, which likely result in being positioned as part of the series 'woman'; however, not every 'woman' is able to menstruate or bear children. In summary, Young proposes viewing gender (but also race and class) as

> a serial collective defined neither by any common identity nor by a common set of attributes that all the individuals in the series share, but, rather, it names a set of structural constraints and relations to practico-inert objects that condition action and its meaning. (Young 1994: 737)

At the heart of Young's undertaking is a critique of societal structures of domination, power, and oppression that govern the formation of serial collectives ('structural constraints' in the above quote). Heteronormativity and the gendered division of labour are two examples of such societal structures (729–32). It is in this regard that Young's conceptualisation of a series leaves Sartre's simplistic foundation behind, thus becoming productive for serialised gender(ing): 'the series women is not as simple and one-dimensional as bus riders or radio listeners. Gender, like class, is a vast, multifaceted, layered, complex, and overlapping set of structures and objects' (728). Sartre's reference to radio listening evokes the originator of one of seriality studies' most productive foundations: Benedict Anderson's 'imagined community' (1995). Both Sartre and Anderson use media consumption – radio listening and newspaper reading, respectively – to demonstrate how collectives come into being through routine media engagements. But, as Young reminds us, societal structures impact the formation of class (Sartre's focus) and the nation (Anderson's focus) as serial collectives. Because the individuals who are positioned in a serial collective through diverse practico-inert relations and histories share only a 'passive unity' at best, for Young, serial gender should be thought of as separate from identity: 'No individual woman's identity, then, will escape the markings of gender, but how gender marks her life is her own' (1994: 733–734). Even though one's position in such a serial collective depends on external factors, this position says nothing about the individual's actions, their responses to this position, or even their awareness of it.

Young's framework allows for a double conceptualisation of popular culture's relationship to gender and seriality: first, as cultural artefacts, television shows serve as practico-inert objects themselves and become influential through processes that align their audience with certain societal serial collectives. Second, 'gender as series' makes visible the processes through which television characters join serial collectives of gender within the fictional storyworld. These characters' relevant practico-inert relationships consist of visual aspects, such as props, setting, clothing, camera perspective, and so on. But characters also form such practico-inert bonds with other popular culture artefacts (through intertextual references), with their viewers (through reception practices), or with author roles (when parallels between author figures and characters are established). To comprehend the serial collectives that characters are positioned in as such, viewers bring their knowledge of societal structures outside of the narrative's storyworld with them. These different societal structures become a shared background through which to 'read' the characters' genders. At the same time, the show's serial storytelling can be understood to function similarly to these societal structures, as it creates the constrictions within and foundation upon which gendered storytelling takes place. Thus, to criticise certain characterisations often involves taking into account the serial storytelling that impacts their formation. These two different alignments occur simultaneously: the viewer places fictional television characters within serial collectives of gender, *and*, through their practice of viewing, audience members may also be aligned with serial collectives of gender.

Because Young's 'gender as series' does not explain how individuals may be perceived by others as belonging to a serial collective, the notion of 'accountability' offers a productive extension. In the gender studies classic 'Doing Gender' (1987), sociologists Candace West and Don H. Zimmerman develop an interaction-based model of gender through ethnomethodological approaches. They emphasise how gender is done through social interactions and 'read' according to the lines of accountability. West and Zimmerman find 'doing gender' to be inescapable, 'unavoidable', and 'omnirelevant' (1987: 137–40; see also West and Fenstermaker 1995: 18).[6] Just as the individuals of Young's 'serial collectives' only occasionally become aware of their positioning, the routine quality of West and Zimmerman's definition veils processes of 'doing' and makes gender performances appear 'natural' or 'evident'. However, it is through external scrutiny, how individuals interpret and 'police' the accuracy of each other's gender performances, that West and Zimmerman can add another dimension to practices of serial gendering: to be successful, enactments of gender 'must be finely fitted to situations and modified or transformed as the occasion demands' (1987: 135). In the process, the pressures of living up to habitualised and institutionalised norms of gender are often rendered invisible as 'naturalised' performances. Through accountability, gender transgressions or deviations of various degrees become culturally legible. This concept also covers the 'specifically unremarkable', which warrants only passing cognitive awareness and, for this reason, serves as an especially successful mode of 'doing gender' because it is 'seen to be in accord with culturally approved standards' (1987: 136; West and Fenstermaker 1995: 21). West and Zimmerman only mention popular culture briefly, stating that it can offer guidelines to 'do' or read gender (1987: 135). However, their notion of accountability is a useful tool for the analysis of serial gender performances in cultural artefacts. For example, genre affordances or viewer reactions place fictional characters within 'serial collectives' of gender and hold those characters accountable to these collectives.

This book employs the term 'performance' to describe the ways in which gender comes into being on a serial basis. Any overview of scholarship on gender constitution would not be complete without the work of theorist Judith Butler, the scholar most frequently associated with performativity. Like Young or West and Zimmerman, Butler is sceptical of understanding gender as rooted in identities: gendered selfhood is not expressed through the performance of subjectivity but constituted through it. Further, because they depend on the process – or West and Zimmerman's interaction – gender identities are never fixed, but always temporal accumulations that are in flux and subject to change. The interest in the temporal dimensions of gender performance are what makes Butler's work relevant for explorations of gender as serial, even though it is not seriality per se but repetition that is at its core: 'The action of gender requires a performance that is *repeated*. This repetition is at once a reenactment and reexperiencing of a set of meanings already socially established; and it is the mundane and ritualized form of their legitimation' (Butler 2008: 191). Therefore, Butler describes gender as a 'stylized repetition of acts' as well as a 'constituted social temporality' (191; 1988: 519–20). Butler does not just emphasise the repetitive and ritualised dimension as relevant to gender performance, but instead centres this functioning as the thing itself; seriality makes gender. Butler's work is subsequently guided by the search for 'the possibility of a different sort of repeating' (1988: 520; 2008: 192), that is, subversive, parodic repetitions that fail to repeat, thus disrupting, if not potentially transforming, normative repetitions of gender.

As the most recent theoretical addition to this framework on serialised gender, I now turn to Judith Roof's *What Gender Is, What Gender Does* (2016). In this work, Roof develops a systems-inspired model of gender as a 'machinic process that perpetually reorganises multiple sets of regimes and operations that link the psychic and the social' (2016: 28). Central to this understanding is the notion of different 'gender regimes' as cultural and psychological 'dynamic architectures of meaning' (21). Due to the overlapping 'polymorphousness' of these regimes, multiple regimes are at work in an individual, with these regimes constantly shifting (12). Roof traces the operations of some of these gender regimes and turns to popular culture to illustrate their workings. For Roof, the artefacts of popular culture 'most unwittingly provide examples of gendering trends and styles' (1). Roof's insightful readings do not grant popular culture the agency awarded to systems of gender. As my turn to seriality studies will demonstrate, popular culture can also be approached as shifting systems of different agencies.

However, Roof's attention to the moving constitution of gender is very compelling: Roof highlights how gender is an unending process – a verb rather than an adjective or noun – and that to gender means to (temporarily) eliminate other options, thus simplifying and reducing complex dynamics. 'Genderings hide the fact that they never organise what they seem to organise', Roof argues and continues that, '[i]n seeming to do what they do, genders never do what we think they are doing' (4). I find such self-aware 'gender regimes' that cover up their own operations a very productive extension of the other theories assembled so far. The notion of 'gender regimes' is sought to remedy the 'illusion of consciousness and will' that Roof explains attaches itself to the concept of performativity (177). Roof criticises performativity as the dominant approach to gender in the wake of Butler's work, as she finds performativity to carry the empty promise of expressing an underlying 'pure' identity and, resultantly, being a tool for conscious self-expression. Nevertheless, this misguided criticism of performativity is inconsistent with Butler's (and most other current gender theorists') scepticism toward gender as an expression of identity. Instead, I place Roof in the critical tradition of Butler, Young, and West and Zimmerman. All thinkers assembled find gender to come into existence in a complex interplay of various positions of undertaking and 'reading' performances, drawing on large cultural, social, and historical repertoires of references in the process.

As another relatively recent endeavour, queer studies is beginning to interrogate issues of futurity and historicity in scholarship interested in queer temporalities. Such work allows for an alternative understanding of seriality as not synonymous with straightforward linear progression but driven by complex and, at times, contradictory re-negotiations. Queer studies' take on temporality highlights how the recursivity of serial identity construction results in nuanced references to the past, present, and future, which always encompass the potentials of failure. What differentiates queer temporalities from heteronormative conceptions of time? In her foundational work, Elizabeth Freeman argues that queer temporalities call into question a 'logic of time-as-productive' (2010: 36) and instead 'propose other possibilities for living in relation to indeterminately past, present, and future others' (xxii). Jack Halberstam describes 'queer time' as impacted by 'the potentiality of life unscripted by the conventions of family, inheritance and child rearing' (2005: 2; see also Edelman 2004). Halberstam further finds repetition to be a postmodern queer method, exploring how queer feminist artists and critics emphasise 'seriality, repetition, absurdity, and anomaly' in their work (2005: 122). In *Ethereal Queer* (2014), Amy Villarejo takes such conceptions of queer temporality to explore shifts in television's organisation of time and space as it relates to discourses of queer visibilities, becoming, and survival. Villarejo describes how television's temporality can be 'segmentation, repetition, seriality, frozen, paused, captured, looped, restored, lost and found' (2014: 10–11). As a result, television becomes a crucial part of the construction of gendered and sexualised forms of identity through its varied temporalities.

GENDER IN SERIALITY STUDIES

The 2010s have seen increasing attention paid to serialised popular culture and its specific textual affordances, production, and consumption patterns. This has less to do with new forms of serial practices or newly emerging cultural artefacts – on the contrary, despite this current fervour, these cultural arenas date to at least the mid-nineteenth century – and more with the emergence of a networked, international field of seriality studies. In addition to the Screen Serialities book series, several vital collections turn to seriality and popular culture (Kelleter 2012, 2017; Loock 2014). So far, seriality studies has largely neglected reflection on how its materials, methods, and approaches are specifically gendered. This study seeks to address this blind spot by introducing intersectional notions of gender to seriality studies, while calling for further work on gender and seriality as mutually entangled in commercial popular culture.

Scholarship tends to agree on fundamental characteristics of serial narratives: a serial cultural artefact has different segments (episodes, comic book issues, etc.) that are released with breaks between instalments. It is usually produced in a collaborative manner with a standardised division of labour, although it may be accompanied by strong authorial presences or 'author fictions' (television's showrunner, cinema's director, comic's creator-writer). Despite following a strategy of relative 'niche casting', it is generally addressed to a mass audience and commercially motivated. This commercial background is also not hidden but self-evident, which is why these artefacts are 'undisguised commodities' (Kelleter 2017: 10).

A central interest of seriality studies is the paradox at the core of serial storytelling: the constraint to repeat in order to provide recognisability (of a plot, character, brand of a show or network, genre, media format) while at the same time creating suspense through new, unforeseen elements. Semiotician Umberto Eco was among the first to diagnose this 'dialectic between order and novelty', or 'scheme and innovation' (1985: 173). Sean O'Sullivan observes that serialised cultural artefacts develop their own understandings of what is 'surprising' versus what is ordinary and 'inevitable' (2017: 206). This particularly applies to narrative interruptions that are so predictable they become 'dead zones' in which the audience has 'little impetus to move, without a central promise of the serial contract, a promise of a "new day"' (208–9). Television studies tends to categorise the ways individual episodes relate to seasons. German scholar Knut Hickethier describes this as television's 'doppelte Formstruktur' ('double form structure') to account for the competing demands of individual episodes and seasons (2003). Other scholars rely on the distinction between 'series' and 'serials' to account for varying degrees of extra-episodic seriality (Oltean 1993). This book employs 'series' as an umbrella term and follows the lead of Gaby Allrath et al., who propose to replace the binary series/serials with a more nuanced view of television's serialisation (2005: 5–6).

Early research on serial storytelling in the nineteenth century highlights how storytelling developed in close interaction with industrialised commercial production (Hagedorn 1988; Hayward 2009). Roger Hagedorn argues that 'commercial exploiters have consistently turned to the serial form of narrative presentation precisely in order to cultivate a dependable audience of consumers' (1988: 5). By contrast, Jennifer Hayward protests any characterisation of the serial consumer as an ignorant dupe lured in by savvy producers of popular culture. Instead, she finds that serial audiences have and continue to 'use their texts and the processes of collaborative interpretation, prediction, meta-commentary, and creation that engage them' (2009: 2).

Although early consumption was itself not gendered – the writing of Charles Dickens had cross-gender appeal for various demographics – Hayward's study demonstrates how serial consumption has long been associated with femininity and/or immaturity (7). Lisanna Wiele follows up on the gendered historical formations of seriality in her work on sensationalist American antebellum city mysteries (2019). In *Having a Good Cry* (2003), Robyn Warhol compellingly develops a theory of the feelings which serial storytelling may evoke in its audience, and how these feelings are ascribed value on the basis of gender. Aside from these exceptional studies, seriality scholarship does not reckon with the long tradition of equating seriality with femininity. If mentioned at all, both the gender representations and the gendered conceptions of production or reception in serialised popular culture are never thoroughly interrogated. With the exception of Warhol's book, seriality scholarship has distanced itself from the female-associated soap opera and the feminist scholarship that analyses soap opera's storytelling, viewing communities, and production contexts. I do not wish to argue that soap operas should be approached as a sort of lone prototype of serial storytelling. However, by framing other serial narratives as unrelated to their soap opera siblings, seriality scholarship largely neglects the gendered discourses of distinction that have long accompanied the understanding of serialised popular culture as feminine (see Warhol 2003: 94). Such an academic (mis)alignment is especially precarious with regard to the preferred materials of seriality studies: male-centric television series heralded as 'Quality TV' to hide the gendered traditions of serial narratives.

Explorations of current reception patterns confirm the 'pleasures for audiences that help explain the continuing popularity of serial narratives' (Loock 2014: 5). Technical innovations like VCRs, DVDs, or online streaming have altered how and when people watch television. Among these, the multitude of ways in which audiences pursue the 'quotidian integration' of serial narratives into their everyday lives (Hämmerling and Nast 2017) have sparked the interest of seriality scholars. Such approaches are based on Benedict Anderson's notion of 'imagined communities' of simultaneous mass media consumption (see Kelleter 2017: 26; Bendix 2013). The current social media-dominated internet culture encourages reception practices in the form of collective 'swarm' intelligence, described by Jason Mittell as 'forensic fandom' (2015: 52, 267). Further, Bettina Soller demonstrates how the creative possibilities of fan fiction continue the serial narratives they evoke (2014). Soller's and Mittell's work is exemplary of the ways in which serial narratives spread into other spaces, ranging from authorised spin-offs or tie-ins to fan art or discussion boards. The tendency to proliferate to such extremes makes serial media what Pat Harrigan and Noah Wardrip-Fruin call 'vast narratives' because they rack up thousands of pages, hours of screen time, or various instalments, and cross over into numerous other media formats (2009). This proliferation illustrates how serial audiences become 'agents of narrative continuation' and not just, as Frank Kelleter reminds us, in the forms of 'active' viewer engagement researched by Soller and Mittell (2017: 13).

Overall, the most productive conceptualisations of seriality highlight that serial storytelling should never be reduced to a mere textual characteristic. Seriality is 'a practice *of* popular culture, not a narrative formalism *within* it' (Kelleter 2017: 15). As a result, studies of serial popular culture have to trace its diverse cultural manifestations. Frank Kelleter and Kathleen Loock's work on Hollywood remakes as 'retrospective serialization' of 'original' films demonstrates how cinema serialises itself and constructs a 'self-reflexive historicity' (2017: 126–7). In *Epic Television* (2018), Britta Lesniak offers a musicologist-ethnographic study of serialised sound in the television series *Ramayan* (Doordarshan, 1987–8) and *Mahabharat* (DD National, 1988–90).

Lesniak finds the music of these religious epics/soap operas to navigate the intricate political and religious concerns in the Indian context of an aspiring radical Hindu nationalism as well as the medialisation of religion. Instead of continuing the traditional media studies triad of production, reception, and text as separate entities, seriality scholarship traces how different production and reception roles shift as '*coevolving* forces' (Kelleter 2017: 24). This book addresses such shifting practices in close interaction with the serial narratives that warrant them as critical, conversational, and authorial modes.

Related to popular series' urge to 'repeat with a twist', serial storytelling struggles to manage competing aspirations toward closure and continuation. From a mere market perspective, its status as a commercial product makes the commodity of a popular series potentially endless. Its serialised production continues as long as the series is commercially successful. However, as viewers, readers, or gamers of serialised popular culture, we anticipate and desire closure and the satisfactory pleasures it promises. This may well be why successful franchises heavily invest in their – almost exclusively male – author fictions in order to assure the audience that even if they feel overwhelmed, there is someone in control of a sprawling franchise (see Mittell 2015: 88–97; Sulimma 2014b).

As Frank Kelleter highlights, the two competing demands of closure and continued renewal only appear to constitute a paradox (2012: 12–13). This is because serial storytelling excels at delivering partial endings while simultaneously tending to postpone any finite conclusion that would cancel further extensions (13). Such deliberations also project notions of self-surveillance on the part of the serialised cultural artefact itself. One of the most important theoretical discussions of seriality scholarship targets popular culture's dynamic of auto-referentiality. Rather than mere postmodern, metatextual play, serialised popular culture's necessity to 'watch itself' is borne out of its commercial imperative for continuation (Kelleter 2017: 17–18). In his conceptualisation of a 'popular seriality' framework, Kelleter argues:

> a text can read itself and describe itself, especially if that text is a serial one – i.e., one that evolves in a feedback loop with its own effects – and if by 'text,' we mean not something that is but something that does: not a single outlook or structure waiting to be decoded or uncovered but an entanglement of textual practices. (Kelleter 2014: 4)

The 'feedback loop' between reception, series, and production is one of the core instruments of seriality research. It is based on the understanding that, unlike stand-alone or self-contained oeuvres, a running series can – and must – observe its effects on its audiences in order to remain commercially successful. A series must adjust its form and content as a consequence of these observations, which is how serial audiences become involved in the unfolding narrative's production, with the lines between producers and audiences becoming ever more unstable. This feedback loop expresses itself because within serial cultural artefacts, 'narrative organization typically takes place on the go' (Kelleter 2017: 16; see Ganz-Blättler 2012: 123–8). Once something is established within the storyworld of a series, it cannot be undone but must be renegotiated in future instalments. Due to their segmented release rhythms,

> producers cannot revise an overall narrative before final publication to get rid of inconsistencies. Popular series therefore have to do their work of coordination, pruning, and coherence-building within the narrative itself. . . . Recursivity here means the continual readjustment of possible continuations to the already established information. (Kelleter 2017: 16–17)

Such serial revision is the result of audiences and producers holding their series 'accountable'. However, just as serial gender performance is never a conscious practice through which an individual expresses 'identity', recursivity highlights a more nuanced logic than mere textual feedback to narrative errors. Rather, through recursivity the horizon of narrative options is staked out: it maps out the ways in which a narrative will progress, and it establishes the ground rules of cultural discourse.

Instrumental for such an understanding of series as self-aware is the advancement of Bruno Latour's Actor-Network-Theory in seriality studies.[7] This methodological approach allows seriality studies to explore series as 'work-nets of agency', as assemblages of individuals, institutions, objects, or technologies, dependent on their shifting connections and interactions (Kelleter 2014: 4; 2017: 25). In order to study 'popular seriality' as a practice, such conceptualisations have to describe the ways these work-nets or assemblages come into being. However, what does this conceptualisation of series as worknets mean for designs of gender? Can gender similarly be thought of as a worknet of agency? While this question could spark an entire book, I want to briefly discuss this theoretical potential. As Kelleter writes,

> we can describe popular series as *self-observing systems*, in the sense that they are never just the 'product' of intentional choices and decisions, even as they require and involve intentional agents (most notably, people) for whom they provide real possibilities of deciding, choosing, using, objecting, and so on. (Kelleter 2017: 25)

It is not coincidental that one could replace 'popular series' with 'gender regimes' in this quotation and arrive at Judith Roof's argument. Gender can also never be understood as a conscious choice that expresses an underlying identity. Moreover, gender performances acquire lasting cultural meanings by gathering the gendered expressions of individuals in collective forms. Here then, we can glimpse what seriality studies can offer gender studies – aside from its nuanced conceptions of serialised popular culture: in seriality studies' conception of the agency of cultural objects, which does not do away with the agency of individuals involved in its complex network, gender studies can find a possible approach to the dilemma of identity. It is this understanding that *Gender and Seriality* wishes to contribute to current feminist theory, and that the following chapters will put to use methodologically. To insist that serial performances of gender create identity, or acquire their own forms of cultural agency, does not mean to strip the persons 'doing gender' of agency. Rather, gender performances provide individuals with options and, in the process, involve them in the continuation of a specific discourse of gender. To become aware of one's involvement in such a performance or 'serial collective' then does not necessarily result in feelings of helplessness or disenfranchisement, of being unable to avoid an externally determined gender performance. Instead, subjects become aware of their own position within a system, their position as 'agents of gendered continuation'.

So where do these brief forays into gender studies and seriality studies leave us in regard to television narratives? They showcase that studying the serialisation of gender *in* popular culture (that is, within narratives as well as the gendered understandings of serial audiences and producers) requires the consideration of gender *as* popular culture (how a show becomes a cultural reference within socio-cultural debates). Serial cultural artefacts depend on gendered discourses and also become part of such discourses. Thus, not only do serial audiences draw on serialised popular culture to 'read' gender, but they are also involved in the continuation of popular culture's repertoire of gender. Consequently, research must focus both on instances in which serialised popular culture depicts conventions of gender as processes, as well as on those instances that are absent from the text, disguising or limiting the efforts, meanings, and interpretations involved in gender enactments. Gender performances are not expressions of some underlying identity; instead, they inherently create gender through the process itself. Research should never attempt to find some sort of hidden truth behind televisual genderings, should not act as a decoding of veiled signs. Instead, scholarship must take the cover-up operations of self-aware popular culture into account and question the ways 'successful' expressions of gender become invisible due to their pliant conformity.

Gender is a 'strategy of survival within compulsory systems', Judith Butler argues, and deviations or failures carry punitive costs for 'those who fail to do their gender right' (2008: 190). Yet, often deviations may be included in changed scripts of gendering. To understand how gender performances need the innovation of such deviations is to return to the two competing demands of closure and renewal as the basis of serialised popular culture. Gender performances are also never final, never completed, and never stably achieved. There are moments in which an individual may become aware of their involvement in a 'serial collective', as Young has it, or in which an individual or a culture holds another's gender performance 'accountable' (see West and Zimmerman), but these are partial endings rather than any finite expression of a lasting 'identity'. Like serial storytelling, gender performances balance competing demands toward closure and continuity. They provide recognisable aspects that are legible, as well as new, innovative elements through which gender and popular series alike avoid becoming a 'dead zone' (see O'Sullivan 2017), more than a clichéd repetition. As Lisa Wade and Myra Marx Ferree point out, 'All of us get away with some rule breaking. Breaking the rules is doing gender. That is, doing gender is about more than conformity. It's also about negotiating with the rules' (2015: 74–5). Whereas West and Zimmerman's understanding of gender accountability sheds light on the ways individuals evaluate one another, the recursivity of serial feedback loops illustrates how such 'rule breaking' becomes part of serialised gender performance. Instead of disrupting the serial collective of a respective gender through deviation, 'rule breaking' results in a repetition with a twist, in an adjustment of gender accountability. Thus, on the one hand, seriality refers to the potentials of naturalising gendered conventions through their repetitions, making gender performances invisible as norms. On the other, seriality also has the potential to refer back consciously, to deviate, and to make this deviation comprehensible as such – because serial repetitions have created a repertoire through which gender has become accountable.

Frank Kelleter describes serial narratives as 'moving targets', because their 'designs keep shifting in perpetual interaction with what they set in motion' (2017: 14). Just as popular series are moving targets, gender performances are also moving targets of endless proliferation. Whereas scholars of seriality studies face a mass of narrative information that appears to destabilise any lasting interpretation, scholars of gender studies struggle to approach ongoing meanings of gender performances. Both interdisciplinary fields attempt to 'redescribe as mobile what has established itself as settled' (Kelleter 2014: 4). *Gender and Seriality* continues both of these undertakings.

OVERVIEW OF THE CHAPTERS

To provide a brief overview of what will follow: Chapter 1 develops the concept of thinkpiece seriality to explore how serial TV criticism is much more than an exterior reaction to television. It explores how *Girls* mobilises the responses of journalists or academics which intertwine with the show's storytelling. As a simultaneous observer of the show and the show's viewer-critics, the chapter identifies textual and discursive trends as practices of thinkpiece seriality, such as ambiguity, metatextuality, or omissions.

Staying with *Girls*, Chapter 2 proposes the metaphor of the carousel to explore the show's gendered identities. It charts how characters move in and out of their critics' (analytical) gazes, as well as run circles around certain cultural types and tropes. Drawing on the sociological framework of gender relations by Raewyn Connell, Mimi Schippers, and Amanda Lotz, the chapter displays how certain genders are positioned as preferred within the narrative.

Chapter 3 traces the show's participation within a postfeminist marketplace. Taking a cue from feminist media scholar Charlotte Brunsdon, the chapter suggests the notion of an ur-feminist impulse that current serial postfeminist media texts propagate to benefit from the relatively recent (commercial) popularity of feminism. For *Girls*, this specifically impacts its viewer-critics' discussions of race and bodily representations.

Chapter 4 conceptualises the serial storytelling of *How to Get Away with Murder* as looped seriality to highlight the show's investment in temporal loops, as well as the loops between viewer responses and the show, recalling the 'feedback loop' of seriality studies (see Kelleter 2017). Three areas emerge as especially interesting to explore the interactivity of looped seriality. First, the chapter relates the 'Who Dunnit' hashtags to the conventions of detective fiction. Second, internet humour in the form of GIFs or memes serves as another crucial site of looped audience engagements. In a third instance, looped seriality is applied to understand the show and the viewers' interactive reciprocity when it comes to the ritualised consumption of snacks and drinks as a different kind of TV dinner.

Detailed readings of the show's protagonist Annalise Keating, her beauty practices, professional appearance, and bisexuality are included in Chapter 5. It employs the metaphor of the outward spiral to capture how the show encourages its viewers' immediate, affective responses. The show's gender performances begin from starting points such as the racialised tropes of black femininity Patricia Hill Collins describes as 'controlling images' (2000). But they proceed to mobilise viewer affect in the form of two distinct, yet similarly affect-driven patterns: first, viewers may recognise themselves in the show's portrayals, and second, they may perceive themselves to be witnesses to a television history in the making.

Chapter 6 demonstrates how with *Murder* network channel ABC stakes its claim to the 'brand' of politically progressive television, turning progressivism, social activism, and identity politics into a kind of narrowcasting technique. The chapter explores how, for instance, *Murder*'s depiction of the US-American legal system as biased in terms of race, gender, or class and in need of transformation allows the show to position itself as such 'political TV'.

In Chapter 7, I argue that any analysis of *The Walking Dead* has to consider how the show aspires to a superior status over the chronologically earlier comic book series which it resigns to the status of paratext. With the notion of paratext seriality, I describe how the show instrumentalises (especially serial) paratexts for its storytelling. Aside from an analysis of gendered and serialised television authorship, two case studies dealing with character deaths and with sexualised violence serve as illustrations of paratext seriality.

As a means to explore gendering, the palimpsest can capture how the comic reverberates in the show's storytelling, which paradoxically both draws on the comic and seeks to overwrite it. Through palimpsest gendering, Chapter 8 explores intentional and unintentional textual echoes in case studies on characters and their popularity with audiences, factoring in the zombie narrative's essentialist gender roles. The chapter offers strategic readings of television characters consistent with their comic counterparts, widely divergent, and of an 'original' creation without a comic book precedent.

Chapter 9 focuses on *The Walking Dead*'s participation in a discourse of survivalism driven by the cultural phenomenon of the zombie apocalypse. I suggest that these practices prepare viewers less for survival within a zombie apocalypse, or any kind of disaster as a matter of fact, and more for competition within a neoliberal marketplace. The chapter turns to readings of genre-related 'zombie literacy', 'zombie consumerism', and 'zombie workout' to demonstrate this understanding of serial survival. Moreover, I speculate on the role of (gendered) survival failure as potentially disruptive refusal of capitalist survivalism in a reading of the 'fringes' of the franchise: minor characters and marginal paratexts.

NOTES

1. I was a member of this Research Unit during its second funding period by the German Research Foundation (DFG) from 2013 to 2016, at which time large portions of this study were written. The different subprojects and associated projects of the group had disciplinary homes in American studies, German philology, cultural anthropology/European ethnology, empirical cultural studies, and media studies.
2. There is still much research to be done on gendered, serial practices in the productions of commercial online providers such as Amazon Prime or Netflix (see Havas 2016) or web series (see Christian 2018).
3. Chapter 4 on viewer engagement on Twitter provides additional methodological embedding in its conceptual overview.
4. Early approaches in gender studies differentiated between a presumed biological 'sex' and a socio-cultural 'gender'. Although this distinction occasionally still surfaces, the understanding that gender constructions inscribe themselves onto bodies and that bodies become cultural sites of gender performances is more current. This theoretical

development of the field is informed by work that explores the historical, medical, and social narratives of a 'biological sex' and the ways they create materialities.
5. Young highlights how the stifling search for a subject has feminist theory and activism either disregard or minimise different experiences in order to cast a generalised, essentialist category of 'woman', or not able to address systemic structures of oppression those perceived as 'women' face (1994: 718).
6. West and Zimmerman's influential 'doing gender' was later refined as 'doing difference' by West in collaboration with Sarah Fenstermaker in order to address notions of race and class.
7. For more on Latour's utility to study serial media see Kelleter 2014: 3–6 and 2017: 25–6.

Part I
Serial TV Criticism and *Girls*

CHAPTER I

The Thinkpiece Seriality of *Girls*

Premium cable channel HBO's massive promotional campaigns in the early 2000s provided a canon of 'Quality TV' drama ready-made with markers of distinction. This campaign coincided with the attempts made by the 'young' discipline of television studies to find a space within universities without being subsumed under film studies. The palatable slogan that the network employed between 1996 and 2009 came to express claims of exceptionality through a schizophrenic refusal of the medium itself: 'It's not TV. It's HBO.' In stark contrast to conceptualisations of television as a 'guilty pleasure', HBO branded its fare as the source of water cooler office chatter. Like both HBO and television studies, moreover, journalistic television criticism underwent a similar process of distinguishing itself as professional against the seemingly lowbrow, mundane associations of its subject. In this chapter, I approach journalistic and academic communities as distinct yet conjoined in many ways. I consider the texts produced by these communities about a television show as that show's respective 'critical sphere'. The chapter argues that texts written by critics, among them journalistic thinkpieces, are not solely accompanying reactions to a show but an essential element of its narrative practices. It is through such serial communication that forms of narration which are seemingly at odds with serial storytelling because they complicate viewer immersion in unfolding plots, expanding storyworlds, or relatable characters – for example, omission, lack of focalisation, or metatextuality – can support a particular kind of seriality in which storytelling is intricately connected with analytical interactivity.

The preferences of critics and viewers often diverge considerably: 'TV seems to play by the rules of a peculiar Faustian bargain: be popular and scarcely acknowledged; or be praised and scarcely watched' (Thompson 2014). A Faustian bargain that is also gendered: the HBO dramas which critics point to as initiators of the canon of 'Quality TV' are set in certain milieus that allow the series to favour a specific type of masculinity and aesthetic. Centring around the prison (*Oz*), the Mafia (*The Sopranos*), or the drug trade (*The Wire*), these shows featured mostly white male protagonists whose 'complex' portrayal as 'antiheros' (Mittell 2015: 142–63) led viewers to explore the limits of morally problematic actions. HBO's gendered use of profanity and graphic depictions of (frequently sexualised) violence, sexuality, and nudity have been promoted by the network as markers of distinction made possible by its exemption from network television's decency regulations (Leverette 2008; McCabe and Akass 2007). While critics responded accordingly, feminist scholarship and journalism have been less invested in the male-centric canon of 'Quality TV'. During the period of HBO's ominous 'Not TV' slogan, female-centred television narratives occurred much more frequently within comedy than drama (Lagerwey et al. 2016) and on network rather than cable (O'Keeffe 2014). Recently, the notion of 'Peak TV' further undermined such a unified canon of 'Quality TV'.[1] Now anxieties centre around the issue of how critical acclaim may be awarded in an increasingly competitive televisual landscape. Both feminist television scholars and critics have shown little preoccupation with such worries due to their continued suspicion of gendered notions of cultural value.[2]

The dramedy *Girls*, which ran on HBO from April 2012 to April 2017 with a total of sixty-two episodes over six seasons, should be understood as a response to the cultural phenomenon of HBO and its masculine-centred legacy of 'Quality TV'. *Girls* tried to mobilise both the engagement of feminist critics as well as critics invested in industry discourses of 'Quality TV'. Its promotional materials introduced four protagonists: the millennial, white women Hannah (Lena Dunham), Marnie (Allison Williams), Jessa (Jemima Kirke), and Shoshanna (Zosia Mamet). *Girls* was about these characters' attempts to build – and at times self-sabotage – their post-college lives: the management of financial and career insecurities, the maintenance of friendships and romantic relationships. The series debut followed comedies such as *2 Broke Girls* (CBS, 2011–17), *New Girl* (Fox, 2011–18), and *Whitney* (NBC, 2011–13), similarly about the struggle urban, white, cis-female characters encountered while making a living in the post-recession cityscape (Negra and Tasker 2014: 14; Dejmanee 2016: 120). While *Girls*'s title and setting seemed to indicate a kinship with these shows, it distanced itself from its network siblings. The dramedy did so through its specifically gendered spin on previous HBO shows and their corresponding auteur roles, as studies of showrunner Dunham demonstrate (Marghitu and Ng 2013; Murray 2018; Nelson 2014; Nygaard 2013; Seaton 2017; Woods 2015; Sulimma 2017).

Lena Dunham is a former darling of the independent movie scene following the success of *Tiny Furniture* (2010), a film she wrote, directed, and starred in. With *Girls*, Dunham's career accelerated; she became a mainstream media sensation and one of the few highly visible female showrunners. She shared the showrunner responsibilities of *Girls* with fellow writers Jenni Konner and Judd Apatow. In a multiplicity of roles that is highly atypical of television's collaborative model of labour division, Dunham is the star of the show, member of the writers' room, producer, and the person to have directed the most episodes.[3] Because the character she plays, protagonist Hannah Horvath, is an aspiring writer herself, the show notoriously blurs Dunham and her character in complicated ways. Apparent in the first episode, the creator-cum-protagonist declares to her parents: 'I don't want to freak you out, but I think that I may be the voice of my generation. Or at least a voice. Of a generation' (1.1 'Pilot'). Utilised for HBO's promotions of the first season, these lines stand as the most frequently quoted of the series, and therefore function as 'one of its most influential self-descriptions' (Kelleter on *The Wire* in 2014: 25). Often Hannah's relativising addendum ('*a* voice', '*a* generation') was neglected, and subsequently, much of the show's controversy resulted from taking her statement at face value. Such readings assumed the character Hannah to be speaking for Dunham and Hannah's fictional memoir to serve as stand-in for the show itself in a kind of 'autobiographical fallacy'.

Many millennial viewers were frustrated with the show that supposedly speaks for their generation (Daalmans 2013: 359). In a similar fashion, academic analyses often treated the show as a document of larger socio-political developments; for instance, of the millennial generation's work choices and economic opportunities (Daggett 2014; Erigha 2014) or dating habits and sexuality (Householder 2015; Tally 2014a). Many observers picked up on the humour and sarcasm inherent in Hannah's declaration because she sidesteps her statement after seemingly realising how worn out and naïve it sounds. Her claim was taken as a metatextual commentary on expectations toward *Girls* that the show would never be able to meet (Gay 2014b: 57; Grdešić 2013: 356–7; McCann 2017: 92). For Katherine Bell, it ironically displays the show's criticism of its own characters' entitlement (2013: 363). Still others understood the lines to embody the search for the self through writing as the thematic interest of the series (Nash and Grant 2015: 979; Witherington 2015: 127). Regardless of how Hannah's statement was interpreted, all these readings touch on certain aspects: the series' investment in metatextuality, the blurring of the character Hannah and her creator Dunham, and the series' tug-of-war between claims to represent a universal 'girlhood' versus the specific story of Hannah, one white (cis-female) New Yorker and her loose-knit group of friends.

Hannah's exclamation, or rather its irony and ambiguity, seems to knowingly trigger such concerns and can be understood as the show instructing its viewers how to watch it, as many serialised narratives are prone to do in their first episodes (Mittell 2015: 56). *Girls* thrives on critical dissection, evades any lasting character or plot developments, and never stopped puzzling critics in their attempts to assess what exactly it represents. Because not all viewers shared the irony of Hannah's statement, one might conclude that the instruction was unsuccessful. Media studies scholar Amanda Ann Klein's response was that the pilot had 'failed one of its primary jobs – to let us know what the series' tone will be' (2012). But Klein followed up this assessment with an elaborate unpacking of some scenes and confessed that these made her 'happy that I study film and television for a living'. This suggests that *Girls*'s ambiguous address of a specific segment of its viewers – the critical sphere – is in fact successfully introduced through Hannah's statement. To highlight how critics' engagements have become part of the show's serial development, this book will refer to the cultural phenomenon that these textual practices result in as *Girls*'s thinkpiece seriality. This is to emphasise the ways the show actively offers textual openings for analysis, discussion, and exploration. *Girls* does so, for example, through ambiguous, fragmented scenes and provocative, metatextual statements. Such instances imagine the viewer-critic's desire to position themselves within the controversies at hand.

This chapter is based on sixty-five academic articles and approximately 250 journalistic pieces of writing. To the best of my knowledge, this corpus consists of all the academic writing on the show between 2013 and 2017 published in one of the three anthologies on *Girls* (Kaklamanidou and Tally 2014; Watson et al. 2015; Nash and Whelehan 2017), a 'Commentary and Criticism' section of *Feminist Media Studies*, and other academic journals and collections. The writers of these texts are largely scholars of media studies, the humanities, or social sciences. Nevertheless, I cannot comprehensively claim to have considered all of the journalistic writing on the show and selected texts based on their prominence. Most of the journalistic writing was published during the first, second, or final season of the show by either freelancers or staff writers.

It is common to use the term 'a writer's writer' to suggest that literary authors' influence can be exempt from mass appeal; *Girls* can be taken to function as 'a critic's show'. *Girls* is credited – and credits itself – with having started a new phase of serial television criticism. Journalists either commend or blame the show for creating 'the over-enrolled *Girls* Thinkpiece Club' (Paskin 2017), the 'think piece industry' (Rose 2017), the 'Think Piece-Industrial Complex' (Saraiya and Ryan 2017), or even the 'thinkpiece revolution' (Raftery 2016). *The New York Times*'s James Poniewozik described the show as 'both the ultimate obsession of think-piece culture and its most astute chronicler. It is a series about precisely the sort of young, wired, highly educated people who would have strong feelings about *Girls*.' (2017).

Journalistic television criticism reaches back to the medium's beginnings and initially functioned similarly to radio or theatre reviews published as retrospective responses.⁴ Overall, the internet drastically changed the temporality, distribution patterns, and communication between the critic, industry, and reader of television criticism. While one may feel frustrated with the increasing commercialisation of previously autonomous fan-created spaces or the ephemerality of online television writing as 'amount[ing] to writing sandcastles' (Juzwiak 2012), the participatory aspects and speed of current television criticism are remarkable. In many ways, online writing has become particularly suited to the rhythms of serialised television. Ongoing television recaps may focus on the smaller units of single episodes, integrating themselves into the weekly flow of a series, and therefore potentially becoming a ritualised part of the viewing experience. Moreover, serial television recaps are often picked up in the deeper dissection and discussion of both the feuilleton and academic discourse. Hence, not only 'formerly academic modes of interpretation migrate in large numbers to the realm of consumer practices' (Kelleter and Loock 2017: 131), but critical writing itself also draws from the textual manifestations of these practices.

A thinkpiece, sometimes also think piece or think-piece, is defined as 'an article containing discussion, analysis, or opinion, as opposed to fact or news' (OED 2018). Within television writing, specifically online writing, the thinkpiece is distinct from the recap or review, even though these different forms of writing overlap one another. While the latter two are concerned with either plot summaries or personal viewing reactions, the thinkpiece is not necessarily published right after an episode airs. It takes up a particular aspect of a show only to veer into larger debates of the media industry, culture, or society. In regard to *Girls*, many thinkpieces tackled questions surrounding representation, access, and accountability, often framed by feminist or intersectional concerns. The amount of writing resulted in critics' attempts to manage the unwieldy debates about *Girls* through catalogues of links or timelines of controversies. For example *The New York Times*'s 'What You Should Read About the "Girls" Series Finale' (Berman 2017) provides an overview of the most relevant thinkpieces for their readers as well as for critics themselves.⁵ That *Girls*'s thinkpiece flood was an indicator of the show's success to the industry becomes obvious when an HBO official told *Business Insider* how thinkpieces rather than viewer ratings proved the relevant metric for assessing *Girls* (McAlone 2017). 'Without "the conversation," it's doubtful *Girls* would've lasted this long', Steven Hyden writes, and continues that it became the show 'that many people experienced solely through think pieces' (2017). As a result, the intense controversies served as a paratext that may also have kept potential viewers from watching the show.⁶

Another important impact of *Girls* was that groups of younger (often female) television critics and academics were able to build careers on their analysis of the show. Television critics like *LARB*'s Jane Hu have reflected on how the show shaped their work:

> I grew up with *Girls* not so much as a, well, girl, but as a critic. . . . *Girls* was the ongoing, open-ended, uneven text that I constantly returned to, all the while adjusting my interpretive capacities, my critical convictions, my personal priorities. (Hu 2017)

While not all journalists or television scholars would describe their fascination with *Girls* as such a career-related coming of age narrative, Hu's engagement is representative of the show's preferred audience, its viewer-critics or critical sphere. Serial TV criticism is much more than an exterior reaction to television; *Girls* stages Hu's uneven textuality through narrative practices to mobilise analytical responses which intertwine with the show's storytelling.

Despite *Girls*'s insistence on having created something new, the thinkpiece has long accompanied serial storytelling in popular culture, as Kathleen Loock demonstrated with reference to the Hollywood sequel (2017: 99). While the urgency, speed, and number of thinkpieces on *Girls* were remarkable, this is not what distinguishes the show's reception from that of earlier critically acclaimed television shows. Instead of locating the show's cultural relevance within its thinkpieces, this chapter argues that *Girls*'s textual attributes actively engage viewer-critics and attempt to further what Andreas Jahn-Sudmann and Frank Kelleter (2012) have termed the serial 'outbidding' of HBO's 'Quality TV' brand. In other words, with *Girls*, HBO attempted to recreate the buzz of its early to mid-2000s watercooler shows by utilising structural changes in how television is evaluated and discussed professionally and increasingly in digital environments. Like earlier shows of the canon of 'Quality TV', *Girls* seeks to generate cultural controversies, but unlike these earlier shows, *Girls* is aware of its role within a recent television history as 'female Quality TV' and employs this role metatextually. The chapter will explore how the show depends on the communication with and through its critics as its particular form of television seriality which requires very different techniques than depictions of profanity, graphic violence, or glamorised sexuality.

NARRATIVE CHARACTERISTICS OF THINKPIECE SERIALITY

Thinkpiece seriality encourages ongoing discussions and interpretation and therefore relies on specific narrative characteristics such as: textual openness and metatextual commentary; a lack of temporal experimentation, but also the tendency toward omission and narrative fragmentation; the cutback of character perspective; and stylistic borrowings from cinematic mumblecore and reality television. Consider this example of the show's use of metatextuality: when Hannah prepares a short story for a public reading, her co-worker Ray responds harshly to her choice of subject, intimacy, by asking, 'what in the world could be more trivial than intimacy?' (1.9 'Leave Me Alone'). Understood as metatextual in journalistic (Holmes 2012b) and academic analysis (Bell 2013: 367; San Filippo 2017: 176; Grdešić 2013: 357), this comment seemed to anticipate some people's dismissal of *Girls* as culturally irrelevant. Further, the scene encourages feminist readings because the female-associated trivial or low-brow is contrasted here with more 'important', high-brow, male-associated forms of cultural production (Levy 2015: 63–70; Tally 2014b: 36).

The show's metatextual inclinations are largely a means through which *Girls* acknowledges its criticism, but it does so in an ambiguous manner that allows for a variety of readings. Critic Alan Sepinwall remarks that scenes in the episode 'Triggering' (4.2), in which Hannah receives criticism for her writing,

> weren't an excuse to lash out at the people who hate *Girls* and/or Dunham, nor were they any kind of stirring defense of either woman. Rather, they took the discussion that swirls around the show and its creator and simply used it to generate laughs. (Sepinwall 2015)

Not every viewer found such scenes entertaining. To maintain malleability and interpretative possibilities, the show never communicated a clear identity of itself as a show. This ambiguity did increase the show's currency for academic and journalistic analysis, but also kept *Girls* from attracting a following of 'casual' viewers not interested in writing about the show, as its continually declining ratings illustrated.[7]

The most remarkable narrative characteristic of *Girls* is the show's approach to temporality. Temporal variation is otherwise a typical feature of the shows associated with the 'Quality TV' label. *Girls* largely lacks temporal experimentation such as flash-forwards, flashbacks, or the speeding up or slowing down of time. Neither does it equip its audience with temporal markers to indicate how much time has passed between scenes, episodes, or seasons.[8] In a typical episode, the narrative 'checks in' with several characters, but never keeps track of all character or plot developments. Frequently, crucial moments of characters' relationships or their reactions after life-altering experiences are absent from the show, which requires viewers to interpret what could have happened. Unacknowledged fragmentation and omission enable its serialised plots: selected scenes are presented without any temporal guidance to indicate how much time or what events have passed since the last scene featuring a character. At first sight, these techniques appear counterintuitive to serial storytelling, which we tend to think of as gradual unfolding of storyworlds, plot, or character developments. However, when taking into account the viewer reactions these techniques manage to mobilise, it becomes clear that *Girls*'s serialisation works not despite of but through these practices, that is, fragmentations and omissions leave room for ongoing audience interpretations as motor for the show's kind of seriality. For example, while each episode of *Sex and the City* includes at least one scene of all four protagonists meeting in a restaurant, bar, or café, which amounts to the show's variation of the sitcom trope of the family dinner, an entire *Girls* season includes only one or two scenes of all four main characters together (Figure 1.1).[9] The lack of such ensemble scenes keeps the nature of the women's relationships with one another hidden from viewers. As a result, viewers' readings diverge widely when it comes to assessments of characters' emotional responses to one another and the status of their friendships.

Moreover, the narration never features diegetic point-of-view camera work, voice-overs, or other modes of providing character perspective, such as dream sequences or hallucinations. Despite the characters' frequent use of social media, attempts at communication with their surroundings never scratch at the fourth wall of the narrative. The characters remain mysterious to their viewers because their motivations and perspectives remain hidden within the diegetic sphere. The effect is one of presumed 'realism' or 'naturalism' and again encourages viewer interpretations. Instead of telling stories from a character's perspective, the show resorts to a mode of *showing* how characters behave in certain situations and environments. Without narratorial guidance to place scenes in connection with previous developments, the series creates the impression that viewers are watching arbitrary moments in the characters' lives, while other moments have been left out without any underlying logic. While this approach to temporality irritated viewers, it is indebted to the cinematic practices of mumblecore, a low-budget subgenre of US-American indie film, and to the surveillance exhibited in reality television.

Characterised by small budgets, a DIY aesthetic, and tuned-down camera and audio, Dunham's celebrated *Tiny Furniture* is considered representative of mumblecore, and HBO emphasised her indie film credentials in promotions (Nygaard 2013; Woods 2015). In terms of style, *Girls* resembles mumblecore films like *Funny Ha Ha* (2002) because it prefers dialogue over plot, indoor locations, low-key aesthetics, 'naturalistic' acting styles, as well as a thematic interest in presumably trivial, everyday lives. I am not the first to point to the show's investment in mumblecore (Ford 2016; Hamilton 2014; Perkins 2014; Scott 2017). Yet, it is important to emphasise that mumblecore's distinct approach to characterisation, to merely exhibit characters and not their inner lives, also poses the largest obstacle for the show's seriality. Unlike stand-alone cinematic mumblecore, the serialised televisual mumblecore of *Girls* is provocative because serial

THE THINKPIECE SERIALITY OF *GIRLS* 33

Figure 1.1 No *Sex and the City* family dinners: rare instances of all female characters appearing together in one scene.

television audiences aspire to forming ongoing relationships with fictional characters and require more insight to do so.

In contrast, *Girls*'s indebtedness to reality television has not been acknowledged, likely because of the show's high production values. The show is linked to this genre by the 'realistic' impression of watching characters behave 'naturally' without assumed outside interference. Such scenes in reality television are, of course, just as manufactured as they are in *Girls*. Evoking modes of surveillance and voyeurism, *Girls* seemed to ask its viewers to maintain a distance and judge its characters. In another context, Chelsea Daggett described this as *Girls*'s 'Brechtian distanciation' (2014: 206), and Melinda Lewis speaks of the show's tightrope act between allowing viewer identification with characters and evaluating their experiences (2014: 177).

However, whereas reality television relies on interview sequences to frame narrative developments and house moments of character motivation, *Girls* never provides reliable insight into characters' emotional and psychological states. Elsewhere, Julia Havas and I argued that the ambiguity of the show's address to its audience highlights *Girls*'s genre hybridity as dramedy, specifically in regard to its 'cringe aesthetics', which causes the viewer to question whether others share their affective response to a scene (Havas and Sulimma 2018: 8–12). Such cringe-worthy scenes often include sexual practices and bodily 'malfunctions'. Reactions to them range from disgust to humour or consternation, which is why they are such effective instances of thinkpiece seriality at work. Overall, the lack of insight into the characters' inner lives enhances the show's relatively low-stake approach to serial storytelling.[10] The refusal of lasting narrative developments can be traced back to its critical sphere: rather than disentangle plots in elaborate recaps, *Girls*'s critics preferred the exploration of various social and cultural themes. Catherine McDermott observes: 'nothing *happens* in Season 2 . . . There is turmoil and insecurity. There are shifts and adaptations, yet no discernible progress is ever being made' (2017: 54). Indeed, when crucial plot developments do occur, such as Hannah's acceptance to the Iowa Writers' Workshop, Shoshanna's relocation to Tokyo, Jessa's university enrolment, or Marnie's marriage, they are quickly reversed. When characters leave these various commitments, the show returns to its narrative status quo of unstable relationships, insecure professions, and unsatisfying living situations.

With that said, *Girls*'s bottle episodes are the show's most critically acclaimed.[11] Far from operating outside the show's serial logic, they provide characterisation through their in-depth focus on the characters' interactions with people of different socio-economic status, gender, or age, such as Hannah's encounters with an upper-class physician (2.5 'One Man's Trash') and with a successful, abusive author (6.3 'American Bitch'), or Marnie's chance meeting with her ex-boyfriend Charlie (5.6 'The Panic in Central Park'). Because such episodes depict a specific moment that one character experiences, they most successfully reveal the character in unmediated fashion. Further, because of their clear temporal and spatial situatedness, they do not have to juggle omissions but commit to a specific narrative scenario. As such, they serve as the purest expressions of *Girls*'s storytelling and most clearly express their limited aspirations to viewers.

Generally, the complaint that 'nothing happens' and the preference for bottle episodes point to the show's minimal interest in serialised story arcs as a way to express the maturation and achievements of characters – despite announcing such progress on promotional posters: 'almost getting it kind of together' (season two), 'nowhere to grow but up' (season four), or 'finally piecing it together' (season five). So, can *Girls* still be understood within the framework of seriality? Again, this chapter argues that the practices that *seem* to complicate *Girls*'s serial storytelling – its metatextual commentary, the complete absence of focalisation, and fragmentation through omission of crucial events – rather function to *support* its particular kind of serial storytelling, thinkpiece seriality, as interconnected with the discussions these practices trigger. There is an unmistakable tension between the lack of plot and character developments and a TV critic's desire to publish a piece on a respective episode every week. Instead of placing an episode within the larger context of the show, critics refined their ongoing arguments with a variety of socio-historical, political, and representational topics (millennials, gender, economic entitlement, social media, the television industry, etc.) as new episodes offered incentives to do so.

THREE WEDDINGS AND A BABY: DOMINANT PLOTS

When Hannah's father Tad informs his wife of his attraction to men in the fourth season, his coming out exemplifies Ron Becker's notion of 'Post-closet TV', a changed representational practice regarding male homosexuality since the late 1990s. Instead of pathologising gay men themselves, narratives have since begun to present closeted gay *masculinity* as a source of pathology (Becker 2006: 127). Tad's late coming out and Hannah's response closely resemble the coming out of the show's other queer character, Elijah. Elijah realises his sexual orientation after having dated Hannah in college. Thus, *Girls* recycles a narrative scenario, and seems only able to imagine one homosexual coming-out experience. Likely indebted to *Girls*'s fragmented storytelling, academic or journalistic writing tended not to address such repetitions of certain plots and narrative scenarios. This invisibility of blatant repetitions serves as an indirect illustration of thinkpiece seriality, as readings of individual scenes and episodes seemed to obscure consideration of the show as a serial text. In the following, I will explore the three most dominant plot repetitions and their implications in terms of sexuality and gender.

The first scenario: during a party in 'Welcome to Bushwick a.k.a. The Crackcident' (1.7), Ray finds himself tasked with looking after his acquaintance Jessa's cousin, his later girlfriend Shoshanna, who panics after having unintentionally smoked crack. The scene mirrors a flashback – the show's only one – to a college party during which Marnie meets her long-term boyfriend Charlie while her pot brownie-induced high renders her paranoid and terrified (1.5 'Hard Being Easy'). These 'Meeting the Guy while High' scenarios are strikingly similar: in both of them the intoxicated female character does not experience joy from recreational drug use, but struggles to cope with anxiety and the loss of control. The intoxicated woman feels even more distress when her neglectful friend, Jessa and Hannah respectively, surrenders her to the care of an annoyed male stranger. Hesitant at first, the male character is charmed by her drug-induced eccentricity. For Katherine Lehman, the combination of drug trips and meeting romantic partners sets 'the link between risk-taking and romance' (2014: 20). This risk-taking is enhanced by the kinds of women Marnie and Shoshanna imagine themselves to be: in control, quick to judge, and unwilling to admit vulnerability. The humour of these scenes derives from their struggle to reconcile the high with their usual behaviour and portrays them as not threatening to Charlie or Ray, who are usually shy and awkward in romantic encounters. Even though scenes of an intoxicated woman meeting a male stranger may evoke the story of 'date rape', neither woman is concerned about sexualised assault, and, likewise, neither male character is positioned as a predatory threat. Rather than solely foreshadowing the romantic potential of Shoshanna and Ray by equating them with the familiar couple Marnie and Charlie, the repetition of the same narrative scenario expresses the show's idealisation of certain gendered relationships: it romantically pairs femininities forced to behave irrationally with nurturing masculinities offering affective labour. Hannah's struggles with mental health during the second season serve a similar purpose to Marnie's and Shoshanna's drug trips, in that she feels abandoned by everyone else and reaches out to her ex-boyfriend Adam to take care of her.

Second, even though many assumed that female friendship would be the central theme of *Girls* (Tally 2014b), the show extensively explores the decline of female friendships due to perceived betrayals, emotional pain, and feelings of neglect. For example, Shoshanna is shown to break all ties to her friends because of the other women's condescending treatment and their unwillingness to confide in her. The primary plot through which the show expresses the deterioration of female friendship is the love triangle between two female friends and an (ex-)boyfriend. The extent to which *Girls* has relied on this plot is surprising as all four leading characters figure in such romantic triangles. When Hannah finds out that her gay ex-boyfriend and current roommate Elijah has drunkenly slept with Marnie, she throws him out of the apartment and while she does not sever ties with Marnie, she repeatedly expresses her hurt (2.3 'Bad Friend'). Shoshanna responds with anger to Marnie's confession of her affair with Shoshanna's ex-boyfriend Ray (3.12 'Two Plane Rides'; Figure 1.2). Lastly, Hannah is shocked to find her ex-boyfriend Adam now dating her friend Jessa (5.7 'Hello Kitty'). Such relationship scenarios uphold an ideal of monogamous romantic structures – polyamorous romantic relationships are never presented as an option in these conflicts. However, because these conflicts primarily play out between the women and not their (former) romantic partners, they contrast temporary romantic relationships with female friendships, which aspire to be more permanent.

Figure 1.2 'I hate you!': Shoshanna reacts with anger to Marnie's confession of her affair with Shoshanna's ex-boyfriend Ray.

Through these plots, *Girls* portrays what is routinely positioned as taboo of female friendship in advice columns (*Dear Coquette* 2015: 'On Fucking Your Friend's Ex'), blogs (*Elite Daily*: 'Oops: What It's Like Sleeping With Your Friend's Ex', Etti 2014), or magazines (*Cosmopolitan*: 'I Slept With My Best Friend's Ex: Learning the Hard Way that Violating Girl Code is a Loser's Game', Choi 2014). The cult film *Mean Girls* (2004) expresses this much-proclaimed 'girl code' in the words of ditsy character Gretchen: 'irregardless, ex-boyfriends are just off limits to friends. I mean that's just like the rules of feminism.' In the early 2000s, Gretchen's ignorance about feminist concerns – and grammar – was played out for the quick laughs of a mainstream audience that was well aware that pink-clad teenager Gretchen was as far as possible from what a feminist was thought to be. Because a friend has likely been a confidante following a break-up, for this person to ally with the perceived enemy – the former romantic partner – is morally dubious in Gretchen's eyes and projects a feminism which occurs in private interactions between women.

A decade later, *Girls* maintains these 'rules of a feminist friendship' by presenting the dating of a former partner as the strongest betrayal of female friendship. As in *Mean Girls*, the conflicts between the female friends at times serve humoristic purposes (Figure 1.2) and ridicule a feminised 'girl culture' invested in 'girl code', but also showcase the emotional pain and guilt they cause. Such portrayals highlight a cultural imaginary without adequate conceptions of female anger, rivalry, or competition, and the ways such conflicts between women may be carried out. As the narrator of Siri Hustvedt's novel *The Summer Without Men* (2011) describes it:

> The duel at dawn, with its elaborate legalisms, . . . the plain old let's-take-it-outside fisticuffs . . . even the playground brawl . . . are all granted a dignity in the culture that no female form of rivalry can match. A physical fight between girls or women is a catfight, one characterized by . . . a scent of the ridiculous or, conversely, of erotic spectacle for male enjoyment. (Hustvedt 2011: 127–8)

Overall, this plot scenario develops a gendered binary between female 'offenders' and female 'victims' fighting over a shared male object of desire.[12] *Girls*'s deterioration of female friendships over such love triangles results in friendships increasingly taking a backseat to the portrayal of romantic relationships. Sociologist Mimi Schippers finds that 'one of the objects given to us by heterosexual culture is the monogamous couple. In order to live a "good life" of sexual and emotional intimacy, we must turn away from other lovers' (2016: 3). The characters of *Girls* routinely fail to turn away from former lovers and in so doing their monogamous relationships become unmaintainable and unsatisfying, yet still paradoxically a norm to aspire to. The love triangle serves to cement *Girls*'s investment in monogamous heterosexuality, especially when combined with its frequent depictions of marriage.

During the course of the show, two of the four women marry and subsequently divorce (Jessa and Marnie) and the sixth season ends with Shoshanna engaged to be married. Even though *Sex and the City*'s premise was the quest for the perfect partner, the show has been understood to criticise its characters' aspirations toward marriage instead privileging female friendship (Gerhard 2005: 38; Henry 2004: 73–5). Within the storyworld of *Girls*, criticism of marriage takes the form of straightforward caricature: Jessa marries a person she barely knows; Marnie marries to keep her relationship from dissolving; Shoshanna's engagement occurs entirely off-screen. These weddings are presented through the prism of intense negotiations of friendship. For example, in 'Wedding Day' (5.1), the women prepare for Marnie's wedding, but the episode ends right before the ceremony. Similarly, Jessa's wedding and Shoshanna's engagement party focus on the other female characters' reactions rather than the event itself. However, all three marriages never raise the possibility of parenthood as a consequence of or reason for those marriages. Meanwhile, for the only character to have a child, Hannah, marriage and a romantic relationship with the child's biological father are not options.[13] Such portrayals serve to disengage marriage from nuclear family-building, and deconstruct marriage as the basis for durable, stable relationships.

Indeed, de-emphasising an apparent cornerstone of life, like marriage, as not life-changing or even durable seems an unusual representation. *Girls*'s portrayal occurs within a cultural climate that simultaneously upholds marriage as desirable and empties it of meaning by positioning it as the romantic conclusion to so many narratives. The controversial franchise *Married at First Sight* (FYI/Lifetime, 2014–) amplifies the contradictions of cultural narratives of (heterosexual) marriage. This reality television show presents romantic love as the idealised basis for heterosexual marriage, but at the same time sets up pragmatically formed marriages based on calculated compatibility and coaching (McKenzie and Dales 2017). Even though the romantic disconnect between some contestants signals their eventual divorce, the show revolves around the question of whether these people will remain married at the end of a season. *Girls*'s debt to reality television suggests itself here, because its viewers also watch mismatched marriages gradually fail. *Girls* does not offer a critique of monogamous partnerships and their investments in 'couple-based' sexual ethics: all the characters aspire to stable and exclusive sexual relationships. Yet no character is able to establish a lasting relationship, and even the one romantic relationship the show arguably depicts as ideal, Shoshanna and Ray, turns instead into a lasting friendship.

After describing how *Girls*'s serialisation relies on triggering discussions and communication, such as through fragmentation, this section had turned to plot repetitions as alternative examples of serial storytelling which were largely disregarded by the show's critical reception. Even though *Girls*'s investment in different versions of family, couplehood, and monogamous heterosexuality are central to its gender politics, critics never perceived the scenarios as serial developments. These plots did not serve thinkpieces as the basis of a larger societal critique, nor did the characters themselves ever express surprise or empathy over their often strikingly similar experiences of divorce, coming out, or heartbreak. This demonstrates how the show and its critical sphere perceive of such repetitions on the level of content as not important for *Girls*'s kind of television seriality, but thinkpiece seriality rather foregrounds narrative and visual techniques that prize ambiguity over clear gender politics. Whereas critics were unwilling or unable to explore these plot repetitions, they certainly agreed to approach *Girls*'s representations of female nudity and sexuality as serialised themes – and thus examples of thinkpiece seriality – due to their metatextual nature.

ON NOT WATCHING CHARACTERS AND GENDERED GAZES

Girls allows significant events in its characters' lives to occur outside the gaze of its viewers. By refusing to narrate what leads up to these events, Jessa's wedding and Shoshanna's engagement are set up as narrative surprises for characters and viewers alike. Such omissions are particularly relevant because, as Frank Kelleter posits, a TV series desires to be watched and to watch viewers watching it (2011: 75). *Girls*, however, often cuts out on the watching and instead relies on fragmentation to trigger discussion. Aside from creating the impulse to analyse and critique, *Girls*'s thinkpiece seriality grants characters agency by denying the audience complete access to their lives. Without such omissions, the show's method of showing characters without focalisation could easily result in the impression of a voyeuristic mode of surveillance, of watching and evaluating characters under a microscope.

Scholarly analysis of *Girls* has turned to Laura Mulvey's ground-breaking essay (1975) to argue that the show 'defies' (Marghitu and Ng 2013: 7) or 'inverts' (San Filippo 2015: 44) the male gaze to overcome female objectification. Connecting feminist film theory and psychoanalysis, Mulvey argued that the camera perspective structures viewing experiences through an objectifying male view of female bodies depicted on-screen. She finds that,

In a world ordered by sexual imbalance, pleasure in looking has been split between active/male and passive/female. The determining male gaze projects its phantasy onto the female figure, which is styled accordingly. In their traditional exhibitionist role women are simultaneously looked at and displayed, with their appearance coded for strong visual and erotic impact so that they can be said to connote *to-be-looked-at-ness*. (Mulvey 1975: 10)

Now over forty years old, Mulvey's work sparked debates within feminist film studies about, for instance, the understanding of femininity as the object and never the driving agency of the gaze. While Mulvey does account for cross-gender identification, she assumes that all viewers adopt the male camera gaze, which turns female characters into an eroticised spectacle. Even though feminist film studies significantly advanced her work toward the female and queer gaze(s), Mulvey's approach to the camera as a gendered apparatus that impacts viewing experiences remains pivotal and can be assumed to have influenced *Girls*'s depiction of female sexuality.

By moving characters outside of the viewer's vision, the series is able to break with what could easily amount to a problematic portrayal of female sexuality. Narratively, sex scenes in *Girls* often begin 'mid-action', a disorienting process by which viewers are not eased into a specific sexual practice or scenario but are immediately confronted with it. In other cases, sex scenes end abruptly and are contrasted with the scenes following them. Furthermore, the show tends to omit scenes of characters' undressing, thus it refuses to engage in a frequent cinematic and televisual (including pornographic) practice of undressing typically associated with femininity, the striptease. These cuts to and from scenes about sexuality create irritation but also deny any build-up of erotic tension and halt the possibility of fetishising female bodies. Jessica Ford describes *Girls*'s camera work as driven by 'stillness':

> the camera rarely travels to meet the characters, but rather the characters move into the frame . . . The sex in *Girls* is largely filmed in medium-long shots and long takes that have little to no movement, either of the camera or of the bodies in the frame. (Ford 2016: 1035)

In contrast with pornographic camera practices such as tracing bodily movements through zoom and panning shots, this stillness may serve to portray nudity and sexuality as determined by characters' agency. Through camera stillness, narrative ellipses, and rapid cuts between scenes with female nudity and sexuality, the show manages to avoid an objectifying gaze.

For example, in the fifth season Hannah is in a relationship with the considerate, gentle teacher Fran who serves as foil for Hannah's occasionally violent former partner Adam. When Hannah discovers that Fran keeps nude 'selfies' that his former partners sent him on his cell phone to masturbate to, she is irritated:

> Hannah: Why would you not just use porn like a normal human male?
> Fran: Are you kidding, Hannah? Porn is disgusting. (5.3 'Japan')

In stark contrast to the first season's portrayal of Adam's porn-inspired sexual encounters with Hannah, Fran finds commercial pornography to objectify women and instead prefers the self-composed pictures without outside mediation. To cope with her jealousy, Hannah consults with Elijah and Ray at the café where they all work. Both men applaud Fran and are unsure how to comfort her. Not at all foreshadowed in their conversation at the café counter, the next scene jumps forward to showcase the solution the trio has come up with for Hannah's dilemma: they apparently closed down the café for a nude photo shoot in order to replace Fran's pictures. Unlike the self-authored selfies of the other women, Ray takes the pictures of Hannah with a phone while Elijah holds a sheet to direct light (or keep Hannah outside of the view of their customers). Ray looks at Hannah through the phone display, but the perspective of the viewers does not align with his, as the camera mostly shows him photographing Hannah (Figure 1.3), filtering the heterosexual male gaze through the medium of his camera – whereas Elijah's homosexual male gaze is direct and receives less attention overall. The scene parodies the commercial sexualisation of femininity as Hannah overdoes the absurd poses of adult magazines. Dunham's physical embodiment of Hannah in this scene is representative of the show's much-lauded body politics. Specifically, Dunham's body type is frequently described as 'non-normative' due to its deviation from standardised cinematic and televisual representations of femininity, in regard to both the slim, toned bodies of actresses as well as practices of lighting, editing, and make-up employed to create an immaculate appearance of already conventionally attractive bodies.

Academic analysis expanded on popular discussions of Dunham's nude performances on the show (Bailey 2015). This nudity has been related to feminist art pornography (San Filippo 2017) and experimental performance art (San Filippo 2015; Thomas 2017). Drawing on Miles McNutt's term 'sexposition' – the relay of information over sex scenes in *Game of Thrones* (HBO, 2011–) – Maria San Filippo finds *Girls*'s 'sexposition' not to provide information on plot or storyworld but 'aimed at critiquing heteropatriarchal representations of sex and women' (2015: 53). The scene discussed illustrates this, as all three characters labour toward the creation of an erotic image, demonstrating

Figure 1.3 The 'erotic' photo shoot breaks with the fetishisation of Hannah's body by, for example, prominently placing photographer Ray within the camera frame.

attempts to mirror prevalent erotic visuality. None of the characters is in a state of arousal but they exhibit critical gazes at the staging of Hannah's body. Their quest for a desirable image illustrates the diversity of eroticisms at odds with the commercial, heterosexual pornographic repertoire that characters and viewers alike are so familiar with. Hannah is understandably unable to follow Ray and Elijah's ominous coaching. She is caught between Ray's intellectualised instruction to provide 'less talking and more animus' and 'a coy smile', and Elijah's suggestion to put on a 'Katie Holmes' look. Only when asked to think of cake, is Hannah able to whip out a smile that both male characters deem attractive enough for the picture, humorously linking food consumption with the consumption of sexuality.

The café setting is also remarkable, as Hannah's nudity occurs in what is simultaneously a workspace and a public space. For Deborah Thomas, Dunham's nudity functions similarly to comedic tropes of male nudity 'generated from the exposure of ordinary, imperfect, male bodies in inappropriate public spaces' (2017: 189) that are rarely employed by female comedians or actresses. However, instead of positioning the 'non-normative' female body as a source of laughter, it is the inappropriateness of the setting as well as the artificial poses of an eroticised femininity that create humour.

Hannah does not self-author her photograph to conform to her own sexual desire, but her body is positioned for the photograph under the critical gaze of her male friends. Unlike the shaky handheld aesthetic of a selfie, the scene uses the camera stillness Ford describes: 'it positions the female body in a deliberately uncomfortable way that emphasizes its blankness' (2016: 1037). The blankness of Hannah's nude body as opposed to an objectified female body serves to disrupt the male gaze but also obscures Hannah's own desires. Hannah's jealousy-inspired goal to be the only source of her partner's sexual desire is detached from their actual romantic relationship. The episode depicts Hannah's attempts to cope, but not Fran's reaction to the erotic image she co-creates. Rather than a negotiation of sexual desire in a heterosexual relationship, the episode centres on Hannah's divergence from bodies typically considered erotic and how she pushes back against such an understanding of female desirability. The scene becomes an experiment in media representation for the character as much as the show.

Within the episode, the plot of Hannah's photo shoot is juxtaposed with two plots in which Jessa and Shoshanna each get to know cis-male characters they desire. When Jessa watches Hannah's ex-boyfriend, the aspiring actor Adam, perform in a mock TV police procedural, his body on-screen becomes more available to her desiring gaze than his actual body on the couch next to her, due to her friendship with Hannah. This depiction showcases Driver's muscular upper body and 'ostensibly revers[es] the gaze, fetishizing the well-built and frequently shirtless Adam' (San Filippo 2015: 49).[14] Meanwhile, Shoshanna lives in Tokyo and is enamoured with an attractive co-worker. She encounters him in explicitly sexualised settings (a spa, an S&M bar) yet only connects with him after he disavows the fetishisation of her white Western femininity. In all of these scenarios, female characters struggle to manage sexualised images of either themselves or their male partners that have been mediated through formulaic and stereotypically gendered Western popular culture, in these cases police procedurals and pornography. The female characters engage these texts with high genre awareness yet seem unsure as to their relation to these texts as an object of desire (Hannah, Shoshanna) or how to handle their own desiring gaze (Jessa). Hence, the show can be taken to express feminist film studies' concerns as to how female sexuality can be depicted without succumbing to practices of fetishisation and objectification. With the variety of disorienting dynamics of thinkpiece seriality, *Girls* found a provocative yet effective combination to engage viewer-critics and mobilise their responses as part of its serial storytelling.

NOTES

1. In 2015, FX CEO John Landgraf used the term 'Peak TV' to postulate that there was 'too much television' (Holmes 2015). Instead of 'Quality TV's' promise of a singular canon, 'Peak TV' laments the seeming problems that arise when everyone watches (and writes about) different shows.

2. For further consideration of the gendered discourse on 'Quality TV', see Lagerwey et al. 2016; Havas 2016; Havas and Sulimma 2018.
3. Over six seasons, Dunham directed a third of the episodes, has single writing credits for thirteen of the sixty-two episodes, and shared credits for twenty-seven episodes. She is also the first woman to have won a Directors Guild of America award for comedy. The showrunner of *Better Things* (FX, 2016–), Pamela Adlon, is another such jackie of all trades. And, Phoebe Waller-Bridge alternately has showrunner, producer, writer, and actor credentials in her different television productions, while Natasha Lyonne stars in and co-writes, co-produces, and directs *Russian Doll* (Netflix, 2019–).
4. From the 1960s onward, the new technology of VCR allowed the industry to provide critics with advance copies and to tap into the promotional purposes of television criticism (Lotz 2008: 26). Critics began to appear more directly as 'professional television viewers, and hence self-appointed taste leaders' (Gray 2011: 115) or 'veritable cultural mediator[s] between the show itself and a broader public' (Polan 2007: 267).
5. Such websites echo another kind of writing that accompanies television, the television guide. However, they do not provide an overview of what is on television, but an overview of the vast online discussions about television.
6. *The New Yorker*'s Jia Tolentino writes about such an experience in 'On Finally Watching "Girls," a Different and Better Show Than I'd Been Led to Imagine' (2017).
7. While television audiences often locate the 'quality' of 'Quality TV' within the respective shows as a text-immanent property, for the television industry the term has always implied that the desired demographic is an educated, urban, upper-middle-class 'quality audience' (Feuer 2007: 147; Mittell 2015: 211). *Girls*'s shift toward viewer-critics as its target audience is in line with such industry approaches.
8. Only twice does the show temporally mark a flash-forward to reveal Hannah in a new relationship or parenting her child (4.10 'Homebirth', 6.10 'Latching'). The show makes use of a flashback only once (1.5 'Hard Being Easy').
9. These scenes include Jessa's wedding (1.10 'She Did'), a flea-market sale (2.3 'Bad Friend'), a shared weekend vacation (3.7 'Beach House'), Hannah's birthday party (3.3 'She Said OK'), a dinner date (5.6 'Close-Up'), Marnie's wedding (5.1 'Wedding Day'), and Shoshanna's engagement party (6.8 'Goodbye Tour').
10. The show's gradual exploration of the dissolution of college friendships may be its only long-term plot investment.
11. Set at a single location with few cast members, bottle episodes have become an industry means of budget allocation to other episodes. The term is taken to stem from *Star Trek* producers who described episodes with few exterior shots as 'ship-in-a-bottle episodes'. Apart from budget-related concerns, within academic and journalistic writing the term is employed for relatively self-contained episodes that provide insight into characters more than they further plots.
12. Tellingly, the easiest 'offence' to forgive is Marnie's sex with homosexual Elijah, since Hannah's hurt stems from jealousy: 'Elijah, I was meant to be your last [female sex partner]', she protests (2.3 'Bad Friend'). This love triangle functions differently, as no potential relationship results from – or is blocked by – Marnie and Elijah's sex, and the three characters eventually make up.
13. One of the rare instances of a major plot point without later revision was Hannah's pregnancy in the final season. A surprising number of characters offer to co-parent her child (former partner Adam offers a nuclear family, Elijah a queer roommate family,

neighbour and single father Laird a patchwork family). In discarding different family scenarios for single motherhood, the show expresses an anxiety toward the family as the basis for stable relationships that haunts all of *Girls*'s romantic relationships, even the only durable homosexual relationship that Elijah has.

14. Driver's bare upper body was so frequently on display that fans created the Twitter account @AdamsChest and the resolution-themed second season's promotional posters had Adam resolve to wear a shirt.

CHAPTER 2

Carousel: Gendering through Controversy

The carousel is one of three analytical metaphors this book introduces to think through the practices by which serial narratives negotiate gender. The narrative characteristics of *Girls*'s serial storytelling – such as metatextuality, textual ambiguity, lack of character insight, a stylistic mode of observation and surveillance, and especially narrative fragmentation – conjoin to allow for carousel gendering. When a carousel rotates, we only see individual horses and riders briefly, in fragments, while they become invisible to us as they go around the back of the carousel, much like the omissions of relevant moments in characters' lives in *Girls*. At the same time, the carousel implies the possibility of a unified whole, though this bird's-eye view is not actually available to any individual spectator. The metaphor of the carousel serves two purposes: first, to explain how gendered performances build on narrative aspects of thinkpiece seriality, such as fragmentation and lack of focalisation, and second, how such performances circle around cultural and intertextual references.

First, the carousel plays off omissions of relevant moments in characters' lives while it simultaneously implies an oversight that it actually lacks. Even though the metaphor of surveillance suggests complete access to the characters' lives, certain moments are elided and deliberately kept from viewers. Riding on the carousel, characters seem to be in constant sight of the bystanding viewer, yet they are slowly turned out of the viewer's field of vision. For example, after an abusive, manipulative bestselling author assaults Hannah (6.3 'American Bitch'), the show never depicts her attempts to cope with what happened. Instead, in Hannah's next scenes in the following episode she finds out that she is pregnant and thus moves from one urgent moment of character development to an unrelated, though also significant, one.

Second, the carousel also allows for a concrete analysis of the ways characters circle around understandings of themselves, understandings which frequently manifest in cultural types and tropes as easily comprehensible popular cultural references. This circularity should not be thought of as incompatible with seriality. Instead of merely referencing, serial narration allows for an exploration of these tropes of femininity and masculinity as self-constituting, integral parts of characters' ongoing gender performances. Rather than trace a non-existent linear evolution of progress and maturity, the carousel here reveals the deep layers of the characters' gendered identities, which turn around these insufficient types.

For example, in *Girls*'s pilot episode, Shoshanna wonders which leads from *Sex and the City* (henceforth *SATC*) her cousin Jessa and herself most resemble, and by doing so, she anticipated that many viewers would employ the earlier show's protagonists as types that the newer show's characters would emulate. The equation of Carrie with fellow writer Hannah, as well as Samantha with the bohemian traveller Jessa, seemed a given. Marnie was less easy to place; some viewers emphasised her professional ambition and read her as Miranda, while others found her to be more like Charlotte: uptight and a driven romantic. Shoshanna, the character most eager to imagine herself within the narrative world of *SATC*, was interestingly the hardest to find a precedent for.[1] As the series progressed, each character's trajectory revealed cultural types to be simultaneously at the core of the character's self-understanding and in tension with their behaviour.[2] Closest to my understanding is the notion that '*SATC* continues to be a type of model, a fantasy to which the characters in *Girls* aspire' (Lewis 2014: 176). Indeed, characters describe themselves and others through such cultural references and labour to follow in the footsteps of these descriptions. Thus, characters mirror the 'quotidian' aspect of *SATC*'s viewers and make it difficult for *Girls*'s critical sphere to apply such descriptions themselves. A frequent narrative strategy of characterisation is to call up popular culture types or tropes, and then circle around them to expose their inadequacy for the show's characters. As Sean Fuller and Catherine Driscoll argue, '*Girls* is also a story about fantasy and type. . . .This includes Charlie's earnest commitment to being a good boyfriend and Hannah's mother's desire for "a lake house" that inspires her refusal to support Hannah any longer' (2015: 256). Ultimately, the characters frequently find themselves struggling with too uncritically adopted, insufficient cultural imaginations that they continue to maintain – often to simultaneously humorous and tragic effect. Even though the show is rich in intertextual references, it does not itself partake in what Jahn-Sudmann and Kelleter have identified as a dynamic of 'serial outbidding' (2012: 215–20), meaning it does not compete with the cultural artefacts it references.

Creating the illusion of progress, the carousel only follows circular motion. It turns around itself in circles and returns its passengers swiftly to their point of departure. Kristen Warner observes that scenes of the pilot could easily have been part of the last season (2017). Despite their constant movement, *Girls*'s characters seem to be running in place. Catherine McDermott labels the show's struggles with serial momentum 'narrative stagnation': '*Girls* produces a type of storytelling that does not comply with traditional narrative convention. The circularity of the series contravenes the most fundamental narrative arc' (2017: 54). This study argues that *Girls*'s circularity is not at odds with its serial storytelling but is a crucial component of serial gendering. While the show may sometimes seem to slow to the point of stasis or stagnation, because there is no fantastic 'operational aesthetic' at play (Mittell 2015: 41–4), the metaphor of the carousel allows for an approach to characters' slow circling around the cultural types they evoke as part of their femininity or masculinity. But it is not only the characters that seem caught up in circularity: the discussions surrounding the show have laboured around similar issues without being able to reach conclusive results, as this chapter demonstrates.

It is telling in this regard that the most frequently employed theoretical frame to approach *Girls* is Lauren Berlant's 'cruel optimism' (in: Bianco 2014; Lewis 2014; Lloyd 2017; McCann 2017; McDermott 2017; Waters 2017; Whelehan 2017). Berlant's interest in subjectivity, attachment, and desire within contemporary neoliberal capitalism lends itself to the paradox of *Girls*'s characters' running in place despite the show's investment in growing up: 'a relation of cruel optimism exists when something you desire is actually an obstacle to your flourishing' (2014: 1). The attachments that one forms and expects to ultimately add up to happiness become the obstacle to what Berlant calls 'the good life' (3). Of course, any serial television can be taken to operate on the promise of cruel optimism, to negotiate viewers' simultaneous need for an ending and the desire for continuation; to keep us watching, television has to make us believe in things adding up. But for *Girls* specifically, academics convincingly argued that the desire 'to become who I am' (as Hannah puts it in 1.1 'Pilot') functions as an impediment to the characters' own good.

The cultural figure of 'the girl' poses an ideal subject for the show to trace processes of self-fashioning: 'as an unfinished business herself, the girl can explore ideas and experiences without committing to a fixed understanding of what they mean' (Waters 2017: 77). In contrast, for instance, with *SATC*'s thirty-something protagonist Carrie Bradshaw, who knew exactly what she was looking for (romance and a pair of Manolo Blahniks), the twenty-somethings in *Girls* are in the midst of figuring out what it is they aspire to, but never arrive at any lasting conclusions. Carrie portrays a confident femininity; in her voice-overs, which frame every episode, she explores urban, single womanhood and draws conclusions from her own and her friends' experiences. Yet voice-overs are unknown in the narrative world of *Girls*, in which viewers watch Hannah and her friends perform an unselfconscious girlhood open to experimentation with sexuality and relationships as a process of learning by doing. This experimentation without any definite results marks the characters as 'disciplinary subjects, stalled in a passive temporal position, always "becoming" in a place where becoming costs so much' (Bell 2013: 367). This is not to say that this search for becoming is only relevant to the female characters of *Girls*; rather, the show explores the costs and limitations of this process for all major characters.

CIRCLING AROUND FEMININITY: WHO'S THE SLACKER NOW?

Employing the metaphor of the carousel, in this section I focus on the two most prominent femininities of the show, Hannah's and Marnie's, and explore how their respective femininity is negotiated as circling around specific cultural types such as the female slacker, the female writer, or popular culture's pretty girl protagonist.

The characterisation of Hannah as female writer evokes a well-established practice of female-centred television and cinema, from *Bridget Jones's Diary* (2001) to *SATC*. Read through voice-over, Bridget's diary or Carrie's column serve as sites of self-writing. Judith Roof finds a circular process in such scenes that intertwines the female writer with the activity of the writing:

> The voice is a guarantee of the personal, simulating a denuding revelation of the 'real' female whose feminizing processes the writing documents. This produces a perpetual cycle of feminizing as the character in the process of perpetual feminization reveals herself to be in the process of perpetual feminization, et cetera. (Roof 2016: 149)[3]

In other words, writing becomes intrinsic to the female writer's gendering, repeated and constituted through ritualised voice-over. However, the lack of voice-over and the absence of Hannah's written text necessarily complicates her gendering in this tradition of feminised self-writing. Even though she aspires to be a professional writer, Hannah does anything but write in the first five seasons. For Stéphanie Genz, Hannah exhibits a 'prima donna mindset' because she looks for 'the recognition and admiration she thinks she deserves' (2017: 22). Indeed, Hannah's struggling writing career is impacted by her procrastination, lack of work ethic, and sense of entitlement to the financial support of her parents, which echoes yet another cultural figure, the slacker, at the core of Hannah's carousel ride.

The slacker is characterised as a pyjama-clad, adolescent or adult protagonist who gets through life with little effort or ambition – and dubious hygiene – and often relies on parents, siblings, or girlfriends to pick up his slack. The slacker may be a stoner, gamer, or nerd, indicating that the figure is part of white- and male-associated youth and subcultures. Hannah is understood to fill a cultural void: *The Guardian* announced, 'The Slacker is Back – and This Time She's Female' (Hoby 2012), and *Forbes* described Hannah as 'slacker sister' (Henderson 2012). Judd Apatow's involvement as co-showrunner of *Girls* furthers this association: he directed the romantic comedy *Knocked Up* (2007), which served many critics as illustration of the slacker's problematic gender politics (Chesaniuk 2016; Denby 2007). Alex Wescott illustrates how – despite the potential to disrupt the productivity of neoliberal capitalism – the slacker's representation 'inhabits a certain deviation from normalcy without quite leaving the privileges his white middle-class heterosexuality often affords' (2014: 22). Female idleness follows a different lineage than male idleness because work, pay, and leisure are coded inversely with regard to femininity. For example, the invisibility of housework as a kind of 'second shift' (Hochschild and Machung 2012) results in the normalisation of female financial dependence on family members or spouses.

Lauding Hannah as a long-awaited female slacker, journalistic critics were eager to explore the figure's gendered implications. For instance, the male slacker is only rarely likened to the author figures of their films while viewers frequently interpret Hannah as a younger, less driven version of Dunham. Some found this unbelievable due to Dunham's professional success, while others located 'a kind of mock heroic pride' (Hoby 2012) in seeing Dunham overcome her presumed slackerdom. Instead of distancing slacker Hannah from the successful media sensation of Dunham, *Girls* continued to uneasily blur them. Further, politicised by virtue of her underrepresentation, the female slacker seemed a more desperate figure than her male counterpart. In scenes that lend themselves to such characterisations, Hannah sits in bed in the dark apartment glued to her laptop screen and wearing an old, oversized t-shirt. While the male slacker prioritises the entertainments of popular culture over work, Hannah is incapable of work because she is frozen in anxiety. In the second season especially, her mental health complicates the characterisation of Hannah as a slacker. As a result of writer's block and stress over a contract for an e-book, Hannah develops an obsessive–compulsive disorder that had lain dormant since her childhood. Such portrayals of female slacking as procrastination caused by severe stress are at odds with male slacking as laziness at the expense of others.

The tension between the female slacker and the female writer characterises Hannah throughout the entire run of the show. Instead of a linear development, Hannah's femininity circles around these two cultural types, and highlights their continued relevance to and insufficiency for her gender identity. Because in general the show only rarely depicts Hannah writing (the process) or Hannah's writing (the result), this allows for further commentary on the practices of writing in the twenty-first century. The opposition of slacker and professional writer does not compromise the depiction of writing, but instead highlights how creative work is driven by moments of non-activity, that is, idleness, pause, and waiting, as much as activity. Invisible within idealisations of self-optimisation, efficiency, and time management, Hannah's slacking hence should not be taken as a foil for the figure of the writer, but constitutes a part of her work, formerly invisible within representations of writing women such as Carrie or Bridget Jones.

An apt contrast for Hannah and her closest friend since college, Marnie Michaels treats popular culture-inspired tropes of femininity as guarantors of her assumed future successes. In many ways, the show presents the former-art-gallery-assistant-turned-aspiring-singer as a mirror opposite to Hannah. Described as 'the most "adult" of the *Girls*' (Turner 2014: 164) and 'possess[ing] the strongest work ethic' (Daggett 2014: 210), Marnie repeatedly casts *herself* as responsible and reliable. Through Hannah and Marnie's friendship, *Girls* shifts the romantic comedy trope of the 'slacker-striver romance' (Denby 2007).[4] Yet just as Hannah oscillates between cultural types, Marnie's striver femininity wavers between being driven versus aimless, thus complicating the template of the striver and slacker.

Marnie physically conforms to conventionally beautiful media representations of white cis-femininity: actress Allison Williams is slim, wears the most cosmetics of all characters, has long hair for the entire run of the show, and has been described as an 'all-American beauty' (Genz 2017: 26; Householder 2015: 26). Rather than evoking only one specific cultural figure or character, Marnie's carousel ride turns around decades of women-centric popular culture that rewards beautiful protagonists. Equipped with high heels and feminine 'body-con' dresses, Marnie is a 'young cliché in the vein of a Carrie Bradshaw in training' (Vayo 2015: 170). The show's greatest aficionada of female-centred popular culture, Shoshanna, also recognises Marnie's resemblance to the femininity prized in such narratives: 'you're like Bella Swan from *Twilight*, and I'm like her weird friend who doesn't understand how fabulous her life is because my boyfriend won't spend four dollars on tacos' (2.6 'Boys'; Figure 2.1). These cultural artefacts instil in Marnie narrow ideals of what her career, relationships, and friendships should look like, precisely because she so successfully fulfils the requirements of normative femininity. Anne Helen Petersen has called this Marnie's 'Pretty Girl Privilege': 'you're a pretty, skinny, moderately intelligent girl, and every piece of media you've consumed has told you that your life would go one way' (2014). On *Girls*, life does not go Marnie's way: after losing her job and long-term relationship, she spends six seasons in search of an ideal of both professional and romantic fulfilment without ever achieving either to her own satisfaction.[5]

Figure 2.1 Shoshanna admires Marnie as the apparent embodiment of her aspirations.

Marnie is often mentioned in writing about the male characters (Dhaenens 2017; Shaw 2015), which illuminates her investment in 'narratives about the erotic power of successful masculinity' (Fuller and Driscoll 2015: 257). From imagining the life of dinner parties and art exhibitions at the side of wealthy artist Booth Jonathan, to the creative romance based on her musical collaboration with hipster musician Desi, Marnie casts potential romantic partners as accessories to narratives of romantic relationships. None of the men Marnie dates can live up to her expectations, resulting in her disillusionment with each relationship rather than with her own expectations. Not even the affair with Ray – who as audience stand-in often expresses the viewers' frustrations with judgemental Marnie – can change her demands for romantic partners. Instead, Marnie appears embarrassed at the less physically attractive, self-styled intellectual Ray possibly being the life partner she is looking for:

> Marnie: It can't be you. It just, it can't. It can't be you.
> Ray: I think it might be me, Marn. (5.9 'Love Stories')

To the viewer, their relationship likely comes off as less of a surprise. A staple plot of romantic narratives builds on the heroine's gradual realisation that her best romantic choice is the reliable masculinity she had previously overlooked. Similarly, the 'mismatched couple', that is, the pairing of a physically attractive femininity with a less conventionally beautiful masculinity, is common in popular culture (Mizejewski 2014: 21; Walsh et al. 2008: 125–7). Their relationship does not last: Marnie struggles to reconcile her needs with the image of herself as a 'good girlfriend'.

Only once does *Girls* allow Marnie to untie 'the handcuffs of her own personality' (Tolentino 2017). In the much-acclaimed bottle episode 'The Panic in Central Park' (5.6), Marnie runs into her ex-boyfriend, Charlie (Christopher Abbott), who had last appeared in the second season and is visibly transformed. Instead of his former slim-boyish figure, Abbott showcases a muscular, bearded, and tattooed body, physically and behaviourally more aligned with the determined, self-assured masculinity Marnie desires. As she follows his lead, Marnie embarks on a romantic adventure that could easily be part of a romantic comedy: it involves a tight red dress, a high society party, drunken dining at an Italian restaurant, and finally a night-time boat ride in Central Park. The episode explores what happens when Marnie's idealised expectations are fulfilled. Marnie is delighted to find in Charlie her male counterpart for such a narrative. When she realises that Charlie enables his confident swagger through heroin and that his drug use is expressive of a psychological crisis, her 'romantic comedy' adventure abandons the genre. By the end of the episode, Marnie has left both Charlie and her husband Desi and arrives at Hannah's apartment to climb into bed with her sleeping friend. This last scene provides one of the rare instances of female intimacy so often omitted from the show – it gives a glimpse into why these women continue to spend time with one another.

Rather than this empathetic moment between friends, the show instead highlights how Marnie's perfectionism has her make petty demands not only on romantic partners but on female friends as well:

> Hannah's father: You look so wonderful.
> Hannah: Thank you!
> Marnie: Doesn't she? I keep telling her she could look like this every day if she wanted to. (3.3 'She Said OK')

This exchange is representative of many scenes in which Marnie polices Hannah's grooming and clothing, without explicitly criticising her friend's figure. The dialogue illustrates how through the 'pretty girl' character Marnie, the show responds to woman-centric popular culture at large and enables viewers to reflect on their own internalised beauty norms, as 'to agree [with such statements] is to align ourselves with the show's most judgmental character' (San Filippo 2015: 50). In line with the discussions surrounding Dunham's body, Williams's conventional beauty led to the depiction of the efforts necessary to maintain it. In holding Hannah accountable for her lack of a beauty regime, Marnie expresses her belief in the importance of such body management, as well as the fulfilment she personally draws from it. As Diane Negra posits in regard to a postfeminist rhetoric of choice,

> perfectionism is the function of a broad promotional rhetoric that (re)assures female clients that they are demonstrating agency and self-management when they avail themselves of such service rather than capitulating to regressive (sometimes misogynist) appearance norms. (Negra 2009: 121)

From the beginning of the series, Marnie's femininity is shown to be the result of a strenuous, highly curated activity. Marnie never questions the labour involved in maintaining her physical appearance; rather, these efforts become the source of her self-esteem. Her tiring perfectionism thus contrasts with Hannah's frequent imperfections, her 'slacking' and wasting time, her food and alcohol consumption. However, Marnie's efforts are not rewarded through the markers of success and validation that *both* Marnie and the audience have come to expect based on previous media representations. In line with a postfeminist media culture in the recession, such ideals are no longer represented as leading toward the fulfilment of life goals (Negra and Tasker 2014: 4). Where Hannah exists in the tension between ambitious writer and female slacker, Marnie runs circles around the idealised 'pretty girl' characters of earlier popular culture and feels lost and aimless to a much larger extent than the other less conforming characters on the show. Accordingly, the prioritisation of certain genders over others becomes visible: unlike popular culture at large, *Girls* does not present Marnie's femininity as ideal, but positions Hannah's femininity as its preferred gender expression. Marnie is redeemed only when she emulates Hannah in cutting herself some slack (as in 5.6 'The Panic in Central Park').

MALE GIRLHOOD? READING MASCULINITIES

From the second season onward, the show narratively expanded its scope beyond the eponymous 'girls' to include male characters, Adam and Ray, Hannah's parents (in the fourth season), and Elijah (in the fifth season). The show upgraded these formerly supporting characters to feature in their own storylines that sometimes did not even incorporate the female leads. To prominently present male perspectives in a show called *Girls* necessarily involves complex methods of gendering masculinities. 'Female masculinity', for example the public performances of masculinity by female athletes or politicians, may be perceived as acceptable when combined with a culturally legible femininity (Halberstam 1998; Sulimma 2014a). But masculinity relies on its discrimination from femininity, hence the performance of femininity is much more elusive for male-perceived bodies. My analysis of the show's management of masculinities draws on Raewyn Connell's sociological understanding of gender hierarchies and order, its advancements by Mimi Schippers and Amanda Lotz, as well as academic readings of *Girls*'s male characters (Albrecht 2015; Dhaenens 2017; Shaw 2015).

Drawing on Marxist Antonio Gramsci, Connell's formative work describes an idealised masculinity, which through hegemony legitimises its privilege over other – 'subordinated' or 'complicit' – kinds of masculinity and femininity. While Connell's concept of 'hegemonic masculinity' has received much scholarly attention, the fluidity within which hegemony is reassigned and the ways in which it relies on other masculinities and femininities for stabilisation have not. Connell has abandoned her original controversial implication that *all* femininities are subordinated to masculinities (2016: 77–9). Instead, femininities are impacted by patriarchal structures as a group, while masculinities are impacted only as individuals. In other words, even though masculinities struggle to live up to a socially and culturally prized ideal of masculinity on an individual level, they benefit from gendered organisations of society through material and symbolic gains called the 'patriarchal dividend' (Connell 2016: 82) or 'patriarchal bargain' (Wade and Ferree 2015: 133).

Sociologist Mimi Schippers extends Connell's work through a needed theory of femininities and finds hegemonic femininity to be composed through 'the characteristics defined as womanly that establish and legitimate a hierarchical and complementary relationship to hegemonic masculinity and that, by doing so, guarantee the dominant position of men and the subordination of women' (2007: 94). Scholars must ask in which contexts and by which processes certain kinds of masculinity and femininity are positioned as hegemonic to function as the '*currently accepted answer* to the problem of legitimacy of patriarchy' (Connell 2016: 77; my emphasis). Marnie's performance can easily be understood in these terms as either 'emphasized' (Connell 2016) or 'hegemonic femininity' (Schippers 2007) due to her attempts to physically, socially, and romantically conform to gender norms. She 'cultivates a hegemonic masculine ideal . . . yet the series does not side with her' (Dhaenens 2017: 128). Accordingly, it is necessary to consider hegemonic gender relations as specific to each cultural artefact 'rather than consistent across texts or within US culture' (Lotz 2014: 20) and not as necessarily mirroring society at large. Amanda Lotz develops a continuum of television masculinity between 'patriarchal' and 'feminist' poles, yet highlights that characters can rarely be positioned definitively on this continuum. This is not to say that narratives do not privilege some behavioural or character traits over others. It is precisely the conflict over which traits of masculinities are presented as best, preferred, or hegemonic within the narrative universe of a television series that illustrates changes of gender scripts as well as the cultural work that television can perform. This chapter turns to *Girls*'s most prominent male characters to illustrate how Ray is established as preferred masculinity, thus hegemonic within the show, and privileged over Adam.

Played by mumblecore actor and director Alex Karpovsky, Ray Ploshansky, or 'Old Man Ray' as other characters nickname him, is first little more than an acquaintance of the female characters. Even though Ray is a bit older than the other characters, his nickname derives from his (self-)fashioning: Ray casts himself as an intellectual, a literary connoisseur, and a sarcastic observer. He takes pride in his ignorance of contemporary popular culture, trends, and colloquial language, in which the other characters are heavily invested. His relationship with fashion victim Shoshanna is 'a study in contrasts' (Daggett 2014: 204), and his later partner – the show's least liked and most conventionally attractive character – Marnie is also his polar opposite.

Working as barista and later as manager of his own branch café, Ray is the only continually employed character of the show and offers a string of characters temporary employment. Fitting Ray's off-putting demeanour, Café Grumpy is an actual New York franchise which functions as a frequent locale and the only consistent public setting of the show. Unlike earlier televisual cafés, such as Central Perk in *Friends* (NBC, 1994–2004), Grumpy is not a space for characters to meet but solely a work environment (Witherington 2014: 125). Because most characters aspire to careers as writers (Hannah), actors (Adam, Elijah, Desi), painters (Jessa), or musicians (Marnie, Desi), Ray sees his non-creative employment as a source of insecurity and ponders postgraduate work in Latin Studies. For Frederik Dhaenens, Ray's perceived career failure exposes 'how a hegemonic masculinity is forcing men to set out ambitious life goals even though these goals have become less evident in a post-recession economy' (2017: 127). However, Ray's vague ambitions are not concerned with traditional markers of success, such as income or security, but are instead situated within *Girls*'s idealisation of creative work (Erigha 2014: 144) and his intellectual aspirations. This chapter argues that what I tentatively call Ray's transparent masculinity is the show's preferred masculinity, that is, a masculinity hegemonic *within* the storyworld of *Girls*, precisely due to expressions of vulnerability, self-doubt, and empathy. I describe Ray's masculinity with the moniker transparent because it is so obviously and easily understood as a performance by characters and viewers alike – a performance which circles around cultural artefacts deemed too absurdly exaggerated or inappropriate for adult male identification.

In a characteristic episode (2.6 'Boys'), Ray embarks on a mission to retrieve his treasured copy of Louisa May Alcott's novel *Little Women* (1868–9), leading to his first encounter with Adam. Mirroring male viewers of *Girls*, *Little*

Women illustrates how Ray's investment in female-associated narratives is policed. After mockingly asking Ray which female characters he identifies with, Hannah and Shoshanna refuse him access by confining him to the novel's (marginal) representation of masculinity: 'you're not a Marmee. You're probably the dad who dies of influenza at the war.' Even though never called out, Hannah's false recollection – Mr. March recovers from his illness and returns to his family – demonstrates how contestable her (and Shoshanna's) gender-based claim to *Little Women* as a book 'for girls' and not 'Old Man Ray' is. The episode ends with Ray crying next to a violent muzzled dog. Ray's failure to bond with Adam leaves only the dog as the witness of his sadness and insecurity. On *Girls*, characters frequently express anger or irritation, but sadness is a rarely depicted emotion. In a culture in which anger alone is considered an adequate expression of male affect, vulnerability and empathy are still coded within the realm of femininity. Scenes in which male characters cry stand out not only within the show but within popular cultural representations in general (Warhol 2003: 29–30). The violent dog here serves as an easily recognisable metaphor for toxic, masculine anger which is held temporarily and inadequately at bay (the muzzled snout) to allow for the expression of other emotions, such as sadness.

Of the first season, Lauren DeCarvalho criticises that Ray serves as a 'voice of moral authority' that puts female characters in their place and ridicules their behaviour as self-centred and naïve (2013: 369). But, as the show progresses, Ray's enactment of such a sarcastic, stand-offish persona is repeatedly interrupted to express empathy, encouragement, and support to male and female characters alike. In such scenes, Ray's performance of sarcasm is highlighted to be just that, an artificial performance of masculinity not convincingly enacted for the other characters, a source of humour for viewers, and altogether quickly discarded in favour of a sincere, empathetic attitude. Ray becomes the person characters rely on in moments of (perceived) crisis. He bails Jessa and Adam out of jail (4.3 'Female Author'), comes to pick up a stranded Hannah (5.8 'Homeward Bound'), and encourages Marnie's musical career (2.9 'On All Fours'). Interestingly, the character least associated with creative fulfilment and troubled by his lack of ambition is also the character most driven by empathy, concern, and care work. Significantly, the show assigns these attributes to a cis-male character.

Ray's prized possession is a life-sized cardboard cut-out of comedian Andy Kaufman in an amateur wrestling outfit, which contrasts with Shoshanna's stereotypically girly Soho apartment in which Ray temporarily lives. Known from the series *Taxi* (ABC/NBC, 1978–83) and *Saturday Night Live* (NBC, 1975–), Kaufman's image and career deteriorated after he turned his comedic attention toward wrestling. Controversially, Kaufman primarily challenged women to wrestle and cast himself as a misogynistic villain, resulting in audiences cheering for his female opponents. Complicating the public perception of Kaufman's delusional wrestling phase as the comedian's descent into madness, Noël Carroll describes it as a continuation of his previous comedic approach 'to make the audience think that they were witnessing a truly awful performance by an inept comic, only to reveal, on the turn of a dime, that they were in the hands of a master' (2013: 334). *Girls*'s Kaufman reference again illustrates how cultural texts become orientation points for gender performances. That Ray cherishes the phase of Kaufman's career in which his conceit became too convincing to be understood illustrates Ray's conception of himself as connoisseur of intricate satire. Just as Shoshanna finds an apt embodiment of the femininity she aspires to in her friend Marnie, Ray becomes fascinated by Adam's masculinity which, in its enigmatic, unclear positioning between knowing deceit and open misogyny, was as controversial for *Girls*'s viewers as Kaufman was for his audience.

Adam Sackler is portrayed by actor Adam Driver, who has risen to indie and Hollywood fame with *Inside Llewyn Davis* (2013), *Paterson* (2016), and *Star Wars: The Force Awakens* (2015). The show introduces Adam as a sexual acquaintance of Hannah's. His absurd re-enactments of pornography-inspired sexual scenarios and disregard of Hannah's needs characterise him as 'as an excessive, comic incarnation of the worst boyfriend' (Murray 2018: 256). Adam's redemption occurs when he points out to Hannah (and the viewers) that she (they) had previously reduced him to the role of a 'sex toy' (Shaw 2015: 84). Viewers were just as torn over the character as Jessa: 'what's the deal with that guy? Is he, like, a great thinker or just a total fucking idiot?' (1.8 'Weirdos Need Girlfriends Too'). More pressing than a question of intellect, Adam's repeated eruption into violence exhibits abusive behaviour toward women only partially explained through his struggle with alcoholism.

In his enactment of what he assumes to be an assertive masculinity, Adam comes across simultaneously as threatening as well as humorous. Adam is a 'man-child' (Kissling 2017: 219) whose blunt enactment of a 'patriarchal masculinity' (Lotz 2014: 34) appears hollow, unconvincing, and childishly immature. Crucially, Adam resorts to this persona when confronted with women's choices, such as reproductive rights or ending a romantic relationship. The strongest exploration of Adam's masculinity as threatening for female characters occurs during a sex scene in which he clearly disregards his partner Natalia's boundaries and leaves her feeling violated: 'that was no fun' (2.9 'On All Fours'). The scene has triggered massive viewer response: *Slate*'s Amanda Hess describes it as 'gray rape' (2013), and Melanie Waters finds it 'stubbornly resistant to tidying. The question of what happened, and why it happened, is left unanswered within the episode but is available for discussion beyond the confines of the small screen' (2017: 81). Feminist academic readings have found the scene relevant for its portrayal of sexualised violence as enacted through a partner, countering the prevalent myth of anonymous perpetrators (Grant and Nash 2017: 68; Tally 2014a: 174; Waters 2017: 81).

In a later sex scene, Jessa and Adam experiment with female consent and male dominance (5.5 'Queen for Two Days'). Orchestrated by Jessa, they enact a sexual scenario in which Adam disregards Jessa's fears of unprotected sex. In an exaggerated, high-pitched voice, Jessa's theatrical objections arouse her but cause Adam to interrupt their pretence to make sure that this is not her actual concern. The scene further stands in stark contrast to Hannah's sex scenes with Adam in the first season, in which sexual fantasies are not co-authored but solely fabricated by Adam. The comparison of Adam's respective sex scenes with Hannah, Jessa, and Natalia illustrate, as Maria San Filippo points out, that 'it is not sexual (self)degradation but its misuse under non-consensual, uncommitted circumstances that is to blame' (2015: 56) for assault. Adam's failure to clearly communicate with his sexual partners positions him as problematic and colours what may be called his enigmatic masculinity.

Academic readings have described Adam as 'a bricolage of various gender discourses' (Dhaenens 2017: 127) and 'the fractured and overdetermined version of masculinity, which leads to a stultifying and incoherent version of self' (Albrecht 2015: 90–1). Like most characters on *Girls*, Adam oscillates between different types – the good guy versus the asshole, the 'great thinker' versus the 'total fucking idiot', the caring boyfriend versus the sexual predator. The show conjoins Adam's repeated struggles with alcoholism, violence, and anger with redemptive portrayals of him as a supportive partner to the women he is dating, including caring for a mentally ill Hannah or financially supporting Jessa's return to college. The character is 'constantly gaining, then losing our sympathy' (Rowe 2014) because viewers can never be sure of the enigma Adam. His gendering omits any indication of what motivates his actions, specifically when he abusively violates boundaries and is unable to communicate.

CAROUSEL GENDERING – APPLIED, IN A BATHTUB

In an example of the show's fragmented storytelling, by the third season Adam and Ray have grown closer, despite not having appeared in any shared scenes since their first encounter. Ray has moved into Adam's old apartment and now becomes a safe haven for Adam to turn to in a conflict with Hannah. In the scene this section focuses on, they talk through their relationship troubles in the apartment's bathroom (3.11 'I Saw You'). This scene functions as a counterpart to a much-discussed bathroom scene from *Girls*'s pilot in which Hannah lounges naked in the bathtub eating a cupcake while Marnie sits on the edge shaving her legs (Figure 2.2). For many critics, this 'tub-cake-gate'

(Wortham 2012) embodied friendship and intimacy (Tally 2014b: 31; San Filippo 2015: 47). This female bonding is disrupted when Marnie's boyfriend Charlie accidentally bursts into the room and immediately retreats without learning that their conversation centres around Marnie's growing dissatisfaction with his seemingly inadequate masculinity. 'You're sick of eating him out. Cause he has a vagina', Hannah quips (1.1 'Pilot'). Her comment 'reveals how Charlie's performance of non-traditional masculinity is less accepted by the women than the men' (Dhaenens 2017: 128), since Ray unequivocally embraces his friend Charlie. Further, the first season juxtaposes the devoted boyfriend Charlie with non-committed, disrespectful Adam (Householder 2015: 26; Shaw 2015: 78–9).

How, then, does *Girls* allow male intimacy to play out in a bathroom shared by male characters? In the scene, Ray stands at the sink to shave, and Adam soaks in the bathtub. Similar to Marnie's shaving her legs as part of her feminine beauty regime, Ray's shaving expresses the management of masculine appearance. While Adam looks up from his lower position, Ray relies on the bathroom mirror for eye contact, avoiding directly facing the naked Adam in the bathtub. Their positioning points to a more loaded engagement with male bodies – compared with the women sitting in the bathtub together – and devices such as the mirror serve to distance the male characters' interaction from the 'threat' of homosexuality. Because the men speak about their romantic relationships with Marnie and Hannah, the dialogue further links both 'bathroom scenes'.

> Adam: I just want some space and I'm sick of fucking explaining it.
> Ray: Yeah, I get that. We can't always justify ourselves, you know?
> Adam: Yeah.
> Ray: Like, recently, I had this thing with a girl, and by all accounts, I should've been psyched. She was beautiful, driven, had an amazing fucking chin. But, I don't know – something about it just didn't feel right.
> Adam: Yeah.
> Ray: And I tried talking to her about it, but, ultimately, I just had to fucking drop the guillotine, you know? Cut bait. And she was like, 'what the.' And I was like, 'you heard me! Slut!' [mumbles] Except I – I didn't really call her a slut, though.
> Adam: Yeah, no! Fuck, fuck. (3.11 'I Saw You')

Adam and Ray's conversation explores acceptable forms of masculinity. Instead of admitting to his disappointment at Marnie's ending their affair, Ray resorts to casual sexism that he likely assumes to be part of cis-male bonding. Yet, Ray makes sure to displace his sexist slur as performative within their

Figure 2.2 Contrasting female and male intimacy in the 'bathroom scenes' of 'Pilot' (1.1) and 'I Saw You' (3.11).

homosocial space: 'I didn't really call her a slut, though.' Having previously nodded enthusiastically, Adam disclaims Ray's response as well ('Yeah, no! Fuck, fuck.'). Adam's comment can be read both along the lines of how 'fucked-up' Ray's employment of the derogative slur in sincerity would have been, as well as how 'fucked-up' Adam's previous acceptance of the sexist utterance was. This exchange thus highlights the difficulty of embodying heterosexual masculinity and closely policing the borders to femininity or homosexuality. Ray's degrading reference to a 'slut' on which a 'guillotine' is dropped is offered as a shortcut for establishing shared male intimacy based on misogyny. Yet, almost immediately, both male characters express their awareness of how problematic the comment is. The scene provides little grounding of male intimacy aside from a shared awareness and inconsistent disavowal of sexism. Its humour results from the contrast of Adam's monosyllabic awe at Ray's tirades, Ray's obscure highlighting of Marnie's chin, or his choice of the guillotine over more current machinations of violence.

Serial television often closely intertwines gendered portrayals of spaces with the gendering of characters. The mise-en-scène of the shared bathroom evokes precisely those social and cultural associations from which heterosexual masculinity seeks to distance itself: the feminised cliché of women visiting the restroom together, or the public toilet as a stand-in for the trope of anonymous homosexual 'cruising'. Yet neither Ray nor Adam comments on sharing the bathroom. Furthermore, the apartment that Adam used to live in and Ray now rents recalls the bachelor pad, a cultural trope that expresses single manhood without responsibility. Overall, *Girls*'s shared apartments have been considered more 'realistic' than earlier New York television apartments, specifically on *SATC* or *Friends*, and represent a 'shift away from decades of inflated images of the middle class' (Witherington 2014: 136). These smaller, darker spaces appear run-down and are furnished with mismatched, relatively low-budget pieces instead of the designer items of earlier TV apartments. However, the apartment looks crucially different when inhabited by the different 'bachelors' Adam and Ray. Adam's apartment is cluttered with indeterminate piles in place of furniture, fabric hangs carelessly across windows, and tools and wood supplies dominate the space. Adam's carpentry has been taken as 'a search for a more primitive physical challenge to ground his masculine sense of self' (Nash and Whelehan 2017: 4). This characterisation is echoed by other characters' responses to the apartment and by extension to Adam: in a mixture of sarcasm and awe, Ray describes it as 'very masculine, primal' (2.6 'Boys'), while Natalia reacts with repulsion: 'this place is just, um I don't know, it's depressing' (2.9 'On All Fours'). When Ray takes over the apartment, it looks tidier and lighter, furnished with bookshelves, his record collection, and framed photographs.

One such decoration features as a cultural reference in the 'bathroom scene'. Next to the bathroom mirror, Ray has hung a framed photograph of silent film actor Buster Keaton. In several camera frames, Keaton extends the twosome of Ray and Adam: adjacent to the mirror, Keaton's portrait joins Ray's reflection in it and both appear to glance at Adam. Like Kaufman, Keaton functions as a crucial example of the cultural types that are evoked in *Girls*'s carousel gendering of Ray. An iconic figure of classic Hollywood cinema of the 1920s, Keaton is known for his stoic, deadpan masculinity which earned him the nickname 'the great stone face' (Sanders and Lieberfeld 1994: 16). Keaton's relatively small physical frame resembles Ray's, suggests how Ray sees himself, and points to the struggles both Adam and Ray have in trying to align emotionality with the performance of masculinity. Significantly, Ray's cultural references are older than the show's characters and not obviously recognisable for his peers – or are deemed inappropriate as in the case of *Little Women*. Meanwhile, Adam's references are so ubiquitous – the man-child, the abusive boyfriend, the male threat, the random sex toy, the simpleton – that they do not require explicit cultural references to the same extent.

Moreover, the theme of contrasting masculinities is relevant to the cultural legacy of Keaton as well, who was known for collaborations with actor Roscoe 'Fatty' Arbuckle. The humorous juxtaposition of two male bodies, neither of which fulfils a cultural ideal, has since become a staple in male-centred comedy. By referencing Keaton, the scene recalls the different bodies of Ray and Adam. The characters also comment on their physical appearance in their first encounter:

> Ray: You know, you and I, we're actually not so different. I may intellectualize everything and you nothing, but at the end of the day, we both get to the same meaty ideas. You know? Maybe it's because we're both honest men.
> Adam: Maybe it's because we're both kinda weird-looking. (2.6 'Boys')

While Ray attempts to establish a common, 'honest' masculinity based on a shared heterosexual investment in (and sexual objectification of) women, Adam rejects the framing of their masculinity as dominant and positions them as marginal, 'weird-looking' outsiders. Both men may not project masculine beauty, yet there is a difference between their 'weird' looks. Ray's smaller frame alludes to his non-conformity to masculine ideals of strength and athleticism, while Adam's larger, muscular frame aligns with conventional beauty norms, with his 'weirdness' indebted to Driver's particular facial composition. As Raewyn Connell points out, 'true masculinity is almost always thought to proceed from men's bodies – to be inherent in a male body or to express something about a male body' which 'drives and directs' or 'sets limits to action' (2016: 45). Just as Charlie's masculinity is limited by an essentialist association with femininity ('possessing a vagina'), Ray attempts to assert himself by bonding with Adam's more affirmed masculinity. However, the show clearly privileges Ray's transparent struggles to align emotionality with masculinity over Adam's less critical 'man-child' persona.

Although these male characters become independent carriers of their own storylines, scenes of cis-male characters' interactions with one another, like the one discussed, are relatively rare in the series. Because, as is the case here, the dialogue of such scenes also centres on women, the show appears to reverse the 'Bechdel Test' by exploring masculinity solely in relation to femininity.[6] Rather than contrast masculinities and their negotiations of male privilege in homosocial settings (as in the bathroom scene), the show relies on male care and empathy for female characters to present its preferred masculinity. What is more, masculinity studies has long pointed to the relationship between heterosexual and homosexual masculinity as burdened with symbolic significance. The show only rarely depicts homosexual and heterosexual male characters in shared scenes, even though Ray and Elijah work together at the café.[7]

When considering hegemony as specific to an individual show (Lotz 2014: 20), *Girls* prioritises non-normative gender identities. Within society at large, Hannah may function as what Mimi Schippers refers to as 'pariah femininity' (2007: 95) because she threatens hegemonic gender relations due to her deviation from practices associated with femininity. Similarly, Ray neither physically (small frame, not normatively beautiful), nor intellectually (too invested in 'old man culture'), nor behaviourally (too empathetic, lack of ambition) performs 'hegemonic masculinity' within society at large. Of all the relationships in *Girls*, the friendship between its preferred femininity (Hannah) and preferred masculinity (Ray) is the one most characterised by an (often unspoken) understanding of one another. The only scene in which Hannah attempts a sexual interaction illustrates their romantic and sexual incompatibility – she initiates oral sex while Ray is driving, and he crashes the car. As an afterthought, the final season introduces Abigail (Aidy Bryant) as Ray's new love interest who partially resembles Hannah in her outspokenness, humour, and divergence from audiovisual beauty norms. Fittingly, Ray's last appearance has him kiss Abigail while riding the historic Jane's Carousel of Brooklyn Bridge Park on New York's East River (Figure 2.3).

In conclusion, the notion of carousel gendering has allowed this chapter to examine the serial fashioning of gendered identities through omissions of crucial plot moments as well as the characters' circling around cultural types or references which become means to narrate gendered selves and read the gender performances of others. The carousel captures the combined influence of ellipsis and repetition on gender performances, that is, the ways in which the show provokes its viewers to speculate and analyse. In other words, carousel gendering describes serial gender as a result of the show and its critical sphere conjoining. The gendered types that the show references and that characters

Figure 2.3 Transparent masculinity: Ray's final appearance concludes with a kiss on a carousel.

and thinkpieces circle around also mark *Girls*'s involvement in recent popular culture; they surface in critical writing where these references are discussed as genre interventions in media history or cultural expressions of the current moment (see Chapter 3).

NOTES

1. Fast-talking Shoshanna has been described by critics as coming 'closest to caricature' (Bell 2013: 364), 'a ball of nervous energy' (Vayo 2015: 170), as well as 'off-kilter, intense, and naïve all at once' (Shaw 2015: 81). Later seasons manifested her role as a sharp commentator of her friends.
2. Because *Girls*'s characters express their love of female-centred television shows like *SATC* and *The Mary Tyler Moore Show* (CBS, 1970–7), academic readings have proposed that *Girls* 'knowingly places itself within a lineage of feminist television' (Ford 2016: 1030; see Fuller and Driscoll 2015: 256), or 'explicitly recall[s] and then renounce[es]' *SATC* (Dejmanee 2016: 127; see Lewis 2014: 176; Nash and Grant 2015: 977; Turner 2014: 156).
3. Hence, gendering can be described as circular motion with no end in sight. More so than Roof's circle, the carousel is such a productive analytical tool because it allows for a conceptualisation of the critic as a bystander who (only) appears to have oversight over the carousel's turns.
4. David Denby finds films such as *Knocked Up* to romantically pair a male slacker with an ambitious female 'striver' to help the slacker mature into a responsible partner and husband (2007).
5. As an example of Marnie's 'failures', she is the only character who must resort to temporarily moving back in with her mother not once but twice during the series.

6. The 'Bechdel Test' has become a popular measurement of female cinematic representation. It originates in a one-page comic strip by artist Alison Bechdel, in which a character gives her criteria for movies: a film includes at least two female characters (1) who interact (2) about a topic other than a male character (3). A reverse Bechdel Test would then avoid scenes without female characters (1) or have women dominate conversations (2), and in rare conversations between male characters, make female characters the topic (3).
7. Elijah is further positioned as the 'gay best friend', a problematic trope of female-centric popular culture. However, the show seems to reflect on this troubling practice of using homosexual masculinity as a prop for heterosexual femininity when Shoshanna parades Elijah as her assistant in order to feign professional success at a networking event (6.2 'Hostage Situation').

CHAPTER 3

Navigating Discourses of Universality and Specificity: The (Feminist) Voice of a Generation?

Three weeks before the first episode aired in April 2012, Emily Nussbaum praised *Girls* as filling a void in regard to female-centric and female-created television. Many critics have since referred to Nussbaum's pre-airing review – quoted in at least fourteen academic essays on the show – making it the 'benevolent patient zero' (Zoladz 2017) of an intense cultural debate. In it, Nussbaum lauded how 'Dunham's show takes as its subject women who are quite demographically specific – cosseted white New Yorkers from educated backgrounds – then mines their lives for the universal' (2012). For Nussbaum, *Girls* served as an industry-made solution to a gender bias she had spent much of her career writing against. Subsequent discussions of both the show and Nussbaum's article connected to a broader cultural conversation, which can be described as a 'discourse of universality and specificity'. This chapter explores how the tension between universal and specific representation has simultaneously served as a backdrop for criticism of the show (for example, in regard to its lack of racial diversity) or praise of it (for its female showrunner, its deviation from norms of cinematic and televisual bodily depictions). *Girls*'s mobilisation of its critical sphere often takes on an almost didactic format: for instance, it combines the show's much-praised 'body politics' with a critique of its representations of race. The resulting controversial constellation of themes in critical television writing is something to which the series reacts but which it never does resolve – and instead continuously evokes as a basis for further continuation. Ultimately, the show's conscious participation in this discourse – by way of the mobilisation of thinkpiece seriality – has particular implications for its investment in feminism.

During the course of *Girls*'s second season, the key interpretative frame employed by its critical sphere shifted from 'generation' to 'feminism'. The three academic anthologies published on the show thus far illustrate this shift through their respective focus. The contributors to *HBO's* Girls*: Questions of Gender, Politics, and Millennial Angst* (2014) approached the show as a socio-historical document of millennial femininity. The collection sought to explore 'how *Girls* is able to reveal contemporary attitudes about young men and women' (Kaklamanidou and Tally 2014: 3), including their dating, work lives, and friendships. The second collection, *HBO's* Girls *and the Awkward Politics of Gender, Race, and Privilege* (2015) is less uniformly positioned and offers readings of the show's representations of bodies (Bailey 2015; San Filippo 2015), masculinity (Shaw 2015), and race (Watson 2015). Meanwhile, *Reading Lena Dunham's* Girls*: Feminism, Postfeminism, Authenticity and Gendered Performance in Contemporary Television* (2017) employs a feminist media studies framework and is interested in the show's position in a postfeminist mediascape.

The trajectory from reading the show through the frame of millennial sociopolitical life toward interpreting it as a key text of feminism or postfeminism connects with the airing of other millennial-centred and millennial-authored TV shows as well as a shift in Dunham's celebrity persona.[1] Like the serial text *Girls*, Dunham's star image progressed in conversation with the serial criticism consistently applied to it (Sulimma 2017). Her branding as a representative of urban, millennial 'girlhood' was increasingly at odds with the multimedia franchise associated with her name, and subsequently, Dunham has been rebranded as a 'feminist media insider', making her a prominent example of controversial 'celebrity feminism'.[2] Academic explorations of Dunham's celebrity feminism highlight how it crosses over several media platforms (Murray 2018; Seaton 2017), such as the email newsletter *Lenny*, the podcast series *Woman of the Hour* and *The C-Word*, or the autobiography *Not That Kind of Girl* (2014). But here lies the conundrum: while Dunham actively claims feminism as an identity for herself and her brand, *Girls* is not promoted as feminist by her, her co-workers, or HBO. Instead, *Girls* has come to exclusively rely on critics for such pronouncements.

Characters utter the word 'feminist' in only a handful of scenes. These scenes deploy humour and irony, thus complicating any easy ascription of feminism to the show or its characters. As an illustration, Hannah mentions feminism in a ridiculously weighty manner to applaud Shoshanna's aspirations to have it all, that is, to spend equal time studying and partying: 'sounds like a really good plan. It sounds smart and strong and feminist' (3.1 'Females Only'). Further, 'feminism' is often evoked in connection with Hannah's writing: she publishes on a 'niche feminist website' (6.3 'American Bitch'), and a classmate at the Iowa Writers' Workshop criticises her writing as based on a 'stunted feminist idea' (4.2 'Triggering'). Overall, the show's characteristic openness allows critics to read their own form of feminism into the series and evaluate its shortcomings. Before this chapter traces the specific forms these discussions have taken, it is necessary to attend to two different, albeit connected ways to understand the tension of the specific and the universal that *Girls* is situated in: narratively – the conflict between 'vast' and 'small' narrative scope – and politically – the conflict of considering a story as representative of a universal condition rather than specifically located.

First, the universal can stand for the narrative containment of multitudes and implies a text's vastness (Harrigan and Wardrip-Fruin 2009). For serial narratives this vastness may translate into detailed storyworlds, elaborate multi-episode-, season-, or even series-spanning plots, and large groups of characters, all of which require efforts to be managed by their viewers. Cross-media franchises like *The Walking Dead* and *Game of Thrones* outline fictional universes within which individual characters may take a backseat to larger themes, such as the post-apocalyptic survival of humanity and the search for good governance. *Girls*, however, stands at the opposite end of the spectrum from such narrative vastness, in that it privileges the navel-gazing of characters, and focuses on spatial and thematic narrowness, an inheritance of both mumblecore and earlier female-centred television. Even though mostly focused on the specific story of Hannah, the show at times flirts with the idea of a universal experience, and has been taken to speak for something larger, such as an entire gender, an entire generation, or an entire nation. Whenever a character goes so far as to express such ideas on-screen, they are quickly put into place by others, or, even more likely, sarcastically negate their statement, as does the 'voice of a generation' Hannah.

Second, the universal appeal of a narrative is inseparable from intersectionality. Narratives that centre around a white male perspective – and are authored by white male auteurs – have never struggled to the same extent with this tension. They are understood as specific stories and are not taken to be representative of all white, heterosexual cis-men, while at the same time they are considered to be of universal appeal for viewers regardless of gender, race, or sexual orientation. As Laurie Penny has argued, 'no male showrunner has ever been asked to speak to a universal male experience in the same way, because "man" is still a synonym for "human being" in a way that "woman" is not' (2017: 143). The specific story of one Tony Soprano (or one David Chase) was rarely even taken to speak for all middle-aged, Italian-American, upper-class, married fathers, but that *The Sopranos* was watched by a diverse audience rarely seems worth pointing out. Such stories are never expected to speak for an entire gender or race to the same extent as 'othered' narratives, that is, the stories of women and people of colour. This is emblematic of a televisual landscape that long lacked female protagonists and protagonists of colour, particularly within the canon of 'Quality TV'. Viewers of colour or queer viewers have long employed resistant reading strategies to locate identificatory moments in such cultural artefacts, often countering narrative underrepresentation and stereotyping. There has also been resistance to considering female-centred popular culture's appeal for male viewers – or to downplay its cross-gender appeal through labels such as 'women's television' or 'women's fiction'.

Girls's viewers thus had to wrestle the show away from the grip of the universal, an interpretative move that was severely complicated by the show's thinkpiece seriality – its textual ambiguity, metatextuality, and vague characterisations. Faye Woods points to both HBO's promotional strategies and early pre-airing reviews like Nussbaum's as having shaped 'expectations of naturalism, realism and universality within its depiction of Millennial women's experience' (2015: 43) Similarly, Maša Grdešić has argued that 'the desire to see *Girls* as universal comes from a specific type of reading and interpretation of the series' (2013: 356) undertaken by both viewers who feel represented through it and those who do not. As so much energy went into determining that *Girls* was one specific story and not a show about a 'universal girlhood', the potential cross-demographic appeal of the story of the white cis-female Hannah and her friends was hard to establish. In the following, the chapter presents the two most prominent instances in which *Girls*'s representation as universal was most challenged (its depictions of race) and most accepted (its body politics).

FAILING THE TEST: 'UNIVERSAL' RACIAL REPRESENTATIONS

A mutually exclusive rhetoric of affirmation or disapproval has structured the charged discussions surrounding the show (and Dunham). Without room for nuance, viewers and non-viewers alike have positioned themselves as either loving or hating *Girls*. This binary is well established as the architecture of social media: the like/dislike button or the swiping gesture of mobile device-embedded dating apps. Several of television's most prominent critics have noted this polarising tendency of the show. Alan Sepinwall, for instance, finds 'no neutral parties in the great *Girls* pop culture wars' (2017). Michelle Dean sarcastically extends the show's reception to national politics: 'who among us did not long for the tone of partisan politics to infect every other aspect of culture?' (2013). Willa Paskin joked: 'who has two thumbs and an opinion on Lena Dunham? And they say there's nothing left that unites this country!' (2017). The foundation on which partisanship in the approval and disapproval camps was established is surprisingly consistent. Opponents of the show found its representations of race or economic privilege problematic. Proponents largely agreed, yet found the show's departure from media norms of representing (white) female bodies laudable enough to outweigh such representational issues. *Variety*'s Maureen Ryan calls *Girls* an 'X-ray show' because 'What a person wrote or said about the show told me a lot about where their head was at' (Saraiya and Ryan 2017). The *A.V. Club*'s Emily VanDerWerff marvels that 'it's possible for me to explain something about the show and say that's why I like it so much, and for you to agree with me *in every detail* and see that as a reason to hate the show' (2013). Hence, *Girls*, ironically, can be evoked as both a beacon of progress and symptomatic of an ongoing malady, depending on a critic's position.

One insensitive phrase encapsulates much of the later controversy: attributing the expression to her fellow critic Willa Paskin, Nussbaum described the show as 'FUBU' – For Us and By Us (2012). Many of her readers understandably took issue with her use of an idiom from African American culture in this context. Female cultural critics of colour pointed toward a questionable generalisation: 'I'm worried that a lot of "us" aren't going to recognize ourselves in this so-hailed feminist milestone of a show' (Shepherd 2012); 'regardless of what Emily Nussbaum says, I do not consider *Girls* to be For Us or By Us' (James 2012); 'They are us but they are not us. They are me but they are not me' (Wortham 2012). These responses were published in the single week between the airing of the first and second episodes. They foregrounded issues that would surface repeatedly in the show's six-season run: the lack of racial diversity and 'white-washing' of New York, the stereotyping of people of colour in marginal roles and cameos, as well as the socio-economic privilege of its female protagonists. Many of these earlier writers' status as 'key commentary' manifested when Anna Holmes referenced and included links to their articles in *The New Yorker* (2012a). Even though these writers were able to gain widespread recognition of their initial arguments, neither they personally nor the websites they published with were lasting core contributors to the cultural dialogue about the show. Instead, the more established cultural content websites included their criticism and in turn exhibited overtly sceptical approaches toward both the show and Dunham. Faye Woods draws attention to feminist-identified, so-called women's websites, such as *Jezebel*, *The Hairpin*, *Racialicious*, or *Feministing*, which initiated debates of the show's racial politics (2015: 45). Ultimately, these websites' criticism resulted in a significant reframing of the initial praise of *Girls*: it highlighted how the show maintained the continual racism and classism of media representations and industry practices. The early reviews became reference points, and many academic texts cited them to signal their awareness of the controversy. For example, Kendra James's article 'Dear Lena Dunham: I Exist' (2012) was cited in at least seven academic articles on *Girls*. While almost all academic essays acknowledge the issue of racial representation, few have focused on readings of race in the show (only Saisi 2014; Hamilton 2014; Watson 2015).

Elwood Watson expresses irritation at the personal tone and intensity of these journalists of colour whose writing to him seems 'as if they are looking for white recognition through Dunham' (2015: 149). And in fact, the writing style of these reviews is marked by a deeply personal tone in which the critics outline excited anticipation of and later frustrations with the show. *The Daily Beast*'s Rebecca Carroll explains: 'I feel somewhat cheated. While I have decided that the show is for me, it has decided that I am not for the show' (2012). Rather than being reprimanded for its confessional tone, this writing should be recognised as being indebted to the self-positioning of feminist methodology.[3] Pointing to their own experiences with race and representation, these writers shaped the subsequent discussions on *Girls*, in regard not only to themes but also to style: the conversation on *Girls* had critics willing to acknowledge how their arguments were framed by their gendered, racialised, and socio-cultural backgrounds. With titles like 'What We Talk About When We Talk About *Girls*' (VanDerWerff 2013), 'What We Talk About When We Talk About Lena Dunham' (Dean 2012), '*Girls* Talk' (Woods 2015), or 'Body Talk' (Marghitu and Ng 2013), the key term of 'talking' highlighted that a dialogue among the show's critics, instead of talking back at the show, became the dominant mode of *Girls*'s reception.

Because the rapid cultural commentary already addressed race in the first week after the show aired, it seemed unnecessarily delayed for Dunham to take three weeks to address what by then had come to be called the show's – and her own – 'race problem', especially considering her outspoken social media presence. Other readings sought to defend Dunham by pointing to the systemic racism prevalent within the entertainment industry, and the possible sexism implied in singling out one of the few female showrunners to shoulder the responsibility of the racial bias of an entire industry. Many pieces quoted renowned writer Ta-Nehisi Coates who in *The Atlantic* argued that *Girls*'s underrepresentation posed a lesser evil than racist stereotyping by insensitive writers (2012). For many thinkpieces, referencing Coates as an author who is taken to represent the racial awareness that Dunham lacks functions as a discursive endpoint to lay the issue to rest. Such readings frequently include the rhetoric of letting an author figure 'write what you know' (Hamilton 2014: 54) and demand the industry should give more television writers of colour opportunities similar to Dunham's (Marghitu and Ng 2013: 22; Saisi 2014: 66; Watson 2015: 162). Specifically, readings point to African American women in the industry, such as Shonda Rhimes or Issa Rae, as possible correctives to Dunham's white millennial femininity.

Overall, viewer-critics talked about the much-awaited series *Insecure* (HBO, 2016–) by producer, writer, and actor Rae very differently from *Girls*.[4] As a consequence of race, *Insecure*'s protagonist Issa (played by Rae) and her friends were not accepted as representatives of the troubling fiction of a universal 'everygirl'. Here again, universality implies not only cis-gendered masculinity but also whiteness and heterosexuality. As Kendra James has asked in response to Nussbaum's prominent review: 'but why are the only lives that can be mined for "universal experiences" the lives of white women?' (2012). Drawing on this question, feminist critic Laurie Penny notes that 'the idea of girlhood as a universal story is a great way to stop individual women's stories being heard' (2017: 144). While universality functions as a dubious goal for narratives, the attribution of 'too much specificity', as experienced by female storytellers of colour, may result in their stories being positioned at the cultural fringes and assumed not to be of interest to those of a different demographic.

As *Girls* progressed, the lack of diversity and racial stereotypes remained central to the discussion surrounding the show, particularly in the second season, when Hannah briefly dates African American character Sandy (Donald Glover) and exhibits precisely the racially insensitive behaviour her author figure Dunham had been accused of all along. Hannah and Sandy's two-episode fling was read as a low-commitment appeasement strategy toward viewers (Marghitu and Ng 2013: 22; Saisi 2014: 68), as a meta-textual commentary (Nelson 2014: 99), and as a knowing exploration of Hannah's racial privilege (Bianco 2014: 83; Lehman 2014: 14; Watson 2015: 156). While the compelling portrayal of Sandy as a black Republican hipster follows a divergent path from *Girls*'s usual establishment of gender identities through references to popular culture types, the minor role provided little more than a critique of Hannah, as evident in her ability to ignore the complex realities of race: 'I didn't even notice you were black – cause I don't live in a world where there are divisions like that' (2.2 'I Get Ideas').

Later seasons did not significantly vary the approach of racial representation. For instance, the sixth season included four narrative scenarios that *Buzzfeed*'s Tomi Obaro has described as 'veer[ing] dangerously close to an archetype often seen in film that refuses to die – the "magical negro"' (2017). In these scenes, Hannah, Marnie, and Elijah each receive advice from or emotional uplift through a person of colour whom they have just met and who disappears from the series after helping them come to a realisation. What is more, in the season finale, Hannah gives birth to a biracial child without any commentary on the part of the other characters (or show's author figures; Figure 3.1). This seeming oversight caused much discussion, as *Vulture*'s Matt Zoller Seitz remarked: '*Girls* should have known that the question would come up and figured out a subtle way to mention it without actually mentioning it' (2017). Obaro and Seitz's recaps highlight how critics' frustrations with racial representation remained an ongoing source of critical conversations throughout the show.

Figure 3.1 *Girls*'s last season did not deviate from its previous textual practices, which also meant that the portrayal of Hannah's parenting a baby of colour was fraught with ambiguity and omissions.

REDEMPTIVE READINGS: BODY POLITICS

While race largely serves as a negative frame of reference, the portrayal of female bodies, specifically Dunham's, unequivocally became a reason to praise *Girls*. Brett Mills finds 'someone playing themselves is quite common in comedy, and comedy remains the only mode within which this is a possibility' (2010: 193). As a genre hybrid, the dramedy *Girls* complicates comedy's equation between performer and character. The conflation of author figure, actress, and character surfaces when Hannah's statements and actions are taken to be the opinions or biographical experiences of Dunham, or, vice versa, when Dunham's autobiography or social media are employed to interpret Hannah. Aside from holding Dunham accountable for the show's problematic racial representations, her celebrity feminism is largely founded on the show's body politics.

Because Dunham's body type is slightly heavier than that of the average Hollywood female star, her appearance can be understood as 'non-normative'. This description refers to televisual and cinematic representation of female bodies rather than societal body norms, as Dunham's body is far more typical of US-American female bodies than those of other female celebrities. Instead, it is the lack of different body types on-screen that makes her non-normative. This non-normative appearance further stems from the show's frequent refusal of cinematic and televisual standards when it comes to make-up, lighting, or editing, practices which are typically used to make already conventionally attractive bodies look even more flawless on-screen. When describing what sets Dunham's physicality apart from media norms, critics described her body as 'short and pear-shaped' (Nussbaum 2012), 'pale, a little pudgy, tattooed' (Thomas 2017: 182),[5] 'non-glamorous and "chubby"' (Tally 2014a: 172), 'non-idealized' (Bianco 2014: 85; Hamilton 2014: 47), '"fat," tattooed and unwieldy' (Ford 2016: 1038), not 'fashion-magazine-slender or even characteristically thought beautiful' (Fuller and Driscoll 2015: 260), as well as 'exceptional or subversive' (Bailey 2015: 29). Many pointed to the didactic potential that Dunham's representation of Hannah may have on audiences who are unaware of their own complicity in mainstream beauty norms (Dean 2014; San Filippo 2017).

Claire Perkins has intriguingly referred to the show as 'television of the body' (2014: 34), in order to highlight the familiarity that viewers acquire with the bodies of the show's characters/performers (42). This does not mean that Dunham's willingness to expose her naked body on-screen was not a continuous source of controversy. Disturbing amounts of sexism, body shaming, and misogyny have been expressed as a reaction to it. Most prominently, radio host Howard Stern famously likened – and would later apologise for doing so – the experience of seeing this 'little fat girl' naked on-screen to rape (Chen 2013). Similarly, during the Television Critics Association press tour, a journalist caused a controversy when he asked Dunham about the 'purpose' of her character's nudity (Molloy 2014). The journalist's question seemed to echo online sexist discussions about whether Dunham was attractive enough to appear nude on television, which accelerated after the episode 'One Man's Trash' (2.5). This bottle episode focused exclusively on Hannah's sexual encounter with the attractive doctor Joshua (Patrick Wilson). Several male viewers found it highly unlikely that Hannah could be sexually attractive to a conventionally good-looking character like Joshua (Haglund and Engber 2013; Martin 2013), which ignores the long tradition of less attractive male comedians being romantically paired off with more attractive actresses. Diametrically opposed to criticisms of Dunham's racial insensitivity, Rona Murray speaks of viewers' 'affective solidarity' (2018: 249–51) with Dunham, to whom most of the show's 'non-normative' body portrayals can be attributed, and against misogynistic viewer responses.

From comedy, specifically female comedians, *Girls* also inherits the exploration of societal restrictions on female bodies. Linda Mizejewski describes how female comedians subvert a 'pretty versus funny' binary with narrow conceptions of Hollywood beauty becoming a source of their comedy (2014: 3–5). TV critic Alyssa Rosenberg concurs that 'if an actress's body doesn't meet those standards, most of the stories she will be allowed to *literally* embody will be drawn from the non-conformity of her looks. . . . *Girls* isn't really content to stay within that expected set of narratives' (2012). Hannah's erotic photo shoot discussed in Chapter 1 warrants such a description, and other examples include her 'unflattering' appearance in a see-through yellow mesh top (2.3 'Bad Friend') or a scanty, green bikini (3.6 'Beach House'). Placed within narrative scenarios that contrast Hannah's body with that of other women, these scenes showcase issues surrounding competition, desire, and acceptance. The show metatextually acknowledges how exceptional such scenes are, when Hannah comments, 'It's a good thing I'm not as susceptible to criticism as I used to be' (3.6 'Beach House'), or 'I worked very, very hard to overcome the challenges of my non-traditional body type and accept myself for who I am' (5.3 'Japan'). These scenes seem to call for analytical unpacking and are destined to illustrate arguments about societal sexism and gendered beauty norms.

The notion of 'unruly femininity' was particularly important for conversations about the show's body politics. Readings of the mentioned scenes have frequently drawn on one of the foundational texts of feminist comedy studies: Kathleen Rowe Karlyn's extension of Bakhtin's theory of the grotesque; her study of the 'Unruly Woman' (employed in Ford 2016; Petersen 2017; San Filippo 2015, 2017; Thomas 2017; Woods 2015). Karlyn traces a tradition that spans from female characters of Renaissance plays to Miss Piggy, Mae West, and Roseanne Barr, all of whom 'disrupt the norms of femininity and the social hierarchy of male over female through excess and outrageousness' (1995: 34). Unruly femininity is described by Karlyn and others through practices and characteristics such as the physical taking up of space, loud laughter, and following one's desires excessively. Further, unruly female characters have been associated with 'leakiness', dirt, taboo, liminality, and disorder. Readings of *Girls* pointed to how Dunham's performance of Hannah follows in these footsteps: 'her image mobilises the effects of camp and the carnivalesque to de-familiarise our cultural notions of beauty and gender performance' (San Filippo 2015: 50). In addition to Hannah's eating and nudity, moments in which Hannah is intoxicated on the dance floor are apt illustrations of unruliness. In these 'drunken dancing' scenes, Hannah projects seriousness through her concentrated facial expression, but she also attempts to present a detached look of coolness. The combination of her serious posture with the dance routines of music videos she imitates results in a parody of sexualised and commercialised dance choreographies. Hannah's dancing is further connected to boundless consumption, as she keeps excessively downing alcoholic drinks and at times grabs the drinks of strangers. In a remarkable scene, Hannah is centred in the camera frame while liquid vomit briefly erupts from her mouth, and the co-workers she had been dancing with scatter away from her in disgust (3.10 'Role-Play'). Surprised by her own body's unruliness, Hannah stands completely still with a blank facial expression devoid of embarrassment and doesn't bend her head or body to avoid staining her light dress.

When Hannah attends a surf camp on a writing assignment but realises she hates surfing and instead parties at the camp's bar (6.1 'All I Ever Wanted'), another interesting scene occurs. She holds onto large, bulbous cocktail glasses during her exuberant dance moves, and repeatedly spills brightly coloured cocktails on herself and the floor. Unlike the interacting crowd around her, Hannah is completely absorbed by herself. The bright red colour of the drink she cannot get enough of, because – as she justifies the next day – it 'tasted like a slushie', seems reminiscent of blood, calling up vampiric associations (Figure 3.2). The artificial neon green and blue lighting of these dance scenes create a glossy, surreal aesthetic more commonly associated with horror.[6] The link of Hannah's consumption with one of the cinematic 'body genres' (Williams 1991), horror, is telling in this regard. Here, *Girls*'s bodily representation calls up cinematic traditions concerned with a direct effect on the bodies of viewers (disgust, fear). However, in a marked difference with body genres, viewers do not share Hannah's affective state. Instead, indicative of the female dramedy's 'cringe aesthetics', such scenes depend on 'viewers' affective distance: we do not cringe *with* but *at* characters' (Havas and Sulimma 2018: 9). In such moments, reductive celebrations of female unruliness are potentially complicated by the viewer's disgust over Hannah's unruly, 'leaky' body. Physicality is attached to the female 'leaky' body self-assuredly bound up in consumption and pleasure: grabbing drinks and threatening not only to stain her own clothes, but to spill onto those surrounding her. Such scenes lead to the frequent description of Hannah (and the show itself) as being unwilling – or possibly unable – to 'tame' her body or her behaviour (Ford 2016: 1038–9).

Figure 3.2 A self-absorbed Hannah cannot get enough of her bright red coloured drink, which evokes vampiric associations of the 'unruly woman' as a parasite.

How does the discussion surrounding the show's body politics as concentrated on the body of Dunham/Hannah relate to this chapter's interest in the universal and the specific? Unruliness in many ways seems incompatible with the universal because the 'unruly woman' is taken to stand out from her surroundings, as Dunham stands out from a perceived ocean of female celebrities with interchangeable, slim bodies. At the same time, for many observers, Dunham's body functions as universal because it is more representative of an 'average' cis-female body than these actresses. The show and Dunham's star image have been walking a tightrope between celebrating its body politics as progressive while acknowledging that this progressiveness stems only from a restrictive media imagination of femininity. Specifically, the criticism of fat activists points toward this discord. In an interview with Dunham, writer Roxane Gay has protested: 'I actually don't think your body is all that unruly, but you know the media certainly does' (2014a). In her own work, the memoir *Hunger* (2017), Gay has engaged with the notion of the untameable, unruly body. Yet for Gay it is the fat body of colour that is unaccounted for in various cultural and social settings. This body causes her real pain and positions her to question socio-cultural norms and hierarchies. Her unruly body forces both Gay and society at large to consider its abilities and makes it impossible to ignore its materiality. This kind of unruliness is harder to celebrate as a kind of 'feminist rule-breaking' because Gay describes it as limiting her life in many ways.

Overall, the unruly body is rarely placed in this position by its own accord, but through outside perspectives. Despite the celebratory undercurrent of Dunham's and other current portrayals of the unruly woman as a feminist agent of change, Karlyn sees the figure of the unruly woman as ambivalent because her subversive potential always carries the weight of misogynist disdain for the female body. This becomes clear in the sexist backlash to Dunham's portrayal of Hannah. Just as the discussions of the show's racial representations have served as a continued site of criticism for the entire run of the series, this singular bodily representation has also remained a source of journalistic and academic praise throughout the show. Different understandings of feminism have become the glue that ties these divergent perceptions of the show together.

THE UR-FEMINIST IMPULSE WITHIN A POSTFEMINIST MARKETPLACE

Discussions of *Girls*'s depiction of race stand in contrast with readings of its norm-breaking potential for bodily representations. Both lines of criticism have frequently been framed within a rhetoric of feminism: *Girls*'s white feminism is perceived as being at odds with intersectional feminisms, and its body politics is regarded as a cause for feminist celebration. This illustrates how *Girls* has maintained its characteristic ambiguity to cater to critics' evaluation of scenes through their own understanding of feminism. In one of the few forays into audience research, Rose Weitz finds the show 'a particularly useful text for exploring the frames young women use to interpret media' (2016: 222). Much writing on *Girls* boils down to the question of whether and how the show is feminist, as well as if it is feminist 'enough' – a debate that frequently overlapped with conversations about the authenticity of auteur figure Dunham's celebrity feminism.

In order to describe what is happening in the discourse surrounding *Girls*, I draw on Charlotte Brunsdon's 'ur-feminist article' as a 'genre' of academic writing (2005: 112). Such writing evaluates the feminist potential of a popular culture research object by moving through different argumentative stages: first, the scholar sets up a feminist 'test' through an 'obvious' reading that reveals the text's or its female protagonists' flaws; for example, by diagnosing a lack of empowerment or an adoption of traditional gender norms. Next, the feminist scholar redeems the text against such a hostile test by employing her own seemingly more attuned feminist reading, which ascribes her research object, her reading process, and ultimately herself greater complexity and a more nuanced feminism. In the words of Brunsdon:

> The author then mobilizes her own engagement with the text, her fondness for the treatment of the dreams and dilemmas of the heroine, to interrogate the harsh dismissal of this popular text on 'feminist' grounds. The author thus reveals the complex and contradictory ways in which the text – and the heroine – negotiate the perilous path of living as a woman in a patriarchal world. The heroine of this genre is both the author and her textual surrogate, while her adversaries are both textual (vampires, lawyers, ex-husbands) and extratextual – censorious feminists who will not let her *like* the story and its iconography, that is, the accoutrements of femininity. (Brunsdon 2005: 113)

Brunsdon demonstrates how another feminist figure is textually embedded as an adversary for the feminist writer in this genre: a personified stereotype of second-wave feminism who is unaware of the pleasures of popular culture and the ambiguities of living as a young feminist within a complex, contradictory media landscape (113). This point illustrates how even feminist critics have internalised the prevalent media tropes of the 'feminist killjoy' (Ahmed 2017: 36–9) and narratives of feminist generational conflicts (Hemmings 2011: 148–51) that researchers like Sara Ahmed and Clare Hemmings have found to populate the stories academic, activist, and popular cultures tell about feminism.

Variations of Brunsdon's concept echo in discussions of a text's pleasures versus dangers for feminism, or the notion of a feminist 'guilty pleasure' enjoyable but at odds with one's activism. Furthermore, Tania Modleski has criticised a 'feminist syllogism' at play in much feminist criticism which she breaks down to the following: 'I like *Dallas*; I am a feminist; *Dallas* must have progressive potential' (1991: 45). Brunsdon's 'ur-feminist article' should be understood as the result of a writer struggling to come to terms with an increasingly complex popular culture that recycles feminist ideas. Foundational work in feminist media studies and cultural studies (Gill 2007; McRobbie 2009; Tasker and Negra 2007) established the concept of postfeminism to interrogate popular culture's representation of feminism as outdated and unnecessary in a society that seems to grant cis-women an abundance of choices and freedoms. Angela McRobbie has described postfeminist culture as 'doubly entangled' with feminism: postfeminism paradoxically has taken feminism 'into account' while simultaneously attacking feminist achievements (2009: 14). Postfeminist media claim that the women's movement has been successful and that women are now able to reap its rewards, free from any constraints of sexism or patriarchy (14). Much feminist analysis has explored postfeminism through iconic media texts considered emblematic of it, such as *SATC* (Arthurs 2007) and *Bridget Jones's Diary* (McRobbie 2009; Negra 2009). Rosalind Gill's conceptualisation of postfeminism as a cultural sensibility has proven particularly productive for exploring femininity through a set of related themes, among them an emphasis on individualism and a rhetoric of choice that are embedded in neoliberal capitalism through practices of consumption, (self-)surveillance, self-discipline, and a 'make-over paradigm' (2007: 149–61).

The question of which forms feminism takes in current popular culture has been central to academic explorations of *Girls*, in which different understandings of postfeminism, feminism, and their relationship are utilised. For some, *Girls* is clearly feminist and has been described as a 'feminist resistance' (Levy 2015: 63), 'fruit of third wave feminism and queer theory' (Turner 2014: 156), or part of a 'fourth wave' of feminism (Householder 2015: 21). Others have argued that *Girls* signals a new era of postfeminist popular culture and should accordingly be referred to as either 'post-post-feminism' (Tally 2014b: 40) or 'post?feminism' (Grant and Nash 2017: 62).[7] Such labels shed light on changed cultural definitions and societal relationships with feminism and/ or postfeminism. If postfeminism serves as a 'productive irritation that helps keep feminist discourse alive in contemporary popular culture' (Fuller and Driscoll 2015: 253), then what kind of feminism is being kept alive through postfeminist media culture such as *Girls*?

As early as 1996, media scholar Bonnie J. Dow described popular culture's 'primetime feminism' as resulting in a strategic 'conflation of feminist *identity* with feminist *politics*' (1996: 207). Two decades later, representations of feminism in popular culture have continued this practice, yet also changed toward a generally more celebratory stance as well as an increasingly commercialised appropriation of feminist images and rhetoric within what journalist Andi Zeisler describes as 'marketplace feminism' (2016: xiii). A far cry from previous unappealing stereotypes of feminists as man-hating, humourless, and unattractive feminist killjoys (Ahmed 2017), brands like Dove or Nike have increasingly attempted to sell their products through themes of social justice and the empowerment of women. However, while the paradoxes of such 'femvertising' (Zeisler 2016: 25) are often easily detectable (for example, a celebration of women's 'natural beauty' in an attempt to sell beauty products), fictionalised cultural artefacts inhabit a less obvious place within what can be called the postfeminist marketplace. Because any representation that is not white, cis-gender male, and heterosexual is currently underrepresented in popular culture, viewer expectations run high when cultural artefacts invest in identity politics. Chapter 6 will explore in more detail how the industry utilises such sentiments to find audiences.

It is remarkable how current media texts like *Girls* outline a depoliticised feminism ready to be awarded through critics within a simple hit-or-miss binary. Consider the implications of commercial feminist co-optation for storytelling and cultural criticism:

> this suggests that feminism is an unvarying entity, a stamp of approval or a gold star, rather than a living ethic at the foundation of a larger system. It suggests that feminism is something that either is or is not okay to consume, rather than a lens through which creators and audiences see stories, characters, and communication. (Zeisler 2016: 108)

The way in which *Girls* triggers evaluations of its potential feminisms textually illustrates that the 'ur-feminist article' has found a new stomping ground within popular culture. The show premediates discussions to such an extent that discussion not only becomes the show's preferred viewing response, but can even be regarded as a textual property of the show, embedded in the structure of the recursive, self-aware, serial text itself. To distinguish this textual property from the piece of writing that Brunsdon identifies, I refer to this embedded triggering of feminist evaluations as *Girls*'s ur-feminist impulse.

The larger discursive patterns of journalistic and academic writing on the show outlined earlier act as the embedded textual 'test' or 'redemption' of the show. Whenever *Girls* is understood as not 'feminist enough', this is likely grounded in readings of its treatment either of race (the lack of diversity, its insufficient acknowledgement of racial privilege, and typecasting of minor characters of colour), of heterosexual sexuality (the subordination of female desire in favour of a heterosexual male sexuality), or of class (the financial support through families, the privilege to pursue creative careers).[8] The redemption of the show through a more nuanced feminist reading occurs when critics describe the show's break with cinematic and televisual conventions through the 'unruly body' of Lena Dunham, its portrayal of women's reproductive rights, or when turning to Dunham as one of the few female showrunners in a male-dominated industry. In its most pronounced, clickbait form, journalistic readings of redemption have been framed around an explicit rhetoric of defence with a myriad of articles titled 'In Defense of Girls'; for example, *The Huffington Post*'s 'In Defense of *Girls*' (Cauvin 2012), *Jezebel*'s 'In Defense of Hannah' (Davies 2013), or *Bustle*'s 'In Defense of *Girls*' Marnie' (Stahler 2014).

As *Girls* illustrates, current popular culture thus presents feminism not as a theoretical approach and activist movement, but as an identity or label to be seized by individuals or objects in a binary of approval/disapproval. *Girls*'s ur-feminist impulse sets in motion a process of questioning whether its portrayals of Dunham's body, her authorship, and the theme of reproductive rights outweigh racial representation to award it the definitive feminist stamp of approval.

Placing *Girls* next to another controversial example of commercialised postfeminist media culture, that of the Ukrainian and increasingly transnational feminist group FEMEN, helps illustrate its cursory ascription of feminism. FEMEN adopts as its signature practice 'sextremism' activism, which builds on the nudity of white cis-female activists. Adorned with make-up, flower crowns, and flowing hair, these women highlight their accordance with feminine beauty norms. After disrobing in heavily mediated public spaces, the activists showcase provocative statements written on their bare upper bodies. FEMEN trades heavily in images without context: its celebrity group members become an irritating, sexualised blend of activists and fashion models. While feminist celebrations of Dunham's 'undesirable', unruly body seem to operate at the opposing end of the model-activists of FEMEN, as cultural phenomena both function along similar lines. They equally reduce feminist issues to questions of the white cis-female body and its ambivalent relationship toward the specific and the universal. Like *Girls*, FEMEN is symbolic of a privileged white feminism for many cultural critics: heavily criticised for performances in blackface and Islamophobic positioning against women's veils, FEMEN presents white femininity as a problematic saviour of Muslimas and women of colour. While they develop very different images of naked femininity and feminism, both FEMEN and *Girls* are interested in fleetingly poking decontextualised feminist issues more so than acknowledging the complexity of these issues and their ongoing socio-political histories. As popular phenomena, they aspire to commercial success and attention in a postfeminist marketplace and mobilise audience assessments of their feminism as a means to these ends.

Lastly, the question arises of who or what the show needs to be defended or redeemed against. After all, with the 'ur-feminist article', Brunsdon demonstrates how persistent stereotypes of repellent second wave-feminists inform scholarship. Within *Girls*'s critical sphere, textual adversaries manifest through the back and forth references to other thinkpieces (or academic articles). For example, readings of the show's feminism are addressed more implicitly to other writers who demonstrate too little understanding of *Girls*'s (or Dunham's) situatedness within a larger popular culture environment and a larger media history. Marcie Bianco, for instance, argues that *Girls*'s feminism is the result of a 'satirical aesthetics', which not everyone is able to observe: 'when critics fail to understand the show as satire, they consequently assert that it is an embarrassment to feminism' (2014: 73, 74). A far cry from the rigorous stereotype of the feminist killjoy, here it is not the feminism of these adversaries that poses a problem and spoils the feminist writer's enjoyment of the pleasures of popular culture, but their inability to spot *Girls*'s knowing, metatextual play. The feminism that Bianco ascribes to the show thus requires an elegant reading of 'satire's rhetorical devices, such as irony, exaggeration, analogy, and juxtaposition' that Bianco then undertakes (74). These assumed adversaries do not recognise how 'knowingly' *Girls* 'plays' with popular cultural tropes or prevalent media practices. The word choice 'knowingly', sometimes also 'self-aware' or 'ironically', becomes a crucial interpretative vocabulary of the redemptive writing on the show (both journalistic and academic). Hannah's ignorant blindness toward (racial) inequality can accordingly be taken as the show criticising her white privilege, or Adam's continually putting his sexual gratification before that of his female partners can become a 'knowing' critique of the ways pornography dictates heterosexual fantasies.

As a textual property, the ur-feminist impulse manifests itself in *Girls*'s heavy use of metatextuality to create the 'knowing' show. Metatextuality serves such serial storytelling as not only a highly valued aesthetic procedure also carries a cultural-economic function: metatextuality becomes the ultimate redeemer of *Girls*'s feminist test. Through metatextuality the show acknowledges the talk about it, but does not 'talk back' to its critics, and rather seems perfectly fine with offering more of the same and 'watching' those critics' discussions. In a way, this reliance on metatextuality is reminiscent of related cultural phenomena like hipster racism or hipster sexism.[9] Unique for a serial narrative, *Girls* never significantly readjusts to incorporate its reception as part of the ongoing narrative, as the feedback loop of serial storytelling is usually prone to do.[10] The ur-feminist impulse helps explain why the critical conversation on *Girls* ran into a dead end during its third season when many frustrated journalists and academics dropped their coverage: it exemplifies how the questions the show inspired seemed to lead nowhere and similar iterations of the same thinkpiece were written all over again.

For feminist media scholar Imelda Whelehan, *Girls* 'makes the activity of feminist critique interesting once more' because the show 'resists the forms of identification and coherent narrative journeys that have become the trademark of postfeminist film and television' (2017: 31, 40). Of such earlier postfeminist media, Whelehan had previously argued that they had become 'un-analyzable' (2014: 247), or 'boring and frustrating' to analyse because their 'message requires little unpacking and lies prominently on the surface of these narratives. For many of us in the business of offering feminist critiques of popular culture in the twenty-first century, it can seem like we're simply tilting at windmills' (2010: 159). It is remarkable that Whelehan finds that the ambiguous show *Girls* revives feminist analysis of popular culture. Rather than serving as an antidote to such dilemmas of feminist criticism, *Girls* has incorporated feminist references in a less obvious, ambiguous, and metatextual fashion that I have referred to as its ur-feminist impulse. The windmills that Whelehan describes as too easy targets for feminist criticism are hence replaced with the carousel gaps of *Girls*. This creates the impression of having to catch up with the show and its complex references, a much more exhilarating, complicated, and rewarding activity than the struggles with docile windmills for viewer-critics. However, on closer inspection, *Girls* provides just as many references on its surface for critics to respond to as these earlier postfeminist texts. Rosalind Gill has recently maintained the continued importance of the concept of postfeminism for feminist analysis, especially in a cultural climate that celebrates a depoliticised version of feminism for sale (2016, 2017). *Girls* illustrates how popular culture has shifted its engagement with feminism enough to make such texts look 'new' and 'different', but on closer inspection reveals only a more sophisticated packaging. Finally, these recent developments suggest that just as we tend to think of Western feminism in terms of historical waves, their capitalist co-optation by postfeminism appears to be going through different waves as well.

This recent wave of postfeminist popular culture prefers ambiguous and distanced engagement over any clear character positioning. These are examples of how television shows pursue self-observation and pop-cultural self-historiography on a serial basis and as a means of distinction: *Girls* signals its awareness of a variety of discourses, from female objectification through the camera gaze to heterosexual monogamy as the final conclusion of stories, but aside from this awareness, it offers little. Overall, the microcosm that is *Girls* and its critical sphere can be taken to express the practices of postfeminist media culture within neoliberal capitalism. The chapter demonstrates that it is not primarily the show's focus on white femininities or white-centric feminism that is problematic in *Girls*, but rather its postfeminist focus on commercially mediated gestures of empowerment. These gestures reduce political practices into seemingly individualised, and, in the worst case, commercialised issues of identity representation. Ambiguous popular culture phenomena like *Girls* position each viewer as a feminist critic and ask them to actively judge the feminist potential of the given text. In this latest postfeminist cultural imaginary, feminism functions as a relative expression of personal taste independent of historical, social, or political practices. The dynamic of the specific and universal is thus reduced to the individual viewer's priorities and respective understanding of feminism. This kind of ur-feminist impulse allows serial postfeminist storytelling to react to political criticism not by adjusting to this criticism but by absorbing it. Hence, any kind of representation on the part of *Girls* is always staged as a metatextual act of observation that allows neoliberal popular culture to absorb any form of theoretical, social, or political critique through interactivity. As this book will continue to argue, the commercialisation of feminism undertaken within the postfeminist marketplace resembles other 'tamings' of previously radical political knowledges and movements.

NOTES

1. To many observers, series like *Broad City* (Comedy Central, 2014–19), *Master of None* (Netflix, 2015–17), *Insecure* (HBO, 2016–), or *Atlanta* (FX, 2016–) portrayed millennial identity with more attention to diversity.
2. As Hannah Hamad and Anthea Taylor have argued, 'celebrity feminists' like Dunham, Beyoncé, or actress Emma Watson claim the label of feminist through their own public position, not their feminist political practices, unlike prominent second-wave feminists such as Gloria Steinem or Germaine Greer (2015: 126).
3. For standpoint theory, see Harding 2009.
4. Protagonist Issa is a variation of Rae's 'awkward black girl' character developed in the precursor web series *The Misadventures of an Awkward Black Girl* (2011–13). The titles of these shows characterised their female leads: women who feel insecure and awkward in social encounters, and thus counter stereotypes of African American coolness and strength (Wanzo 2016: 45).
5. Barely any attention has been paid to Dunham's tattoos, even though current feminist analysis of the pathologisation of 'heavily tattooed women' (Thompson 2015) suggests itself for such an argument.
6. The well-established comparison of vampiric blood-drinking with excessive sexuality is also evoked when Hannah is drawn out of her self-contained dancing to realise her sexual attraction to her surf instructor.
7. Others have explored its characters' 'postfeminist entitlement' (DeCarvalho 2013: 368), highlighted how these characters are influenced by postfeminist discourse (Ford 2016: 1032; Lewis 2014: 176), and argued that postfeminism is parodied in the show (Bell 2013: 363; Seaton 2017: 154).
8. Discussions of economic privileges of characters were extended to claims of nepotism surrounding the show's actresses' celebrity parents: Dunham's mother is the artist Laurie

Simmons (and her father the painter Carroll Dunham), Zosia Mamet is the daughter of playwright David Mamet, Allison Williams is the daughter of *NBC Nightly News*'s anchor Brian Williams, and Jemima Kirke's father is drummer Simon Kirke of the band Bad Company.

9. Similar to 'retro sexism', 'hipster racism' reproduces racially insensitive and offensive comments under the guise of their being outdated, thus humorous. Several critics found the show's racial politics to resemble such 'hipster racism' (Saisi 2014: 67; Watson 2015: 153; Woods 2015: 47).

10. In other words, viewer criticism has not changed the show's storytelling aside from metatextual acknowledgements (for example, its racial representation was not significantly altered despite Sandy's brief appearance).

Part II

Television Audience Engagement and *How to Get Away with Murder*

CHAPTER 4

The Looped Seriality of *How to Get Away with Murder*

In September 2014, *The New York Times*'s chief television critic Alessandra Stanley published a controversial piece on the upcoming show *How to Get Away with Murder* (ABC, 2014–; henceforth *Murder*). In a sloppy argument, Stanley evoked a racist stereotype, the 'angry black woman', as something both the show's implied author Shonda Rhimes and its leading actress Viola Davis overcame (2014).[1] After being called out by Rhimes and Davis on Twitter, white woman Stanley proceeded to justify her article by arguing that 'Twitter culture' was to blame for the controversy, because Twitter users were unwilling to read beyond the length of a tweet (Prince 2014). Stanley's commentary demonstrates her disregard for social media interactivity and its cultural function for television narratives, particularly the shows associated with Rhimes's production company Shondaland. Along with *Scandal* (ABC, 2012–18) and *Grey's Anatomy* (ABC, 2005–), *Murder* formed ABC's scheduling block TGIT, short for 'Thank God It's Thursday'. The offering of three continuous hours of Rhimes-associated television has provided the network ratings success in this competitive Thursday night primetime slot. It also serves as a self-aware reference: in the 1990s, ABC's sitcom block TGIF ('Thank God It's Friday') was advertised as suitable for the entire family to watch television together on Friday nights. ABC explicitly promotes TGIT as women-centric television, but (like TGIF) the network highlights live viewing with others as a major pleasure of the programme. Albeit virtually: producers and viewers alike turn to social media and primarily to Twitter to react, discuss, and promote these shows, building communities with others who are watching at the same time. This chapter turns from the analytical engagements of viewer-critics to viewers who are interested less in composing elaborate readings, but more in sharing immediate, affective viewing experiences on Twitter.[2]

The phenomenon #TGIT signals a return to an 'appointment-based' model of television viewing, which many critics assumed had been replaced by a more flexible 'engagement-based model' that emphasises the availability of television in digital environments (Jenkins et al. 2013: 116). The success of #TGIT confirms the work of seriality scholars, who argued that long-running serial popular culture is at its most appealing when it becomes part of the everyday practices and routines of viewers as a kind of 'quotidian integration' (Hämmerling and Nast 2017: 248–9). Despite all the new options available for accessing television, serial audiences apparently continue to find pleasure in sharing the viewing experience with others. While seriality scholarship has utilised Benedict Anderson's concept of 'imagined communities' (Kelleter 2014; Bendix 2013), feminist audience studies engaged Stanley Fish's notion of 'interpretive communities' (Radway 1984; Bobo 1995) to explore such practices. The cultural phenomenon 'Black Twitter' – into which Twitter conversations surrounding *Murder* frequently bleed – is one such imagined and interpretative community. This chapter will explore how the show at times consciously mobilises practices connected with Black Twitter, and at other times blurs such associations to appeal to different audience segments.

On Twitter, users of colour are anything but a minority: study after study highlights the disproportionately high usage of Twitter by people of colour and specifically African Americans. While not every black Twitter user necessarily participates in Black Twitter and Twitter is not representative of a homogenous 'black experience' of some sort, it has received widespread recognition due to its ability to initiate awareness of systemic racism through a variety of hashtags, most prominently #BlackLivesMatter, and to foster a remembrance culture to keep the names and stories of the victims of racial injustice circulating. Black Twitter has been described as a community based on racial identification (Stevens and Maurantonio 2018: 183), a 'social space' (Florini 2014: 235), a 'social public' (Brock 2012: 530), and a 'counterpublic sphere' (Chatman 2017: 301). As Pritha Prasad highlights, 'Black Twitter functions not just as a tool or accompaniment to "real" protests elsewhere, but as an alternatively embodied, relational rhetorical imaginary that affords multiple simultaneous spatialities and temporalities' (2016: 56). Humour- and entertainment-oriented cultural commentary is not antithetical to but accompanies the political dimensions of Black Twitter. André Brock describes Black Twitter as 'ritual drama' because it employs 'cultural touch points of humor, spectacle, or crisis to construct discursive racial identity' (2012: 537). For instance, tweets and hashtags attributed to Black Twitter include performances of black vernacular (Florini 2014: 235), celebrations of black cultural achievements, and a call-out culture that draws attention to stereotypical misrepresentations of people of colour.

Conceptualisations of 'social television' or 'second screen' viewing have been intrinsic to the thinking of media industries and media scholarship.

While Twitter was initially conceived of as a sort of backchannel for television, recent studies have increasingly considered it as a 'return channel' (Harrington 2014: 242) or 'direct line of communication between audiences and production' (Navar-Gill 2018: 415–16). Based on different studies on television viewing and Twitter (Harrington 2014: 240–1; Auverset and Billings 2016: 10), the following Twitter reactions are typical for serial television: in their tweets, viewers attempt to guess future narrative developments, respond to surprising plot twists – often through jokes, seek the attention of production personnel or actors, and protest portrayals they deem problematic. Even without direct engagement, Twitter offers the possibility to imagine oneself within a larger collective, an 'imagined community', on the basis of shared media consumption (Anderson 1995: 6). Generally, *Murder*'s second-screen viewing favours cursory glances rather than in-depth engagement or conversations: viewers scan tweets and pay attention sporadically, switching their focus between the different devices.

So far only three academic articles have explored the Twitter activities of *Scandal* or *Murder* viewers (Williams and Gonlin 2017; Warner 2015a; Chatman 2017). In the only big data analysis, Apryl Williams and Vanessa Gonlin find that around 65 per cent of *Murder*'s viewers are female, and most of the tweets originated from geographical locations with a predominantly black demographic (2017: 990).[3] I observed live-tweeting practices organised through the hashtags #HTGAWM, #DatMurda, and #TGIT from the second to fourth season (September 2015 to March 2018) on the original day of the broadcast and three subsequent days.[4] The examples of tweets referenced in Chapters 4–6 are representative of larger trends or themes of *Murder*'s Twitter discourses. The Twitter platform is under constant change, which creates some problems for researchers. Because some of these tweets have since been deleted or set to private, I reproduce them anonymously without usernames. Furthermore, Twitter displays results which the website's invisible algorithms deem of interest to me based on the data it has collected on my internet behaviour. I attempted to control such filtered displays by repeatedly accessing Twitter through newly created accounts with disposable email addresses, from different computers with different IP addresses. This strenuous approach was necessary due to the lack of efficient software available to researchers. While sophisticated research tools exist, the pricey subscription models place them out of reach for individual researchers and cater toward companies interested in information about their consumer base. Further, the overlap of *Murder*'s Twitter conversations and Black Twitter also necessarily creates culturally specific instances that remain illegible for me as a white German researcher. Despite these two methodological caveats, this chapter offers essential new insights for the ways serial storytelling interacts with ongoing social media conversations.

Murder is set in Philadelphia where its protagonist Annalise Keating (Viola Davis) works as a prominent law professor and defence attorney. Annalise's different (nick)names demonstrate the different layers of her character: her husband Sam calls her Annie, her students dub her AK, her relatives continue to use her birth name, Anna Mae, and most viewers referred to her as Anna. In her first appearance, Annalise introduces not only her fictional university lecture but also the series itself through the much-quoted lines:

> Good morning. I don't know what terrible things you've done in your life up to this point, but clearly your karma is out of balance to get assigned to my class. I'm Professor Annalise Keating. This is Criminal Law 100. Or as I like to call it, how to get away with murder. (1.1 'Pilot')

In addition to serving as the unofficial title of her diegetic lecture, the show's title functions as its guiding idea, because Annalise, her employees, and students not only defend their clients against murder charges, but also become ensnared in a series of murders, suicides, and fatal accidents themselves. Among the students awed by her entrance, five are highlighted: Michaela (Aja Naomi King), Connor (Jack Falahee), Laurel (Karla Souza), Wes (Alfred Enoch), and Asher (Matt McGorry). These students of widely diverse ethnicities, sexual orientations, and class backgrounds are called the 'Keating Five' because they join Annalise's law firm as interns assisting her two other employees, Bonnie (Liza Weil) and Frank (Charlie Weber). The show's premise and these characters' joint endeavour become the cover-up of Wes's murder of Annalise's husband Sam by means of various schemes that result in a chain of follow-up murders, as well as the uncovering of long-past crimes prior to the show's story-present. Many episodes also contain episodic trials in which her students and employees assist Annalise in the defence of various clients.

Murder shares several stylistic and narrative features with the other #TGIT shows: aside from large, ethnically diverse casts, these shows also mix a variety of genres (melodrama, soap opera, romantic comedy), as well as settings familiar for various work dramas – for *Murder* these are crime series and legal drama.[5] Like *Scandal*, *Murder* relies on fast-paced plotlines in combination with what Anna Everett has called their '"WTF"-plot points' (2015: 38), bizarre narrative twists and cliffhangers. This kind of fast, flashy, and often sensationalist television melodrama has aptly been called 'hyperdrama' (Paskin 2014) because it thrives on 'hyperbole and hybridity' as well as 'narrative velocity, fast-paced dialog, fast camera movements, and fast cutting' (Puff 2015: 114, 118). These features provide compelling invitations for viewer engagement; hence, reactions to and discussions of such 'WTF' scenes drive the #TGIT Twittersphere.

Murder's strongest divergence from the template of its prominent older TGIT sibling *Scandal* is the show's elaborate temporality, which abounds with innumerable flash-forwards and flashbacks. On average, every episode spends about a third of its running time on such scenes, and often frames or interrupts the story-present with temporal jumps. On Twitter, viewers repeatedly express their confusion caused by such timelines. This chapter traces the show's serial storytelling by means of an analytical metaphor, the loop: as episodes include multiple jumps forward and backward, the loop illustrates the constant shifts between temporal positions. The first season, especially, jumbles its flash-forward scenes to lead viewers to false conclusions. At the same time, the show assists viewer comprehension through montages of already established visual cues (the murder weapon, a shot of the victim, or a blood-smeared wall), or a rewind sequence in which characters move backward – next to a rewinding time marker – to a moment previously omitted. Each of these devices results in rapid temporal movements that allow for new narrative reveals. Looped seriality thus results in a thickening of meanings, as gaps are filled in and new gaps only gradually become apparent to audiences.

My conceptualisation of *Murder*'s looped seriality draws on Robyn Warhol's and Julia Leyda's respective analyses of the experimental temporalities in the fourth season of *Arrested Development* (Comedy Central, 2003–6; Netflix, 2013).[6] In a stark departure from its earlier seasons, *Arrested Development* switched between different focalising characters in every episode to expand on previously minor plot points. Warhol finds that 'the constant looping back through time within and between episodes establishes a new way to structure serial narrative' (2014: 146), which Leyda deems a 'recursive synchronic structure' (2018: 353). Both wonder how compatible this kind of storytelling is with seriality, and they maintain that it is positioned 'completely outside the forward moving timeline that has been one of the defining features of serial form' (Warhol 2014: 156). Rather than contend that this recursive temporality is out of sync with serial storytelling – as is arguably the case in *Arrested Development* – I contend that through temporal experimentation and the slowly progressing murder mystery plot, *Murder* draws audiences into weekly serial rhythms. Whereas the shift in focalisation allows for *Arrested Development*'s constant refocusing, *Murder* more consistently balances different temporal modes with the promise of narrative resolution. Here, looped seriality is plot-driven, not character-driven.

Despite the amused confusion its viewers so often expressed, *Murder* follows a relatively simple formula that the first three seasons have implemented with surprising consistency. The first half of each season follows two related plotlines: a future crime, the eponymous murder, is hinted at in a series of jumbled flash-forwards, and the present-day plot leads up to this murder as the season progresses. This present-day plot operates as the show's story-present and is introduced through temporal markers that highlight the countdown toward the events of the flash-forwards.[7] The mid-season finale acts as a particular transition, when the present time plot connects with the future plot and culminates in a murder; some viewers have begun to refer to this episode as 'murder night'. The first two seasons specified the 'murder night' victim at the beginning of a season (Annalise's husband Sam in season one, prosecutor Emily Sinclair in season two), and created a mystery out of the murderer's identity and motivations. Seasons three and four, however, built suspense by keeping the identity of the murdered (or life-threateningly injured) character a secret. Hence, these seasons' flash-forwards slowly omit potential candidates, while viewers deducted who the possible victim and murderer could be. The second half of each season also juggles two related plotlines but is generally driven not by future-oriented glimpses, but by looking backward. Here, the story-present is interspersed with flashback scenes to a time even before the first half of each season. The second half of a season's story-present manages the long-term repercussions of 'murder night' on individual characters, while the past-oriented second plot presents these characters' motivations as based on their – at times surprising – biographies.

In addition to the explicit temporal markers that precede scenes, different plotlines are also distinguished visually. The future-oriented flash-forwards of 'murder night' are shot with a blueish-green tone that creates an almost forensic atmosphere with a detached effect on viewers primed to look for clues. Each mid-season premiere prominently includes a moment in which the more 'realistic' mode of the story-present switches into the well-known blueish-green – typically as the sun sets in the narrative – which indicates to viewers that the moment of conclusion has finally arrived. In stark contrast, the past-oriented flashback scenes are often tinted in sepia tones and create a more mellow, nostalgic feeling. Usually, these scenes take place during the day, in well-lit, sunny environments. They indicate a time well before the murder, a time when all still appeared to be well.

Through its elaborate plotting, *Murder* demonstrates its indebtedness to the long-running storytelling of soap operas, which combines quick plot twists with the deep narrative reveals of long-term storytelling. Abigail De Kosnik's notion of soap operas' 'rippling narrative style', in which one resolved plot conflict traces subsequently related narrative conflicts in its wake, can thus account for *Murder* as well (2013: 358). Most prominently, one murder results in even more deaths to cover up the initial crime, with one corpse begetting even more dead bodies. But while ripples initially act as apt descriptors, *Murder*'s temporal dimensions complicate the understanding of the show as a legacy of soap operas. In *Murder*, rippling occurs inwardly as well as outwardly and intensifies through the backwards and forwards motion of the different flash-forwards and flashbacks. The first season's murder loops forward into future cover-up crimes but also traces back to past crimes in connections that are not initially exposed.

As different characters become murderers for various reasons, and their friends and co-workers protect them for even more complicated reasons, *Murder*'s serial storytelling loops back to the past to keep these characters' outrageous behaviour emotionally accessible for viewers – if not always logically believable. In rare instances, dialogue metatextually acknowledges the challenges of this form of serialised storytelling. When Michaela runs from a crime scene, she is stopped by another character who points out in cold blood: 'you've done this before'. Despite her assertion, 'Exactly. I'm not doing it again', Michaela will end up interwoven into many further elaborate schemes (2.9 'What Did We Do?'). 'You just never learn', Annalise tells Michaela and her co-conspirators two seasons later, recognising the exhaustion many viewers articulated in the face of the show's storytelling (4.9 'He's Dead').

This exhaustion becomes an indication of this specific form of serial narrative. Both Robyn Warhol and Julia Leyda find the difficulty of binge-watching *Arrested Development* to be an indicator of its different serial format: the 'altered temporalities . . . created a stop-and-go pace that is the antithesis of the compulsive binge-watching style that made Netflix (in)famous' (Leyda 2018: 353). *Murder* also repeats scenes from previous episodes, at times in painstaking detail: 'not the cheerleader again!' one Twitter user lamented, commenting on a prominent visual cue, a twirling cheerleader at a social college function, that signals the flash-forward plot in the first season. Such repetitions may create a sense of boredom when watching episodes back-to-back. They also explain why *Murder* struggled more than *Grey's Anatomy* or *Scandal* to attract new viewers, as repetitiveness created disincentives to catch up outside of the live broadcasting block of #TGIT. Seriality studies has theorised the interactions between viewers and serial artefacts as a feedback loop (Kelleter 2017: 13–16). Accordingly, future narrative developments must adhere to past storytelling efforts as well as audience reactions to them. When viewers respond to *Murder*'s narrative developments on their second-screen device during the broadcast, the episode itself continues but these tweets cognitively loop back.[8] Next, I turn to three instances in which the interactivity of *Murder*'s looped seriality surfaces in the show's Twittersphere.

#WHODUNNIT: DETECTION, TWITTER, AND TEMPORAL UNRELIABILITY

Through the prominent fading-in of suggestive hashtags during the broadcast, *Murder* initiates audience interactivity. Often these hashtags centre around a season's mystery, such as the question of a culprit's identity, known in detective fiction as the 'whodunnit': #WhokilledLila, #WhokilledSam, #WhokilledRebecca, #WhoshotAnnalise, or #WhokilledWes.[9] This section takes up the impetus behind these questions – which drive narrative progression and audience interactivity – by exploring *Murder*'s indebtedness to and variation from detective fiction. *Murder* evokes detective fiction by engaging its defining characteristics and characters: false clues, the corpse, and the detective figure, or in this case, team.

A poignant example of its distinctive mise-en-scène, the 'client shot', allows the show to mobilise modes of detection as a viewing position. In such a scene, the camera is positioned behind and slightly above a client of the law firm and displays the group of student interns and employees spread across the room. The cast listen with varying degrees of involvement as their client presents her or his case. Overall, the client shot displays the large cast as mostly immobile and mirrors the show's promotional posters in staging (Figure 4.1). The stillness, attention to detail, and wide angle of the client shot recall the visual technique of the tableau, found in painting, photography, Vaudeville, and early film.[10] Regardless of medium, the term 'tableau' has been taken to stand for elaborate depictions that inspire awe and admiration in the observer. In its client shots, *Murder* appears to imitate aspects that film theoretician David Bordwell finds characteristic of early European and US-American cinema, such as a fixed camera setup and distant framing to control the viewer's gaze. Significantly, Bordwell points to the tableau shots' resemblance to theatre rather than cinema due to its 'optical projection [which] means that cinematic space is narrow and deep, while stage space is broad and (usually) fairly shallow' (2017). How does this characteristic shot serve *Murder*'s serial storytelling?[11]

The tableau staging highlights the show's diversity, for example by consciously placing African American (Annalise, Michaela, Wes), Caucasian (Bonnie, Frank, Asher, Connor), Latinx (Laurel), and Asian American characters (Oliver). Most straightforwardly, it characterises its large cast through visual juxtaposition of placement, body language, or facial expressions. For example, Annalise is often seated at the centre of the shot with other characters standing, sitting, or leaning around her. Reminiscent of a monarch's position in a court painting or the head of a family in family paintings and photography, this visualisation highlights her exemplary status as head of the firm and central character of the show. Her prominent position forms a direct contrast to that of white man Asher, the only student not involved in the first season's murder, who is frequently clueless about the group's social dynamics. Asher is often sulking in the background, crossing his arms in front of his body in either a refusal to engage or an attempt at critical distance. This posture illustrates not only his initial position within the group, but also his insecurity with exhibiting a professional persona. Even though traditional scripts of professional conduct are most accessible to white cis-man Asher, through his uneasiness at embodying them and his goofy behaviour, the show makes its most privileged character likeable for audiences.

Figure 4.1 Tableau staging in a 'client shot' and promotional poster from the second season. This distinctive display characterises by contrast, highlights the cast's diversity, and positions the characters as jury-detectives.

The tableau-inspired client shot establishes characters in the process of judging a client's case, which is embodied, for example, by some characters taking notes. The characters' facial expressions vary from empathy to disbelief or repulsion as they develop their interpretation of a case – which may be challenged by the narrative developments of the episode. The characters thus become a variation of jury and detectives because they try to plan a court strategy but also labour to reconstruct what happened. As jury-detectives, the characters occupy a cognitive position similar to that of *Murder*'s viewers, who also watch their television sets and write down interpretations to share on Twitter. Like the show's characters, viewers are thrown off by false leads or misinterpreted clues and may misjudge a suspect's motivations and actions. While characters mirror their viewers as jury-detective in these episodic cases, viewers occupy this position throughout the entire season when trying to figure out the murder mystery of the mid-season finale. Classic detective fiction with its investments in logic, deduction, and reconstruction, appears to have little in common with this show's sensationalist, melodramatic representation of murders spiralling out of control. However, through the viewing position of the jury-detective established through the client shot, the show recognises the pleasures to be found in collecting clues and developing theories.

In *Murder*, temporal variation complicates the way viewers deduct their investigative results. We do not enter a story which begins with a dead body and encourages us to deduce in retrospect who killed this person, but, instead, we find a crime that takes place in the future and is foreshadowed through flash-forwards. *Murder* dangles the carrot of a neat conclusion in front of its viewers, as something they may be able to piece together and share in Twitter conversations. But, due to its serial storytelling, the show's narrative closures are consistently spiced with new mysteries. In her work on early detective film serials of the late 1910s and 1920s, Ruth Mayer holds that dynamics of detection and concealment proliferate over serial instalments. Despite the appearance of narrative resolution, the detective genre has always lent itself to serial storytelling: 'a closer look at its workings reveals that it operates by reeling off ever new beginnings, or rather, loops of action' (2017: 21). Mayer's description of new narrative developments as 'loops of action' resonates well with *Murder*'s looped seriality. Unlike classic detective fiction, in which the relevance of clues is not always clear to the audience, *Murder* abounds with false clues that lead viewers to wrong interpretations which are often already ruled out in the following episode. Twitter responses indicate that such misleading clues inspire pleasure and frustration in equal parts. However, surprisingly often, frustration is expressed with one's own naïvety – along the lines of 'I should have known better' – and not with author figures Rhimes and Nowalk. Instead of being annoyed at how fruitless one's previous attempts to reconstruct the puzzle were, viewers express surprising acceptance and pleasure in loops revealing inconsistencies of earlier clues. For example, viewers eagerly followed the seemingly chronological flash-forwards of the third season to figure out which main character would die in the mid-season finale and engaged in lively discussions under the hashtag #UnderTheSheet. After the process of elimination left only Frank or Nate as potential victims, the mid-season finale revealed a scene to be chronologically out of order, surprising viewers with the sight of Wes's corpse underneath the coroner's body sheet.

In murder mysteries or detective stories, the crime itself is rarely present in the narratives but is rather displaced and only manifests through the dead body/bodies and the accounts of others. Traditionally, the victims of these stories have amounted to little more than ciphers and causes of investigations, 'simply a signal for a battle of wits to begin between murderer and sleuth and, often, between author and reader' (Herbert 2003: 201). Never merely a corpse, characters like Annalise's husband Sam (Tom Verica), Emily Sinclair (Sarah Burns), or Wes are actively involved in the narratives, and viewers screen their interactions for clues about the events that will lead to their deaths. In place of a detective figure as a focalising instance, the viewers follow potential murder suspects and potential victims to answer the driving question of #whodunnit. Even after their death is established in the story-present, dead characters can never truly be forgotten on the show. Their memory continues to haunt other characters in melodramatic loops back to the past.

The crime of 'murder night' becomes an anticipated moment for many viewers as it finally offers the relief of relative closure. In cinematic detective serials, temporal constraints limit characters' actions (Mayer 2017: 26), but in *Murder*, time becomes a flexible structuring device for the plot. Time is sped up, rewound, or paused for narrative purposes. Similar to the structuring figure of the detective in classic detective fiction, temporal alterations provide viewers with clues to the future crime and allow for the pleasures of figuring out both the circumstances as well as the larger repercussions of the 'murder night' through forward and backward loops.

Even though the central hashtags occur in the format of the whodunnit, the show and its viewers are also highly interested in the related question of *why* an established character is driven to murder. Positioned as jury-detectives through looped storytelling, *Murder*'s viewers are ultimately interested – more so than the 'forensic fans' that Jason Mittell has explored (2015) – in evaluating whether the sympathetic murdering characters should, in fact, 'get away with murder'. Therefore, neither false clues nor the lack of a focalising detective figure significantly disturbs audiences' pleasure in figuring out what will be morally justifiable for these characters, that is, which emotional circumstances justify murder. Like the employees of Keating's firm, the viewers immerse themselves in the (fictional) cases and change their initial impressions of characters after looped storytelling offers new realisations that disrupt previous understandings of each 'murder night' case.

DID NO ONE LOCK THE HOUSE?: MEMES, GIFS, AND INTERNET HUMOUR

Most viewers tend to respond to *Murder* by retweeting or 'liking' others' comments through Twitter's heart icon, not by engaging in dialogue. Visual, humorous displays are the most dominant viewer reaction to the show. Such tweets may reduce the absurdities of *Murder*'s elaborate plotting to a sarcastic byline or viral video that generates thousands of retweets. Repetition is inherent to this authorless visual internet humour, evident in the resurfacing of popular pictures and video clips via new posts each episode. Even though media scholarship has increasingly turned to the new phenomenon of 'memes', creating and sharing memes continue to be notoriously under-considered serial practices of television audiences.

Within online cultures, the word 'meme' has acquired a specific cultural meaning that departs from the neologism's origins in biologist Richard Dawkins's work. It is generally understood to refer to a digital image or video clip that incites humorous reactions, is spread by a multitude of users, and often inspires copies or variations. Colloquially a 'meme' refers to a recognisable picture, often a screengrab that is overlaid with two lines of text. Often a seemingly harmless comment is positioned on the top of the visual and juxtaposed with an ironic punchline at the bottom. A prominent example of such a 'classic meme' is a screenshot of Annalise's townhouse on fire in the third season that was shared with the caption 'The whole season happened – because the door wasn't locked.' This meme is so meaningful because of the significance of this house to the narrative of the show. As the central setting for the first three seasons, Annalise's house amounts to more than her home and workplace – the law firm – but also constitutes a major crime scene. The show's many deaths spread throughout the house are reminiscent of the board game *Clue/Cluedo*'s many possibilities for murder: Wes bludgeons Sam to death with Annalise's statue in the living room, Bonnie suffocates Rebecca with a plastic bag in the basement, and a hitman strangles Wes in the hallway. Annalise's house accordingly inverts the locked room of detective fiction: it is a porous space entered by a variety of suspects, witnesses, and victims.[12] These murders become possible only because her home is repeatedly left unlocked and people slip in unnoticed. While Annalise is frustrated that Frank forgot to lock up in the first season, later seasons do not even attempt to justify why Annalise lets herself live and work in this constant state of intrusion and even insecurity. Annalise's acceptance of the conflation of her private and professional lives stands in stark contrast to white lawyer Alicia Florrick (Julianna Margulies) in *The Good Wife* (CBS, 2009–16), who struggles to keep her home free from interference by her professional life (Kanzler 2015: 149). Significantly, the home has never been an entirely private space for many women of colour who found employment as domestic workers for upper-class households – a profession that *Murder* even acknowledges in the cameo of a woman of colour as houseworker for Asher's parents.

While such 'classic memes' focusing on, for instance, Annalise's house, therefore convey significant meaning, what most social media users consider a meme has been subject to gradual change. Currently, screenshots frequently take the form of collages – they include stills from different popular culture texts – and less standardised placement of written text. Such memes make up a large percentage of *Murder*'s social media activities. A prominent example (Figure 4.2) combines three different screenshots of Annalise in different emotional or physical states and equates these to users' viewing experience. First, Annalise looks confident and amused ('Start of the show'), then focused and slightly confused ('This is me . . . 15 minutes in'), and in the last shot lies unconscious in a puddle of her own blood after being shot in the second season's 'murder night' ('Me . . . at the end of every episode'). Like many similar memes, this example humorously likens viewing experiences to the characters' suffering.

Anna Everett has compared the 'delighted shock and awe' *Scandal*'s viewers feel at the show's outrageous developments to the pained pleasures to be found in the horror genre (2015: 36–7). Everett's description brings to mind Linda Williams's understanding of cinematic horror as a 'body genre' in which viewers mirror the affect of characters on-screen – in this case, fear (1991). However, unlike Williams's body genres, memes demonstrate the difference between characters and viewers in a humoristic fashion. Like Figure 4.2, these memes are entertaining precisely because they only *claim* to function like Williams's body genres: unlike the shared emotions of fear in horror, sadness in melodrama, or arousal in pornography, viewers do not actually feel the physical or emotional pain of the characters depicted. Instead, when viewers claim to do so, humour arises from this claim amounting to the same exaggerated dramatic mode that *Murder* excels at. Struggling to keep on top of confusing plotlines is not the same as being strangled or shot, hence the drama of such responses loops back the drama of the show and becomes another site of entertainment for other viewers. As a practice, these memes deepen the pleasure of the show's outrageousness through its adoption as an affective mode in social media. Were viewers to truly feel the slightest version of the emotions they lay claim to here, their frustrations would result in turning the television off rather than sharing viewing reactions with the 'imagined community' of Twitter viewers.

Still more effective than mere text-based communication, within social media conversations, GIFs – or short video clips – serve as 'embodied emotional displays' (Tolins and Samermit 2016) of a person's affective and (physical) reactions. I would estimate that at least a third of all tweets on the show – likely even more – include GIFs.[13] The appeal of GIFs lies in their easy emotional access

Figure 4.2 By dramatically comparing being shot to the attempt to follow the show's complex timeframe, this meme adopts *Murder's* melodramatic mode.

and their temporality: the GIF repeats an action in loops until a user scrolls on. The GIF calls to mind the repetitious movements of early nineteenth-century zoetropes or phénakisticopes, whose moving images similarly repeat (Eppink 2014: 298). Moreover, GIFs evoke 'pleasure in the familiar when reliving such moments of emotional acuity and then reliving them again and again as they repeat' (Newman 2017). Because *Murder* is so invested in temporal loops – and relies on loops between viewer responses and the show itself – the GIF becomes a particularly crucial site of negotiating viewer reactions.

Linda Huber describes Twitter as a 'remix culture', an understanding that resonates in the word choice of other researchers as well (2015). Media scholars refer to GIFs as being 'lifted', 'yanked', 'severed', or 'appropriated' from their original popular culture texts. Scrolling through the #HTGAWM Twitter feed during the live-airing of an episode, one can routinely encounter GIFs extracted from a wide range of reality television shows, documentaries, or music videos, often from the late 1990s or early 2000s. A GIF of reality television persona New York attacking another dating show contestant on *Flavor of Love* (VH1, 2006–8) alternates with one of Will Smith's character in a celebratory dance on *The Fresh Prince of Bel-Air* (NBC, 1990–6) and an unknown talk show audience member breaking into excessive tears. Their popular culture origins, low resolution, and dramatic air confirm Limor Shifman's observation that '"bad" texts make "good" memes in contemporary participatory culture' (2014: 86). Clips from *Murder* also frequently resurface not only on its own Twitter hashtags but for more generic searches on the database giphy.com.[14] The popularity of GIFs taken from the show can thus also be understood within the implied value hierarchy Shifman has in mind, as the show's association with melodramatic 'guilty pleasure television' places it similarly within the gendered category of 'bad text'.[15]

Because bodily gestures drive the reaction GIF, the question of whose bodies are depicted should be of great relevance to studies of GIFs. Because GIFs can be described as an 'affect bomb you drop to express your reaction in a given moment' (Newman 2017), race or gender factor into the GIFs' explosive emotionality. This is troubling because, aside from age-specific associations with youth culture, memes occur in a specifically racialised context. GIFs disproportionately depict the bodies of black reality television actors, black athletes, black musicians, and anonymous people of colour. Such GIFs lead the search engine results and enjoy popularity with social media users of all races. This preference for GIFs that depict people of colour recalls racist stereotypes of African Americans as excessively emotional. Lauren Michele Jackson aptly locates the appropriation of black images within the tradition of minstrel performances and conceptualises them as 'digital blackface' which 'does not describe intent, but an act – the act of inhabiting a black persona. Employing digital technology to co-opt a perceived cachet or black cool, too, involves playacting blackness in a minstrel-like tradition' (2017). Hence, to share a GIF of Viola Davis performing as Annalise may become an instance of 'digital blackface' when carried out by white social media users. The most popular GIFs taken from *Murder* confirm such ascriptions of emotionality: Annalise fiercely stands her ground in court, dances with her fingers snapping at a family gathering, or breaks into tears with eye make-up streaking her cheeks. In such scenes, Annalise performs what Brandy Monk-Payton has described as 'important modes of black girl humor' (2015: 22), the interlaced black feminist and black queer cultural practices of 'sass' and 'shade' (15). For white viewers accustomed to the 'post-racial' brand of #TGIT, digital blackface becomes a deracialised practice with problematic outcomes.

Even though the appropriations of white viewers complicate how viewers of colour re-emphasise race in post-racial television (Warner 2015a: 41–50), this is not to say that their reinvestments are rendered culturally meaningless. Instead, as Sesali Bowen has illustrated, such 'black memes' become crucial tools for women and girls of colour to inhabit identity and sexuality, often within the same online spaces that appear hostile or restrictive to them (2016: 21). GIFs used to talk about *Murder* on Twitter as well as GIFs created from scenes of *Murder* to express viewers' emotional responses thus demonstrate what Lisa Nakamura elaborates: 'women and people of color are both subjects and objects of interactivity; they participate in digital racial formations via acts of technological appropriation yet are subjected to it as well' (2008: 16). *Murder*'s prominent hashtags become an assemblage of the practices of both white viewers – digital blackface – and Twitter's users of colour, who share the same black memes in a celebratory fashion. In the stream of live-tweets, it often becomes impossible to distinguish between these coexisting social media performances, when unknowable viewer profile pictures complicate who is 'authentic' and who is 'appropriating'.

TELEVISION DRINKS: CONSUMPTION DURING AND IN #TGIT SHOWS

If a Twitter user new to the #TGIT shows were to check out the shows' prominent hashtags before the live broadcast, that person would likely be surprised by the number of snapshots depicting a still life of red wine glasses, bowls of popcorn, or bags of crisps placed prominently in front of television or laptop screens. Looped seriality helps to understand the show and viewers' interactive reciprocity evident in the consumption of alcoholic beverages and snacks on- and offscreen. The practice of eating in front of a television screen dates to the beginnings of television as a mass medium and the invention of the TV dinner in the 1950s. For television historian Lynn Spigel, television viewing in social settings created new chores for women held accountable to an ideal of gracious hosting; the TV dinner was 'the perfect remedy for the extra work entailed by television, and it also allowed children to eat their toss-away meals while watching Hopalong Cassidy' (1992: 90). *Murder*'s consumption loops translate the practices of the older television dinner into a more current (and postfeminist) ethos of neoliberal 'self-care'. Such a practice of individualised consumerism values impulsivity (to treat oneself to yet another drink, snack, or episode), and characters become relatable when they exhibit similar behaviours, to be celebrated emphatically by the show's Twittersphere. For the viewers of serial television, snack preparations turn serialised viewing by appointment into media rituals, as Christine Hämmerling demonstrates for viewers of the long-running German crime series *Tatort* (ARD, 1970–). However, #TGIT viewers diverge significantly from the participants in Hämmerling's study (2016), because the shows themselves suggest specific drinks or snacks through characters' consumption patterns on-screen.

On the day of *Murder*'s premiere, Shonda Rhimes introduced Annalise through her preferred drink and invited viewers to drink along with the character: 'put down the red wine. Pick up the vodka. And get ready to meet Annalise Keating!' All of the #TGIT show's leading characters have a signature drink, such as the tequila shots of *Grey's Anatomy*'s Dr Meredith Grey (Ellen Pompeo) or the long-stemmed glasses of red wine which political 'fixer' Olivia Pope (Kerry Washington) likes to pair with bowls of popcorn on *Scandal*. Viewers frequently express pleasure at recognising their snack and drink consumption mirrored on-screen or complain about the cravings such depictions cause. Official promotions have also embraced interactive consumption loops: lists of emoticons 'needed' for viewing include a bowl of popcorn or a glass of red wine, the official website sells #TGIT wineglasses as merchandise, and television ads show the leading actresses drinking wine together on a large couch in satin pyjamas (Figure 4.3). Such paratextual materials position viewers' consumption as part of an elegant, feminised setting in which one should not feel guilty for treating oneself to a glass of wine, a bowl of popcorn, or three hours of seemingly 'guilty pleasure' television.

Foundational scholarship of feminist audience studies has highlighted the pressure that the audiences of feminised, 'guilty pleasures' like romance novels or soap operas negotiate when it comes to their enjoyment of cultural artefacts versus the stigmatised external perception of this enjoyment (Radway 1984; Ang 1985; Bobo 1995). *Murder* and its #TGIT siblings cleverly evoke these negotiations of feminised culture in glossy defence of the pleasures to be found in them. Like the professionalised protagonists of these shows, female viewers – especially black female viewers – may manage tiring, hostile work or social environments. Setting the stage for ritualised consumption, indulging oneself is presented as an essential form of self-care enjoyed by a large community of

Figure 4.3 Leading ladies Kerry Washington, Ellen Pompeo, and Viola Davis share red wine and popcorn (with one another and with their viewers) in this #TGIT advertisement from September 2017.

people who sip wine along with Olivia Pope. *Murder* draws on such viewing pleasures but has also increasingly come to complicate them.

Food items and drinks tend to amass intersectionally gendered associations, such as class-belonging, which are inscribed in diets through various sociocultural factors. Alcoholic drinks, in particular, mobilise gendered belonging. For example, expressions of masculinity may be compromised through the consumption of 'frisky', sugary cocktails, wine coolers, or even just wine. Instead, drinks associated with masculinity such as bitter liquors, beer, or, most notably, whiskey tend to possess more cultural cachet. 'When men enjoy something, they elevate it', culinary website *Taste*'s Jaya Saxena criticises, 'but when women enjoy something, they ruin it' (2017). In this context, the legitimising strategies of self-care that #TGIT offers gain resonance for female viewers. However, Annalise's choice of drink is also specifically gendered. In line with her show's general (self-)presentation as a darker, 'rawer' or 'realer' show than *Scandal*, Annalise prefers neat vodka shots and frequently eats calorie-rich potato crisps straight from the bag. As many viewers comment, Annalise gulps vodka like water with a superhuman tolerance for alcohol. As a hard liquor, vodka tends to be associated with its Eastern European origins. The anaesthetic taste of vodka stands diametrically opposed to sweet and fruity flavours, and the person drinking vodka with a straight face is likely a seasoned drinker.[16] Through her choice of drink, Annalise is marked as no-nonsense, direct, and able to hold her own.

Rather than the glamorous portrayal of *Scandal*'s Olivia, Annalise's consumption aspires to 'authenticity' and relatability. Her eating and drinking often occur to humanise the mysterious, successful woman as driven by impulse. Frustrated with the healthy stock of her kitchen shelves, Annalise prefers 'real food' such as 'Chips, dip, anything with chocolate' (3.6 'Is Someone Really Dead?'). The disconnect between Viola Davis's beautiful, athletically slim figure and Annalise's unhealthy diet and lack of exercise is frequently joked about in tweets, yet never addressed in the show.[17] Repeatedly, other characters attempt to change her diet of packaged and processed junk food. Her husband Sam frequently asks her if she has eaten, and prepares and organises their dinners; employee Bonnie's attempts to care for Annalise involve throwing away her alcohol or junk food;[18] and, on-and-off-boyfriend Nate memorably prepares her a green smoothie which Annalise tosses into a bin as quickly as possible. As Black Twitter demonstrates, references to certain food items may become expressions and markers of African American identities (Stevens and Maurantonio 2018). However, many scholars and activists point out that class-based food divisions remain stark because many urban communities of lower- and middle-class people of colour lack access to fresh produce. While relatable to these viewers, Annalise's preference of a heavily manufactured diet is at odds with her upper-class status and the resources it affords her.

Because Annalise also drinks to calm herself down when the group's elaborate cover-up of various murders threatens to collapse, her drinking as a coping behaviour echoes the show's viewers: 'after that episode, I need alcohol. I need Annalise to drop by with her giant bottle of vodka', as one tweet humorously puts it. Not surprisingly, *Murder* has inspired a variety of drinking games to humorously cope with both the show's outrageous plots and its frequent repetitions: 'take a gulp, if . . . there is a bonfire flashback (double if they show the cheerleader's flying stunt)' (Piwowarski 2015). In a departure from the #TGIT shows' attempts to mirror and approve their viewers' ritualised consumption, by the third season, *Murder* began to portray Annalise's frequent drinking in a surprising light. Initially, Annalise strategically claims to be an alcoholic to escape disbarment for unethical behaviour. However, viewers, as well as the character herself, slowly began to understand her alcohol consumption as an addiction. This example of the show's looped seriality adds a new layer, albeit one that offers surprising implications for viewers whose pleasure of 'drinking together' with the characters on-screen was called into question through Annalise's alcoholism.

Three dominant viewer responses subsequently emerged as attempts to reconcile the dilemma: first, a large group of viewers disentangled their drinking from that of Annalise. These viewers were able to worry about Annalise's relapses and celebrate her continued abstinence while they continued to drink alcohol while watching the show. They rooted for Annalise to battle her addiction as a more radical form of self-care but did not connect this reading to their own drinking practices. Second, an initially large but dwindling group of viewers continued their equation of drinking with Annalise because they refused to acknowledge her addiction. These viewers humorously positioned her destructive drinking binges as 'so me' without worrying that this might characterise them as alcoholics. Third, another common practice of viewers was to refocus the pleasure of shared consumption from alcoholic drinks to snacks or non-alcoholic beverages. Responses to a scene in which Annalise opens and smells wine bottles at a store and only at the last minute turns to buy a stack of candy highlighted such celebrations of her conquering her addiction.

In conclusion, this chapter's conceptualisation of *Murder*'s serial storytelling derived from the show's investment in temporal loops, its narrative flashforwards and flashback plots, as well as the loops between viewer responses and the show itself, the 'feedback loop' of seriality (Kelleter 2017). Compared with thinkpiece seriality (Chapter 1) and paratext seriality (Chapter 7), *Murder*'s looped seriality resembles the most widely used, standardised forms of serial storytelling in popular culture. Looped seriality allows *Murder* to gradually thicken and extend meanings, open new gaps, and continuously renegotiate previous storytelling and characterisation. Like so many shows in the digital television age, *Murder* unfolds like a game between producers and viewers. It aspires toward immediate affective reactions rather than the removed detective pleasures typically associated with its genre(s), theme, and extreme temporal experimentation. Unlike *Girls*'s serial reception practices, *Murder*'s hashtag viewing is not about elaborate interpretations but expressive communication. Three areas emerged as especially relevant to the interactivity of *Murder*'s looped seriality and the show's Twittersphere. First, the 'whodunnit' hashtags and *Murder*'s client shot encourage viewers to discuss how morally justifiable the extreme actions of the characters are. With their literal video loops, GIFs provide interesting openings to further examine exaggerated viewer responses. In a third instance, I applied looped seriality to understand the show and the viewers' interactive reciprocity when it comes to #TGIT's ritualised consumption.

NOTES

1. While the main executive force in the background of *Murder* is male and white, the show's public authorial face is female and black: producer Shonda Rhimes is much more prominent than showrunner Peter Nowalk.
2. Launched in 2006, Twitter has steadily expanded its user base and rose to public awareness following 2010. Its brief tweets lend themselves to fast, immediate circulation and real-time commentary. Furthermore, they are typically publicly accessible – a remarkable feature in times in which cultural anxieties surrounding online privacy and

surveillance abound – and are marked by the platform's refusal to take measures against racism, sexism, and anti-Semitism.
3. *Murder* does not garner the same activity as *Scandal* – with an average of 133,000 tweets – or *The Walking Dead*, which was the most talked-about show on Twitter for three years (2015–17) with an average of 435,000 tweets (Kissell 2015). *Murder*'s second season premiere garnered 289,000 tweets by 85,000 unique users (TV by the Numbers Editors 2015). In its fourth season, original posts (no retweets) by 25,000 unique accounts were counted (Martinez 2017).
4. Both Rhimes and Viola Davis favourably acknowledged the hashtag #DatMurda, but its users tend to understand it as a less authorised, more racially specific site for conversation.
5. Meanwhile, the hospital-based setting of *Grey's Anatomy* allows for a variation of medical drama, and *Scandal*'s Washington DC setting takes a page from the playbook of political thrillers.
6. Umberto Eco employs the loop to describe types of serial storytelling as well (1985: 168–9). While his understanding of 'loop-series' as flashback-heavy explorations of new narrative possibilities is close to my use of the term here, my analysis does not concord with Eco's finding that such temporal experimentation does not affect the already fixed characterisation (168). On the contrary, I explore the particular possibilities for characterisation that looped serialities offer.
7. For instance, the fourth season led up to its mid-season finale with temporal markers such as 'Three Months Later' (episode 4.1), 'Two and a Half Months Later' (4.2), 'Two Months Later' (4.3), 'One and a Half Months Later' (4.4), 'Two Weeks Later' (4.5), 'One Week Later' (4.6), and '48 Hours Later' (4.7). The nit-picky narratologist may prefer to understand the future-oriented plot as the show's story-present and the present-day plot as a series of flashbacks. However, because the present-day scenes occupy the largest part of an episode and are stylistically most concordant, I approach them as story-present.
8. In general, social media conversations follow a looped logic: while Twitter's timeline seems to display tweets chronologically (yet, guided by invisible algorithms), loops occur when tweets are retweeted or responded to.
9. Sometimes understood as a subgenre of the detective story or an alternate moniker, the whodunnit is short for 'who has done it?' The readers or viewers follow a detective figure through the process of solving crimes. This may take on a playful element in board games like *Clue/Cluedo* or interactive murder mystery dinner theatres.
10. Tableau staging derives from the *tableau vivant*, French for 'living picture', a style of painting or photography prominent in Europe in the late nineteenth and twentieth centuries, which emphasises large groups of subjects arranged in deliberate, detailed costumes, settings, and poses (Brandl-Risi 2012).
11. The tableau shot is so characteristic of the show that it has strategically employed obvious deviations from it. For instance, in the second season, Asher attempts to deliver an emotional speech in a parody of the shot. The other characters refuse to listen attentively and keep moving in and out of the frame.
12. Because Annalise's house is such an open and porous space, it is not surprising that most of the show's most intimate dialogue takes place in cars. The car here becomes an enclosed space that offers more privacy for confidential conversations and fewer opportunities for disturbance or intrusion than the house.
13. GIF is short for 'graphics interchange format' and refers to seconds-long moving images without sound taken from various popular cultural artefacts.
14. While 'traditional' memes were created by users themselves, GIFs have meanwhile become a profitable business. As a result, various companies create GIF sets, and social media websites include GIF search engines.

15. Scholarship on GIFs has raised the question of whether GIFs retain or empty their original source material's cultural meanings to be emotionally effective (Bowen 2016: 7; Huber 2015). In regard to television viewers, such concerns should take into account the sophisticated, intertextual knowledge of the audience.
16. Aside from these masculine connotations, vodka is also a preferred drink of those concerned with their weight as it possesses relatively few calories.
17. Overall, aside from its awareness of the underrepresentation of bisexual orientation and racialised beauty norms, *Murder*'s body politics take a relatively traditional and normative form. By this, I mean the glamorised, feminised ideal of slim beauty that the female characters adhere to.
18. Bonnie is the only female murderer of the show's main group of characters, and many viewers found Bonnie to be an unlikeable character early on. As a white woman, Bonnie's policing of a black woman's – albeit unhealthy – diet and drinking further added to many viewers' perception of her as problematic.

CHAPTER 5

Outward Spiral: Gendering through Recognisability

This chapter uses the outward spiral to examine how *Murder*'s looped seriality results in processes of gendering. The outward spiral demonstrates how gendered identities signify culturally and socially in expanding circles with recourse to viewer responses. Unlike a serialised characterisation which emphasises the development of characters as a journey or process, *Murder* retrospectively introduces new aspects of characters' past lives and – often through flashbacks – affirms these as central to their identity and motivation. For instance, an unwelcome visit of her estranged mother reveals Michaela's family background as the adopted child of a white lower-class family of the Appalachian region (3.9 'Who's Dead?'). This reveal reframes Michaela's aspirations to an affluent marriage – she mentions the Obamas as her ideal of professional and private partnership – and her search for a black female professional mentor. The materialistic markers of success such as her treasured, self-bought Vera Wang wedding dress or the Louboutin high heels her new employer gifts her take on new significance as embodiments of Michaela's personal from-rags-to-riches story. As this example illustrates, spiral gendering does not reposition previous characterisations but reveals new layers of them. As looped storytelling jumps back and forth to dissect new layers of characters' intersectionally gendered identities, social media commentary reaffirms connections to broader social, cultural, or political conversations that these layers evoke.

This chapter focuses on *Murder*'s central character, Annalise Keating, and teases out two dominant themes impacting the gendering of black femininity. My readings elaborate on television's participation in contested discourses of 'colourblindness' or 'post-race'. Post-racial ideology claims the 'pastness' of racism and similarly assures 'the dominant white culture that colorblindness represents a position of tolerance and acceptance' (Nilsen and Turner 2014: 3).

Murder offers a variation of post-racial television that acknowledges racism or sexism in its own peculiar ways. Viewers of colour have often lauded Annalise as a response to the 'colourblind' portrayal of *Scandal*'s protagonist Olivia. As the much-acclaimed first black female lead on a television show since the brief Blaxploitation series *Get Christie Love!* (ABC, 1974–5), Olivia Pope is often related to the 'controlling images' of black femininity that Patricia Hill Collins has identified (2000: 76–106). Research on *Scandal* interrogates Olivia's characterisation against such racialised imagery (Warner 2015b: 18; Puff 2015: 104; Gomez and McFarlane 2017: 366). These scholars find Olivia to complicate 'controlling images' such as the mammy, jezebel, matriarch, or sapphire because her characterisation affirms and subverts these racist types simultaneously. Research on how viewers respond to these presumed 'problematic' portrayals resonates most with my understanding of *Murder*'s spiral gendering of black femininity. Such approaches emphasised how viewers find pleasure in the characters' ambiguity, which envisions black femininity beyond the scope of racist stereotypes or 'respectability politics' (Warner 2015b: 18; Chatman 2017: 310).

Instead of approaching black femininity through the 'controlling images' so wearisome for scholarship on *Scandal*, this chapter revolves around the assumption that *Murder* speaks back to such images and positions viewers to do the same. For *Scandal*, Stephanie Gomez and Megan McFarlane propose the notion of 'refraction' which, like a prism, 'speaks to a both/and tension [rather than either/or] that ultimately depoliticizes race and gender, while it seeks to conceal the depoliticization' (2017: 364). *Murder* does something similar, yet because its temporality is much more complicated than *Scandal*'s largely linear storytelling, the more dynamic movement of the spiral serves best to explore *Murder*'s expanding, layered processes of gendering. Instead of turning around cultural types like Chapter 2's carousel, spiral gendering reveals serial television's use of cultural types as a starting point to connect with larger social or political discussions and mobilise social media commentary. Spiral gendering thus describes the ways in which viewers react to gendered and racialised characterisations and how these interactions become part of the narrative.

VISUAL ASSEMBLAGES OF BLACK PROFESSIONAL FEMININITY IN THE COURTROOM AND HAIR SALON

This section traces how Annalise deviates from previous representations of professional femininity in her navigation of professional and private modes of (self-)fashioning. The assemblage of Annalise's appearance spiralled into cultural significance for many of the show's viewers regarding racialised notions of beauty, professionalism, and authenticity. Annalise Keating's first appearance convinces viewers of the iconic, rockstar-esque status she occupies within *Murder*'s storyworld, because her excited new students were gushing about her only seconds before she burst into their lecture hall. Annalise's outfit communicates this characterisation with a fitted burgundy leather jacket, black pencil skirt, high heels, and a short brown-haired wig. Costume and make-up are important devices of gendered characterisation within audiovisual media. Nonetheless, aside from the extravagant costumes of period dramas like *Mad Men* or *Downton Abbey* (ITV, 2010–15) and fantasy hybrids like *Game of Thrones*, visual appearance is often not granted exceeding analytic attention. Especially within serial storytelling, consistent or changing appearances materialise as crucial sites of gendering. Focusing on Annalise's fashioning and the depiction of practices required to assemble it, this chapter asks how her portrayal contrasts with previous representations of white female lawyers in popular culture. The white protagonist of *The Good Wife*, Alicia Florrick, operates as a productive counter example for my analysis. Second, this chapter turns to black hair culture as relevant to Annalise's portrayal as a woman of colour. Here again, *Scandal*'s Olivia and her much-discussed 'unrealistic' hair (Warner 2015a: 43–4) are points of departure for the show and its viewers.

Overall, formerly male-dominated professions are more open to women today than they were a few decades ago. At the same time, the issue of 'work-appropriate' clothing highlights the complex societal demands directed at feminine gender performance in such spaces. In the cultural imaginary, femininity is too often perceived as incompatible with professionalism, while the 'lack' of femininity is felt to be inauthentic. More than twenty years ago, Kathleen Hall Jamieson referred to this catch-22 as a 'double bind': 'women who are considered feminine will be judged incompetent, and women who are competent, unfeminine' (1995: 16). Feminist political science has long understood political offices and institutions to possess a gender or race as a consequence of former personnel associated with the positions. Historically, cis-women and people of colour have been held in place by the law, unable to make legally binding decisions or rely on legal institutions to enforce their needs. As such, the judiciary has long appeared as the domain of white cis-masculinity. Female attorneys and attorneys of colour are always already out of place, interlopers under the burden of proof that they do belong in the legal profession, whereas it is taken for granted that white masculinities do. As in other gendered professional settings, clothing here becomes a mechanism of distinction.

Lawyers are a sartorial exception in US-American courts, which are generally spaces of ungendered uniforms. The black gowns of judges, the jumpsuits of the charged prisoner, or the uniforms of police officers and court personnel contrast with the lawyer's self-chosen clothing (Figure 5.1). However, influenced by the corporate clothing styles of business accountants and bankers, male lawyers found an expensive, yet failproof uniform in the standardised suit.[1] Female lawyers cannot become part of what ethnologist Viola Hofmann deemed the aesthetic of the row – the row of similarly looking suits (2007: 162). Instead, even accidentally wearing the same outfit poses a competitive faux pas as embodied in the 'Who wore it best?' feature of women's magazines. The female-centric phenomenon of 'Dresses the Same' points to the 'embarrassment' of wearing a mass-produced consumer good, as well as requirements to individuality expressed through clothing that are unparalleled by male clothing in professional contexts.[2] An armada of magazines, websites, personal shoppers, and image consultants emerged to advise female lawyers' fashion choices. Notably, their counsel differs widely when it comes to female lawyers being noticed for their clothing. For instance, one lawyer finds 'fashion is a way for lawyers to say what they mean and mean what they say without having to voice a single objection' (Slotnick 2014), while a law professor warns that 'attorneys have to make sure that their clothes don't speak louder than they do' (Coe 2013). Television's female lawyers from *LA Law*'s Grace Van Owen clad in silky blouses (NBC, 1986–94) to *Ally McBeal*'s tight skirts and large suit jackets (Fox, 1997–2002) seemed to have adhered to – and possibly inspired – the first suggestion. Most prominently, *The Good Wife*'s Alicia has become emblematic of female professional fashion (Miller 2017: 155). Even though Alicia begins her professional life in plain suits, as she rises in the ranks of her firm, her designer fashion choices grow increasingly more colourful, tailored, and confident throughout the series. Audiences also began to pay more attention to these fashion choices, coveted interviews with costume designers, and purchased (budget) versions of the clothing seen on-screen through websites dedicated to this purpose as well as an 'official' tie-in clothing line.

Unlike Alicia, Annalise is already an established lawyer at the beginning of *Murder* and showcases her professional and sartorial confidence in form-fitting, sleeveless dresses, bold colours, ostentatious jewellery, and high heels. For example, in her first court scene, Annalise wears a tight black dress and several pieces of large silver jewellery. This appearance violates rules number 4 ('Don't wear a dress without sleeves') and number 6 ('Don't overaccessorise') of *Marie Claire*'s 'Alicia Florrick Guide to Looking Good in an Uptight Office' (Valenti 2015). However, Annalise's portrayal highlights the exclusionary racial politics that accompanied earlier representations of female professionalism. As a dark-skinned woman of colour, Annalise cannot blend into the gendered and racialised space of the courtroom, and therefore her fashion choices frequently do not aspire to do so. Renata Ferdinand points out how her clothing 'propels viewers to see the dark skin. And this is dark skin with confidence – not the usual portrayal of dark skin as deviant, criminal, uncivilized, threatening, or violent' (2015: 336). Viola Davis's darker complexion stands out among other

Figure 5.1 In contrast with the prisoner's uniform of her client Rebecca, Annalise's outfit negotiates the pressures placed on black professional femininity within the racialised and gendered space of the courtroom.

representations of typically lighter-skinned black femininity in popular culture (Williams and Gonlin 2017: 986). Throughout her career, Davis has often been lauded as a much-sought representation to counter such colourism.

Notably, in most episodes, Annalise wears the same dress in her lecture hall as in these later court scenes but loses her elegant trench coats or suit jackets to argue her cases. These sleeveless ensembles, outfits which many have pointed out would not be entirely appropriate in actual courts, showcase Davis's athletic arms. Viewer tweets have recognised and appreciated this portrayal's reference to the cultural fascination with former FLOTUS Michelle Obama's muscular arms displayed in public appearances. Here then, as an example of spiral gendering at work, Twitter conversations link the cultural significance of black professional femininity and the ways its enactment may take different routes than those suggested by white femininities. Even though *The Good Wife* demonstrates how Alicia can transcend the visual double bind by linking professionalism and femininity, such a look of professional white femininity is not accessible to Annalise who has to manage two double binds (race and gender).

Instead of the inadequate uniform, the notion of clothing as armour surfaces as an appealing description within discourses of female fashion.[3] *Murder*'s costume designer Linda Bass echoes the cultural currency of armour in her account of Annalise as totally put together in hair and makeup and what she wears. So that when she walks out of the house, when she's in the courtroom . . . She's an imposing force partly because she is so pulled together in what she looks like. (Hoo 2015)

The connections between the armour of 'looking pulled together' and the management of affect appear at the core of current female-centred television series. As Jorie Lagerwey, Julia Leyda, and Diane Negra observe:

> chic tailoring functions as a conspicuous symbolic correlative for controlled affect. In contrast to the exuberant and excessive fashion (and affects) of *Sex and the City* . . . perfectly tailored but relatively austere professional women's wardrobes in *The Good Wife*, *The Honorable Woman*, *The Fall*, and other series signify [a] newly prominent form of female performance and limited affect. (Lagerwey et al. 2016)

Even though Annalise's professional presence in court partially resembles the controlled white female professionalism described, she repeatedly transgresses through her appearance and demeanour – through her bare arms or her emotional outbursts in the face of injustice. As a black female lawyer, Annalise's visual and behavioural deviations never signal unprofessionalism but frequently bolster her successes. Julia Havas argues that Alicia's distanced, 'Sphinx-like reticence' serves *The Good Wife*'s aesthetic aspirations to distinguish itself from 'network television's "feminine" reliance on verbosity and displayed affect', the latter of which Havas ascribes to shows like *Scandal* or *Murder* (2016: 226). Instead, I contend that Annalise's performance of black female professionalism knowingly evokes the practices of white female lawyers as a reference point. It does so in order to present these practices of white femininity as unobtainable and undesirable, and thus, it creates moments of resonance for viewers of colour. Even though *Murder*'s costume designer understands Annalise's visual 'put togetherness' as affect control on par with the white characters mentioned above, the show places Annalise in a different representational context determined by her gendering as an African American woman. In this cultural tradition, mental preparedness for conflicts surfaces not in chic tailoring, but in the dispersal/the taking off of items which 'put one together' visually.

Most prominently, the first season's episode 'Let's Get to Snooping' (1.4) ends with a two-minute-long scene of Annalise lost in thought during her night-time routine, which turns out to prepare her for confronting her husband Sam about his infidelity rather than for simply going to bed. About this scene black viewers pointed out: 'nothing is Blacker than a Black person "fixing their face" right before a confrontation' (Young 2014); 'you can't fight if you're too worried about your wig getting snatched' (Robinson 2016: 50). This describes a preparedness for physical conflict rather than the verbal fights the female white protagonists engage in. Annalise is 'at home' in both modes of hostile encounter. As she sits at her dresser in a blue satin robe, the camera alternates close-ups of her face and hands with widened shots which capture Annalise's gaze at her mirror image. She begins to disassemble her usual professional appearance by taking off her wedding ring, jewellery, and artificial eyelashes. The camera then zooms in on her hands, which lift the wig off her head. Subsequent scenes showcase Davis's natural hair through frames that encompass her head or Annalise again looking at her reflection in the mirror. Next, she rubs off her make-up, her eyeshadow, lipstick, and foundation. A close-up of her face reveals the different textures of the skin still covered with make-up and parts of her face already cleaned. Lastly, Annalise picks up a staple of black skin care, cocoa butter, and rubs it on her hands and neck. The nondiegetic ambient and hip-hop song 'No One's Here to Sleep' (2013) by Naughty Boy and Bastille provides the score for the scene. Through the slow, driven beat and lyrics, the scene acquires an eerie sense of foreboding: 'you were always faster than me. I'll never catch up with you. Oh I can feel them coming for me.' In addition to foreshadowing future developments, these lines transmit a loss of control, anxiety, and possibly betrayal. The addressee of these lines becomes clear as Sam steps up behind Annalise. An initial shot reveals only his white dress shirt behind Annalise's reflection in the mirror. A startling contrast with the more mellow tones of the scene, the brightness of Sam's shirt signals an emotional change of its introverted atmosphere. Therefore, it is not only Sam's cis-masculinity in this space of feminine beauty practices but the allusion to his whiteness that disrupt Annalise's self-care and reflection and signal the beginning of their confrontation. Even though the show's Twitter account had promoted the episode through the claim that the viewer's 'jaw will hit the floor with Viola Davis' last nine words', it was not the diegetic marital conflict hinted at but the scene's break with limited televisual conventions of representing women of colour in popular culture that stood out to its viewers.[4]

The 'reveal' was hailed to be 'unlike everything we've ever seen on television before' (Young 2014) or 'THE SINGLE GREATEST MOMENT IN BLACK WOMEN TELEVISION HISTORY' (Robinson 2016: 49). The latter quote's all-caps excitement echoes the immediate responses of many black viewers following the episode. Viewers of colour wrote or posted links to commentaries and thinkpieces on the scene to affirm its cultural significance. Twitter users not familiar with the show expressed their desire to watch it because their Twitter feeds erupted into discussions after it had aired. Davis's Annalise was understood as a portrayal of authentic black femininity in which many black female Twitter users saw themselves affirmed (Williams and Gonlin 2017: 995). The connections between the scene and the lived realities of black women in the US were so poignant for viewers that the separation between character and actress collapsed in most tweets. In repeated calls to award her the Emmy she would later actually receive, viewers applauded Viola Davis's decision to appear without make-up and wig on-screen. Somewhat paradoxically, many tweets affirmed Davis's 'natural beauty' alongside the 'courage' or 'bravery' this scene required. Through their praise of her appearance, composers of such tweets characterise themselves as outside of a cultural mainstream that does not appreciate Davis's beauty – hence, it takes courage on her part to present herself this way. Many Twitter users of colour responded to the prevalent inability of white viewers to recognise the cultural significance of the scene immediately after it had aired. Their tweets frequently joked about having to explain it to white friends and co-workers and protested its comparison to a scene in *Dangerous Liaisons* (1988) in which the white Marquise de Merteuil (Glenn Close) takes off her make-up. Unlike white cis-feminine beauty routines, these tweets clarified that the scene's significance stemmed from its acknowledgement of race as impacting notions of beauty.[5]

Williams and Gonlin captured immediate Twitter reactions to 'the reveal' (2017: 985). They found the scene to spark emotional reactions, in that viewers described it as 'real', 'raw', 'powerful', or 'inspiring' (993). Especially the word 'real' takes on varying meanings: 'at times "real" means authentic. Sometimes "real" means exciting or dangerous. Still at other times, "real" means relatable' (995). In such discussions, an ideal of 'authentic blackness' is linked to 'natural hair' discourse (995). Through their connection of 'natural hair' with racial pride, these tweets draw on cultural frames popularised through the Black Power Movement of the 1960s. In a refusal of procedures such as chemical relaxers or hot combs that straighten curls to comply with Eurocentric hair norms, this cultural moment linked black hair practices and political activism. Former Black Panther Angela Davis has notably reflected on her signature afro:

> It is both humiliating and humbling to discover that a single generation after the events that constructed me as a public personality, I am remembered as a hairdo. It is humiliating because it reduced a politics of liberation to a politics of fashion. (Davis 1998: 23)

Such a selective cultural memory establishes the basis on which many viewers of colour interpreted the scene. These viewer practices highlight the rippling cultural impact of spiral gendering: through such responses, viewers thus immediately understood this depiction of daily rituals associated with African American femininity as not only an issue of (self-)fashioning but a remarkable political moment.

From this scene onward, hair care and hairstyles emerged as crucial sites for viewer conversations. The show demonstrates how heterogeneous and expansive both black hair culture and the serial gendering of characters are. Each season would equip Annalise with a different 'signature wig' with varying lengths, colours, or textures. From the third and fourth season onward, she wears sew-in weaves while the flashbacks depict her younger self with braids or an afro. At night, Annalise wraps her hair in a turban. Further, when Annalise goes to prison in the third season, her high-quality weave becomes an indicator of upper-class status, and she chops it off with a razorblade. Such depictions are diametrically opposed to previous, limited representations of black hairstyles in mainstream popular culture. Millennial comedian of colour Phoebe Robinson laments that during her childhood 'there were typically three options for black women's hairstyles depicted in the media: the bank teller style, . . . Pocahontas hair, or . . . short dreadlocks' (2016: 27). Hence, black female viewers enthusiastically remarked on changes to Annalise's hairstyle, as well as the items and practices associated with caring for these styles.

To black viewers, such scenes were indicative of *Murder*'s evolution from #TGIT's dominant 'colourblind' characterisation. Specifically, viewers were long frustrated by the way *Scandal*'s Olivia lacked 'cultural markers such as vernacular, diction, fashion, hairstyles, extended family, or accompanying traditions associated with kinfolk' (Erigha 2015: 11). Black female viewers were especially puzzled by Olivia's 'magical hair' – which preternaturally withstands all tribulations and never requires any time-consuming care (Warner 2015a: 43). Kristen Warner demonstrates how *Scandal* viewers' Twitter responses counter post-racial representations because they reinvest the portrayal of Olivia with cultural specificity. Through the character Annalise, *Murder* acknowledges such practices of #TGIT viewers.[6] For this purpose, Annalise gains more and more cultural markers of black femininity during the course of the show, such as her culinary preferences, her family traditions, the relationship with her mother, as well as her references to systemic racism.

In March 2018, the double-episode crossover 'How to Get Away with Scandal' aspired to let *Murder*'s culturally specific black femininity actively feed back into its sister show. In these episodes, both series' storyworlds overlap when Olivia becomes a supporter of Annalise's efforts against the racial bias of the judicial system. Annalise's presence in *Scandal* temporarily counters Olivia's lack of emotional connection with other black women, her apparent unawareness of racism within US-American society, and even the issue of her 'magical hair'. In a scene set at a hair salon, initial conflicts in their working relationship surface while Annalise and Olivia get their hair done.[7] Annalise openly addresses colourism and class as differentiating their experiences of black femininity. She confronts lighter-skinned Olivia as having judged her

> like a white man in a boardroom looking down on me because my hips are too wide and my hue too dark. . . . You think we soul sisters just 'cause you rented out a hair salon for a few hours on the black side of town? Please. I've dealt with plenty of bougie-ass black women just like you. (*Scandal* 7.12 'Allow Me to Reintroduce Myself')

In this scene, Annalise becomes a mouthpiece for many of *Scandal*'s viewers of colour. That this scene takes place within a black hair salon, a specific sociocultural space, which *Scandal* had never depicted before, makes it even more culturally significant.

Scholars describe black female hair salons – and their equivalent black male-centric barber shops – as 'safe spaces' (Boylorn 2017: 283), 'counterpublic spheres' (Chatman 2017: 301), or 'loci for sharing information about the nuances of black femininity itself' (Bowen 2016: 34). The symbolic resonance that the physical space of the salon acquires for black women becomes obvious in the many tweets that responded to its portrayal within the #TGIT block. While a novum for *Scandal*, *Murder* had already introduced Ro's in its third season, a hair salon Annalise frequents to get her hair done by stylist Ro, played in a celebrity cameo by rap pioneer Mary J. Blige. In the first scene at the salon (3.5 'It's About Frank'), Annalise participates in joyful teasing and call outs. Her ease in this setting stands in stark contrast to her usual guarded behaviour around her students, employees, and clients. Robin M. Boylorn of the Crunk Feminist Collective finds that the dissemblance of appearance within the black female hair salon creates community and emotional vulnerability: '"at the shop" we were sisters, even when we were strangers, because being without a done 'do was like being naked' (2017: 283). In a later scene, it is in the salon that Annalise first admits that she is an alcoholic and allows herself to be comforted by Ro (3.9 'Who's Dead?'). The salon plays a significant role in Annalise's rivalry with DA Renee Atwood (Milauna Jemai Jackson) as well. Annalise finds out that Atwood got her hair done at Ro's on the pretence of being Annalise's friend while actually conducting a criminal investigation against her. For both the character and the show's viewers of colour, Atwood's behaviour was an intrusion on the community that salons provide black women: 'That's low. You don't gather intelligence in a woman's salon . . .'; 'Home girl tried to snoop at her salon !!!!?!?!? Gon head on na!'

For black viewers, representations of the salon were instantly recognisable and created 'black scenes' or 'black moments' within the show. As spiral gendering reaches beyond the screen, viewers of colour connected these depictions with their private lives and media histories that neglected black femininity. Again, jokes about white viewers' inability to understand the cultural relevance of the scene indicated the pleasure not only of feeling part of an in-group but also of being acknowledged by 'our Shonda'.[8] White viewers largely commented less on these salon scenes, similar to their delayed acknowledgement of the 'wig scene'. Nevertheless, some white female viewers perceived the scene along the lines of 'girl time' or 'girls' night' and found the depiction to resonate within their female friendships. Such readings disentangle these scenes from the political and cultural meanings of black beauty politics. Instead of faulting these white viewers' inability to appropriately 'read' such scenes, their comments should be understood as demonstrations of the solid foundation of #TGIT's colourblind portrayals because even obvious cultural markers of race can be reframed by such tweets.

It is telling that the visual assemblage of professionalism made so appealing for black femininity remains invisible for white femininity. Katja Kanzler points out how *The Good Wife* 'draws attention to the work behind the scenes of the courtroom-theater, the work of orchestration that prepares for and seeks to optimize every detail of the decisive courtroom performances' (2015: 141). However, the efforts the female lawyer (or those she hires) invests in the establishment and maintenance of her professional femininity are conspicuously absent from these shows. With the character of Annalise and her many varying hairstyles, *Murder* accentuates the investment and procedures Annalise has to undertake to achieve her professional appearance in court. Thereby, Annalise's labour is illustrated while Alicia's fashion and beauty efforts are obscured and invisible in the show itself, befitting a white middle-class version of feminine modesty and decorum.

NEW LAYERS: SERIALISED BISEXUALITY

In order to protect her student-employees, Annalise ruthlessly frames her devoted lover Nate (Billy Brown) for the murder of her husband Sam. Annalise haphazardly expresses the conviction that Nate will be released soon because she hired 'the best lawyer I know' to defend him (2.1 'It's Time to Move On'). So promisingly introduced, this character is Annalise's former Harvard Law classmate, white woman Eve Rothlo (Famke Janssen). Annalise's trust in Eve's capabilities – which are confirmed when Eve wins Nate's case – is at odds with her critical stance toward the systemic racism and sexism of the law that fuels Annalise's behaviour throughout the show. With this plot, *Murder* sets up a complicated love triangle between Annalise, Nate, and Eve. By doing so, the second season reveals not only Annalise and Eve's past romantic relationship but also Annalise's bisexuality as a crucial layer of her characterisation. 'A black queer character', a reviewer on the lesbian culture website *Autostraddle* jubilates, 'who gets to kiss Jean Grey, leading an entire hour of television? I live. I am seen' (Autostraddle Editors 2017).[9] With her stylish, fitted apparel, long, straight brown hair, and calm, confident demeanour, Eve resembles another television lawyer, by now well established as a significant reference for *Murder*: Alicia Florrick. Through the romantic coupling of these two kinds of femininity, *Murder* again responds to the white female lawyer figure's centrality and refuses to position Annalise as a variation of the femininity established by Alicia. On par with the reveal of her natural hair discussed earlier, Annalise's bisexuality caused a peak in Twitter activity. Viewers were eager to address the new layer of the character and often related their own experiences with sexual orientation. Through the outward spiral, this representation can be understood to purposely mobilise viewer practices of meaning-making and pronouncements of cultural significance.

While some viewers tweeted that Annalise and Eve's intimacy and erotic tension led them to anticipate the reveal, most expressed their surprise at it. Many expressed the desire to pause and rewind to better comprehend what had just happened. Early on, several tweets noted the exceptionality of a bisexual or queer lead of colour on a network show (Figure 5.2). These viewers often shared their own experiences with fluid sexual orientations. Effectively timed, the episode aired the day after Bisexuality Day (23 September) and coincided with Bisexual Awareness Week, as some tweets acknowledged. In this line of response, viewers expressed an understanding of themselves as witnesses to (television) history in the making. Their tweets neatly align with *Murder*'s aspiration to be 'political television', as is evident when actors or producers retweeted such messages on their celebrity Twitter handles. Some immediate responses to the episode, however, took a 'less progressive' form, not desired by the show's producers.

First, some viewers refused to accept Annalise's relationship with Eve to be sincere and instead argued that her past relationship with Eve was the result of meaningless 'college experimentation'. Other tweets assumed Annalise's kiss and the (implicit) sex scene should be understood as a means to manipulate Eve to defend Nate, hence as an expression of Annalise's willingness to

Figure 5.2 Annalise kisses Eve goodbye on her porch. Some black female viewers found Annalise's willingness to wear a turban in front of her love interest to be an indicator of their strong connection.

do anything to protect those she loves rather than indicative of her sexual orientation. In a third opposing stance, viewers accepted Annalise's bisexuality but expressed their annoyance at *Murder*'s portrayal of diversity in terms of sexual orientation: 'Oh hell naw!!! They done turned Annalise gay. WTF! Is everybody in Shondaland gay or bisexual?' Such comments voiced the worry that sexual orientation may take precedence over representations of race in the #TGIT shows. Further, as a last prominent viewer position, many undecided tweets favourably responded to Annalise's bisexuality, yet also expressed their wonder at *Murder*'s looped storytelling: 'So now Annalise is gay??? I can't even keep up lol.' This tweet is illustrative of how many viewers simultaneously celebrated the show's 'revolutionary' potential and outrageous narrative twists and turns. In my reading, the reveal of bisexuality becomes another form of a surprising 'WTF' plot and thereby stabilises the 'shock value' of bisexuality. Bisexuals have long struggled against pathologisation as deceptive and untruthful, and *Murder* affirms the stereotypical deceptiveness of bisexuality by capitalising on its unexpectedness. Many viewers worried that Annalise or Eve would fall victim to a problematic, yet surprisingly persistent plot development, the notorious 'Bury Your Gays' trope, which often results in the death of queer characters shortly after they have acted on or expressed their sexual desires. Such worries were called for because the season's flashforwards depict a lifeless Annalise in a puddle of blood with another dead body being carried away by paramedics.

Generally, *Murder* is invested in the portrayal of Annalise's complex female mentor–mentee relationships (with her student-interns Michaela and Laurel or employee Bonnie), female rivalries (with her sister-in-law Hannah or prosecutors Emily Sinclair and Renee Atwood), as well as relationships with women who shifted between positions of confidante and antagonist (with university president Soraya or fellow lawyer Tegan). Annalise's bisexuality caused viewers to re-examine these relationships for possible sexual attraction. Moreover, the spiral gendering of Annalise's sexual orientation depends on the show's looped serial storytelling, as flashbacks flesh out the past relationship between Annalise and Eve. To understand the larger implications that spiralled out of Annalise's bisexuality for many viewers, the scarcity of bisexual representations on television – especially of women of colour – must be taken into account.

Annalise joins a relatively small group of bisexual characters on television, which has become slightly larger compared with earlier television seasons.[10] Quantitative bisexual representation on television is disproportionately lower than its assumed percentage within the US-American population, especially since almost all bisexual television and film characters are gendered female.[11] Race also factors into cinematic and televisual representations of bisexual femininity, as this femininity is overwhelmingly cast as white. As a bisexual person of colour, Annalise follows in the wake of popular *Grey's Anatomy* character Callie Torres and Kalinda Sharma of *The Good Wife*. *Bitchmedia*'s Jordan McDonald places Annalise in the company of bisexual black women Nova Bordelon of *Queen Sugar* (Oprah Winfrey Network, 2016–) and Nola Darling of *She's Gotta Have It* (Netflix, 2017–19) and argues that these portrayals share a biphobic take on a 'controlling image' of black female sexuality, the promiscuous, immoral jezebel (2018). I disagree with such an assessment because Annalise's sexual encounters are almost exclusively shown to be part of serious long-term investments that sometimes span decades.[12] Repeatedly, Annalise shares incriminating confessions with these romantic partners and relies on their help despite her usual guardedness. The portrayal of Annalise's bisexual relationships instead demonstrates *Murder*'s acknowledgement of such racist tropes. Again, this illustrates the limited utility of a trope-based analysis to approach serialised processes of gendering, specifically when attempting to understand their mobilisation of and interactions with viewers.

In general, the continued lack of bisexual representation both within fictional realms and society has sparked controversy: *The Advocate* deemed 2014 – the year before Annalise's reveal as bisexual – the 'Year of Bisexual Invisibility' (Cruz 2014). Crucial theoretical impulses regarding the cultural phenomenon of 'bisexual invisibility' centre on bisexuality's troubled relationship with both heterosexuality *and* homosexuality. Legal scholar Kenji Yoshino refers to an 'epistemic contract of bisexual erasure' to describe the agreement of heterosexual and homosexual identity positions to disavow bisexuality in a shared investment in stabilising sexuality (2000: 388). Feminist media scholar Maria San Filippo's groundbreaking study of bisexuality in popular culture, *The B Word* (2013), further explores how 'compulsory monosexuality', defined as 'the ideological and institutionalized privileging of *either* heterosexuality *or* homosexuality as the two options for mature sexuality', structures socio-political perceptions of sexual orientation (2013: 12). As a result, bisexuality's existence is called into question through stereotypical representations of bisexuality as a phase concluded by clear positioning as either heterosexual (in the case of bisexual women) or homosexual (in the case of bisexual men). To counter such stereotypes, activists and educators define bisexual orientations as not related to whom a person sleeps with at the moment. As Robyn Ochs writes, 'I have in myself the potential to be attracted – romantically and/or sexually – to people of more than one sex and/or gender, not necessarily at the same time, not necessarily in the same way, and not necessarily to the same degree' (2017). Audiovisual media have long depicted sexual orientation through the shortcut of a character's sexual partners. Bisexuality causes a representational dilemma; it raises the question of how to represent bisexual characters per Ochs's definition, that is, without depicting bisexual characters as sexually insatiable, commitment-phobic, or dismissive of their past lovers through their new relationships.

Serial television storytelling is, in theory, ideally suited to counter this representational challenge of bisexuality. After all, its ongoing and expanding dynamics operate very differently from the traditional narrative chronologies of cinema that according to Maria Pramaggiore privilege closure and thus 'reinforce notions of coupling' (1996: 277–8) by affirming one relationship as superior and worth ending the narrative on. Serial storytelling allows for sexual orientation 'to unfold over time, necessary for the accumulation of experiences that renders bisexuality not practically *viable* – for any individual is potentially bisexual, no matter her or his behaviors to date – but rather representationally *legible*' (San Filippo 2013: 204). Nevertheless, this potential for serial storytelling to render bisexuality visible as such a serialised sexual orientation is rarely realised.[13] It is telling in this regard that the reveal of Annalise's bisexuality occurs through the contrast of her relationships with men and a woman in the form of a staple of bisexual cinematic representation: the love triangle.

The love triangle has become popular culture's go-to device to organise and suggest bisexuality by simultaneously depicting same-sex and opposite-sex attractions. However, the majority of cinematic representations imagine bisexual triangularity as temporary because these films centre on bisexuality as a narrative enigma to be resolved by the revelation of a character's 'authentic' monosexual orientation (San Filippo 2013: 37; Pramaggiore 1996: 273). Affirming stereotypes about bisexuality – as a phase, as rooted in sexual insatiability or romantic indecisiveness – the bisexual love triangle focuses on a woman and often involves her preference of an opposite-sex relationship even though the possibility for same-sex romance is maintained for 'narrative suspense' (San Filippo 2013: 39). *Murder* abounds with love triangles. Romantic regroupings occur frequently, and every main character at one point or another struggles to cope with the overlap of their current and past romantic involvements.[14] This is not to say that such love triangles mean romantic, polyamorous investments between all three partners, but rather that one character is torn between feelings for two other partners who compete for her (rarely his) attention.[15] In the first season, Annalise negotiates her feelings for her paramour Nate and her husband Sam. After Sam's death, the second season portrays her at the core of a romantic triangle with Eve and Nate, while the flashbacks reveal that Annalise had left Eve for Sam. This establishes another 'historical' bisexual triangle.

These flashbacks transport viewers back a decade, not to Annalise and Eve's college romance but to a moment in which Annalise reaches out to Eve after an extended period of estrangement. This past relationship takes on a platonic form, in which neither woman expresses physical desire. In this exchange, Eve pressures Annalise to admit that shame for their same-sex relationship was the reason that Annalise left her for Sam:

> Eve: Just say it, Annalise. You didn't have the nerve to tell me back then, but I – I need you to say it now.
> Annalise: Say what?
> Eve: That you got scared. That's why you left me.
> Annalise: No, I left you because I'm not gay.
> Eve: Bull.
> Annalise: Alright. – I needed something in my life, someone who loved me. You did that, and I loved you back. But not in a way that either of us deserved.
> Eve: I don't even know what that means.
> Annalise: It means you live your life, I live mine, straight or gay, whatever you want to call it.
> Eve: I am gay. That's – that's what I call it. (2.12 'It's a Trap')

While Annalise ultimately does acknowledge that she loved Eve, she backpedals: 'not in a way that either of us deserved'. This comment seems to confirm Eve's point that Annalise cannot fully inhabit her same-sex attractions and so turned to an opposite-sex relationship. Instead, Annalise specifies that she cannot label her sexual orientation ('whatever you want to call it'). Eve counters Annalise's unspecific phrase by explicitly claiming the label of gay for herself and implicitly admonishes Annalise for not being able to do so. Annalise's weariness at this exchange highlights it as a repeated incident. In a later scene in the story-present, Annalise and Eve respond to the advances of two men in a bar, Eve by firmly positioning herself as gay/lesbian, while Annalise comments, 'It's complicated' (3.4 'Don't Tell Annalise'). In both scenes, Annalise's unwillingness or inability to announce her bisexuality – despite her obvious practice of it – follows a long lineage of bisexual screen characters. Maria San Filippo finds that 'the explicit articulation of the B word itself matters less than its enunciation in practice' (2013: 240). Even though many viewers took Annalise's expression that she is 'not gay' as an affront to Eve, others were more understanding. Especially since a few episodes earlier, Annalise admits to Eve in the story-present what she could not in the flashback dialogue: 'It was good with you. And real. Too real. So I got scared. And I left. But you're the most beautiful thing that ever happened to me' (2.2 'She's Dying'). Even though Annalise fails to affirm her queer identity verbally, she is never hesitant to act on her desire and initiates all sexual encounters with Eve.

Twitter reactions to the flashback sarcastically commented on the divergence between her self-understanding and her actions: 'That one time you're not gay, but your lover is a woman'; 'Well if you not gay, why was u with her Annalise? LOL.' Instructed to do so by the show's looped seriality, viewers connected the flashback with the rekindling of their relationship in the present and pointed out how, ten years later, Annalise was still having sex with a woman. Other viewers expressed their frustration with Annalise – '"I'm not gay" part of me wanna say to Annalise "girl bye"' – or their empathy for Eve – 'I can't believe Annalise just said "I'm not gay." Eve must be beyond hurt.' Some viewers did take Annalise's statement to express that her relationship with Eve was 'only' based on her loneliness and not any 'authentic' physical attraction. Meanwhile, other viewers found pleasure in the interpretation that Annalise had 'played that white girl', assuming for the character a position of power through a sexual desirability typically not awarded (especially dark-skinned) women of colour.

Further, many viewers were quick to refer to Annalise as bisexual; at times, they took care to correct other viewers who in their tweets referred to her as gay or lesbian. Such viewers filled the textual void and were willing to 'speak the word' for the character:

> 'You're not gay but you were just "experimenting" girl bye you know your ass is bisexual.'
> 'Annalise, you're bi, and it's beautiful.'
> 'Annalise: I'm not gay. Me to my screen: BI. SAY IT WITH ME NOW. BI.'

Specifically the last tweet's challenge to 'say it with me now' highlights the position of viewers willing to fill in the blanks of Annalise's suggestive bisexuality. These viewers evoke Annalise's initiation of sexual encounters with Eve in the story-present to counter her past refusal of a queer identity, and, by doing so, they extend her characterisation to connect with cultural conversations on bisexuality. As a driving dynamic of spiral gendering, recognisability is especially relevant to such discourses. It becomes explicit in bisexual and lesbian viewers' confessions to see their earlier selves represented in this portrayal of Annalise: '"I'M NOT GAY" yo Annalise, that was me 3 years ago too'; 'Chile been there done that . . . run girl run.' For many viewers, Annalise's confusion at inhabiting a bisexual identity – despite her obvious practice of one – speaks to the larger cultural tensions surrounding bisexuality in a monosexual culture. Instead of faulting *Murder*, these viewers extended Annalise's sexual orientation through spiral gendering and connected it to broader cultural concerns as well as to their own personal experiences.

It is telling that neither Eve nor Nate is able to occupy a public, legitimate position as Annalise's spouse, while white man Sam becomes her husband and the person whose last name she takes. Her marriage with Sam thus enjoys a visibility that Annalise's other relationships lack – especially her same-sex relationship. Further, her same-sex relationship differs from her opposite-sex relationships, in that Eve herself is not part of her own love triangle but is exclusively invested in Annalise.[16] Unlike responses to Annalise's simultaneous relationships with Nate and Sam, the audience did not as uniformly receive her romantic entanglements with Eve and Nate (Figure 5.3).[17]

Generally, there is a lightness to Annalise and Eve's interactions that is unusual compared with the show's (melo)drama. Both women reminisce about their past, flirt, and laugh with each other in several scenes. Eve exudes calmness and repeatedly affirms Annalise: she accepts Annalise's judgement of Sam's murderer (Wes) as someone who is worth protecting and firmly insists that Annalise is a 'good person'. Many viewers found this a reason to 'ship' 'Annaleve' or 'Evalise': 'every time Eve is around, Annalise actually smiles. I am all for it.' These viewers' desires for their romance as 'endgame' were disappointed when in the third season, Eve moves across the country to be with another woman. Most viewers expressed understanding: 'Annalise can't really expect that Eve will be there ready and waiting for her whenever Annalise wants her. Acting like a man.' Because Annalise wishes her ex-girlfriend well, tweets lauded her sacrifice as an expression of true love, even though many found it troubling that Eve's well-being was placed before Annalise's: 'WTF kinda line is this about letting yourself being loved – for Eve – an insert white woman support role? What about ANNALISE!' Eve's timing

Figure 5.3 Annalise arranges for Eve to defend Nate. Viewers were as torn as the character herself over whom they wanted Annalise to pursue a relationship with.

seemed particularly off, as Nate had previously also left Annalise: 'I WAITED FOR NATE TO LEAVE AND WHEN HE DOES EVE IS WITH SOME-ONE???' Annalise's love triangle does not end with her picking one partner over the other. It collapses in order to set the stage for Annalise's descent into alcoholism as sparked by her loneliness.

However, Nate continues to be a significant presence in the show, and the potentiality of their opposite-sex romance carries with it a suggestive air of ultimate romantic coupling. *Murder* here seems to take a cue from soap opera's signature 'long-arc romance', of which Abigail De Kosnik says, 'the most popular romantic entanglements begin and end countless times over many years; marital infidelity, furtive encounters at public events, and a wish to keep the relationship concealed from the eyes of the world are typical features' (2011: 236). Like many of the show's viewers, Annalise's family and her mother approve of charismatic Nate as opposed to their disapproval of white upper-class professor Sam. But, unlike the obvious romance of *Scandal* – the much acclaimed #Olitz of Olivia and Fitz – Annalise's bisexuality allows for different romantic options aside from Nate. My reading of Annalise's bisexuality illustrates how a dismissal of her relationship with Eve as a 'short-lived indulgence . . . that reveals the character's manipulation and carelessness' (McDonald 2018) cannot capture the serialised dynamic of Annalise's romantic entanglements. Throughout the show, she struggles not to harm any of her partners yet neither Annalise nor *Murder* has the vocabulary to create polyamorous partnerships. Overall, the portrayal of the open communication, understanding, and agreements at the core of such relationships are of little interest for a show so invested in dramatic confrontations, narrative surprises, and 'WTF' reveals.

Ultimately, through the portrayals of Annalise, her beauty practices, or sexual orientation, *Murder* highlights its own deviation from established US television standards, not unlike *Girls* does when consciously circling around cultural types from other postfeminist storytelling (Chapter 2). Just as viewers of colour responded to depictions of black beauty practices by connecting these both with their personal lives as well as with a larger cultural history, Annalise's bisexuality mobilises similar viewer responses through spiral gendering. Altogether, the resultant Twitter conversations exhibit remarkable flexibility: side by side, viewers intimately connect Annalise's experiences with their personal lives, while at the same time, they situate the character, the show, and by extension their own lives within a broader cultural or political history. Accordingly, through spiral gendering, the intersectional gendering of characters becomes more and more nuanced and emotionally resonant for viewers. Just as the show expands its offerings for intimate recognisability, increasingly, *Murder* also aspires toward political branding.

NOTES

1. Regardless of gender, dressing 'expensively' is often taken as a measure of a lawyer's success. This concept of dressing to display economic power calls to mind the practice of 'conspicuous consumption', which sociologist Thorstein Veblen outlined in *The Theory of the Leisure Class* (1899).
2. How female visual uniformity becomes a death sentence is explored in *The Good Wife*: when Alicia aspires to be elected to political office, a campaign crisis occurs after her opponent releases a video of his mother wearing the same dress (6.9 'Sticky Content').
3. In *House of Cards* (Netflix, 2013–18), Zoe, who has an affair with protagonist Frank, heads straight to his wife Claire's closet at first opportunity. 'It's like steel', she marvels in wonder and alludes not to the material but the purpose of one of Claire's dresses (1.11 'Chapter 11'). The understanding of an appropriate, beautiful, and fitting item of clothing as protection within hostile surroundings informs this scene and the discourse of female professional fashion.
4. Annalise begins her confrontation by calmly asking one of the show's most outlandish lines of script, 'Why is your penis on a dead girl's phone?', which was immediately turned into one of *Murder*'s most prominent memes.
5. There are two different approaches to beauty in feminist scholarship: one camp approaches beauty as a problematic and oppressive notion rooted in sexist structures, whereas another understanding considers beauty and beauty practices as potentially expressing forms of female agency. Black feminist thought has found its own uneasy positioning in this regard to address the necessity to redefine and widen Eurocentric beauty ideals.
6. This is not to say that *Murder* always gets black hair practices 'right'. For example, viewers tweeted about a scene in which Annalise's mother combs her hair without the required fine-toothed comb or moisturiser (Williams and Gonlin 2017: 998–9).
7. Despite this scene, their collaboration is characterised by mutual admiration. Celebrating the crossover, many viewers used the popular hashtag #BlackGirlMagic.
8. Such moments affirmed *Murder* as the 'blacker' show in comparison with *Scandal* and exhibit the relatively low relevance that white male showrunner Nowalk held as the show's author figure.
9. Janssen played Jean Grey/Phoenix in the superhero film *X-Men* (2000), a paratext that affirmed Eve's desirability as a romantic partner for Annalise when tweets called her Jean or Phoenix.
10. In the television season that showed Annalise's 'coming out', 2015/16, GLAAD found 14 per cent of all LGBTQ characters on broadcast television to be bisexual (2015: 26). By the 2017/18 season, this increased to 28 per cent for all of television, yet broadcast networks lag behind this figure compared with online and cable providers (GLAAD 2017: 24–5). Such numbers should be considered with caution, because, as Rebecca Beirne points out, queer representations in popular culture are 'marked by advances and retreats, breakthroughs and hiccups, sometimes even within the same program' (2012: 3).
11. The unique representation of bisexual and lesbian femininities allows for a 'queer commodification' by appealing to queer viewers as well as awarding heterosexual male viewers voyeuristic pleasures (San Filippo 2013: 22; Beirne 2012: 3).
12. This places Annalise in stark opposition to *The Good Wife*'s Kalinda, of whom Taylor Cole Miller has argued that in contrast to white heterosexual female characters' professional agency, Kalinda's only source of power is her bisexual eroticism, which she utilises to gain information and which positions her as 'exotic other' (2017: 160).

13. Critics have lamented a prominent case of serial storytelling undermining bisexual representation: Alice Pieszecki (Leisha Hailey) on *The L Word* (Showtime, 2004–9).
14. For example, Laurel dated Frank for the first two seasons, then began a romantic relationship with Wes in the third season, but rebounds with Frank. Meanwhile Frank began to sleep with Asher's ex-girlfriend Bonnie.
15. However, the only other implied bisexual love triangle involves heterosexual Michaela, her bisexual fiancé Aiden, and homosexual Connor. None of the characters discusses the possibility of Aiden's bisexuality, but Michaela struggles to understand how Aiden's past involved homosexual encounters (with Connor).
16. Meanwhile Nate is torn between Annalise and his wife, while Sam seeks to keep his affair with student Lila a secret.
17. Most viewers preferred Nate over Sam for Annalise. While this might be attributed to the unacknowledged difficulties of interracial romance – #TGIT shows are infamous for their post-racial depictions of interracial relationships – it was likely due to Sam's fate as dead man walking as well as viewers being enamoured with Nate themselves.

CHAPTER 6

Evoking Discourses of Progressivism, Social Activism, and Identity Politics: Such an Important Episode!

The CEO of the media monitoring organisation GLAAD (formerly Gay & Lesbian Alliance Against Defamation), Sarah Kate Ellis, opened an annual report on media representation as follows: 'the critical and commercial success of series like *Empire*, *Transparent*, and *Orange Is the New Black* can serve as an example to network executives that audiences are looking for stories they haven't seen before' (GLAAD 2015: 3). It is this claim to represent something as yet un-televised, meaning characters that had been under- or misrepresented along the lines of race, gender, and sexuality, that enables *Murder* to project itself as progressive *and* rooted within the contemporary popular mainstream. The reports by 'media watchdog' GLAAD serve as orientation points for viewers, journalists, the television industry, and scholarship. *Murder* is the steady darling of the NGO because of its depiction of ethnicity, sexual orientation, and HIV-positive status. *Murder* has been widely praised for its portrayal of an HIV-positive queer person of colour, Asian American Oliver Hampton (Conrad Ricamora). GLAAD finds it remarkable that his HIV status is 'presented as just another facet of his life, as opposed to an obstacle to overcome. Oliver is also the only regular character on all the platforms tracked to be HIV-positive' (2017: 23). Always described as 'groundbreaking', the story of Oliver and his serodiscordant romantic relationship with student Connor acts as a central building block of the show's participation within a cultural discourse of progressivism and the 'previously untelevised'.[1] Against this background, this chapter argues that *Murder* brands itself as 'political television' by participating in discourses of progressivism, social activism, and identity politics. This kind of progressive narrowcasting is a form of marketing that resembles the commercial phenomenon known as 'cause-sumption'. In an age of narrowcasting and online TV criticism, *Murder* and other 'progressive' shows aspire to appear as cultural markers of a zeitgeist and to appeal to audiences that desire 'alternative' portrayals.

Murder paratextually links its claim to televise previously unaired identities with the show's casting politics and crew diversity. For her performance of Annalise, Viola Davis became the first woman of colour ever to win an Emmy for a lead role in a drama series, in September 2015.[2] The exceptionality of this Emmy illustrates the problematic lack of diversity that haunts so many television dramas – and especially those cable shows that are considered 'Quality TV' and are thus canonised and legitimised by academia and TV criticism. Instead of merely accepting the award as praise for her achievements, in her acceptance speech, Davis drew attention to the lack of substantial roles for women of colour on television. Appealing to producers to grant others the opening she had with this role, she said, 'The only thing that separates women of color from anyone else is opportunity. You cannot win an Emmy for roles that are simply not there.' Davis's comment became a crucial paratextual accompaniment for the reception and self-branding of *Murder*. The positive media buzz of Davis's Emmy performance elevated the show to a rare cultural artefact.

As I argued in the previous chapter, *Murder* presents Annalise Keating with racial markers, such as black beauty culture. This chapter interrogates *Murder*'s aspirations as a racially specific variation of post-racial television that appeals to diverse audiences. Even if not all white viewers can understand the show's 'winks' to audiences of colour, they could at least potentially turn to the connected online discussions of the Twitterverse to learn more. These social media conversations affirm the show's cultural, socio-political importance in the mould of airing something previously not depicted accurately. Watching and reacting to *Murder* on social media for its viewers takes the form of a – highly decontextualised – television history in the making in which one may participate in an almost epiphanic way. This kind of branding lends itself to the digital loops of social media discussed in the previous chapters: the retweeted message by actors, the GIF-able gesture, and/or meme-suitable dialogue in the show. Through *Murder* then, the auteur brand of Shonda Rhimes, Shondaland, and the #TGIT shows have been able to poignantly position themselves within a changed cultural discourse in which progressive politics do not alienate but attract television audiences.

Even though it is necessary to remain sceptical toward some television shows' self-professed progressivism and capacity to respond to a cultural void – not least because of the commercial rewards associated with such claims – viewers can indeed find socio-political value in these shows to inspire them, extend their knowledge about unfamiliar lifestyles, and motivate manifold forms of activism. Rather than implying, however, that the airing of previously invisible aspects of identity politics is per se political, *Murder* relies on viewers to make such connections through their tweets, memes, and GIFs. As I argue in the conclusion to this chapter, 'political television' can never be political in itself, despite all claims to the contrary, but viewers' readings and discussions of these scenes may spark political activism. Serial popular culture, in particular, augments the interaction of 'political' representations on-screen and audiences' political activity.

'LET'S TEACH THESE BASTARDS A LESSON': THE CASE OF THE WEEK

In episode 4.12 ('Ask Him About Stella'), Annalise travels to Harrisburg to meet with the Supreme Court of Pennsylvania and discuss a class action lawsuit she is preparing. While she waits in a conference room, the camera captures the way she looks up at the prominently placed portraits of white male former chief justices of the US, including Salmon Portland Chase, Melville Weston Fuller, and Roger Brooke Taney.[3] Staring down at the anxious Annalise, such white male embodiments of the legal establishment highlight the lack of diversity at fault for the gendered and racialised institutions of the law that Annalise increasingly begins to target in her work.

Throughout the series, *Murder* propels narrative action through the major characters' motivation to keep either themselves or those they care about from being persecuted by the law. The series here strays far from the cultural stereotype of the cunning lawyer able to twist the law to literally get away with anything. Instead, it presents the ability to 'get away with murder' as possible only if one can dodge legal charges and a trial. That these lawyers and law students are so paradoxically determined to avoid courtrooms at all cost sheds light on *Murder*'s understanding of the law, the judicial system, and court proceedings in the US. Through its mostly episodic court cases, the show embarks on plotlines that explore how the alleged neutrality of the law amounts to a gendered, racialised, and classed version of justice. Before turning to those cases, I comment on the political implications of the show's eponymous murders, which the main characters either commit or help cover up. With their extralegal settlement of justice outside of the courtroom, the killings are suggestive of the distinct US-American discourse on the right to bear arms and the right to self-defence in the face of corrupt institutions. However, the show does not develop some sort of left-leaning or progressive variation of the conservative, right-wing fantasy surrounding militant citizenship. Alternatively, *Murder* meticulously portrays the traumatising aftershocks of the violent acts characters committed or witnessed. In the wake of violence and death, shell-shocked characters employ a variety of coping mechanisms but struggle to continue with their lives. Through the killings, the show unfolds an ethical dilemma for the characters and viewers, and yet, because shock, guilt, and trauma clearly haunt the murderous characters, most viewers find them to be redeemable. Further, characters do not kill out of self-serving reasons or out of planned calculation, but because they seek to protect others and feel emotionally driven to the bloodshed. Overall, these narrative scenarios do not envision extralegal, vigilante violence as admirable or heroic, but imply that citizens are civilians who should never be forced to pursue such 'justice' or protection. *Murder* envisions all acts of violence as profoundly destructive, to both victims and perpetrators. This explains why even privileged white characters Asher, Frank, and Bonnie need Annalise's protection even though they do not face the racialised bias of the law: broken legal institutions have failed them as well, made their extralegal violence necessary, and, as a consequence, they are traumatised by the desperate violence they commit.

Reviewer Kayla Kumari Upadhyaya wondered: 'as silly as *How to Get Away with Murder* can often get, is any other show on network TV as critical of American institutions?' (2016). It is the episodic 'case of the week' in particular that advances this portrayal of the judicial system. The teenage son of an abusive police officer who kills his father to protect his mother from domestic violence (1.5 'We're Not Friends'), a refugee who risks deportation to keep his daughter from being prosecuted for a harmless marijuana possession (3.1 'We're Good People Now'), a heavily tattooed former gang member imprisoned for the suicide of his girlfriend and unable to get a fair trial due to his appearance (4.3 'It's For the Greater Good'): these are examples of the clients that Annalise and her firm defend in the show's first four seasons.[4] All of the cases position Annalise and her firm on the morally 'right' side. This does not mean that her clients are always innocent, but that their actions are the result of desperate situations caused by a broken system. Such a pattern is visible, for example, in the case of the teenager who shot his father. As we find out later, the son and his mother were unable to report domestic violence to the police because officers were unwilling to act against their colleague.

In another episode, 'Two Birds, One Millstone' (2.6), Annalise gets an emergency phone call from her colleague, the trans-female professor Jill Hartford (Alexandra Billings). Both women are shown to be very close, and Jill is upfront about having just killed her husband in an altercation. Annalise rushes to the crime scene and throughout the episode varies between being Jill's lawyer and a close confidante attempting to comfort her friend (Figure 6.1). Jill's marriage is revealed to have been strained by her cis-male husband's domestic abuse. In one of their consultations, Jill brings up her fears of following a similar fate as the real-world case CeCe McDonald, a trans woman who made headlines in June 2012 for being sent to a men's prison after her self-defence resulted in the death of her transphobic assailant. And indeed, Jill's treatment by the police appears to follow along similar lines when one of the detectives accuses her of

Figure 6.1 Annalise comforts her friend and client Jill before the transphobic behaviour of the authorities requires her to adapt her defence strategy.

having 'lied' to her husband 'about what you are'. The detective speculates that the altercation must have been brought about by Jill's husband having 'finally found out what you hid from him'. Just as Annalise has no doubts that Jill's act of murder was justified, viewers firmly aligned with sympathetic Jill and hence rejoiced when Annalise tells her client and friend: 'let's teach these bastards a lesson'. The police and District Attorney's office are incapable of looking beyond Jill's gender identity as a trans woman to understand what *Murder* presents as the true crime of the episode, the ongoing domestic abuse Jill suffered at the hands of her husband. Annalise utilises the prosecutor's bias to frame the murder case as a hate crime investigation in which the authorities become complicit due to their transphobic bias. Lauded for casting prominent transgender actress Billings as Jill, with this episode *Murder* connected to an ongoing conversation surrounding trans people's visibility.[5] In May 2014, a *TIME* cover with trans-female, iconic celebrity actress Laverne Cox proclaimed the 'transgender tipping point' and declared trans identity-related issues to be 'America's next civil rights frontier'.

The Good Wife approaches judicial institutions very differently from *Murder*. Through its focalising character Alicia, Katja Kanzler argues,

> the audience shares an experience of the law as a system whose rules of operation are hard to understand and sometimes even harder to endorse ... because this system presents itself as self-contained and self-sustaining, operating in considerable detachment from the

presumably absolute values it is supposed to represent and serve – truth and justice. (Kanzler 2012: 73)

With her increased sense of the system of the law and her growing skills in navigating it, Alicia begins to question her formerly firm grasp of moral right and wrong as she navigates the law as a 'universe of uncertainty' (73). *Murder*, in contrast, insists on a moral right and wrong, as well as firmly established understandings of justice and truth. However, the show represents the law as antithetical to such justice and truth in its gendered, racialised, classed, or transphobic biases. *Murder* asks under which circumstances criminal actions are justified within a broken system that fails those dependent on it. In lieu of judging along with the character of the judge who presides over each trial, viewers are aligned with Annalise, her employees, and students (for example, through the jury-detective shot discussed in Chapter 4) and have likely already formed their opinions before any scenes in court. Accordingly, the show devotes relatively little time to actual courtroom scenes and rarely characterises judges or prosecutors, who do not receive much screen time, barely utter lines, and do not reappear in later episodes.[6] Courtroom scenes become occasions for Annalise to convince the system of its own faults, rather than settings in which lawyers play the law like 'legal roulette' (Kanzler 2012: 76).

Only in rare instances does Annalise take on clients whose accusation is not shown to be a consequence of systematic prejudice. These clients are all upper-class, narcissistic white men who exhibit misogyny and an assumed entitlement over the women in their lives. When they are found innocent, like one client who murdered his first but not his second wife (1.2 'It's All Her Fault'), or a stalker who terrorises his ex-wife and is framed by her for murder (2.7 'I Want You to Die'), Annalise's defence appears justified, especially as she does not tolerate any inappropriate behaviour on their part. The only exception, a client whom tabloids nickname 'the callgirl creeper', is clearly positioned as guilty of murdering a woman unwilling to have sex with him (3.3 'Always Bet Black'). Like her female students, Annalise struggles to keep her antipathy for the client in check, and after she wins his case, cannot restrain herself from slapping him in the courthouse, an action that is satisfying to the other characters (and viewers) but later causes her attorney licence to be temporarily suspended. Further, through flashbacks, Annalise's unique relationships with Bonnie and Wes are framed as retribution for the guilt she feels at successfully defending guilty clients that have wronged Wes's mother and Bonnie.

Clients are typically not as straightforwardly open with Annalise as her friend Jill is. On the contrary, her cases are often not what they appear to be initially, and clients are unreliable, keep secrets, or hide their motivations. For example, to the shock of her family, the docile 'soccer mom' Paula turns out to be an internationally sought terrorist, who utilises her trial to help her partner in crime escape (1.3 'Smile, or Go to Jail'). The small and larger secrets that Annalise's clients keep from her often require her to wildly improvise her court strategies in compelling plot twists. 'The question I'm asked most often as a defense attorney is whether I can tell if my clients are innocent or guilty', Annalise lectures her students. 'I don't care. And it's not because I'm heartless, although that's up for debate – but because my clients, like all of us here in this room, lie' (1.2 'It's All Her Fault'). In her conception of the profession, Annalise does not assume that a lawyer owes her client a contractually agreed upon service. Instead, she casts lawyers as powerful, somewhat parental protectors who have their clients' best interests in mind in hostile surroundings. These interests may not be initially obvious to her clients or may be sabotaged in a client's attempt to protect somebody else, which makes Annalise's notion of the lawyer as a protector not always legible for her clients (or the viewers).

Altogether, it is not pre-planned strategising that predominantly drives the show's court scenes, but surprise, spontaneity, and emotionality. Legal dramas conventionally rely on the theatricality of the courtroom to educate and mobilise their viewers on a variety of social, political, or ethical concerns (Kanzler 2012: 64–6). In *The Good Wife*, in particular, preparation for courtroom performances – the 'work of orchestration . . . [that is] a highly specialized, hyperprofessional business' – drives narrative impetus and becomes the central pleasure of its viewers (Kanzler 2015: 141). *Murder* rarely zooms in on the preparation of Annalise and her employees: in place of strategically mapping out potential courtroom scenarios, Annalise frequently improvises and changes her strategy mid-trial. Almost all trials involve employees or interns rushing to deliver last-minute information or evidence and Annalise resourcefully utilising new findings. Unlike the 'intellectuality and powerful reticence', which Julia Havas attributes to *The Good Wife*'s protagonist and its many central characters (2016: 229), Annalise's court strategies centre on emotional criticism of the law. Furthermore, her courtroom performance is indebted to a different understanding of the law, professionalism, and a lawyer's responsibility; Annalise often appeals to emotions, exhibits recalcitrant behaviour, and is willing to pursue alternative, non-legal strategies to protect her clients from prosecution. Over the course of the series, Annalise has perjured herself on the stand, waived attorney–client privilege, tampered with evidence, established false witnesses, blackmailed, or knowingly framed innocent people. Again, rather than search for legal strategies, Annalise's disillusionment with the law as biased drives her to alternative means to fulfil her ideal of justice.

Various websites have turned to actual criminal defence attorneys to 'fact-check' the show. As one would expect, such accounts find (almost) every aspect of its depiction of law school, court proceedings, or the day-to-day business of lawyers to be unrealistic. However, some lawyers do point out that 'a show all about law school would be terrible. It's a lot of work, heavy old books, weekends in the library, and it costs an arm and a leg to boot. Law students wouldn't even watch a show about law school' (Hope 2014). Such reception practices again point to the different conceptions of the law in comparison with *The Good Wife*, which was often lauded for its accurate portrayal of trials and the work of a law firm. #TGIT viewers rarely express annoyance with inaccurate depictions of 'the law'; instead, there is consensus on how the show 'gets' the racism and sexism of institutions. Hence, *Murder* does not represent the experiences of lawyers or judges as players of the legal system, but the perspective of looking in from the outside. In lieu of actual judicial proceedings, the show captures the helplessness of those dependent on the system and unable or unwilling to understand its injustices. Herman Gray argues that television fictions run into difficulty when trying to portray 'the systemic way in which processes of racialisation, gender subordination, and class inequalities are central to the structure of legal practice and the law' (2005: 22). Even though *Murder* calls for a reform of the biased judicial system, it also exhibits these difficulties because the show problematically positions a singular character, Annalise, as capable of bringing about systemic change.

Annalise's improvisation, disregard for court procedures, and rebelliousness in the courtroom signify her disappointment with 'the law' as a gendered and racialised apparatus. Through her urgent, emotional monologues, often either a trial's closing speech or her reaction to a hostile, privileged witness, she is positioned as an exceptional renegade lawyer figure. Rather than reflecting the stereotype of witty lawyers as unpredictable truth-twisters, the long speeches position Annalise as a lawyer-truthteller able to persuasively describe the injustices she perceives and, in the process, move judges to consider structural racism, sexism, and classism in their rulings. Specifically, *Murder*'s 'case of the week' plots insist that institutionalised prejudices continue to exist and are not the result of personal responsibility, as the notion of post-racial accountability would have us believe. In other words, instead of blaming people of colour for 'choosing' to see race everywhere, as common racist diction and right-wing conservative rhetoric argue, the show foregrounds an awareness of the systemic roots of injustices. However, as truthteller, one individual person is shown to possess the superhero-like ability to change systemic discrimination through her appeal to common sense. In the same breath, judges reprimand Annalise for disregarding court etiquette and pronounce their judgments as influenced by her words. Annalise's speeches mobilise rulings through which these judges hold the system accountable, offer redemption or reconciliation, and generally express the responsibility to right the wrongs to which an individual has been subjected.

One such example occurs in the first season (1.6 'Freakin' Whack-a-Mole') when Annalise stops everything she is doing to rush into the retrial of a case, which we learn has been troubling her since her college days. Death-row candidate David has been imprisoned for twenty-one years and is now allowed a retrial before the Supreme Court of Pennsylvania. A victim of a corrupt judge, African American David was charged with the murder of his girlfriend, an activist, who at the time of her death mobilised against a real-estate tycoon's displacement of working-class black residents. In a grand sweep, the episode dizzyingly targets the death sentence, the criminalisation of men of colour, the racist casting of white women (the girlfriend) as victims of African American men (David), the corruption of the judicial system, as well as the racial and classed effects of 'gentrification'. Before the Supreme Court Annalise attacks the real-estate tycoon, now a prominent senator, and holds a characteristic monologue in which she points out the racism of David's prosecution as well as the real-estate policies of said senator. Despite being reprimanded incessantly, Annalise continues her rapid-fire argument: 'the majority of [people displaced by his actions] are poor, powerless, and didn't bear the color of skin desirable to your business interests'. Following such monologues, viewers and her interns alike routinely express awe for Annalise. Their admiration is not shared by the judges, who in their ruling, like so many of their colleagues, criticise Annalise's conduct: 'you've operated with blatant disrespect for this court and its protocols, and your argument, when isolated from all the bluster, seems to consist entirely of speculation'. Regardless of their criticism, the judges rule in David's favour. Despite their frustration with Annalise's court performance, they cannot help but be persuaded by her emotional 'truth talking', pronounce David 'free', and order an investigation into the corrupt senator. With her idealistic monologues, Annalise's court performance stands in direct contrast to the opposing lawyers and prosecutors she argues against. Often their major legal strategy appears to be a personal attack on Annalise's credibility. Over the course of the series, such slander has singled out her marital infidelity, speculations as to her involvement in Sam's murder, and her ongoing struggle with alcoholism. Through personal attacks, the show appears to suggest that Annalise's 'truth talking' is beyond questioning or doubt, leaving these responses as the only option.

Even though her employees and students support her, Annalise is a singular agent. Her attempts to reform legal institutions are not embedded within a movement, and her moments of victory are not acquired through collective group efforts but through her own brilliance. As an exception, in the fourth season, Annalise temporarily teams up with the new employer of former intern Michaela, the talented lawyer Tegan, to negotiate the custody hearings of her complicated enemy-friend, university president Soraya. Set in wide camera shots, the negotiation scenes markedly highlight the ethnicity and gender of the two opposing councils (Figure 6.2): whereas Soraya's white ex-husband and his white male lawyer sit on one side of the table, the four women of colour,

Figure 6.2 In a rare scene of collaboration (4.4 'Was She Ever Good at Her Job?'), Annalise joins the defence team of fellow lawyer Tegan and her former intern Michaela to defend their client Soraya.

Annalise, Soraya, Tegan, and Michaela, sit opposite them. Viewers' tweets celebrated the singular collaboration of the four 'powerful' women as a kind of superhero team-up.

In contrast to Alicia's position vis-à-vis the law in *The Good Wife*, which is subject to change as she painfully comes to realise the 'limited nature of her own agency on the legal stage' (Kanzler 2012: 74), Annalise is already disillusioned with the judicial system and verbally responds with anger and impatience to its apparent faults. In a straightforward, essentialist understanding of right and wrong, truth and justice, her heroism results from her ability to transcend the limitations of her position as a female lawyer of colour and utilise her perspective as an insider ally to the disenfranchised to reason for change. Through Annalise's monologues, the show expresses poignant social criticism and develops a beautiful fantasy: it only takes a sole brave, capable, and eloquent individual (Annalise) to speak the truth (expose racism or sexism) in the right setting (a courtroom) to the right people (an elderly white cis-male judge) to end systemic injustices. Ultimately, this is a trivialisation of the ongoing, complicated labour and actions of various social movements to achieve social reforms. Social change becomes a mere issue of addressing the 'right people' in the 'right manner'. As a consequence, the individual carries the power – but also the responsibility – to change institutions, which have formed long before her birth and that she can transform at a rapid pace if she is able to choose the right words. This is not to say that fantastic transformations of systemic racism cannot be very satisfying for viewers. Because the other #TGIT shows so frequently disregarded the systemic implications of race, gender, or class in favour of a merit-based, post-racial depiction, *Murder*'s consideration of these issues is immensely pleasing to the show's viewers. Annalise's lines circulated endlessly in tweet quotations and GIFs replaying her moments of victory. In particular, the show's fourth season included several such instances: departing from its explorations of the legal system's bias through the 'case of the week', *Murder* presented a season-long arc in which Annalise prepares and argues a class-action lawsuit in front of the Supreme Court of the United States.

In addition to its inclusion of theatrical elements and the revered setting of the Supreme Court, the trial also features several of *Murder*'s characteristic ingredients for Annalise's court performances: she emotionally and eloquently utters commanding phrases such as 'Racism is built into the DNA of America', or 'the promise of civil rights has never been fulfilled' (4.13 'Lahey v. Commonwealth of Pennsylvania'). She is reprimanded by the hostile chief justice – an older white man – whom she ultimately manages to convince. Her intern Michaela delivers the last-minute finding that makes up the centrepiece of Annalise's improvised closing remarks. As the face of the class-action suit, Annalise has – to melodramatic effect – chosen Nate's estranged elderly father, an African American man imprisoned for most of his life and, despite his mental health issues, mostly left in solitary confinement. Among her awed viewers, not only Nate and her interns feature prominently but also Annalise's proud mother Ophelia as well as her new ally Olivia Pope. Overall, Annalise's solitary position invokes US-American tropes of individualism and heroism, subsequently undermining the fantasy of effecting change through the simple critique of legal institutions. By investing in the fantasy that an individual, heroic figure can undo systemic discrimination, *Murder* develops its own specific brand of 'colourblindness'. The show demonstrates a surface awareness of institutionalised racism and sexism, but significantly downplays the durability and opaqueness of institutions.

HOW POLITICAL IS POLITICAL TV?

In *Was macht Populärkultur politisch?*, Kaspar Maase distinguishes between: 'what makes popular culture *political* and what popular culture *does* politically itself' (2010: 13).[7] Maase proceeds to explore these two dimensions as separate and also conjoined, the political as an attribute of popular culture and popular culture as an active participant in political processes. My interest in *Murder*'s participation in a political discourse of social justice and progressivism relates to his assertion that it is mainly in times of social unrest and anxiety in which popular culture can position itself as political through transgressions of aesthetic norms as well as disregard of a mass audience's desire for normality (44). Similar to the serialised cultural artefacts Maase considers, it is in *Murder*'s reception that politics develop in close relationship with the show itself. However, in times of social insecurities and power struggles regarding racialised and gendered inequalities, *Murder* positions itself as a champion of its diverse viewers rather than an educator of the ignorant, apolitical masses that Maase envisions.

Conventionally, the ability to address current social and political issues has been attributed to premium cable or online providers like Netflix or Amazon Prime, because they do not have to appease fickle advertisers to the same extent that network television does. In such an understanding, references to political issues are contrasted with advertisers' commercial interests because they could split a mass demographic into smaller political camps. In the occasional 'special episode', network television had found a vehicle to embed television shows with political timeliness without placing either shows or the network too clearly on a political spectrum. The current cultural moment demonstrates how prior industry beliefs have changed because political positioning has become a more and more viable means of promotion not only for television shows themselves but also for the brands that advertise in their commercial breaks. Increasingly, various companies have realised that professing to stay out of politics may be less economically lucrative than actively communicating political positions to potential consumers.[8] Despite their inaccurate assessment of the current televisual landscape and its viewers, the ominous notions of 'Peak TV' and 'too much television' have promoted a competitive atmosphere in which shows may rely on issues surrounding identity politics to garner attention and pursue cultural value. *Murder* here joins television shows like *Orange Is the New Black* (Netflix, 2013–19), *Transparent* (Amazon, 2014–19), *Master of None* (2015–17), or *Grace and Frankie* (Netflix, 2015–), which all aspire to be associated with subversive or progressive themes. These series are heavily interested in exploring gender as intersectional and highlight televisually – and socially – marginalised identities; for example, in relation to age (*Grace and Frankie*), race (*Orange is the New Black*, *Master of None*), or transgender identities (*Transparent*). Notably, issues of class have received less consideration, and most shows do not scrutinise their characters' immense financial health (especially *Grace and Frankie* and *Transparent*, but also *Murder*). While, again, many of the series are premium cable or online provider productions, network channel ABC stakes its claim in the 'brand' of politically progressive television with *Murder*.[9]

ABC's aspirations appeared to be undermined when first lady Melania Trump said that *Murder* was her favourite television show in December 2017. Entertainment news headlines ranged from outrage to ridicule of Trump for her televisual preference. Several of the show's actors have reacted with frustration and annoyance to this public endorsement. Interestingly, these responses affirm *Murder* as a politically progressive television show and position celebrity viewer Melania Trump as either incapable of understanding the show's political aspirations or as masochistically embracing 'the enemy', that is, the dissident voices critical of her husband's political administration. For example, a tweet by actor Matt McGorry during the fourth season explicitly addressed the perceived political disconnect between the show and its celebrity viewer: 'very proud to be a part of this episode with some incredibly important messages about the racism built into our criminal injustice system. YOU WATCHING THIS MELANIA???? SHOW THIS EPISODE TO YOUR DAMN HUSBAND!!!' Several tweets by viewers also noted how the social justice commitments of characters like Annalise Keating and, to a lesser extent, Olivia Pope become outstanding in contrast with the lack of similar aspirations by actual politicians: 'when fictional characters are giving you the inspiration your country's leaders aren't'. Such tweets position *Murder* as a politically progressive narration that steps into a void created by real-life politics. When a television show is upheld as inspiration to political constituency as well as didactic play that could even educate the seemingly lost cause of a right-wing president, popular culture appears to be affirmed as an important political player intervening in social and cultural struggles for equality.

In a parallel to lawyer Annalise as a truth-talker who possesses the gift of gab and transforms the system of the law, producer Shonda Rhimes is presented paratextually along similar lines. Rhimes is cast as an exceptional author figure who challenges the racial and gender bias of the contemporary media industry through her presence. However, Rhimes's star image has considerably shifted with changing cultural contexts: from her previous insistence on a merit-based, 'post-racial' public performance in connection to her successes with *Grey's Anatomy*, she has increasingly begun to acknowledge race as relevant to the #TGIT shows and her public persona. Tracing Rhimes's different promotional performances, Ralina Joseph has referred to her self-branding as 'strategic ambiguity' and understands it to be a twenty-first-century version of respectability politics (2016). Rhimes's strategic adjustment of her public image in 'the pre-Obama era to the #BlackLivesMatter era', Joseph argues, 'demonstrates that, in the former moment, to be a respectable black woman is to not speak frankly about race, while in the latter, respectable black women can and must engage in racialized self-expression' (2016: 306). Rhimes's star image then crucially draws on the political brand of *Murder* to achieve this currently attractive, strategic evocation of identity politics.

Coinciding with the Melania Trump news item, the 2017 Emmy celebration hosted by comedian Stephen Colbert mocked the Trump administration and portrayed the media industry as an active oppositional force against it. Such self-congratulatory positioning seems irreconcilably at odds with the struggles of women and people of colour within the industry and their continued quantitative exclusion on and off screen – particularly, when a few months later #MeToo drew attention to the prevalent sexism of the industry. As *Variety*'s Maureen Ryan wrote about that Emmy ceremony,

> it wasn't the real world of TV, which still has miles to go when it comes to matters of representation, diversity, and inclusion, but instead a place where the industry reassured itself that it was doing the work necessary to resist the worst of the present moment. (Ryan 2017)

Isabel Molina-Guzmán refers to this as 'Hollywood's diversity paradox' (2016: 439) to describe how the increased attention to diversity is a result of the industry adjusting to its demographic, while at the same time these portrayals still remain minimal and their equation with social and political progress is at best ambiguous (444). Like many other observers, Molina-Guzmán warns against equating representational visibility with structural improvements, especially since – despite the presence of exceptional individuals like Shonda Rhimes – 'the racial, ethnic and gender privilege of Hollywood's power structure [is left] uncontested' (445). I read Melania Trump's endorsement as another indicator of Molina-Guzmán's 'diversity paradox'. In place of understanding Trump as misguided and unable to truly comprehend *Murder*, her viewing preference illustrates that the politically progressive aspirations of the show do not as neatly map onto actual political progress as tweets suggest. Instead, claims to diverse media depictions as indicators of systemic change rather gloss over continuing power structures.

Addressing the understanding that representation is central to many cultural struggles for recognition, Herman Gray writes: 'the problem is less with specific images than with the investment in a conception of cultural politics that continues to privilege representation itself as the primary site of hope and critique' (2005: 2). A preoccupation with 'wrong' or 'missing' portrayals has motivated much of the scholarship on *Scandal*'s Olivia and her overlap or divergence from tropes of black femininity. In Chapter 3, I found related concerns (albeit surrounding racial diversity) to drive scholarly and critical interest. For example, Hannah McCann raises similar questions about *Girls*: 'what are we hoping to achieve in demanding greater representational diversity from the show?' (2017: 97). McCann concludes that such demands may have to do with the television screen being 'a relatively simple realm within which to address inequality around issues of race, when circumstances off-screen are so dire' (100). Thus, when done 'wrong' (as in the case of *Girls*) or done 'right' (as in the case of *Murder*), the political aspirations of serialised 'political television' amount to fictional imaginations of political struggle and activism as 'do-able' and rewarding.

Through its self-promotion, *Murder* offers its viewers the appeal of being part of a socially progressive demographic. The 'political television' brand accordingly comes with a corresponding 'political viewer' offering. Even though the show has proven so popular with (especially female) viewers of colour, its audience construction is diverse and does not require viewers to be of the same racial, gendered, classed, or national background. The ease and effortlessness with which white viewers can appropriate the show's depictions of black beauty culture as 'girl time' or employ GIFs of characters of colour as careless 'digital blackface' (Jackson 2017) demonstrate its 'open' audience construction. Viewers are united through the conception of themselves as sociopolitically progressive and aware of the ways that sexism, racism, and classism continue to shape US-American society. Therefore, targeting a 'progressive audience' serves as a particular kind of narrowcasting in the current political moment. However, I do not want to cast viewers as cultural dupes falling for the show's commercially motivated brand of 'political television'. On the contrary, it is my firm contention that such representations can inspire and fuel the politics of its viewers. One does not need to look far to support such an understanding, as the #TGIT responses of viewers frequently overlap with the hashtag activism of #BlackLivesMatter within the cultural space of Black Twitter. Rather than consider hashtag activism as solely a means of mobilisation for 'real' or 'more serious' politics outside of digital spaces, the Black Lives Matter movement conjoins both. For this reason, hashtag activism constitutes an equally viable or socially relevant arena of politics to activism outside of the internet. The commercial motivation of 'political television' complicates a celebration of the politics of its viewers when it draws on viewer discourses as paratextual accompaniments. In other words, watching 'political television' is in and of itself not political activism, but when audiences engage and further the themes evoked in it, this acquires political dimensions. Moreover, when television series then again refer back to these political viewer engagements and attempt to instrumentalise them for their own promotions, political activism and commercial interest become inseparably entangled. Serial television narratives are uniquely suited to feed on political viewer activism.

Throughout the book, the perspective I take is that of a second-degree observer when I observe a show in connection with its viewers' reactions. This perspective allows me to distinguish between the political self-staging of a show – for example, its branding of itself as feminist or political television – and its implicit or even concealed dependence on commercial success.

In conclusion, this chapter argued that *Murder* participates in a discourse of progressivism, social activism, and identity politics, especially relevant within the political climate of the Trump administration. To position itself as political, a serial television show has to keep up with current developments and needs the affirmation of certain institutions – such as GLAAD – as well as its viewers' acknowledgement of its exceptionality and political impact. Echoing Chapter 3, these practices serve as a further example of how radical criticism can be contained in neoliberal popular culture. For *Murder*, this radical criticism concerns systemic and institutionalised racism and everyday police brutality in the US. The show turns issues such as discrimination, exploitation, and oppression into tweetable moments which may feel empowering to viewers yet negate any awareness of socio-economic structural or systemic dynamics of racism. This permits the show to stage acts of protest and resistance against racism in a similarly selective manner as individualised and effective heroism. Unlike the intellectual argument of ur-feminist impulse discussed in Chapter 3, these viewer responses often take a purely affective, emotional route of affirming *Murder*'s status as much needed 'political television' as corrective to a current political crisis.

NOTES

1. 'Serodiscordant' is the expression used to describe couples with different HIV statuses; 'seroconcordant' describes couples with an identical HIV status. The AIDS crisis is currently nearing its fourth decade, with scholarship and activists speaking of a 'New Era' of prevention, activism, and treatment. In addition to their ongoing stigmatisation, HIV and AIDS have become relatively displaced from cultural representation.
2. The 2015 Emmy Award nominations were also remarkable for their uncharacteristic consideration of 'older' actresses: thirteen of the eighteen female nominees were over the age of forty – Davis was forty-nine at the time of her win. Still, only white people were nominated for the categories of female lead in comedy and male lead in drama.
3. Chief justice Roger Brooke Taney is often remembered for delivering the majority opinion in *Dred Scott v. Sandford* (1857), which held that African Americans were not to be considered citizens of the United States.
4. Remarkably, unlike other legal dramas, *Murder* has not yet introduced a case that draws attention to its materiality as a television show. Typically, such self-reflexive trials involve television writers, media producers, or television viewers and raise questions of responsibility, copyright, or audience expectations.
5. The casting of trans-female characters with cis-male or cis-female actors has increasingly become a means for actors to achieve credentials; yet in a marketplace offering few roles for trans actors such casting practices have become problematised as 'trans-face' (in an analogy to blackface) by LGBTQIA audiences. Films like *The Danish Girl* (2015), *Dallas Buyer's Club* (2013), and the television series *Hit & Miss* (Sky Atlantic, 2012) have faced scrutiny for their passing over of trans actors. The Netflix show *Transparent* on which Billings also appears as a recurring character has cast several trans actors, but protagonist trans woman Maura is played by cis-male actor Jeffrey Tambor. For television shows with prominent transgender cast and crew, for example, *Orange is the New Black*, *Sense8* (Netflix, 2015–18), or the web series *Her Story* (Independent, 2016), discussions surrounding casting become crucial paratexts. With the casting of Billings, *Murder* seeks to participate in this cultural conversation.
6. This stands in stark contrast to *The Good Wife*, which depicts a legal community of different, recurrent prosecutors, opposing lawyers, and judges, each with their own preferences and quirks. Often, Alicia and her colleagues have to 'read' their judge

and adjust their behaviour or alternate counsel to receive a favourable combination of prosecutor, defending lawyer, and judge.
7. The title of Maase's monograph can be translated as *What Makes Popular Culture Political?*; in German the quote reads: 'was denn Populärkultur *politisch* mache, wie daran was Populärkultur politisch *mache*' (2010: 13).
8. Brands such as the shoe manufacturer TOMS or the toiletry producer Dove have been economically successful due to their strategic employment of political activism to promote their brands and market their products through what has come to be called 'cause-sumption'.
9. This gains resonance when considering other prominent network fare unreflective of its inherent misogyny and problematic gender politics; for example, *Two and a Half Men* (CBS, 2003–15) and *The Big Bang Theory* (CBS, 2007–19).

Part III

Television Authorship and *The Walking Dead*

CHAPTER 7

The Paratext Seriality of *The Walking Dead*

Girls and *Murder* share a distinct feature that amounts to an anomaly within the current television-scape: a highly visible female author figure.[1] Lena Dunham and Shonda Rhimes are prominent examples of the 'showrunner'. The showrunner is television's central instance of authorship, a previously relatively invisible, loosely defined position in television production (Newman and Levine 2011: 49). Television studies has been exploring how the notion of authorship oversimplifies television production and blurs the medium's collaborative nature. Jason Mittell emphasises that television author figures communicate 'authority, mastery, and control of fictional universes', characteristics that in the cultural and social imaginary are gendered and racialised (2015: 103–4). In a highly competitive field, few female or non-white writers have been able to rise to the position of showrunner, and even fewer have managed to garner the celebrity status of some white cis-male showrunners associated with the canon of 'Quality TV'. The significance of such gendered and racialised figures forms the foundation of this chapter, which explores how paratexts – and especially ones that are themselves serial – serve as a means to establish and contest television authorship. Unlike the two other shows discussed in this book, *The Walking Dead* deliberately refrains from positioning itself in current socio-economic controversies. It further – or possibly because of this – is one of the few contemporary US television shows whose fan base reaches across all political camps. Rather than mobilising wider audience discussions and reactions, *The Walking Dead* is more interested in curating fan activities and controlling the forms they take. This is why Chapter 7 focuses on official paratexts as one such means of authorial control and their involvement in serial storytelling. The chapter will explore how serial authorship develops in and through paratexts, the multiple forms it takes at different stages of the franchise (for instance, from a model of inheritance to a kinship-based collaboration), and the role that gender plays in constructions of television authorship (such as the differentiation between male-associated creativity and female administration).

While models of authorship are subject to historical change, they often express more about a cultural artefact's reception than its actual production. Michel Foucault's 'author function' speaks to television studies and seriality studies in productive ways. Foucault explores how an author's name carries out a classificatory function within narrative discourse by allowing us 'to group together a certain number of texts, define them, differentiate them from, and contrast them to others' (1998: 210). The author in this argument becomes the 'author function', 'a projection . . . of the operations we force texts to undergo' (213–14). Jason Mittell expands the notion by describing television's showrunner as a manufactured reference point for audiences' meaning-making strategies: 'we can look at authorship as one of the key products of television programming, its industrial practices, and its cultural circulation' (2015: 95). Jonathan Gray calls attention to the temporal dimensions of authorial practices: 'asking *when* the author is, in other words, may help us to answer the thornier question of *what* an author is' (2013: 89). He suggests focusing on both the text and the 'moments of its authoring' (108). Gray's understanding of 'clusters of authorship' (103) is useful in considering the changing, multi-faceted, conflicting authorship of serial texts. Moreover, Frank Kelleter and Daniel Stein find conflicts of authorisation to contribute to the stability of the serial text, rather than threatening it (2012: 269). In this sense, such conflicts function as spaces of self-observations for serial texts, spaces in which texts test the possibilities and methods of their continuation (278).

Numerous different individuals have acted as author figures for the multi-protagonist drama *The Walking Dead*. One of several franchise properties with the same name, the television series *The Walking Dead* (henceforth *TWD*) has been airing on the basic cable channel AMC since 2010. The show is based on a comic book series that was published by Image Comics from 2003 to 2019. At the time of writing (January 2020), the show has concluded its tenth season, and Image published the last comic issue #193 in July 2019. Both TV and comic series brand themselves as 'stories of survival horror' and focus on the social interaction in communities that humans formed to survive hostile surroundings after a zombie apocalypse. My readings explore how the show's serial storytelling, production, and reception follow the model of what I call paratext seriality. Through this concept, I address, first, how the television show *TWD* relies on its paratexts for narrative developments, storyworld or character continuity, authorship performances, and the management of viewer responses. Second, I examine how the show subjugates other components of the franchise, most prominently the comic book, to the status of televisual paratexts for these purposes.

The concept of a 'paratext' was coined by literary theorist Gérard Genette, who described it through spatial metaphors: paratexts are 'thresholds', 'vestibules', 'zones', 'edges', or 'fringes' (1997: 1–15). These kinds of materials *present* the literary or cultural artefacts they accompany, but also in the process *make* such artefacts *present* in the sense of 'ensur[ing] the text's presence in the world' (1). Genette argues that paratexts support reception practices, whereby he specifies that through them readings become 'more pertinent, of course, in the eyes of the author and his allies' (2). This potential 'multiplication of authorizing instances' (Birke and Christ 2013: 70) embedded in Genette's concept of the paratext offers a starting point from which to explore the multi-authorial self-presentation of television shows.

Overall, this chapter develops an understanding of authorisation and paratextuality as a conjoined, crucial aspect of contemporary television series. Paratexts (especially those that are themselves serial) often serve as the glue of the 'work-nets of agency' (Kelleter 2014: 4) that make up serialised cultural artefacts. While the materials that I considered in previous chapters also have a paratextual relationship to the TV series they accompany, what distinguishes the types of cultural artefacts in this chapter is their (self-)positioning as 'authorised' paratexts: they claim to be valid interpretations or commentary as part of a show's canon. In order to become authorised – meaning that they are both canonised and able to communicate authorship performances – these paratexts require a person or agency with legitimising influence to position them as valid in relation to the text. Paratexts become demonstrations of textual authority, both because personified authorial presences are established in them and because they communicate the intent of those author figures. Authorised paratexts insist on the authority of their readings as opposed to viewer-created paratexts, while at the same time creating the illusion of representing fan communities. They take up criticism in affirmative ways, thereby smoothing the waters for a series' continuation. In doing so, they become prime examples of serial texts' feedback loop, requiring author figures to turn their authorship performance into a serial project enacted in paratexts.

A genre hybrid, *TWD* can be situated within both horror and melodrama. Privileging literature and cinema as the genre's prime habitat, horror on the small screen is often perceived as less innovative, less scary, and less engaging: television appeared as 'a cultural site that is assumed to be alien to the genre and a space where horror supposedly does not belong' (Hills 2005: 111). Lorna Jowett and Stacey Abbott find televisual horror to surface when 'TV movies, series and serials stop trying to be like cinematic or literary horror but embrace the televisual' form (2013: 55). *TWD*'s self-understanding as the 'zombie movie that never ends' is so remarkable because repetition is among the core indicators of this embrace (Platts 2014: 294; Hills 2005: 46–70). *TWD* has no complex mythology or chronology to manage, because it narratively decentred the cause of the zombie outbreak as non-essential. Altogether, *TWD*'s temporality is chronologically linear; it rarely employs flashbacks. Time jumps in-between individual episodes and scenes may indicate how characters settle into new communities, but for the most part viewers accompany the survival struggle as an unmediated phenomenon in 'real time'. Most episodes check in with two to four groups of characters in different locations and on different 'missions'. The show expands its storyworld as new characters join the main collective of survivors, other characters die, and new spaces for settlements have to be found when previous shelters become uninhabitable. The show's driving narrative momentum comes from the reunion of separated members of the survivor collective, battles with hostile groups and hordes of zombies, and, to a lesser extent, the ways characters cope with past traumatic experiences.

While some paratexts reference only the television show, others align themselves with the comic, and a large group attempts to associate themselves with the franchise in general. This illustrates a management strategy that Clare Parody refers to as 'franchise storytelling', which she defines as 'the creation of narratives, characters, and settings that can be used both to generate and give identity to vast quantities of interlinked media products and merchandise, resulting in a prolonged, multitextual, multimedia fictional experience' (2011: 211). Elsewhere I have argued for the necessity of conceptualising the relationship of simultaneously progressing television shows and book/comic series beyond the suggestive frameworks of adaptation studies or transmedia storytelling (Sulimma 2014b). I now explore the processes through which television shows claim other instalments as paratexts.

THE MANAGEMENT OF MULTI-AUTHORSHIP THROUGH PARATEXTS

Speaking of *The Wire*, Frank Kelleter highlights that paratexts 'suggest how the series wants to be watched' (2014: 6). To extend this idea, *TWD* suggests how it wants to be discussed through *Talking Dead*, a talk show that airs immediately after each new episode, as well as through the comic's letter column 'Letter Hacks'. *Talking Dead* premiered during *TWD*'s second season in 2011. Ratings indicate that a large percentage of viewers continues to watch AMC after each episode of *TWD*, making the talk show a highly visible paratext in the franchise.[2] Hosted by Chris Hardwick, *Talking Dead* has a generic live studio audience and living room setting in which two to three cast or crew members are joined by celebrity 'super fans' to share their impressions of the prior episode. Each episode features viewer reactions, initiated by a question from a pre-selected audience member, phone call-ins, or social media posts. Like the comic's letter column, the talk show engages in a kind of 'authorised interpretation'. Suzanne Scott describes the celebrity fans' responses as a kind of 'quality fandom', because they refrain from appearing either too critical or excessively emotional, or from bringing up erotic readings (2014). Indeed, celebrity fans are always willing to defer their interpretations to the comments of present cast and crew, as well as to host Hardwick (specifically: he always has the last word).

Black cis-female comedian Yvette Nicole Brown is the celebrity fan who veers most from the established forms of how one should 'talk dead'. Brown brings her viewing notes and is humorously framed as a kind of 'geeky smart girl'. Disregarding the franchise's authorised readings, Brown often offers alternative interpretations. Scott argues that Brown's fandom resembles unauthorised 'fan talk' which visually makes *TWD*'s cast and crew uncomfortable because these viewing responses challenge authorial intent (2014). Through Brown, the most frequently invited celebrity guest on *Talking Dead*, the franchise can acknowledge fan practices without having to address their concerns. Any potential controversy is reframed as a question of misunderstanding on the part of the fan rather than a conflicting interpretation. *Talking Dead* thus curates which narrative moments are worthy of debate and attempts to smooth plot inconsistencies by affirmatively discussing them as possibilities for future storytelling. Through such an approach, the talk show seeks to complement *TWD*, not to overpower or undermine it. In this way, the franchise can comprehensively establish what it considers to be the official canon and which viewer responses are inadequate.

Hardwick's fan persona serves as the strategic centrepiece of *TWD*'s management of preferred readings of the show. It is significant that Hardwick acts as a mediator: he shifts from personifying the viewers of the show, more specifically the uncritical fan position the franchise encourages its viewers to take, to representing the franchise when speaking with actual viewers or celebrity guests. As a kind of chameleon authority, Hardwick may switch from appearing as an industry insider, who is part of the production processes, to portraying an unknowing outsider shocked by plot developments. Always clad in a fitted suit and enthusiastically promoting the franchise's merchandise, he avails himself of different modes of professional white masculinity as well as the cultural type of the nerd. Hardwick's exaggerated combination of these two modes serves to ridicule both: for example, he races through his talking cards as a parody of prepared professionalism, and he sarcastically jokes about his emotional reaction to certain scenes.

Having appeared on *Talking Dead* fourteen times, the comic's writer Robert Kirkman is the most present author figure, followed by special effects designer and co-producer Greg Nicotero (twelve appearances), executive producer Gale Anne Hurd (seven), and showrunner Scott M. Gimple (twelve) (Figure 7.1). These repeated appearances demonstrate how the talk show manages a variety of authorial voices that claim to represent the franchise in a carefully orchestrated web of authorship. I will chronologically trace three phases in which strategies for communicating authorship shifted significantly. The phases correspond with the different 'reigns' of showrunners Darabont (season one), Mazzara (season two and three), and Gimple (season four onward).

On the first season's DVD bonus material, both Kirkman and Darabont position themselves as long-time fans of the horror genre, who share their search for a like-minded partner to creatively pursue horror storytelling. Darabont expresses that he 'always wanted to play in that sandbox', and was searching for a project that would allow him to do so. Kirkman similarly emphasises his search for someone able to do justice to 'his' material. He continues that Darabont proved himself by expressing that the comic is not about the zombies but about the characters' struggle to survive (Ruditis 2010: 10). The pairing hinges on the description of Kirkman's supposed 'test', through which Darabont demonstrates his 'worthiness'. Such a litmus test appears to be a common rhetorical device for establishing authorship performances when it comes to 'simultaneous series', that is, crossmedia franchises with two parallel progressing series (Sulimma 2014b: 133). For instance, *Game of Thrones* showrunners David Benioff and D. B. Weiss frequently claimed that the novels' author George R. R. Martin asked them who the mother of character Jon Snow is, one of the franchise's most discussed mysteries, to demonstrate their competence to adapt the novels to screen. Those 'tests' present comic or book authors as genius creators who function as sole authorities, but who willingly share authority with showrunners after having discovered them to be kindred minds. Out of touch with the realities of copyright and contract negotiations, such romanticised stories of searching for a worthy candidate and crowning a successor are fantasies of rightful succession and inheritance. These fantasies are gendered because they recall Western conceptions of (inherited) property ownership that historically have excluded women. The pursuit of the best successor is tied to an understanding of property as a masculine right.

(White) masculinity is intrinsic to those narratives because, in order to translate their 'creative vision' into another medium, 'original creator' figures search for someone they perceive as 'equal'. Darabont's horror fandom becomes a prerequisite for understanding *TWD*'s initial two author figures as like-minded. Both Darabont and Kirkman repeatedly expressed their fandom of cult director George A. Romero. The cinematic zombie narratives associated with Romero become intertextual frames for *TWD*, but Romero himself also becomes a source of authorisation for Kirkman and by extension Darabont. Novelist Jay Bonansinga or special effects designer Greg Nicotero – who both worked with Romero first– deliver a rhetoric of such kinship. For example, Bonansinga lauds Kirkman for 'reinvent[ing] an entire genre in comic book form' in the tradition of the zombie genre's 'inventor' Romero (2011: 56).[3] The conception of Kirkman doing for comics what Romero did for film claims a similar position in a righteous line of succession for Kirkman.

Figure 7.1 Top to bottom: first-season showrunner Frank Darabont with comic book writer Robert Kirkman; *Talking Dead* appearance by Kirkman, Laurie Holden (Andrea), and showrunner Glen Mazzara (1.13); Kirkman, showrunner Scott M. Gimple, Jeffrey Dean Morgan (Negan), and Norman Reedus (Daryl) (*Talking Dead* 5.16).

Readers of the comic are asked to 'trust' in Kirkman, his creative authority, and horror fandom, as well his surrogate, Darabont. Suzanne Scott described the authorial identity that straddles the positions of producer and consumer as the 'fanboy auteur': such author figures claim to know their audience's desires because of 'their fan credentials, which are narrativized and (self)promoted' (2012: 44). When included in the same paratexts, executive producer Gale Anne Hurd complicates the 'fannish author bromance' between Darabont and Kirkman because her mere presence draws attention to the gendered exclusivity of their fan collective. As a basis for authorship, horror fandom relies on an understanding of horror as a male genre, a genre that 'social misfits' like Kirkman and Darabont bond over with one another (as well as with their viewers) but that a middle-aged, professional career woman like Hurd cannot possibly enjoy. Even though *Talking Dead*'s making-of sequences at times depict Hurd and other female production personnel such as co-producer Denise Huth during the filming of gory action scenes, the franchise largely perpetuates a gendered depiction of female managerial work and male creativity.

The franchise sought to create a legitimate space for Hurd's authorship. It has done so by portraying Darabont and Kirkman as visionary, struggling artists unable to make themselves heard within the entertainment industry. By highlighting how Hurd swiftly found a network that would finance the development of the show, such narratives showcase Hurd as a well-connected industry insider (Platts 2014: 296). Though uncharacteristic of accounts of the media industry, this narrative depicts a woman's ability to make herself heard and speak on behalf of less established men. This authorship narrative likely says little about the show's actual creation history.[4] It offers a gendered specialisation of authority in order to reconcile conflicting demands: whereas Darabont's and Kirkman's positions of authority rest on their claims to represent the interests of viewers and fans, and position their creative genre knowledge as a means to do so, Hurd represents the industry. Instead of the fannish enthusiasm to 'talk dead', she brings her personal connections, boardroom negotiation skills, and the ability to 'speak business'.

The first season's primary authorship performance of two equal 'fanboy auteurs' within a lineage of zombie fan-creators was abandoned when Darabont abruptly left the show during the production of the second season. Journalistic accounts by, for instance, *The Hollywood Reporter* speculate that AMC fired Darabont over budget negotiations (Masters 2011).[5] Darabont's departure posed an authorship crisis: if Darabont's authority is equal to that of Kirkman, how could the showrunner possibly be replaced? In this impasse, a relatively unknown member of the writers' room, Glen Mazzara, was promoted to showrunner. Mazzara's eligibility for the position was based on a description of him as Darabont's mentee: as the official *TWD* website expressed in September

2014, Darabont 'recognized his writing skills and ability to manage staff – a rare combination of talents – and brought Mazzara on-board as his #2'. Again, a legitimate line of succession presents Mazzara as the next best thing. Yet Mazzara never positioned himself as a horror fan or even as a fan of the comic series. Mazzara's insufficient fan credentials were mended through the extension of Kirkman's authorship to the television show as well.

Though Kirkman had previously expressed his unfamiliarity with large-scale television production in the first season's DVD interviews, Kirkman was announced as a permanent member of the show's writers' room and presented as a 'steward' of the brand following Darabont's departure.[6] Never explicitly specified, this authorship position appears to be a genuine feature of large crossmedia franchises and complements the televisual showrunner by offering a broader vision of storyworld continuity. Such a presentation characterises Kirkman as ultimate canon authority, someone who oversees and protects the franchise, again enhanced through his fan credentials. When Glen Mazzara also left the show just eighteen months after Darabont's departure, his voice had become one of many different authorship performances subordinated to Kirkman.[7]

After Mazzara's departure, Scott M. Gimple, who had been a member of the writers' room since the second season, became the new showrunner. When asked about the frequent change of showrunners during an AMA (short for 'ask me anything') on Reddit in March 2014, Kirkman highlighted each showrunner's contribution. Whereas he found the show to be influenced by Darabont's 'directing and visual style' or Mazzara's 'level of energy' and pacing, Gimple's accomplishment is that he 'honestly knows more about this world than I do'. Rather than a 'labour of love', Gimple's appreciation of the franchise is expressed in rational, analytical terms. In his paratextual appearances, Gimple enacts hyperprofessionalism, often clad in a suit and tie, as compared with Darabont's Hawaiian print shirts and Mazzara's jeans and trainers. In a departure from Darabont's enthusiastic horror fandom, Gimple demonstrates his knowledge of cinematic horror, the comic, and the franchise as a source of expertise and not affective connection. No excited 'fanboy auteur', soft-spoken Gimple could be described as a '(horror) connoisseur auteur', who calmly intellectualises his fandom. Whereas Suzanne Scott's 'fanboy auteur' utilises his – the gendered pronoun here serves as a reminder that popular culture does not offer an equivalent 'fangirl auteur' – fan credentials to claim to know his audience, because he is one of them, the connoisseur auteur insists he is *not* a fan like his viewers. Evoking an older, savvier brother, he positions himself as able to provide a service to the fan community due to his exceptional merit. Instead of claiming to know what viewers want because he wants the same thing, the connoisseur auteur claims to know what viewers *should* want.

Overall, Gimple's authorship performance continues the show's shift toward professionalisation and specialisation. Kirkman's claim to 'stewardship' of the franchise has been undermined by a web of professional experts, of which Kirkman is only one. These experts stand in for different fields of the production process, such as the writers' room, the special effects department, and set organisation. Enactments of fandom, which had previously been crucial parts of Kirkman's and Nicotero's star personas, have been tuned down to accord with this more rational specialisation. Potential authorship conflicts between Kirkman and Gimple are addressed through their mutual affirmation of the other's capabilities and responsibilities. The above example of Kirkman modestly claiming that Gimple's knowledge of the franchise exceeds his own – awarding Gimple the highest honour of being on par with the franchise's steward – is exemplary of this attitude. It is in regard to their performance of authorship as dynamic and unstable that authorised paratexts like *Talking Dead* become interesting for critical analysis: instead of accepting a unified author figure, due to their own seriality, these figures have to continuously include more authorial voices and present deeper insights into production procedures. In this context, serial performances of authorship simultaneously take place within paratexts and themselves function as paratexts. The serialised extension of *TWD*'s authorship has allowed the work of other crew members to become visible. For the most part, however, this has not upended the invisibility of other writers and lower ranking, below-the-line labour typical of media production (Caldwell 2013).[8]

Further, writer Angela Kang has recently been announced as taking over the showrunning responsibilities for the ninth season. Prior to this, Kang had not publicly appeared as an author presence; she has never been a guest on *Talking Dead*. Kang's promotion in light of the show's declining ratings is an example of what has come to be known as the 'glass cliff' in leadership studies: the appointment of women to leadership positions during phases in which companies or institutions are in crisis situations (Ryan and Haslam 2005). The readings I provided offer productive points of comparison for analysis of Kang's current authorship.

'I DON'T WANT TO KILL ANY OF YOU': THE AUTHORIAL POWER TO KILL

Right from the start of the comic series *The Walking Dead*, readers discussed its potential for being adapted into a film, TV series, or miniseries in the letter column 'Letter Hacks'. After AMC picked up the rights to the comics, Kirkman announced the development in the letter column (#65). The comic's letter column provides a site in which Kirkman's authorship, or 'stewardship', of the entire franchise is established. Chronologically, the comic book series precedes the television series. Prior to the first season, the comic book served as an 'entryway paratext' (Gray 2010: 10–11), hence making the comic book readers a 'built-in' audience for the show in its first season. By now, the comic book supplements the show as an 'in media res paratext' (23–5). Simultaneous instalments often deal with similar narrative scenarios or themes. For example, in comic #139, Michonne returns from a lengthy leave to cope with her 'survivor's guilt' and depression. At the same time, in the fifth season of *TWD*, Michonne joined the pacifist community Alexandria, where she aspires to change her survival 'lifestyle'. The continued thematic relationship between show and comic serves as the basis for the show's paratextual storytelling. Relegating the comic to a paratext, the television show also draws on the comic's column. Especially during the first and second seasons, the show and comic routinely took up the same amount of space in the columns. I will consider the letter column of comic books #1–143, consisting of more than 550 pages of letters written over a period of twelve years.

Visually, the simple do-it-yourself aesthetic of the 'Letter Hacks' recalls independent or alternative comics, especially since the comic is in black and white.[9] In the column, Kirkman and his respective editor 'hack' into the letters and emails of readers to respond to questions, criticism, and feedback.[10] Different fonts indicate different authorial voices – yet Kirkman's response is always the last, allowing him to definitively settle the score. Letters also often respond to the previous debate, which creates the effect of an ongoing conversation. Aside from being a space for communicating preferred readings, the letter column serves as a site in which authorship is challenged and extended. Based on *Batman*'s letter columns, Daniel Stein observed how the writing of a letter transforms (comic) readers into (letter) writers, and (comic) writers into (letter) readers (2013: 168). Through the practice of letter writing, readers insert themselves into the franchise and become authorial presences themselves. More than one reader proudly announced the publication of their letters on *TWD*-related message boards or YouTube videos. By turning to social media, these writers continue the discussions their letters raise – without the authorising voice of Kirkman or the editor.

The overall tone of the 'Letter Hacks' is one of informal speech and sarcastic humour. Very often letter writers curse Kirkman out, even though swears are frequently turned into praise ('You bastard, how could you do this to me! I loved it!'). Many curse words employ sexist speech to feminise supposedly inappropriate responses. For instance, Kirkman repeatedly insults those letter writers who express sadness or shock as 'pussies'. For such language to be insulting, the letter column has to be gendered as a homosocial space in which it is offensive to be feminised. Even though the comic has a relatively large female readership, letter writers appear overwhelmingly male, and if they do not indicate their gender, Kirkman or the editor assume them to be ('this guy', 'dude'). Female readers who write letters tend to highlight their gender and make their perspective as female readers visible. Just as *Talking Dead* invites celebrity fan Yvette Nicole Brown to share her readings, Kirkman and his editor address these 'exceptional' letters with uncharacteristic sincerity. Despite their inclusion, non-white and non-male viewing positions are marked as 'other', as deviating from the viewer or reader imagined by the franchise. Hence, they require special attention and encouragement and cannot be humorously berated in the way that the normative white, presumably heterosexual male fan can be.

One of the most prominent letters (#104) highlights an ongoing topic of the column: Kirkman's presumed 'power to kill' (characters). It was referred to by a variety of news outlets, and later letters agreed that this was the 'best *Walking Dead* letter column'. Published in comic #102, the letter was written by actor Steven Yeun in response to the brutal death of Glenn, the character he portrayed on the show. Yeun imitates both the sarcastic tone of other letters (and includes colourful insults), as well as their fannish excitement. Yeun's letter affirms Kirkman's authority for the entire franchise because it makes Kirkman personally responsible for the death of comic book Glenn and assumes that television Glenn would now also soon die, making Yeun effectively unemployed. Yeun's letter is one of the most common types of audience reactions featured in the letter column: the letter writer pleads with Kirkman not to kill a certain character, suggests which character to kill next, bets on which character might be the next one to go, or complains after a character has died. Again and again, readers threaten to drop the comic to prevent a death in the comic, as well as on the show. Such letters perceive the 'power to kill' to be Kirkman's prerogative, because he is the creator of the franchise and the only person involved in producing both the show and the comic. The power over the life and death of characters paints Kirkman's authorship as that of a god-like creator figure. Rather than frame this authority as a benign presence able to give life to new characters, which might carry feminised associations of giving birth and biological reproduction, paratexts highlight Kirkman's power to kill as the male author's most robust demonstration of authorial power.

As genre hybrids of horror and melodrama, all instalments of the franchise revel in spectacular, bloody deaths and extended narratives of characters coming to terms with the loss of their friends and family members. *TWD* thereby joins a group of current television shows that do not shy away from killing their central characters, like *Game of Thrones* or *Sons of Anarchy* (FX, 2008–14). These shows break with a long-held industry taboo of killing off central characters, a taboo that supports the requirements of episodic television and the need to reset for the next episodic adventure. While character deaths guarantee media buzz, they showcase serial storytelling because they establish unchangeable narrative 'facts'. Such plot developments create unexpected narrative voids in which mourning viewers (and characters) are unsure how to proceed, and new narrative possibilities arise in the form of minor characters filling the void. For example, *TWD* often envisions a single character as the group's moral compass (Hershel, Dale, Tyreese), until the character dies tragically, and the show begins to establish another character as capable of fulfilling this role. The fluctuation of characters promises serial innovation but risks the possibility that viewers cannot develop emotional investments: frustrated with the show, television critic Emily Nussbaum wondered 'how often your heart can break' following frequent character deaths (2013).

Glenn's death scene, one of the most severe cases of such 'heartbreak', functions as a meta-moment in the comic and reiterates a central self-understanding of the franchise: none of its characters is safe from death. Villain Negan has captured a group of main characters and threatens to kill one of them to set an example. He lines up the group and explains, 'I don't WANT to kill any of you . . . let me make that clear right from the get-go. I want you working for me. And you can't very well do that when you're fucking DEAD, now can you?' (#100) (Figure 7.2). Negan's comment serves as a recognisable reference to the ongoing controversy over character deaths. Whereas Negan claims that he has to kill to demonstrate his authority and leadership, Kirkman claims that killing characters is a necessity of the franchise's brand of survival horror. He insists that, like the audience, production personnel also struggle with character deaths. For example, when a letter laments character deaths on the show's fifth season, Kirkman objects, 'It's tough for us to lose those characters, too, but that's kind of what we signed up for, you know?' (#139). The comment implies a contract between storytellers and story consumers, the ones that signed up to kill and the ones that signed up to expect losses. As a kind of self-reflective author stand-in, the character of Negan complicates Kirkman's casting of himself as someone who 'only kills because he has too'. When Negan claims that the act of killing is an obligation, a responsibility even, this stands in stark opposition to his obvious enjoyment and pleasure in the power he embodies at that moment.

Swinging his deadly bat, Negan looks over the kneeling main characters and narrates the dilemma of deciding upon a victim. He successively rules out a young mother, teenager Carl who should not be killed 'before your story ends, too fucking interesting', as well as African American Heath and Asian American Glenn because of the 'race card'. In this monologue, Negan's character voice seems to overlap with that of author figure Kirkman. Through Negan, Kirkman comments on the storytelling process, expressing considerations as to which characters still have a story to tell (Carl) and how to maintain the group's racial and gendered diversity. When Negan comments, 'I'm a lot of things but I'd never want to be called a racist. No fucking way', this authorial self-reflection echoes past discussions of the letter column in which some

Figure 7.2 Villain Negan's speech implies authorial self-reflection and reveals him to be a stand-in for Robert Kirkman (#100).

letters did call Kirkman a racist for choosing to kill the 'wrong' character. As a deliberate announcement of authorial self-reflection, Negan's speech indicates that Kirkman's power to kill poses a dilemma for the author figure because there is no fair choice that will satisfy all readers.[11] Ultimately, Negan decides by employing the nursery rhyme 'Eeny, meeny, miny, moe', which creates the impression of arbitrariness as part of the authorial killing process – ironically, without considering the racist heritage of American versions of the rhyme.

Even if character deaths may at times feel senseless or arbitrary in the world of the zombie apocalypse, a result of 'bad luck' just as often as of 'bad' survival choices, to many viewers the deaths of fan favourites – if they have to occur at all – should at least feel 'meaningful'. What makes a character death meaningful varies for different viewers and readers, but often involves setting (which episode or issue), narrative repercussions (how other characters are affected), as well as the kind of death (how long, how gory, how much agency a death involves; does the character get to 'come back' as a zombie?). To briefly elaborate: Glenn's death(s) occurred in the much-anticipated anniversary issue (#100) as well as the seventh season premiere, highlighting how endings of major characters become narrative events that are framed as milestones in 'special' comic issues or episodes. In letter column #120, a letter writer complains to Kirkman about the fast death of a favourite character: 'you said on *Talking Dead* recently that the more important a character is, the more dramatic you make their deaths'. As a form of reader or viewer obituary, such responses retrospectively protest not the deaths themselves, but the relative lack of impact awarded to the character. This letter holds Kirkman accountable to his previous paratextual authorship performance, reads the show (and comic) through his commentary, and turns to another paratext (the letter column) to protest inconsistency.

The paratextual negotiations of the 'power to kill' often skirt tensions because they reveal an underlying hierarchy between storytellers (among whom Kirkman as 'brand steward' is elevated), story consumers, and the actors/cast members. As Steven Yeun's letter demonstrates, the killing of characters involves another authorial presence as well: the actor rendered unemployed. As a partial authorship performance, *Talking Dead* invites the show's actors to speak as authority about their characters' emotions, motivations, and decisions. Host Hardwick often asks actors how they felt in a certain situation or why they behaved in a certain way, as though they were the characters they portray. Actors (and viewers) understand the rhetorical equation and answer by combining the character's name with first person singular pronouns and verb forms. By doing so, actors inhabit an authoritative insight into the characters' inner lives – because they rhetorically are affirmed *to be* this person. When a character dies on the show and the actor who played them is invited to *Talking Dead* for the last time (or even for the first time in the case of minor characters), the equation creates a curious tension. Frequently, Hardwick jokes in a semi-sincere tone, 'I'm so sad you died!', while the actor is humorously disgruntled and expresses mock anger. A curious example occurred in the *Talking Dead* episode that aired after the seventh season premiere in which Negan (Jeffrey Dean Morgan) killed Glenn as well as Abraham (Michael Cudlitz). As Morgan entered the stage, Cudlitz got up to provocatively gesture toward his genitals – while smoking a cigar and drinking bourbon. The exaggerated performance of hypermasculinity typical of Cudlitz's character (implying that Negan can 'suck Abraham's dick' and enjoying the whiskey and cigar as symbols of a masculinised good life) served to call out 'his murderer' and offered viewers (and fellow cast members) the pleasure of directing frustrations at a willing target, the actor portraying Negan, rather than toward the storytellers Kirkman and Gimple, who were also on stage.

Sometimes, when 'official' author figures are present, the hidden hierarchy of storytellers and actors becomes tangible: actor IronE Singleton jokingly asked Gale Anne Hurd what he did wrong to have his character T-Dog killed (2.4); Chad Coleman expressed his gratitude toward Nicotero (and Gimple) for granting his character Tyreese such a 'meaningful' death (4.9); and Emily

Kinney repeatedly broke into tears while Robert Kirkman, who was sitting next to her, seemed mortified by her sadness over her character Beth's death (4.8). In these examples, author figures visibly cringe, demonstrating feelings of irritation or discomfort. Of all three interactions, Coleman's response appears the least awkward because he affirms the franchise's preferred reading that all deaths are inevitable, and hence a meaningful death is all viewers and actors can ask of their author figures. Kinney and Kirkman's lack of interaction, uneasily mediated by an overwhelmed Hardwick, demonstrates the least 'appropriate' response and curiously is also the most gendered. The young white woman's act of weeping (essentially over losing her job) may echo a frequent viewer response to fictional deaths, but through paratext seriality the show asks its viewers to continue watching and learn to cope with the death as part of the genre, as something they should be able to embrace as (horror) fans.

Just as Kinney's tearful *Talking Dead* appearance significantly deviates from the 'accepted' gratitude that actors express toward the show's author figures, some fans similarly deviated from the show's intended viewer response: in December 2014, viewers drafted a petition to 'Bring Back Beth' on change.org and sent spoons to AMC to protest the character's death.[12] The petition was never acknowledged in the show's authorised paratexts. Moreover, the mostly female petition signers were ridiculed by other viewers as unable to comprehend the premise of the franchise. These female fans – just like Kinney – were seen as breaching the 'contract' that author figures and especially the author figure with the 'power to kill', Kirkman, have with their viewers.

RAPE, REVENGE, RACISM: THE ADAPTATION OF CONTROVERSY

The show's depiction of sexual assault serves as an example of paratext seriality: the comic's earlier (racialised) rape-revenge plot of protagonist Michonne and the authorial dispute it caused in the comic's letter column ultimately influenced the show's adaptation of this narrative scenario. The notion that narratives of sexualised violence activate audiences because 'images of rape function as the site of collective identification' (Horeck 2014: 9) is a cornerstone for the following reading. For serialised popular culture, viewer discussions of sexualised violence tend to address author figures and demand that they 'take responsibility' for representations understood as offensive or inadequate.

In the third season (3.7 'When the Dead Come Knocking'), the franchise's most popular romantic couple, Glenn and Maggie, is captured by a hostile group, whose leader, ominously named 'the Governor', tortures them to reveal the location of their community. Whereas Glenn is physically abused, Maggie is psychologically threatened with the possibility of sexual assault.

When Maggie refuses to give up her group, the Governor has her undress and drags her into the cell in which Glenn is imprisoned and tortured. The scene juxtaposes Glenn's severely injured body with Maggie's body, which is bare but intact, suggesting an entirely different kind of suffering.

One episode later (3.8 'Made to Suffer'), the Governor is involved in a brutal, lengthy fight scene with Michonne. Michonne had joined the Governor's community with her friend Andrea, but grew suspicious of their leader and left. Unaware of what exactly causes her distrust of the Governor, Michonne returns to kill him. Even though it clearly presents the Governor as an antagonistic character, the television series provides no justifiable motivations for Michonne's and his mutual hatred – other than jealousy over Andrea that was not significantly explored. In the subsequent *Talking Dead* episode, Hardwick, Kirkman, and celebrity guest *Lost* showrunner Damon Lindelof discuss the fight scene but not the reasons for Michonne's animosity. The antagonism between Michonne and the Governor serves as an illustration of the show's paratext seriality, because Michonne's need for revenge in the show makes sense when viewed through the frame of reference the comic establishes.

In comic #28 it is not Maggie but Michonne who is imprisoned, tortured, and repeatedly raped by the Governor. The comic never visually depicts the rape scenes, choosing to show black panels over which speech and sound bubbles document the Governor's violence and pleasure, as well as Michonne's screams, and disturbing close-ups that subsequently depict her mutilated body. Many readers felt that such 'off-panel' presentation was appropriate because Michonne's revenge is much more explicit. But most readers found the rape scenes problematic, especially since the comic's author figure is a heterosexual white man and its readership was similarly assumed to be majority normatively male and white. In the column of comic #32, a letter by a self-identified reader of colour spoke up against what he called 'a kind of chocolate rape fantasy'. The reader's impression aligns with the work of feminist media scholars: Sarah Projansky diagnoses a 'cultural willingness to do/see violence to African American women (in this case through particularly explicit, on-screen rapes), to let the rape of a Black woman stand as a marker of generic racism' (2001: 195). Kay Stieger found the scene to reinforce 'a historical reality that still hasn't been fully acknowledged or reconciled', namely the sexualised violence that women of colour were systematically subjected to at the hands of white men in pre-civil rights US-America (2011: 102–3). Letter writers were also troubled by the continued structural racism and sexism of the comic industry and the question of point of view: with which character does the imagined comic book reader align himself in this issue? A later letter provocatively expressed: 'If you want the honest truth Mr. Kirkman a great deal of your white readers probably whacked off to that issue' (#35). The letter columns #35–51 were dominated by the controversy – in #36, 38, and 39 every letter responded to it. Regardless of their position, the letters held Kirkman accountable to the larger-than-life authorial presence he projects. The letters implicitly agreed upon not finding pleasure in the rape plot – they are not the ones to 'whack off' to racialised violence. But they wondered if it was Kirkman's responsibility to have such a readership in mind when telling stories.

Serial television narratives bring their own discursive history of representations of sexualised violence. After all, many shows of the canon of 'Quality TV' rely on combinations of violence, sexuality, and profanity as markers of distinction (McCabe and Akass 2007). Prominent examples demonstrate the abstruse tensions such plots build up: the rape of Jennifer Melfi by a stranger in *The Sopranos* (3.4 'Employee of the Month'), the rape of Joan Hallway by her fiancé in her boss's office in *Mad Men* (2.12 'The Mountain King'), or protagonist Tommy Gavin raping his ex-wife on *Rescue Me* (FX, 2004–11) (3.4 'Sparks'). For viewers of these and other shows, the immediate reaction appears to be suspicion: about whether such scenes are 'necessary' for character or plot development, if they are 'appropriately' filmed (whether they are pointlessly cruel or too stylised as erotic), or whether they reduce female agency (by taking up the point of view of a helpless male bystander). Narratives of rape appear to cast viewers outside of immersive storyworlds and activate them as critical witnesses to what a show is 'trying to do' in those stories. TV scholar Jason Mittell described the effect of an 'operational aesthetic' of serial television, which positions viewers to 'enjoy the [narrative] machine's results while also marveling at how it works' (2006: 38; see also 2015: 41–4). Representations of sexualised violence can thus be understood as an unintended effect of an operational aesthetic at work. Unlike the 'narrative special effects' Mittell describes, they lack playful components and instead have viewers wondering if the show should be allowed to 'pull off' such a narrative manoeuvre.

Televisual adaptations reinforce viewers' moral positioning to critique representations of rape. In these cases, via paratext seriality, viewers can compare the show's depiction of sexualised violence with that of the earlier source material. Just like the novels it is based on, the *Song of Ice and Fire* series, *Game of Thrones* sparked heavy scrutiny for its extensive and frequent rape scenes. The most controversial scenes of the show were criticised for deviating from the novel in ways that viewers found problematic. For example, the fourth season replaced the novel's consensual sex scene between characters Cersei and Jaime with a scene in which Jaime rapes Cersei (4.3 'Breaker of Chains'). The blog *The Mary Sue* announced that it would suspend all recaps of the show following this change: 'The show has creators. *They* make the choices. *They* chose to use rape as a plot device. *Again*' (Pantozzi 2015). This illustrates how rape representations lay bare some of contemporary culture's fascination with television authorship, especially when negotiations of authorship are multiple and contested.

Ever since Michonne's rape-revenge plot proved to be a 'hot topic' in the comic's letter column, readers speculated if and how it would enter the show. The fan-managed *The Walking Dead Wiki* dedicates a specialised header to comic book plots, which are 'violent and graphic moments that may not make it on to the television show'. Through viewer practices like these, author figures become graspable as the ones who make decisions on the show's narrative developments from among the possibilities the comic offers. 'Michonne Raped' and 'Governor Tortured and Mutilated [and Raped]' received the wiki's header, but the television series attempted a variation of the controversial scenes. Dan Hassler-Forest finds that Maggie's assault is rendered suspenseful through the implicit 'question whether the action will follow the same trajectory' (2014: 101). Hassler-Forest's impression aligns with the series' preferred reception of the scene: on the subsequent *Talking Dead* episode, Yvette Nicole Brown and host Hardwick both pleaded: 'please, don't go there', and expressed gratitude that they were 'spared' such scenes (2.7). Again, these viewing responses highlight how televisual adaptations of sexualised violence enable a specific kind of 'operational aesthetic' in which viewers hold author figures accountable through paratext seriality.

Overall, the show's rape scene shifts its characterisation of the villain: in contrast to his counterpart in the comic, who tortures Michonne for sadistic pleasure, the Governor appears to be rationally motivated by the well-being of his community. Whereas Michonne is both physically and psychologically tortured in the comic, the show 'parcels' the abuse and abusers. Glenn faces physical torture at the hands of henchman Merle, while Maggie faces sexualised psychological torture by the Governor. These adjustments sought to avoid another 'Letter Hacks' controversy because even if the show depicts abusive behaviour, it did not allow for the sexualised objectification of white woman Maggie to the same extent as it did of black woman Michonne in the comic. However, the show does not reflect the criticism expressed toward Kirkman in the letter column. In place of acknowledging the historical and social contexts that the sexualised objectification of Michonne plays into in the comic, the show appeared more comfortable with avoiding such discussions altogether by replacing Michonne with white woman Maggie, rather than addressing them in more aware ways. *The Daily Kos*'s Chauncey DeVega found that writing Michonne out of these scenes 'remove[d] Michonne's power': she 'has to suffer at the hands of the Governor so that she can evolve and grow into an even more essential character who is (at least) as important and capable a leader as Rick' (2012). DeVega's comment is interesting because many viewers were willing to accept Michonne's centrality in the show as based on her overall centrality in the franchise.

Instead of framing the show as an adaptation having to satisfy both comic book readers and new audiences, notions of paratextuality impacted the different versions. Paratext seriality here explains how the show relies on the comic for Michonne's characterisation, even if her character follows a different path in the show. This becomes an explanation for how easily Michonne's revenge quest from the comic continues within another medium, the show. To understand the antagonism of Michonne and the Governor within the show, *TWD* relied on the precedent that the comic had established.

The narrative inevitability of Michonne's revenge is an intertextual reference to the horror subgenre of the rape-revenge film. In *The Last House on the Left* (1972) or *I Spit on Your Grave* (1978), a (typically white) female character is brutally raped, presumed dead, and left behind by a group of men. The former victim transforms herself into an avenging figure to hunt down, torture, and kill her rapists. Carol Clover finds similarities between this avenging figure and 'the final girl' of slasher films: both undergo processes of masculinisation, which depend on the castration and demasculinisation of their former rapists or the serial killer of the slasher film. Through such processes, female characters become instances of cross-gender identification for what Clover assumes to be largely male audiences (1992: 43). In comic #33, the former victim Michonne appears to be 'redeemed' through her violent revenge. Over nine pages, Michonne violently drills holes into the Governor's body, removes several of his body parts, and ultimately rapes him. She foreshadows her cruel practices by describing her torture instruments in a display of 'torture technology', which for Julia Reifenberger is a crucial component of the rape-revenge genre and allows the female heroine to acquire a symbolic masculinity through phallic instruments (2013: 98–9). Because those violent scenes are recognisable as genre conventions of the rape-revenge narrative, many letters expressed that retrospectively they approved of the cruelty of earlier sexualised violence as necessary for her characterisation.

It was after Michonne had demonstrated her revenge as a form of coping mechanism that female letter writers intervened in the letter column. These readers pointed out how the previous conversation had excluded the perspectives of women as well as of sexual assault survivors (#39, #41). Uniformly, female letter writers responded positively to Michonne's violent act of vengeance, resilience, and strength. In an uncharacteristic lack of response, neither Kirkman nor his editor 'hacked' into the letters by female readers, thus decreasing their authorial performance in light of experiences they cannot weigh in on. These 'unhacked' letters challenged the invisible gendering of the letter column/comic book readership as male and white, but also complicated the formulaic equation of readers with the masculinised 'final girl'. By positioning their own gendered experience as giving them insight into Michonne's story, female letter writers insisted on Michonne's rape and revenge as gendered stories of relevance to female readers and readers of colour, not merely part of a narrative formula that uses rape and revenge to create an appealing character for male readers.

In conclusion, this chapter explored how the authorship of *TWD* manifests in various paratexts, and changes to at different moments encompass the entire franchise and at others only the television show. The complexity and multiplicity of *TWD*'s authorship are possible because its viewers' knowledge of the show's production constantly expands through serial paratexts such as *Talking Dead* or the comic letter column. Following my discussion of the god-like power to kill characters, the depiction of racialised sexual violence provided another example of how author figures are held accountable and how they defend their authorial powers in paratextual negotiations.

NOTES

1. Aside from Rhimes and Dunham, showrunners like Tina Fey (*SNL*, *30 Rock*) or Mindy Kaling (*The Mindy Project*) are prominent because they also star in their respective shows, whereas Julie Plec (*Vampire Diaries*), Amy Sherman Palladino (*Gilmore Girls*, *The Marvelous Mrs. Maisel*), Jenji Kohan (*Weeds*, *Orange is the New Black*), Michelle King (*The Good Wife*), or Liz Meriwether (*New Girl*) maintain a public profile due to dedicated fan followings of their shows. In contrast, Carol Mendelsohn, Pam Veasey, and Ann Donahue (all *CSI* franchise), Jam Nash (*Rizzoli & Isles*), Michelle Ashford (*Masters of Sex*), or Kerry Ewin (*Bates Motel*) are relatively absent from popular discussions of authorship in US television series.
2. During *Talking Dead*'s first season, on average a sixth of *TWD*'s live audience watched the talk show, a number which grew to a third of *TWD*'s viewers during *Talking Dead*'s fourth season (Bibel 2015). During mid-season and season finales this number routinely increases to half of *TWD*'s viewers.
3. Romero never endorsed but criticised the *TWD* franchise. Those framings of Romero as the 'father' or 'inventor' of the zombie genre are complicated when one considers the popular cultural figure's Caribbean origins and the historical processes of colonialism and postcolonialism that shaped it.
4. Rather than an issue of 'being heard', timing appears to have played a crucial role in this negotiation because the network AMC had been searching for horror-related material as well: the network rebranded its Halloween scheduling block 'Fearfest' in 2008 and sought an original production to promote horror films (Platts 2014: 297).
5. Despite intense public interest, Darabont and AMC avoided commentary, due to their ongoing involvement in lengthy legal battles over Darabont's right to proceeds from 'derivative work' such as *Talking Dead* or *Fear the Walking Dead*. This is the franchise's second high-profile trial: artist Tony Moore sued for proceeds after he was replaced with Charlie Adlard following comic #7.
6. To my knowledge, the first (self-)description of Kirkman as the entire franchise's 'steward' occurs in the letter column of #126.
7. Ironically, Mazzara's authorship was affirmed by those viewers who expressed disappointment with the second season and found Mazzara to be at fault for its shortcomings.

8. So far, twenty-one writers have been credited for an episode of the show, of which the gender ratio is seventeen to four, while eighteen writers are white, and three are minorities (Asian American, Hispanic). No African American writers have worked on the show so far. Angela Kang has the most writing credits (seasons 2–8: twenty-four episodes), followed by Gimple (seasons 2–8: twenty-two episodes), Matthew Negrete (4–8: twenty episodes), and Channing Powell (4–8: fifteen episodes). Kirkman has not received primary writing credits since the sixth season (1–6: six episodes).
9. *The Walking Dead* is one of the most successful series of publisher Image Comics. Because Image's business model allows comic book creators to retain original copyright, it projects an appeal of 'doing things differently' on par with the cultural framing of premium cable television.
10. So far, the letter column has had three editors – Aubrey Sitterson (until #71), Sina Grace (#72–96), and Sean Mackiewicz (#97 to present) – all of whom are white men. The editor's position in these conversations resembles Hardwick's chameleon authority. The editor may open the column by expressing his surprise and shock at the comic's developments – mirroring readers' reactions – but he also serves as a mediator between readers and Kirkman.
11. The authorial self-reflection that the character of Negan offers for Kirkman continues throughout the comic. After the main characters defeat Negan's group, Negan is imprisoned in Rick's basement. A form of self-chastisement, the author stand-in becomes a prisoner of his characters who refuse to work for him any longer.
12. In 'Still' (4.12), Beth finds and keeps a silver spoon. The franchise represented characters by means of objects in their possession. For example, the opening credits highlight Glenn's silver pocket watch or Rick's sheriff star, and characters like Michonne (katana), Daryl (crossbow), or Tyreese (hammer) possess signature weapons in the superhero-comic tradition. That Beth's fans chose an expendable, everyday item reflects the character's marginal status within the show. The spoon also carries associations with the domestic labours that primarily characterised Beth.

CHAPTER 8

Palimpsest: Gendering through Accountability

Even though *TWD*'s first episode (1.1 'Days Gone By') featured no female characters – other than female zombies – its male characters had much to say about gender. In a flashback to the period before the apocalypse, two white cis-male police officers muse about 'the difference between men and women'. Rick (Andrew Lincoln) and Shane (Jon Bernthal) are childhood friends whose rivalry drives the first and second season. They are rivals for the love of Rick's wife Lori (Sarah Wayne Callies), as well as for the leadership of their group. In this flashback, chauvinistic Shane asserts that he 'never met a woman who knew how to turn off a light', and how irrationally and irresponsibly emotional 'chick[s]' or 'pair[s] of boobs' behave. Shane consciously employs this exaggerated hypermasculinity to cheer up Rick, but this sexism foreshadows Shane's aggressive survivalist masculinity. Rick, meanwhile, confesses his marital troubles and describes his wife's behaviour as abusive: 'the difference between men and women?! I would never say something that cruel to her.'

This exchange raises the question of the significance of gender roles in the show. After all, the technological ineptitude or emotional cruelty that Shane and Rick respectively diagnose in women might actually be advantageous in a zombie apocalypse. However, the series instead imagines male characters as 'naturally' capable of survival. Ashley Barkman relied on the show to confirm her essentialist understanding of gender: 'where survival is only of the fittest, the necessary qualities of a leader comes to entail masculine traits that are generally lacking in their female counterparts' (2012: 102). In a much more helpful argument, Pye and O'Sullivan argued that, within the zombie apocalypse, gender roles become 'cultural baggage' that should be left behind (2012: 117). Similarly, many viewers refused to believe that *all* men would be better at survival than *all* women, or that characters of colour would have a lesser chance of survival than white characters. '*The Walking Dead* most definitely has race and gender issues. It's ugly, and it's obvious, and it's mostly just stupid' (Burton 2012). The franchise observed such criticism and in its later seasons and instalments introduced survivors and even leaders who were not white and cis-male. Such responsiveness to the audience is an indicator of serialised popular culture's feedback loops, although the show's author figures avoided acknowledging any racial or gender bias on their part. Instead, their frequent stance was that female characters were established on a survivalist learning curve. *TWD* initially presented female characters as 'bad at survival', but eventually adjusted its sexist gender roles by including characters that were capable female survivors.

This chapter proposes the palimpsest as a model for exploring how traces of the comic book influence the show's gendering. As a metaphor, the palimpsest is part of the repertoire of literary and cultural theory of the late twentieth and early twenty-first centuries. Derived from the Greek words 'pálin' (again, back) as well as 'psēstos' (to scrape clean, scratch off), the palimpsest refers to a reprocessed page. Palaeography employs the term for the historical practice of scraping writing off parchment for reuse. Yet earlier inscriptions cannot be entirely cleaned off, and leave traces. Their fragments remain visible in the new texts written on that parchment.[1] Due to this persistence of what is meant to be erased, postcolonial theory found the palimpsest to be a significant symbol for colonial processes of appropriation, overwriting, and superimposition of meanings. The palimpsest therefore tells dual stories, and it is this duality that allows the palimpsest to describe current forms of storytelling/gendering while tracing how they are enabled and influenced by what has been erased – the previous storytelling/gendering of the comic or other instalments of the franchise.

This concept of palimpsest gendering evokes Frank Kelleter and Kathleen Loock's notion of remaking as 'second-order serialization' (2017). For Kelleter and Loock, Hollywood remakes never entirely erase or override the prior film, but consciously reference the earlier film(s) as a kind of 'self-reflexive historicity' (2017: 126–7). Just as references between different films allow Kelleter and Loock to understand remaking as serialisation, 'conversations' between the comic and television show are relevant to their interrelated storytelling. Enabled by paratext seriality, the gendering of characters follows processes of palimpsestic reinscription. Not all of these processes of overwriting are envisioned by the show's production. Often traces of the comic remain even if the show does not intend viewers to perceive characters in this way. Just as paratext seriality develops strong authorial presences that viewers hold accountable, it also allows viewers to hold the show's gendered performances accountable to the comic.

In the following, I first turn to those television characters that are fan favourites, before proceeding to disliked characters. I read the television characters that are consistent with (Michonne, Lori) and diverge from (Carol, Andrea) the comic's characterisation, as well as an 'original' creation without comic book precedent (Daryl). Viewer responses derive from my observations (from 2012 to 2017) of the show's official Facebook page, the *Walking Dead Forums* (www.walkingdeadforums.com), Reddit's *The Walking Dead* subpage, and *The Walking Dead Wiki*.

BELOVED SURVIVORS: GENDERED AND RACIALISED 'STRENGTH'

In the cliffhanger of the second season's finale, a hooded figure flanked by two jawless zombies on a leash (Figure 8.1) emerges to save another female character from the undead through expert slashes of her katana. Even if non-comic book readers had missed the social media rumble and Chris Hardwick's gushing on *Talking Dead*, this scene itself signalled that someone important had entered the show. Played by Danai Gurira, Michonne stands in stark contrast to the other, mostly white female members of the survivor collective in the comic and the show. Her introduction is emblematic of the character's role as the first woman in the franchise not to depend on male protection, leadership, and decision-making. Michonne is the longest-surviving person of colour in the different *Walking Dead* instalments. She signals a welcome departure from a gendered inheritance of the zombie narrative: a model of helpless white femininity established by the catatonic Barbra of *Night of the Living Dead* (1968). Unlike Barbra or the female characters of *TWD*, Michonne enters the narrative 'already made': she does not undergo a *Bildungsprozess* of learning to fight and kill. These narrative ellipses of her early days as a survivor allowed Michonne to appear as a more empowered femininity – while also relying on a one-sided depiction of (racialised) strength and resilience.

In many ways, Michonne is a successor to the white 'warrior women' or 'female action heroes' of popular culture at the turn of the twenty-first century. Xena (*Xena: Warrior Princess*, NBC, 1995–2001), Buffy (*Buffy the Vampire Slayer*, The WB/UPN, 1997–2003), and Sydney Bristow (*Alias*, ABC, 2001–6) appeared to incorporate strength at the expense of further characterisation. Michonne's strength is racialised: her apparently innate survival drive and ability to cope with traumatic situations (such as the horrific rape I discussed in Chapter 7) evoke the racist 'controlling image' of the 'strong black woman' (Collins 2000: 76–106). Patricia Hill Collins explains that

> images of Black femininity reinforce notions of an inappropriate, female strength. Whether working-class 'bitches' who are not appropriately submissive, bad mothers who raise children without men, or 'educated bitches' who act like men, this Black female strength is depicted and then stigmatized. (Collins 2005: 179)

178 TELEVISION AUTHORSHIP

Figure 8.1 Michonne equipped with her katana and zombie escorts/pets in the comic book and television show.

Tamara Winfrey Harris describes how such images of strength affect African American women and become a threat to their well-being: 'It is easy to forget that people who are strong need support and relief. It is sometimes depressingly hard for even black women to remember that they are not, indeed, superwomen' (2015: 92). Whereas *Murder* employs controlling images of black femininity as starting points from which its protagonist Annalise proceeds and which its viewers negotiate through spiral gendering (see Chapter 5), *TWD* does not consciously evoke racialised imagery. Rather, as a form of palimpsest gendering, it shimmers through and affects Michonne's characterisation in unacknowledged ways that have been frustrating for viewers.

The iconic visual of Michonne with her leashed 'pet' zombies is one of the most reproduced images in *TWD*'s merchandising. The two zombified escorts serve to disguise her human scent and keep the undead from attacking her. Like another black female zombie-apocalypse survivor, Sugar of the film *Sugar Hill* (1974), who calls on voodoo zombies to aid her quest for revenge, Michonne mastered what is threatening to others, zombies. Robin Means Coleman argues that as protagonists of horror, black women face a 'battle [that] is often much closer to home' (2014: 170): they struggle to survive continued racism and sexism as much as the supernatural threats of the genre. As Michonne's racialised rape-revenge plot in the comic demonstrates, in these stories white cis-men pose a much larger danger for women of colour than zombies do. In general, the crossmedia characterisation of Michonne carries specific racialised meanings that the franchise is hesitant to acknowledge. For example, not solely a protective measure, her zombie escorts are also a bizarre form of 'emotional baggage': they are the revived bodies of two black men, Michonne's former boyfriend and a friend. *Salon*'s Lorraine Berry connected this barely addressed aspect to the racist stereotype of black femininity as a harmful, 'castrating' presence in the lives of African American men (2012).

TWD aims not to differentiate between its characterisations of black woman Michonne and white man Daryl as 'strong, silent types' who struggle with their need for community in the face of the trauma they have endured. Through characterisation, the show takes its place in a group of 'colourblind television' shows that Sarah Nilsen and Sarah E. Turner outline (2014). 'Colourblind' or 'post-racial' characterisations ignore the impact of intersecting race and gender. These intersections resurface as palimpsestic echoes that the show often appears to understand only retrospectively (as in the rape-revenge controversy). For example, after Michonne expertly slaughters a large group of zombies, she smiles and exhales in satisfaction. This prompts another character to ask her if she 'get[s] off on that!?' (3.5 'Say The Word'). Whereas this portrayal might provide a quick laugh when applied to a white male character, framing the fighting of a woman of colour as sexualised recalls racist imagery and controlling images of the hypersexual black woman. For instance, Michonne's use of the katana requires close combat, which lends itself to the equation of fighting with sexuality, while white female characters typically protect themselves from a distance with guns. Even if the palimpsest gendering of Michonne's strong femininity aimed to overwrite racialised and racist tropes like the 'strong black woman' or 'the magical negro', these images nevertheless surface in viewer responses and thus have to be managed by subsequent instalments.[2]

To break with Michonne's characterisation as solely a 'strong black woman', the franchise presented glimpses of Michonne's past life and the painful memories she represses. In the episode 'After' (4.9), a flashback (revealed to be a dream) shows a different version of Michonne: instead of her leather pants, combat boots, and katana, Michonne wears a flowing skirt, make-up, and an elaborate hairdo. To emphasise this feminine, upbeat appearance, she prepares food while laughing with her partner and cuddling her child. The comic includes scenes in which Michonne talks to herself for comfort, revealing her to be more than a stoic bastion of strength. Furthermore, a special issue developed a similarly contrasting pre-apocalypse femininity: in high heels and an office suit, lawyer Michonne runs past zombies in a futile search for her family – and finds her signature weapon, the katana, instead.[3] Because both the comic and the show tend to avoid flashbacks, such attempts to ground a character primarily understood through her physical strength are unusual. As palimpsestic forms of overwriting the 'strong black woman', these explorations of Michonne's past provide fragments of her emotional struggles.

Palimpsestic reinscription potentially allows the show to create a 'better version' of the comic's characters, as can be seen in the figure of Carol (Melissa McBride). In both show and comic, the character is a domestic assault survivor whose husband dies early on in the zombie apocalypse. Whereas the loss traumatises comic book Carol, who seeks new romantic relationships and the security and comfort they offer her, the show's Carol discovers new autonomy. In the comic, Carol is a normatively attractive, slim woman with long, blond hair. She embraces the gendered leadership structure and fulfils the menial tasks the group assigns her. Rather than learning how to defend herself, Carol expresses an interest in needlework, crafting, and books, and during their shared domestic work becomes the confidante of Rick's wife, Lori. When her partner Tyreese leaves her, Carol has an emotional breakdown and pursues different community members. These romantic and sexual advances are foremost represented as consequences of trauma and not indicators of her sexual desire: Carol proposes a polyamorous relationship with Rick and Lori, which the shocked couple declines as inappropriate. Rick and Lori's insistence on monogamy in a setting dominated by displacement, death, and insecurity never appears to require justification. Instead, Carol's proposal is reframed not as an example of her desire for bisexual, alternative romantic structures, but as an embodiment of her desperation. This understanding is affirmed when

Carol proceeds to pursue another 'inappropriate' romance: she seduces the teenager Billy and then takes her own life.

Carol's method of suicide – she offers her body to a female zombie who resembles Lori – as well as her last words, 'Oh good. You do like me' (#41), allow for a queer reading in which her proposal was a genuine expression of interest in a polyamorous relationship with Lori and Rick. The affirmation Carol finds in the zombie's feeding on her appeared absurd within the comic's survivalist setting – of course, the zombie will devour her! – but gains significance when reading her as a queer character who through this choice of death realises the possibility of physical consumption with another female body, albeit a consumption that ultimately destroys Carol. The willingness to conform to her group's expectations and the prioritisation of romantic connections (even over her daughter Sophia) made the character an example of a 'weak', frustrating femininity.

Television Carol is older than her comic book counterpart: the quiet, middle-aged woman with short, grey hair rarely stands out among the other group members. Her marriage to the abusive Ed was 'uncomfortable' to watch because Carol appears 'desperate to hang on to Ed despite the fact that he mistreats her' (Stieger 2011: 112). After Ed's death, Carol is simultaneously relieved and in mourning, demonstrating the complicated dynamics of their relationship. At first Carol relies on the other men of the group for protection, but from the third season on, Carol shoots guns, uses knives, and develops an autonomous, no-nonsense approach to survival. Without any scenes of training, Carol evolves into the longest-surviving female character on the show. In the fifth season, Carol singlehandedly brings down the cannibal community Terminus and saves her entire group from certain death. Whereas Michonne is an example of continued characterisation from the comic, Carol's popularity with viewers stems from her radical departure from the comic counterpart's investments in docile gender roles.

The next fan favourite is an 'original creation' for the show without precedent in the comic. Hence, the palimpsest serves a different purpose in my readings of Daryl Dixon (Norman Reedus): Daryl is often given relationships, plots, or conversations which the comic attributes to other characters. By doing so, he is contrasted with these characters and their televisual counterparts. As Rick's closest confidant, Daryl is involved in plots that in the comic are occupied by characters like Tyreese, Abraham, or Michonne. Jeffrey Sartain finds the change from black man Tyreese as Rick's right hand to 'hillbilly' and 'racist' Daryl problematic (2013: 262). Whereas the show carefully distinguishes Daryl from his racist neo-Nazi brother Merle, such changes limit the impact of television's Tyreese. Also, since in the comic Michonne is Rick's most trusted ally, the show struggled to find an equal space for her with the addition of Daryl in this position. From its sixth season onward, Michonne and Rick become a couple. Whereas the show imagines nuanced forms of white homosocial friendship, it reduces this interracial and differently gendered relationship to a romantic bond that continues to sexualise Michonne's survival.

Initially a minor character, Daryl's entrance established him as a tight-lipped, stand-offish man through his appearance. In 'Tell It to the Frogs' (1.3), Daryl steps out of the woods carrying his signature weapon, the crossbow. The leather cut-off he wears emphasises his muscular arms but is adorned with a patch of angel wings instead of biker gang paraphernalia, suggesting a romantic hero rather than a tough biker. A survivor of child abuse, Daryl was raised by his alcoholic father and older brother Merle in rural Georgia and is somewhat prepared for the zombie apocalypse by virtue of his wilderness skills. Joining the group of survivors with his aggressive brother, Daryl struggles to connect emotionally and only develops trust in his substitute brother Rick after Merle is separated from the group.

From the second season onward, Daryl is presented as the group's muscle – alongside Michonne. These characters perform the most elaborate fight scenes and willingly take risks for the group. Even though they are Rick's confidant(e)s, Daryl and Michonne rarely question Rick's decision-making or offer their own perspectives. Instead, they demonstrate their willingness to do what Rick considers best for the group. For example, in the episode 'Judge, Jury, Executioner' (2.11), Daryl puts aside his moral objections to torture a captive for information. Many viewers objected to the ways in which white man Rick strategically employs the fighting skills of black woman Michonne. Meanwhile, viewers have overall been less critical of Daryl's characterisation as Rick's muscle, perhaps because Daryl and Rick are presented as equals, enacted, for instance, through their shared term of endearment for one another: 'brother'.

Moreover, Daryl's gendering is less impacted by palimpsestic reinscriptions because there is no comic book precedent, but also more importantly because he is one of many white cis-male survivors. Repeatedly, Daryl is placed in opposition with other men to highlight his being 'so much more' than a biker survivalist. Such scenes mobilise palimpsestic viewing positions, but instead of contrasting televisual and comic versions of characters, they ask for an intratextual comparison of masculinities. Daryl can be understood as what Amanda Lotz calls 'reconstructed masculinity', which is positioned as a more appropriate, possibly 'feminist' alternative to the 'patriarchal masculinities' it contests (2014: 34–42; see Chapter 2). Each season, the show establishes different versions of 'patriarchal masculinities' to juxtapose Daryl with: in the second season, Daryl competes with ruthless Shane for the position as leader Rick's confidant. In the third season, Daryl is reunited with his brother Merle who, like Shane, stands for a more cut-throat, Machiavellian lifestyle. In the fourth season, Daryl encounters an all-male gang of brutal pillagers. 'When men like us . . . cooperate a little bit', their leader Joe tells Daryl, 'the world becomes ours' (4.15 'Us'). Daryl appears to fit right in with the group, which bristles with leather and heavy weaponry. Joe especially looks like an older version of him, thereby suggesting who Daryl might have become without the 'humanising' influences of his survivor family. Through such contrasts, Daryl's violence is redeemed as a means by which he exhibits care, loyalty, and love for his collective and thus as much more than a struggle for power or resources. Whereas this form of reconstructed masculinity legitimises the 'strong white man' Daryl as a caring presence, Michonne's comparison with other (white) women renders the character's strength visible and enables the problematic equation with the 'strong black woman' trope.

Alternatively, the palimpsest of Daryl reaches beyond the screen: the character is impossible to separate from the large fandom surrounding the actor portraying him, Norman Reedus. Reedus easily inhabits a fannish persona that his past roles lend credibility to; for example, as one of the vigilante brothers in the 'cult' film *The Boondock Saints* (1999). He successfully employs social media to interact with his fans and maintains the show's most active Twitter account, where the number of his followers surpasses that of all other individuals associated with the franchise. With Reedus's personal Twitter account serving as a significant promotional paratext, Daryl might give the show a runaround in being possibly the only character who is unlikely to be killed off. To counter the franchise's claim that 'No one is safe', Daryl fans have long made clear that 'If Daryl dies, we riot.'

Despite the way that Reedus is sexualised by many of his devoted fans, Daryl has never expressed sexual desire or pursued romantic relationships throughout ten seasons of the show. Some viewers expressed their understanding of the character as a gay man who could potentially take over the plots of prominent gay characters in the comic. Daryl's close friendships with Beth and Carol in season five led different camps of viewers to announce a '[relation] shipping war' between the proponents of two potential romantic couplings: 'Caryl' versus 'Bethyl'. Such viewer practices affirmed the character's heterosexual desirability against queer readings of Daryl as a 'closeted' gay man. The most obvious reading of Daryl as an asexual man, who aspires toward emotional connections without sexual relationships, has not been pursued so far by either viewers or author figures. By combining asexuality with a successful, preferred masculinity, the show could extend Daryl's masculinity toward a disentanglement of physical ability from heteronormative sexual conquest. However, for the most part Daryl's asexuality has been implied to be the traumatic consequence of childhood abuse. As with comic book Carol's 'shocking' interest in polyamorous relationships, the franchise again relegates all relationship forms and sexual orientations that do not result in stable monosexual couplings to the status of mental deviance. Even though – or rather because – asexual Daryl is uninterested in heteronormative romance, biological reproduction, and the establishment of a nuclear family, he develops alternative bonds with the children in the survival collective. Like Carol, Daryl treats children as equals with the same rights and responsibilities as other members of their group. Thus, the show contrasts surrogate parent figures like Carol and Daryl with biological parents, foremost biological mothers, who are unwilling to adjust pre-apocalypse notions of childhood and nuclear families, as the following discussion of Lori will illustrate.

The depiction of Daryl in the opening episode of the fourth season ironically comments on his popularity. In two different instances in one episode (4.1 '30 Days Without an Accident'), white cis-male teenagers exhibit an almost fannish infatuation with 'survival expert' Daryl, which irritates and embarrasses him (Figure 8.2). Through such scenes, the show comments on the absurdity of a superhero-like character like Daryl – or Michonne and Carol – in a franchise that insists on everyone's expendability. Further, white male fandom becomes a source of humour, especially since these teenage fans do not stand a chance and die soon after. Those scenes also highlight the social awkwardness and emotional insecurity of strong characters like Michonne, Daryl, and to a lesser extent Carol. All of the fan favourites mastered the blank, calm expression of the 'poker face' as a response to the various challenges of the zombie apocalypse. Even though the characters prize the well-being of their chosen families over their own security, they rarely express emotions. Michonne 'apparently has a face set on scowl' (Burton 2012), and similar observations can be made about Daryl and Carol as well. As the above example illustrates, viewers enjoy humorous scenes in which the characters' emotional reserve and social awkwardness are 'used against them', meaning scenes in which these survival experts are overwhelmed by social interactions, displays of emotion, or social rituals.

Carol, however, knowingly plays with the stereotypes of middle-aged femininity as seemingly incompatible with strength. Repeatedly, she puts on an act of harmless, naïve femininity when she encounters strangers. For example, in the show's fifth season, Carol is interviewed by Alexandria's community leader Deanna and cultivates the cheerful, unpractical housewife image:

> Carol: I did laundry, gardened, always had dinner on the table for Ed when he came home. I miss that stupid, wonderful man every day. You know, I really didn't have much to offer this group, so I think I just sort of became their den mother. And they've been nice enough to protect me.
> Deanna: Where do you think you'll fit in?
> Carol: Oh, um, hmm. Well, I'd like to be involved in the community. Do you have anything like a Junior League? I'm a real people person. (5.12 'Remember')

Figure 8.2 The brief appearance of Daryl's 'fanboys' Patrick and Zack in the fourth season amuses Carol and allowed the show to reflect on the idealisation of its most popular character.

For the audience the description of Carol's abusive husband Ed as a 'wonderful man' whom she misses was a clear indicator of how much of a performance the hardened survivor puts on in this dialogue. Carol is able to conspire against Alexandria's leadership because they underestimate her as an invisible 'old woman' (5.13 'Forget'). Carol demonstrates her ability to 'read' others and utilise their prejudices against her. Those reoccurring scenes allow both the show and viewers to pat themselves on the back for not underestimating 'older femininity' and being willing to look past such stereotypes to recognise Carol's competence.

What differentiates Daryl from Michonne (and, at first sight, Carol) is how his survival expertise is not a new habitus he is forced to adopt in the zombie apocalypse but has been part of his lifestyle for a long time, due to his lower-class background, lack of parental support, and necessary self-reliance. The other characters (and viewers) realise this when the group reaches the secluded, gated community Alexandria in the fifth season. There, Daryl is the only character who is not glad to be 'back in civilisation', to 'play house', but behaves as an antisocial loner incapable of opening up to strangers. Whereas the other characters' post-apocalypse gear is a matter of necessity rather than preference (even Michonne dons a dress in Alexandria), it constitutes Daryl's identity. Unlike Michonne, who had been a successful lawyer before the apocalypse, the show implies that Daryl's survival lifestyle has not considerably changed. Meanwhile, housewife and mother Carol has to learn to survive in the zombie apocalypse, but the remarkable self-reliance and resilience she exhibits stem from her past as a survivor of domestic violence. In episode 4.4 ('Indifference'), Rick is surprised to learn that Carol taught herself to relocate her own shoulder to cover up her husband's abuse. Carol's character echoes and shifts understandings of domestic assault survivors as weak and helpless victims unable to respond to their spouses' ongoing abuse. As a domestic assault survivor Carol shares a particular bond with Daryl. Such portrayals imagine the survivor of domestic and sexualised assault (also Michonne in the comic) as uniquely suited to the horrors of the zombie apocalypse.

In a franchise in which characters are under constant threat of being killed, Michonne, Daryl, and Carol serve as 'easy emotional investments' for viewers due to their extraordinary survival skills. In rooting for such fan favourites, viewers are less at risk of 'having their hearts broken', because these characters are less likely to die. Yet, the depiction of 'strong characters' runs the risk of relying on their one-sided strength at the expense of other features. Whereas white man Daryl's emotional investments in his survivor family are highlighted through the contrast with 'patriarchal masculinities', and white woman Carol knowingly plays with stereotypes of 'older femininity', *TWD* proved to be surprisingly tone deaf to the racialised implications of 'strong black woman' Michonne.

DIFFICULT WOMEN: ANTAGONISTIC TELEVISION WIVES AND INCOMPETENT WARRIORS

Despite the presence of horrific white cis-male villains like the Governor and Negan, the franchise's most disliked characters have been white women who were not *intended* to cause such negative emotions. Viewers were frustrated by these characters' poor romantic choices, their dependence on men for protection and decision-making, and their overall inability to adapt to the zombie apocalypse. As my reading will illustrate by means of the palimpsest, viewer responses were often brought about by too little characterisation (Lori) or characterisation inconsistent with the comic (Andrea).

At the San Diego Comic-Con in 2010, actress Sarah Wayne Callies introduced the character she plays as 'Rick's wife and Carl's mom. And those are probably the two most significant things that she would say about herself.' Like Callies, the show struggled to come up with anything else for Lori. Neither the comic nor the show imagines any other aspirations or attributes that go beyond Lori's relationships with male characters: as Rick's wife, Carl's mother, and Shane's lover. Five years after her demise in the third season, lists of the 'worst characters' of the show still include Lori. Many viewers took issue with the survivor collective's gendered division of labour and leadership: 'some of the worst gender dynamics in today's world are replicated in the ones with murderous zombies' (Stieger 2011: 105–6). Whereas some female characters are frustrated, Lori accepts the new status quo and her unique position in the group as the romantic interest of its respective leaders Shane and later Rick.[4] It is unclear how much of a change these gender roles pose for Lori because the show never addresses her past education or professional experiences.

Because Lori is reductively characterised through her primary roles as mother and wife, her 'failure' to successfully inhabit those roles is one of the reasons that 'worst character' lists feature her. Often Lori appears too preoccupied to engage with her young son Carl, who consequently wanders off into dangerous zombie encounters. Lori's neglectful parenting involves not only her inability to watch her son but also what was perceived as her misgivings about his growing up in the zombie apocalypse. In both the comic and the show, Lori clashes with Rick over their different parenting styles. Whereas Rick wants Carl to learn how to shoot a gun, Lori insists on a pre-apocalypse understanding of childhood: 'He's SEVEN YEARS OLD for Christ's sake! This is NOT a good idea' (comic #5). In the show, Lori expresses, 'I'm not comfortable with it. Oh, don't make me out to be the unreasonable one here. . . . I don't want my kid walking around with a gun. . . . It feels wrong' (2.6 'Secrets'). To the other characters (as well as the viewers and readers), Lori's appeal to her emotions as a basis for her argument indeed results in her appearing 'unreasonable', especially since she relies on the group to protect her and her son.

Through mother Lori, both comic and show raise the theme of parenting in the zombie apocalypse. This theme centres around the question of whether parents should shelter children or teach them to fend for themselves, an undertaking fraught with morally ambiguous consequences. In its different instalments, child survivors take the form of either helpless, 'innocent' embodiments of childhood (Sophia in both the show and comic) or capable but psychotic 'child killers' (the comic's Ben, the show's Lizzie). The franchise's central child character, Carl, oscillates between these poles. The clash between his parents, Rick and Lori, thus not only signals their different parenting styles, but also outlines different possibilities for the kind of person Carl could grow up to be in the storyworld of *TWD*. For the gendering of his mother, Lori, the parenting conflict contributes to the character's apparent inability to comprehend – and respond to – her changed surroundings. Just as her difficulty with shooting weapons endangers her own survival, her unwillingness to let Carl learn such skills becomes a risk for the survival of her child. The theme of parenting thus juxtaposes an ignorant, neglectful biological motherhood (Lori) with a more pragmatic, 'realistic' biological fatherhood (Rick), as well as a similarly practical substitute motherhood (Carol, comic book Andrea).

Moreover, because Lori pursues a romantic relationship with Rick's friend Shane after she assumes Rick has died, some viewers see her as failing in her second role of wife. The first two seasons and first fifteen comic issues position

Lori so as to contrast the two different masculinities of her husband Rick and lover Shane. She amounts to a prize for which both men compete, just as they also compete for the leadership of their group of survivors and the role of being a father figure for Carl. Because Lori rebuffs Shane's advances once she learns of Rick's survival, some viewers were willing to 'forgive' her marital infidelity. Overall, Lori's behaviour privileges the nuclear Grimes family as dominant over the chosen family of the survivors in the franchise's early instalments. Her choice of Rick over Shane is justified by the show presenting Rick – just like his 'chosen brother' Daryl – as a 'reconstructed masculinity' in contrast with Shane's 'patriarchal masculinity'. For example, Rick accepts Lori's pregnancy and infant Judith as his own, despite Shane's biological fatherhood, as an illustration of his benign influence. Meanwhile, Shane aggressively tries to 'win' Lori back, going as far as physically assaulting her (1.6 'TS-19'). Whereas the love triangle serves as a productive means of characterisation for male characters, for Lori it manifests her ineptness as a romantic partner as well as her reduction to a 'trophy wife'.

Several recappers likened Lori to Lady Macbeth (Rodriguez 2013; Barry 2012) because Lori persuades her husband to murder Shane to stabilise her position within the group. However, when Rick follows through on the murder Lori suggests, she responds with shock, grief, and anger at Shane's death. Lady Macbeth finds herself unable to cope with guilt over her power-hungry manipulations, yet Lori's behaviour again is instead framed as either emotionally inconsistent, irrational, or the result of erratic plotting at the expense of a little-formed character.

In the parenting conflict and Lori's 'Lady Macbeth' plot, viewers were aligned with Rick's position and wondered about Lori's motivations. This constellation of viewer alignment with husbands in heterosexual marital conflicts at the expense of their wives has been well established by other prominent serialised television dramas. As is the case with 'unpopular' Lori, the privileging of male perspectives in the respective storyworlds likewise translated into viewers expressing hostility and frustration with female characters. The perspectives of television wives like *Breaking Bad*'s Skyler White (AMC, 2008–13), *Sons of Anarchy*'s Tara Knowles, *Dexter*'s Rita Morgan (Showtime, 2006–13), and *Boardwalk Empire*'s Margaret Thompson (HBO, 2009–14) tend to be similarly obscured in their marital struggles when their spouses serve as protagonists, more prominent characters, or narrative centres of the shows. For *Breaking Bad*, Jason Mittell argues that even though viewers are so familiar with protagonist Walter's perspective, his wife Skyler's alternative 'story is there, creeping toward the narrative center as the series progresses' (2015: 257). Mittell's argument can be extended to the other examples: by their mere presence, these television wives reframe the ethically questionable, yet very entertaining behaviour of the shows' antihero protagonists as abusive, cruel, and narcissistic. Viewers perceive these female characters as antagonistic because they disturb the characterisation of their husbands and even the narrative focus of those shows.

The white antagonistic television wife turns grandiose stories of drug cartels, biker gangs, serial killers, or prohibition-era crime and politics into smaller-scale narratives of the various power struggles, neglect, abuse, miscommunication, boredom, and dissatisfaction women may experience in heterosexual marriages and shows how they often lack the tools to adequately cope due to various forms of societal sexism or classism. These wives are antagonistic not because they are classical villains but because they disrupt the anti-hero protagonist's story. Hence, it is unsurprising that viewers respond by attempting to push back against the way these characters reframe the narratives. Within toxic fan cultures, practices of pushing back may involve targeting the actresses who portray these characters. After playing Tara on *Sons of Anarchy*, Maggie Siff described her shock at viewer responses: 'the amount of vehemence or anger or righteousness that people can feel when they say, "She should be shot. She should be killed." That's most startling and disturbing, when you really sit down and think about it' (qtd in Ross 2013). The producers and writers of all of these shows sought to counter misogynistic fan responses by positioning such hostility as mere 'misreadings', yet those readings can be grounded in the narrative structures, which privilege male perspectives and render female views disruptive. For viewers accustomed to the antagonistic television wife from other shows, Lori serves as a palimpsestic echo of these figures. It is remarkable, and indebted to the franchise's elaborate authorship performances, that many viewers took authorial defences of Lori to be an illustration not of their own misreading, but of failure on the part of the show's storytellers.

Whereas Lori's reduced characterisation on the show was in line with her comic version, another contestant for the show's 'worst character' caused frustrations due to her blatant divergence. The introduction of Andrea (Laurie Holden) initially appeared to conform to the comic's depiction of the 'badass' sharpshooter. In a deserted Atlanta shopping mall, Rick encounters members of his future survival collective, among them a blond woman who aggressively shoves a gun in his face. Later Rick condescendingly reveals to Andrea (and the audience) how unthreatening she was to him: 'little red dot means it's ready to fire. You may have occasion to use it' (1.2 'Guts'). Rick's snide comment reverses the image of a capable woman that Andrea's initial appearance seemed to establish and contrasts Rick's suitability for post-apocalypse survival with her inexperience. This somewhat stereotypical gendering is furthered when the two characters search the department store for survival gear and Rick asks Andrea if she has found something she 'likes'. The scene intertextually references the mall setting of *Dawn of the Dead* (1978, 2004): while Andrea and Rick scan the goods inside the store, zombies claw at the glass windows and hungrily stare at the human characters on display. The scene employs the theme of consumerism to establish its gender politics, rather than the surface critique of capitalism that director George A. Romero's films became known for. Reminiscent of a male breadwinner 'treating' a female partner to a shopping trip, Rick encourages (or: 'allows') Andrea to take a necklace. Their exchange signals the shift from their previous positioning: Rick only recently woke from a coma, and seemed out of touch with the realities of survival – for instance, by riding a horse directly into zombie-infested Atlanta. It is nonetheless he who tells Andrea that the breakdown of society renders her 'looting' of the necklace insignificant. The scene highlights Rick's growing awareness of what it takes to survive but does so by contrasting his character with Andrea's inadequacy.

The necklace Andrea takes resurfaces in what amounts to the scene most often analysed in scholarship: the first scene to depict the transition of a human into a zombie. But what remains rarely acknowledged is that the scene also makes Andrea the first female character to kill a zombie.[5] In 'Wildfire' (1.5), the survivor camp recovers from a zombie attack. Among its casualties is Andrea's sister Amy (Emma Bell). Even though the group members (and viewers) worry that Amy may revive as a zombie any minute, Andrea fights them away from her sister's body to say her goodbyes. Lovingly, Andrea places the necklace around Amy's neck, and calmly glances into the zombie's eyes as if to search for remaining signs of her humanity, before she delivers a headshot. This emotional scene benefits from the specific affordances of serial televisual horror (Jowett and Abbott 2013: 32) and extends the comic's version – which only dedicates two panels to it – to establish 'the melodramatic payoff fans expect from *The Walking Dead* in whatever medium' (Jenkins 2013: 377). It is highly relevant that the show presents such a crucial, emotional journey not only as one woman's survival struggle, but as a universal experience of loss and pain rarely explored through the eyes of female characters in popular culture.

The audience was taken with Andrea after the first season. After all, in the comic, Andrea evolves to become the group's best sharpshooter. In the process, she embodies the old superhero paradigm that any (white cis-)'man' has the potential to greatness in 'him', that is, to become a superhero if the circumstances call for it. Even though Andrea also carries out more traditionally female tasks – she is the group's best seamstress – she insists on her flawless markswomanship: 'Hold on, Rick, I should be on the other side of this fence with you guys. I'm the best shot in the group, in case you've forgotten' (#13). The other characters agree with her self-assessment, and Andrea's contributions are the deciding factor for their victories in various battles. The show appeared to envision a similar path, yet in the second and third seasons shifted Andrea's characterisation. Increasingly, Andrea was considered not to have lived up to the potential of her comic book equivalent. In the 'Letter Hacks', a disappointed viewer laments: 'she went from favorite character in the book to least favorite in the TV show' (#93). Such responses indicate how the comic's Andrea became her television equivalent's 'downfall', because her characterisation affected the show in palimpsestic gendering.

In the second season, Andrea is physically transformed; she has replaced earrings and a delicate flower-patterned blouse with a leather waistcoat and combat boots – a more practical and militarised look. On the DVD bonus material, actor Holden maintained that the character evolved 'from being a scared woman who is not able to defend myself [sic] to being just a powerhouse warrior' (featurette 'She Will Fight'). However, subsequent scenes undermine such a characterisation. Because Andrea struggles with depression and contemplates suicide after Amy's death, the male characters restrict her access to firearms. Pye and O'Sullivan point out that the men take Andrea's gun away right after she learns that 'guns are where the true power lies' (2012: 113). Andrea's position within the hierarchy of the collective is compromised by her constantly having to prove that neither her gender nor her mental health should exclude her from putting her sharpshooting skills to best use. In 'Chupacabra' (2.5), Andrea mistakes Daryl for a zombie and shoots him. The scene is absurd as a group of men is already approaching the assumed zombie, and the group previously discussed their ammunition shortage. Her irrational behaviour is a marked instance of Andrea's deviation: it demonstrates her desire to prove herself through a flashy show of her abilities (whereas, in the comic, Andrea's excellence is enhanced by her calm confidence and understatement) – and her poor shooting skills because Daryl is not seriously injured (whereas comic book Andrea would likely have killed him). Just as the show (and comic) continually undermine Lori's conception of herself as a good mother, the show (in contrast to the comic) undermines Andrea's conception of herself as a great sharpshooter. Had the show not called Andrea's ability into question, her desire to prove herself competent despite her gender could have allowed the show to criticise the sexism of the survivor collective. Notably, her divergence from the group's gendered organisation is called out by Lori, the female character who most conforms to the collective's gender roles *and* who most benefits from its hierarchical structure. In a crucial scene, Lori questions Andrea:

> Andrea: I contribute. I help keep this place safe.
> Lori: The men can handle this on their own. They don't need your help.
> Andrea: I'm sorry. What would you have me do?
> Lori: Oh, there's plenty of work to go around.
> Andrea: Are you serious?! Everything falls apart, you're in my face over skipping laundry?! . . .
> Lori: We are providing stability. We are trying to create a life worth living. (2.10 '18 Miles Out')

This dialogue seeks to contrast the two different female characters via their survival lifestyles. It is fitting that their conversation takes place in the kitchen of the farm, where the group found refuge, and while Lori is occupied with domestic tasks. The kitchen is her 'natural habitat', the scene suggests, a place where she feels at ease. Meanwhile, Andrea remains in a fixed position and appears to be an intruder. In their conversation, Lori polices Andrea's divergence from the gendered division of labour their group established and criticises her 'selfishness' for opting out of the group's work of social reproduction. Andrea feels certain of her contribution as a protector rather than caregiver. Each woman is convinced that her role in the group is necessary and, in the process, downplays the other woman's contributions as insignificant. Had the show established Andrea's skills more clearly at this point, that is, given her more than merely 'the *appearance* of the strong, independent woman' (Burton 2012), viewers would have better comprehended the distinct female characters' positions. As such, the dialogue *seeks* to present these women as different, whereas to many viewers they both resemble an illogical femininity out of tune with the necessities of survival.

Another dominant source of frustration for many viewers was how Andrea's behaviour was impacted by her romantic relationships. A small group of viewers regarded Andrea (like Lori) as overly promiscuous because she engaged in more than one sexual relationship. Most viewers, however, did not find Andrea's acting on desire problematic in itself, but rather her choice of sexual partners and the way she prioritised romantic relationships over her survival collective or her friendship with Michonne. In the comic, Andrea has long-lasting romantic relationships in the form of durable partnerships among equals – first with Dale, and after his death, with Rick. By contrast, on the show, Andrea ignores warnings and naïvely trusts her partner, the villainous Governor. Indicating to many viewers her lack of self-awareness, Andrea does not question her lover's character, the scope of his cruelties, or his disregard for her. As the partner of the Governor, Andrea occupies a similar 'first lady' position as Lori in their initial survivor collective. Andrea now appears to crave 'a life worth living', thus, retrospectively, the show positions Andrea as having more in common with Lori than with her comic counterpart.

TWD did attempt to redeem these 'unpopular characters' through their deaths. Both women were awarded what the franchise considers 'good deaths'. They die exhibiting selflessness (Lori willingly dies from her caesarean section so that her child can live; injured Andrea commits suicide by headshot, so that her friends do not have to kill her as a revived zombie). They are mourned and 'remembered' within the narrative (through burial sites or Rick's hallucinations of Lori). However, these redemptive deaths perpetuate the characterisation that had resulted in the viewer rejections of Lori and Andrea in the first place. Even in her death scene, Andrea's survival skills appear disappointing within the frame established for her as possible – this time not only by the comic but by the show itself. Andrea dies after her former lover, the Governor, ties her to a chair and leaves a zombie to kill her. Nine episodes earlier, Glenn was put in the exact same situation and managed to kill the zombie with parts of the chair he was tied to. Andrea is unable to save herself in time. Just as Andrea's discordant characterisation continues in her death scene because she cannot live up to the potential of her comic counterpart, Lori, too, continues to be characterised reductively as solely a mother and wife. Amanda Rodriguez finds her death during childbirth 'punishment for her affair and for the continued implication that she's a bad mother' (2013). The circumstances of Lori's death (a caesarean performed with a pocketknife without anaesthetic) aspire to redeem the character through her extensive suffering (Figure 8.3). Her death confirms Lori's kinship with other antagonistic television wives who die in gruesome ways to further their husbands' narrative development (*Sons of Anarchy*'s Tara is stabbed in the head with a carving fork by her mother-in-law, and a serial killer preps the body of *Dexter*'s Rita for her husband to find).

To conclude, this chapter used the notion of palimpsest gendering, or palimpsestic reinscription, to describe how the gendering of *TWD*'s characters contains several layers. These layers should not be understood as a purposefully complex characterisation but rather – as the term 'palimpsest' suggests – as an at times unintended continuation of meanings from earlier episodes just as much as from other parts of the franchise. The palimpsest can capture how

Figure 8.3 Her selfless and gruesome death – a caesarean performed with a pocketknife – aspires to redeem the most disliked character Lori (3.4 'Killer Within').

the comic's storytelling reverberates in the show's storytelling and gendering, which paradoxically both draw on the comic and seek to overwrite it. In other words: any attempt of the television show to 'learn' from the controversies of the comic book, that is, to adjust overly traditional and sexist gender representations, can never be entirely successful. These adjustments always run the risk of not being convincing enough to overwrite previous characterisations, or of being revealed as overly strategically motivated. In the case of unpopular characters, palimpsestic echoes are not envisioned by the show's production but become a by-product of the show's paratextual relationship with the comic.

NOTES

1. The multifaceted nature of the palimpsest has attracted structuralist and poststructuralist thinkers such as Roland Barthes, Michel de Certeau, Jacques Derrida, and Gérard Genette, all of whom have relied upon it as an allegory in their thinking.
2. As an example of the later racist trope, feminist blogger Megan Kearns finds Michonne to resemble a 'magical negro' because she often serves as a black caretaker and protector for white characters (2013).
3. Michonne's backstory was first published in *Playboy* in April 2012 and not in the comic series. When letters expressed annoyance, Kirkman defended the publishing decision as expanding his readership (#97). This continues the gendering of the franchise's audience as primarily male and heterosexual, hence the appeal of *Playboy*, but also ensures a more prominent position for Michonne's backstory with regard to the viewers of the show.
4. In the comic, white woman Donna wonders, 'I just don't understand why we're the ones doing the laundry while they go off and hunt. When things get back to normal, I wonder if we'll still be allowed to vote' (#3). In the show, black woman Jacqui (Jeryl Prescott) adds a *Gone with the Wind* (1939) reference: 'can someone explain to me how the women wound up doing all the Hattie McDaniel work?' (1.3 'Tell It to the Frogs').
5. In the comic, Andrea is also the first woman to kill a zombie. This, however, is not her zombified sister, because Andrea shoots Amy's corpse before Amy revives (#5). Instead, many issues later, a panel depicts Andrea casually shooting a random zombie the group encounters (#12).

CHAPTER 9

Neoliberalising Discourses of Serialised Survivalism: You Make It . . . Until You Don't

In the two previous chapters, survival appeared as a crucial theme of *TWD*: be it the ill-advised behaviours of Lori or Andrea, the exuberant fighting skills that made Michonne, Daryl, and Carol fan favourites, or the 'power to kill' that distinguishes Robert Kirkman from other author figures. This chapter explores how thematic concerns of the show's storyworld translate into a larger discourse of serialised survival that involves neoliberal understandings of preparedness, success, and failure. Despite the franchise's insistence that 'no character is safe', it imagines that specific body politics, consumer practices, and forms of media knowledge promise better odds of survival. Survivalist fantasies almost exclusively take place in homosocial spaces and bring forth a strict masculine imagination. However, even though *TWD* does trade in such survivalist fantasies, its kind of survivalism, and physical–mental zombie workout treasures neoliberal ideas of individualised assertiveness and resilience for a wider audience. As a way to emphasise its televisual *and* serialised horror, *TWD* encourages viewer interaction through different survival scenarios with narrative repercussions not only in the television series itself but also in its paratextual extensions. Promotional quizzes explicitly ask viewers, 'How long would you survive?' and the show implicitly encourages viewers to see themselves as one or more of its characters by presenting characters as symbols for viewers' capacity to survive the zombie apocalypse. Even if viewers do not find their specific 'survival choices' or 'survival profile' represented within the show, countless other instalments allow them to discover how long they would be able to 'make it' in a storyworld in which 'no one is safe'.

TWD illustrated these themes from the beginning: in the first episode, black man Morgan and his son Duane are the first survivors Rick encounters after waking from a coma in an abandoned hospital. Naturally, Morgan instructs

Rick (and the audience) about the changed surroundings following the zombie outbreak. In Rick's deserted family home, they interpret missing photographs as evidence of Lori's escape: 'My wife. Same thing', Morgan muses. 'There I am packing survival gear, she's grabbing a photo album' (1.1 'Days Gone By'). Such comments set up the contrast between practical masculinities and femininities out of touch with the necessities of survival, which shaped the reception of Lori's character.[1] However, Morgan's later inability to shoot the zombie that used to be his wife shifts the character from a guiding presence to a contrast foil for Rick. While Rick swiftly shoots the horrifically decayed 'bicycle girl' zombie, Morgan can only helplessly watch his zombified wife (Figure 9.1).[2] The scenes reveal a staple of the zombie narrative: the willingness to accept – and act upon – the infection of a friend, family member, or ally as a litmus test for a character's eligibility for life in a zombie apocalypse. Again, white woman Barbra of *Night of the Living Dead* initiates the trope because she cannot comprehend the danger her zombified brother Johnny poses. Gender plays a huge role in this survivalism. Self-doubt and indecision may be – temporarily – tolerated in male characters such as Morgan, while such behaviour is almost always considered a 'survival failure' when exhibited by female characters.

When Rick re-encounters Morgan in the third season, the implications of Morgan's 'survival failure' have become tragically concrete: his zombified wife has killed his son Duane. Traumatised Morgan has withdrawn from all human contact and fashions himself as a fatalistic 'cleanser' who excessively kills zombies to atone for not saving his family. Rick protests Morgan's state of mind with a meta-commentary: 'We both started out in the same place. Things went bad for you. Things went bad for me. . . . This can't be it. It can't be. You gotta be able to come back from this' (3.12 'Clear'). By stating that both Rick and Morgan 'started out in the same place' three seasons ago, the show remembers its origins in a language reminiscent of gaming. In the narrative scenario of survivalism, everyone has the same shot at survival, and individual choices determine the outcome. The comment also alludes to the possibilities of future world-building: whereas *TWD*'s narrative followed Rick's survivor collective and the perverse multitude of 'things going bad' for these characters, multiple other narrative scenarios are also possible. Accordingly, the show and its extensions may (and do) explore 'things going wrong for other characters', such as Morgan or the protagonists of the prequel series *Fear the Walking Dead*.

Rick's refusal to accept that Morgan is beyond saving, 'You gotta be able to come back', rings hollow in light of some viewers' demand to 'bring back Beth', as discussed in Chapter 7. When Morgan does 'come back' in a later episode, he contemplates, 'Everything gets a return' (5.16 'Conquer'). Morgan's return is exceptional, because unlike other characters, he gets a 'second shot' and joins Rick's survivor collective. Viewer responses were overwhelmingly positive to

Figure 9.1 Screenshots from the first episode (1.1 'Days Gone By') illustrate the comparison between Rick, Morgan, and the female zombies they set out to kill.

the uncharacteristic 'reset' of the character. In his first *Talking Dead* appearance after the episode, actor Lennie James suspected that it was Morgan's inability to shoot his zombified wife which 'opened a door for certain fans' and allowed for a different kind of emotional engagement (4.16). Whereas the show and its viewers embraced emotional 'survival failure' on the part of a warrior figure like Morgan, they were unwilling to imagine 'weak' female characters like Beth (or Lori) in this manner.

ZOMBIE LITERACY VS ZOMBIE CONSUMERISM: THE CULTURAL PHENOMENON OF ZOMBIE PREPAREDNESS

The second and third seasons of *Talking Dead* featured a segment called 'Survival Tips' hosted by Matt Mogk of the popular website *Zombie Research Society* (zombierresearch.org). In the segment, Mogk addresses the audience with props on hand and advises how to assemble a 72-hour emergency kit, how to turn random objects into improvised weapons against zombies, and how to scavenge in deserted areas. Through such paratextual accompaniments, *TWD* participates in a cultural discourse of zombie survivalism as a tongue-in-cheek version of survival, which rewards fan practices of horror genre literacy, but also seeks to give the impression of actual 'didactic' disaster preparedness.

The *Zombie Research Society*'s Management Team and Advisory Board consists mostly of white male academics with film or media studies backgrounds or storytellers like the much proclaimed 'father' of the zombie narrative, director George Romero. Mogk himself has few wilderness or public health credentials but is the author of *That's Not Your Mommy Anymore* (2011) and *Everything You Ever Wanted to Know About Zombies* (2011). Mogk's work is representative of a group of zombie-themed guidebooks, such as Max Brooks's *The Zombie Survival Guide* (2003), John Austin's *So Now You're a Zombie* (2010), and Roger Ma's *The Zombie Combat Manual* (2010). These guidebooks essentially catalogue genre conventions; they are guidelines distilled from their authors' media literacy of zombie horror. Matt Hills finds one of horror's central appeals to be the connoisseurship which allows audiences to classify and enjoy texts on the basis of their knowledge of the genre and its production practices (2005: 115). The guidebooks are the result of those practices but also address readers as fellow horror fans who can appreciate their detailed catalogues of narrative conventions. Because he writes for less aware 'fans', the writer of a guidebook performs a similar authorship to that of showrunner Scott M. Gimple: he functions as connoisseur auteur (see Chapter 7). Not coincidentally, all of the author figures are white male horror enthusiasts, and non-cis-male survival issues that are not explored in zombie narratives are absent here as well (for example, how to improvise menstrual hygiene products during a zombie apocalypse).

One year after its facilities served as a shooting location for *TWD* (1.6 'TS-19'), the Georgia-based Centers for Disease Control launched a 'zombie preparedness' campaign. The CDC was one of many US-American governmental institutions, universities, and businesses that employed the zombie as an educational tool for emergency or public health management in 2011 and 2012 – and which had to specify that they did not expect a zombie apocalypse to happen. The campaigns are aesthetically similar to the survival guides and thus also had to clarify that they were employing the narrative scenarios of the zombie apocalypse as a metaphor to communicate disaster education-related 'facts' rather than entertainment. Whereas the success of these 'official campaigns' depended on the negotiation of the zombie's popularity with the 'serious topic' of preparedness, the franchise of *TWD* has benefitted from treating its survival theme as merely a pastime or harmless thought experiment, while also presenting genre-based media literacy as relevant survival knowledge. Such flexible positioning of survival surfaced in the open-access 'massive open online course' *Society, Science, Survival: Lessons from AMC's* The Walking Dead, offered by the University of California, Irvine, in cooperation with AMC in 2013. Taught by professors of public health, social sciences, physics, and mathematics, this interdisciplinary course introduced various approaches to survival – and also served as an entertaining tie-in to the show's fourth season. The course and Mogk's 'Survival Tips' enable the show to simultaneously appear as an actual survival guide and also reward viewers for the development of genre- and franchise-specific media literacy.

When it comes to surviving the undead, media-savvy viewers have an advantage over the franchise's characters because the storyworld of *TWD* does not seem to include the zombie as a cultural figure. Without zombie films or other forms of zombie narratives, the characters are initially not aware what these creatures are, how to respond to the threat they pose, or even what to call them – their preferred expressions vary but always steer clear of the z-word: walkers, lurkers, biters, roamers, or deadheads. Meanwhile, the show's viewers are encouraged to draw on media literacy in their reception. As a result of paratext seriality, viewers may employ their knowledge of the comic *and* draw on genre knowledge of horror or cinematic zombie narratives. Whereas in the show those viewing positions are mobilised through intertextual references, specific paratextual accompaniments also address a media-transmitted survival literacy.

One such example is an online multiple-choice test released on AMC's *TWD* website during the first season, which allowed viewers to find out which 'survival profile' based on the show's characters 'fit your personality'. This test introduced viewers to the show's cast through simplified stereotypes as possible test results, like 'Alpha Male' (Shane), 'Strong Mom' (Lori), 'Hillbilly Survivalist' (Daryl), or 'Tough Chick' (Andrea). The test already indicated that certain survival strategies would be more successful than others, since the too reckless test taker or horror novice could get the result 'walker'. A similar online test during the show's third season emphasised the punishment/reward logic of survival decisions. Different responses yielded results varying from 'You'd survive for three months', 'You're still alive. But you're missing a leg', to 'You'd be the first one to die.' From the second season on, such survival testing as an immersive practice has become a part of the show's popular 'Social TV' service Story Sync. This second-screen app accompanies the broadcast of the show and provides 'judgment polls', in which viewers evaluate a character's actions or decisions, and 'decision polls', which ask viewers how they would react in some of the show's narrative scenarios (Auverset and Billings 2016).

In US-American culture, multiple-choice testing is associated either with the sampling of knowledge within classroom settings or with the profile-based, 'customised' lifestyle advice of magazines aimed at women and girls. The various tests and polls of *TWD* aspire to neither. They do not test for actual disaster preparedness, nor do they provide advice, that is, they do not inform test takers which alternative answers might have resulted in a more desirable outcome. Instead, because the tests mobilise the audience's familiarity with the horror genre and zombie narratives, they encourage viewers to watch the show to develop the kind of media literacy these tests ask for. Rather than pursuing didactic aims, the serial quiz highlights ludic pleasures and depends on serialised interactivity. Jonathan Eburne argues that intradiegetic and extradiegetic elements of play are central to horror narratives: 'any fictional character who stands a chance of survival must play the part of reader (or aspiring writer); any reader is interpolated as a fictional character' (2014: 396). This playful element accounts for the pleasures to be found in the sober compilations of genre conventions that zombie guidebooks and *Talking Dead*'s 'Survival Tips' offer. It also indicates a possible viewing position of ludic detachment from which audiences may evaluate characters' survival decisions and the successes or 'failures' (i.e. death) they result in – without having their 'hearts broken' over every character death. These accompaniments claim to be 'orienting paratexts' (Mittell 2015: 261), because they provide an overview of the storyworld's zombie apocalypse; yet, their easy applicability for disaster preparedness disturbs readings of these paratexts as mappings of a fictional storyworld.

In *Talking Dead* episode 3.9, Mogk's segment gives host Hardwick the occasion to promote an official 'Walking Dead Survival Kit' (Figure 9.2). Among other items, the kit includes emergency food and water rations, a first aid kit, 'space blankets', and waterproof matches – in a messenger bag with the show's logo. The AMC website sells the kit among 'regular' merchandise such as action figures of Michonne, bedsheets with a dreamy-looking Daryl, or a zombie-shaped night light. The 'Survival Kit' serves as the franchise's foray into survivalist shopping motivated by the zombie apocalypse. Sociologist Todd Platts finds consumerism at the core of the cultural phenomenon of zombies, or 'zombie culture' (2013: 555). Being prepared – for natural disasters as well as zombies – comes with a hefty price tag (the 'Survival Kit' costs $149.99). In addition to rations, weapons, tools, and clothing, the survival-anxious consumer can also acquire survival bicycles, container houses, or even the 'silo condos' sold in Kansas in 2012. Even though these consumption practices arguably partake in more general disaster preparedness, the zombie apocalypse is attractive packaging for those commodities. This is a remarkable cultural manoeuvre because, after all, the early zombie films of director Romero are commonly understood as a critique of capitalist consumerism. Romero has himself criticised the shifted cultural 'afterlife' of the zombie. For him *TWD* is an embodiment of these developments: 'Basically it's just a soap opera with a zombie occasionally. I always used the zombie as a character for satire or a political criticism and I find that missing' (qtd in Roberts 2013). Regardless of Romero's approval, the zombie possesses infinite possibilities to become a cultural allegory. Academic research has struggled to pin down the zombie's proliferating cultural meanings and in the process appears to create ever new zombie metaphors. Remarkably, for such a vast franchise – and here I agree with Romero – *TWD* adds very little to zombies' potential cultural or political meanings. In this regard, it lends itself much more to 'training' to survive than to criticism of socio-economic structures.

Figure 9.2 *Talking Dead*'s sequence 'Survival Tips' featuring Matt Mogk (2.14); the 'Survival Kit' of AMC's online shop.

The understanding of the zombie as a mere obstacle and the zombie apocalypse as a stand-in for a disaster of some kind – hence, requiring more than media literacy – accounts for the franchise's appeal within audience segments that can be described as 'doomsday survivalists' or 'preppers'. For instance, on *The Prepper/Survivalist Forum* (prepperforums.net) the show has provoked extensive recaps and commentary. In their conversations, forum participants criticise individual characters' decisions, lament the absence of specific aspects of apocalypse survival, or suggest 'more appropriate' strategies. Narrative locations like the fortified prison in which characters grow crops and tend to livestock (seasons 3 and 4), camps secured by zombie traps, or a church surrounded by stakes (season 5) seem to gesture toward such viewers. The discussions do not evoke horror genre conventions – at times lengthy conversations exclude any mention of zombies – but take the form of 'realistic' strategic planning for various catastrophe scenarios with posted links to purchase recommendations (typically for weapons or emergency rations) or to building instructions (for shelters, fences, water purification devices). Forum participants are divided on their affective responses to the show – some express fandom, others dislike – but univocally employ the show to illustrate their own survival fantasies.

Prepper viewers of *TWD* find in its storyworld an appealing background against which to imagine various forms of preparedness. Disastrous dystopian aspects of the zombie apocalypse thus acquire an aspirational, compelling, and almost utopian undertone when addressed in discussions of how to best plan and prepare for them. In such a cultural imagination, the zombie apocalypse becomes a metaphor to express the desire for a 'simpler' life. Nonetheless, in order to locate utopian elements in the *TWD*'s survival struggle, prepper viewers have to prepare themselves 'while they still can' to enable the fantasy of a good life within the ruins of a collapsed society. A paradox at the core of these online prepper forums, participants live out the narrative desire for a collapsed civilisation by drawing on the resources of participatory and digital cultures: they educate themselves with digitally available expertise, purchase emergency goods online, and 'test' their strategies with their peers in online communities. In the homosocial spaces of prepper forums, participants cast themselves as part of an elite, as opposed to the unknowing, unprepared, and therefore doomed masses. Dystopian narratives like *TWD* offer similar imaginary sites in which the labour and inconvenience of survival preparation are rendered investments that will pay off. Several studies have shown how earnest discussions of survivalism tend to take place within homogenously gendered (cis-male), sexually oriented (heterosexual), and classed (middle-upper class) spaces (Rahm 2013; Foster 2014). Remarkably, such cultural conversations never incorporate the practices of refugees and other displaced people whose self-sufficient, autonomous behaviour and inability to rely on official infrastructures have much more in common with the survival skills prized in Western zombie narratives like *TWD*.

Through their readings, the show's prepper viewers highlight tensions in the franchise's survival theme. In their inability to appreciate the media-savvy, intertextual layer of zombie survival, these viewers take *TWD*'s survival 'too seriously'. Atia Sattar argues that the core of zombie consumerism is the belief that a zombie apocalypse remains 'fictional enactment, firmly fixed within the cultural imaginary. It can be allowed to function in society merely as an empty signifier, as a repeated performance that remains just that, a performance' (2014: 273). Due to their lack of detached, even ironic zombie literacy, such viewers' interest in the minutiae of preparedness is framed as 'taking things too far'. For instance, even though Kirkman presents himself as zombie authority, he refuses to cast his story as primarily a survival manual. When letter writers point out 'better survival strategies', he typically brushes them off: 'at times things just need to be inaccurate for story purposes' (#103). Just like its tongue-in-cheek presentation of genre conventions as a means of disaster preparedness, the consumption of survival items should indeed be viewed as a performance, a reception practice, and not actual preparedness. Paratextual extensions like the 'Survival Tips' or 'Survival Tests' celebrate survivalism as 'not too serious', communal entertainment, not an actual lifestyle. Despite its survival content, as a commercial enterprise, the franchise may seek to appeal to prepper audience segments but does not wish for its viewers to withdraw from society, to become self-reliant, autonomous, and in essence, media-averted.

RESILIENT BODIES AND ZOMBIE WORKOUTS

Several entertainment websites, such as *Uproxx*, *Buzzfeed*, and *The National Post*, have published 'infographics' about characters' kill scores that web forum users evoke to comment on individual characters' 'usefulness' during a zombie apocalypse. Echoing the rhetoric of AMC's 'Survival Test' profiles, these discussions evaluate characters based on the number of zombies (and sometimes humans) that they have killed. Some of the show's most prominent killers are highlighted by the signature weapons they carry.[3] However, perseverance in the television series is not primarily expressed by survivalist equipment but rather by the physical bodies of the characters/actors that are positioned as weapons or tools of survival. For instance, after his paramilitary militia failed to defeat the survivor collective in the third season, in an embodiment of prepper survival fantasies, the Governor returns to attack the group with a tank in the fourth season. Yet, Daryl disposes of the tank with surprising ease. In contrast to the Governor's group, the multi-protagonist group at the centre of the franchise is overall less militarised, as they employ simpler technologies and weaponry or ride horseback. For the show's characters, surviving requires a combination of physical prowess, the ability to defend oneself and others, and the mental resilience to cope with the violence of a post-apocalyptic world.

Of fellow zombie apocalypse expert, Alice (Milla Jovovich) of the *Resident Evil* franchise, Roth and Shoults write that 'there is something oddly fascinating about watching Alice in combat. She is lithe, athletic, and graceful, more like a dancer than a fighter' (2015: 230). Even though the glamorous, cocktail-dress clad appearance of Alice appears to operate differently from that of the more practically oriented *TWD* survivors, the show seeks to inspire a similar impression of athletic feats. However, it depicts fighting less as effortless, graceful, and dance-like than as an exhausting activity that resembles a hard, sweaty workout. The fighting scenes take the form of close physical combat, in which characters utilise their surroundings to manage large groups of zombies by picking them off one by one. For example, in episode 7.12 ('Say Yes'), Michonne and Rick are chased by a group of about seventy zombies in a deserted fairground. Throughout, they remain calm and confident, strategising how to most efficiently separate the zombies and dispatch their attackers with calculated blows to the head. As the zombies' bodies fall one by one, the human survivors' bodies are splattered with blood and drenched in sweat.

Emblematic of aspirational sportswear commercials, the scenes show experienced athletes engaged in well-practised routines necessary for them to maintain their level of sports(wo)manship. Those moments displace the notion that Rick and Michonne are slaughtering human figures. Taking the form of rewarding labour, such a 'zombie workout' enables these bodies to maintain their lean, attractive forms. The configuration of zombie battle as workout for long-lasting survivors almost lets viewers forget that survival is at stake in the demonstrations of resilient bodies.

The journalistic promotion extends the show's celebration of the athletic physicality of its actors. Danai Gurira (Michonne), Lauren Cohan (Maggie), Norman Reedus (Daryl), and Andrew Lincoln (Rick) have given interviews about the physical demands of shooting the show, their workout schedules, and their diets for *Men's Fitness*, *Men's Health*, *Esquire*, and *Vogue*. Full of praise for these actors' 'amazing condition', a cover photographer for *Entertainment Weekly* noted, 'That's not something you always see with people who are not athletes' (qtd in Smith 2014). The physicality prized by *TWD* and its reception signals an update of the masculine, muscle-packed, bodybuilder performances of Arnold Schwarzenegger and Sylvester Stallone in what Yvonne Tasker describes as the 'muscular action cinema' of the 1980s (2008: 35). Instead of emphasising masculine muscles and strength, regardless of gender and race, the show features slim and agile physicalities represented as persevering and resilient. They are staged in scenes that combine influences from action cinema, the inspirational dynamic of sports coverage or sportswear commercials, and the horror genre's fascination with the destruction of bodies.

What the show and its viewers celebrate through the athletically capable and visually appealing bodies of Gurira, Reedus, or Lincoln is the efficiency, self-management, and self-regulation that their physique epitomises. In this regard, *TWD*'s resilient bodies have a place within a larger neoliberal body politic. The complex economic and political undertaking that is still best described by the worn-out denominator 'neoliberalism' subordinates all political and social areas to the logic of the 'free' market. Generally assumed to have taken hold in Western societies from the 1980s onward, neoliberalism becomes a catch-all phrase to describe the increasingly globalised deregulation of economies, the privatisation of formerly public sectors, and the acceleration of capitalist synergies. Feminist social scientists have long argued that not only do bodies make politics, that is, the bodies of political actors and institutions, but that politics also inscribe themselves into the bodies of human actors. Within neoliberal agendas, bodies should be emancipated from any 'flaws' or 'deficiencies' through self-management. Addressing an 'autonomous, calculating, self-regulating subject', neoliberal body politics emphasises self-monitoring and optimisation – in accordance with postfeminism (Gill and Scharff 2011: 7). Through its resilient bodies, *TWD* in many ways demonstrates the dynamics of neoliberal capitalist organisation, most prominently, competition: textually, the human survivors compete with other hostile groups for resources, with zombies for their own bodies, and with fellow group members for their position within the collective. Extratextually, characters compete for viewers' recognition through zombie kills, fighting abilities, and even through the forms their deaths take.

Within discourses of disaster preparedness and recovery, neoliberal logics bring forward a notion of individualised resilience, as Julia Leyda and Diane Negra demonstrate: 'resilience discourse often enables the elision of questions about the origin of systemic failures and displaces responsibility onto the individual rather than the social institutions charged with disaster preparedness and response' (2015: 16). Moreover, Sara Ahmed describes resilience as a 'deeply conservative technique' that drives subjects toward the acceptance of increasing pressures and demands which are

> well-suited to governance: you encourage bodies to strengthen so they will not succumb to pressure; so they can keep taking it; so they can take more of it. Resilience is the requirement to take more pressure; such that the pressure can be gradually increased. . . . Damage becomes a means by which a body is asked to take it; or to acquire the strength to take more of it. (Ahmed 2017: 189)

Even though it casts its survivor collective as a chosen family that endures together, the show imagines survival as an individualised experience through its body politics. Again and again, the collective survives because it has exceptionally capable and resilient individuals – like Michonne, Daryl, Carol, or Rick – without whom its chances are relatively bleak. In this regard, the survivor collective echoes its 'production family': despite the paratextual maintenance of a web of specialised authors, exceptional figures such as Kirkman make a hierarchy of authorship tangible. Accordingly, we find neoliberalism's emphasis on individual responsibility, rather than forms of social collectivity, to constitute a body politics that turns bodies into ideal vehicles for political regulation.

Questions of materiality become central to the differentiation between the bodies that serve as obstacles to be disposed of and the bodies that become active agents 'mastering' other bodies: the show juxtaposes the visually impaired, stumbling bodies of zombies with the agile, defined, controlled bodies of its human characters. In a reading of the pastiche novel *Pride and Prejudice and Zombies* (2009), Andrea Ruthven describes human bodies as appearing 'contained' when contrasted with the 'messy, falling apart, and contagious' bodies of zombies (2014: 342). In my understanding, these resilient bodies are 'contained' not only because they are mostly unharmed, free of infection or injury, but also because they aesthetically conform to an athletic ideal of contoured, defined, and lean physicalities.[4]

TWD's zombie fight scenes call up the horror genre's interest in bodily metamorphosis and destruction. Horror viewers' disidentification with the repulsive sight of destroyed bodies is particularly fruitful for understanding how human characters (rather than zombies) become such privileged sites of viewer identification in these scenes. Barbara Creed suggests that 'the experience of viewing horror, the subject's encounter with abjection, might also serve to reinforce in the viewer a sense of bodily purity, wholeness, and selfhood' (1995: 157).[5] In *TWD*, the reinforcement of bodily ability and wholeness is embodied in human characters through contrast with the zombies' bodies. In order for zombie killing to be framed as a kind of admirable physical workout to be emulated by viewers, zombies have to be understood as 'killable' without moral complications, that is, they have to be stripped of their former humanity. For the most part, the show aligns viewers with the perspective of its resilient human characters and frames zombies as mere 'things' that these characters have to dispose of. In an illustration of serial television narrative's 'one-upmanship' or 'outbidding' (Jahn-Sudmann and Kelleter 2012: 211–15), zombie obstacles become visually and narratively more spectacular as the series progresses, hence surpassing not only former special effects but also the athletic challenges for characters and their actors.

Although itself a product of televisual work division (among actors, director, special effects teams, etc.), resilient bodywork is intra- and extratextually celebrated as an individual character/actor's achievement to be emulated by audience members. The cultural phenomenon of zombie survivalism easily incorporates practices of personal fitness and physical activity: either playfully – for example, in the personal training app *Zombies, Run!* and exercise classes with names such as 'Zombie Fit' and 'Zombitsu' – or, more implicitly, through the idealisation of able-bodiedness, health, and endurance in zombie narratives like *TWD*. Because bodies become the most significant tool in the fight against zombies, they either ensure or endanger survival. It has become a staple of zombie narratives and survival conversations to consider people with non-conforming and specifically fat bodies to have little chance of survival. In the first minutes of *Zombieland* (2009), a voice-over of protagonist Columbus relates 'Cardio' as the 'First Rule of Survival' overlaying an image of zombies chasing a fat person. Through such 'fat-shaming', zombie narratives promote societal prejudices that mistakenly assume that fat bodies are incapable of athletic achievement and that all slim bodies are. In this reductive understanding, the athletically toned 'resilient body' is the means to survival but also a productive result of the zombie workout.

To recap my argument: different activities become entertaining pastimes that prepare viewers less for the survival of any real disaster than for survival and competition within a neoliberal, capitalist marketplace. Through zombie literacy, that is, the knowledge of the zombie narrative's genre conventions, a survivor/neoliberal subject is expected to know 'the rules' of the zombie apocalypse/the capitalist marketplace, to make educated guesses based on this knowledge, and to predict best strategies for a desirable outcome. Zombie consumerism, meanwhile, calls for the subject to make investments at strategic moments, that is, to buy survival goods and prepare in advance because such investments promise rewards at a later moment. Through consumer practices, subjects can position themselves as separate from an unknowing mass that is unaware of the risks and chances of the apocalypse/capitalist competition. And lastly, zombie fitness rewards the willingness to persevere and be disciplined. Framing body practices of fighting as an enjoyable workout conceals the neoliberal logics of optimisation, productivity, and self-regulation that exert influence on these bodies.

DEAD YOURSELF: THE LIBERATING POTENTIALS OF THE FAILURE TO SURVIVE

In the episode 'Clear' (3.12), Michonne risks her life to bring Carl a photograph of his deceased mother, Lori. In one of the show's rare instances of humour, Michonne brushes off Carl's feelings of guilt and gratitude: 'I was gonna go . . . anyway. I couldn't leave this behind.' The tacky cat statue she proudly presents amuses Carl (and the viewer) because it appears to be a blatant lie told to comfort the teenager (Figure 9.3). In a series so focused on survival (as both a theme and reception practice), it seems absurd that one of the most successful survivors would risk her life for something as irrelevant as a crude decorative object. After all, in the first episode, Rick and Morgen bond over their 'misguided' wives prioritising items with emotional value instead of survival equipment. And yet, the scene hints at a compelling potential counternarrative to the show's straightforward prizing of survival. What if Michonne were to lose her life over an item that others would consider insignificant? Can the show imagine circumstances under which the refusal to survive is a legitimate reaction rather than a sign of personal failure and weakness? Is there a possibility for a 'good death' outside of the narrow definition of the franchise, one in which trivial pleasures, such as cat-shaped objects, become more meaningful than the sweat, blood, and labour necessary to stay alive in the zombie apocalypse? The following section cannot provide definitive answers to these questions, primarily because they are of so little relevance to the show itself. Instead, these questions allow me to identify small disruptions in the show's preferred understanding of survival and the discourse of (neoliberal) serialised survivalism.

Figure 9.3 Survival essentials worth risking your life for: colourful cat decorations.

Alternative narratives of survival failure arise through fringe characters and minor paratexts. It is necessary to turn to alternative narratives, because unlike *Girls* and *Murder*, which centred their reception practices on their viewers' understandings of feminism and postfeminism (Chapter 3) and progressivism and identity politics (Chapter 6), *TWD* steers curiously free of any form of political or socio-economic commentary – as prominently reflected in Romero's criticism. In early seasons, the exorbitant use of weapons, sexist gender roles in the main survivor collective, and the early deaths of survivors of colour appeared to indicate a conservative, possibly right-wing politics. In subsequent seasons the show has increasingly put its diverse cast to better use by introducing more capable female survivors and by letting several characters of colour survive. Again, this adjustment occurs as a form of post-racial television, without any acknowledgement that race or gender impact the different survival strategies of its characters.

Some people who have experienced sexualised violence question the label of 'survivor' as an adequate (or desirable) expression. As one contributor to the collection *Not That Bad: Dispatches from Rape Culture* (2018) expresses, 'I resent having to face up to it. I resent having to be a survivor. "Survivor" is the "special needs" of victimhood. If I say I have survived, I'm fooling nobody. I didn't' (McKenna 2018: 81). To consider oneself a survivor rather than a victim of abuse has been a crucial terminological trajectory for early activism and research on sexualised violence. Such rhetoric may empower and award agency, yet also culturally prizes the process of surviving, the overcoming of trauma as an indicator of individual resilience and progress. As argued before, notions of resilience and strength in the face of adversity lend themselves to the kind of ongoing survival horror *TWD* undertakes, and not coincidentally, many of its 'strongest' survivors have endured sexualised violence or abuse (Carol, Michonne in the comic, Maggie in the show, Daryl).

Within *TWD*, the failure to survive becomes most pronounced when characters refuse to engage with the practice of survival at all and opt out: through suicide. Suicide becomes an act in which the label 'survivor' is stripped of its aspirational appeal and instead reframed as an exhausting activity not beneficial to coping with trauma. Characters commit suicide when the struggle for survival becomes too costly or when they are too traumatised to continue without a foreseeable end to their hardships. The show (and many viewers) find little to redeem in characters who prove 'too weak' to even try to survive, especially when the bodies of those who have committed suicide revive as zombies and attack their former friends and families. *The Walking Dead Wiki* differentiates between characters who commit suicide and characters who sacrifice themselves for others. For instance, in the seventh season, Sasha (Sonequa Martin-Green) strategically commits suicide so that her zombified body may kill villain Negan. Many of the chosen deaths collected in this category appear to be the show's version of what anthropologist Karin Andriolo has described as a 'masked suicide' predominant in 'warrior cultures'. This form of suicide occurs when 'an individual arranges for a high chance to have himself killed by others while performing an act that is culturally approved, even highly esteemed' (1998: 40). Such martyrdom is evoked in the show, and except for Sasha, largely gendered cis-male. Self-sacrifice or 'masked suicide' becomes a 'productive' form of suicide that rewards characters with a 'good death' because they heroically die to protect others. Meanwhile, to kill oneself out of desperation and hopelessness becomes an expression of 'weakness'.

The episode '30 Days Without an Accident' (4.1) provides an example of the disruptive potential that female suicide possesses, not only as survival failure but also as an expression of female characters' agency. In the forest, Rick encounters Clara (Kerry Condon) and first mistakes her unkempt, neglected figure for a zombie. This not only foreshadows Clara's fate, but is also telling because Clara is unwilling to accept her husband's zombification as an end to their relationship. However, Clara is not helplessly killed because she is unable to recognise how her zombified husband has changed. She skilfully maintains their relationship, sleeping next to the undead body, and intends to 'feed' Rick to him. When Clara realises that she cannot sacrifice other humans to the zombie, she decides to kill herself as an alternative to maintaining her relationship. 'I can't be without him. . . . Let me be like him. Don't stop it. Don't end it after. Let me be with him.' Overall, Clara is presented as a tragic figure rendered mentally unstable over the loss of her spouse – and thus serves as a cautionary contrast for Rick who mourns his wife Lori. Without her husband,

Clara finds too little reason to continue living, and instead, the afterlife as a zombie becomes a preferable option for her.

What is compelling about *TWD*'s gendered portrayals of death is that zombification severely complicates the visual practice and gendered aesthetic of the beautiful female corpse. Edgar Allan Poe prominently mused that 'the death, then, of a beautiful woman is, unquestionably, the most poetical topic in the world' (1846: 166). Elisabeth Bronfen has unpacked this cultural fascination with femininity and death that echoes in the displays of beautiful female corpses in popular culture (1992). Further, sociological studies have found the methods of suicide to be profoundly gendered: according to the 'beautiful corpse hypothesis', women are more likely to kill themselves in ways that impair the appearance of their bodies as little as possible (Stack and Wasserman 2009: 13–20). While we have to treat such generalisations with caution – for instance, they do not accurately represent aspects of race, class, age, and bodily impairments – they resonate with the aestheticisation of female death in contemporary popular culture, which extends back at least to the nineteenth century. Even in death, this research suggests, women have internalised the demand to appear normatively beautiful. The female zombie, however, is neither still nor beautiful. If the female corpse is often displayed like an art object on exhibition, which allows a mourning male spectator the full spectrum of sadness, desire, and loss (Bronfen 1992: 95–102), the female zombie never stops moving and poses a threat to any spectator. Within the storyworld of *TWD*, an aestheticisation of death and femininity therefore becomes challenging to pursue. In order to commit suicide and not revive as a zombie, characters have to destroy their brains. When a minor cis-female character in the community of Alexandria commits suicide through one of the methods which sociological research suggests is gendered as 'feminine' – she slits her wrists – she revives as an unappealing zombie. The female zombie is thus a counterfigure for cultural imaginings of the beautiful dead woman.

Elisabeth Bronfen's work also describes possibilities for countering such gendered forms of objectification in death. She finds that suicide can become a form of female authorship:

> Dying is a move beyond communication yet also functions as these women's one effective communicative act, in a cultural or kinship situation otherwise disinclined towards feminine authorship. It involves self-reflexivity in so far as death is chosen and performed by the woman herself, in an act that makes her both object and subject of dying and of representation. (Bronfen 1992: 141–2)

Because male-centric authorship performances and authorised paratexts so thoroughly seek to frame the show's interpretations, minor female characters' acts of suicide have the potential to become disruptions and establish divergent cultural meanings. Along with that of minor character Clara, Carol's death in the comic book is another compelling example because, as I argued in Chapter 8, it visually suggests Carol's unspoken same-sex desire for her friend Lori. Even though the suicide is framed as the result of an insecure and mentally unstable woman seeking the security of a romantic relationship at any cost, as a self-authored act, Carol's suicide expresses her desire for life beyond the reductive nuclear family structures her group has established. She refuses the responsibilities of biological motherhood, that is, to keep living solely for the sake of her daughter. Instead, Carol is shown to gladly embrace death as a self-chosen act. Just like Clara, Carol prefers to be a zombie in the company of other zombies, rather than to endure survival among humans. The transformation into a zombie may offer liberating potential because characters refuse to continue holding onto their lives in a surrounding in which they experience so much loss and danger. As zombies, these characters join collectives (Clara can be spotted in crowds of zombies in later episodes), they freely roam the storyworld, and only follow their own desire (for human flesh).

In rare, but very remarkable moments, the show breaks with its usual portrayal of zombies as mere obstacles for its resilient survivors to 'dispatch'. The scenes often involve zombified major characters, whose relatives or friends struggle to kill them (Morgan's inability to kill his wife, Andrea's emotional killing of her sister Amy). Sometimes, characters' emotionally resonant encounters with zombies break with their characterisation as mere fodder for athletic fighters. Stephen Shapiro argues that cultural artefacts with zombie protagonists, such as *Fido* (2006), *Warm Bodies* (2013), or *iZombie* (The CW, 2015–19), allow for a 'Janus-like form of representation . . . increasingly both against and with the zombie' (2014: 217). A related manoeuvre occurs, for example, when Maggie discovers the zombified body of an abducted woman who had died forgotten in the trunk of a car (5.10 'Them'); or when Carol and Daryl encounter a zombified mother and her child in a domestic abuse shelter (5.6 'Consumed'). In those moments, characters pause to 'read' the bodies of the zombies before them, are overwhelmed by the memories of past human suffering they find there, and draw unexpected parallels between themselves and these figures (Maggie's sister Beth was also abducted; Carol and Daryl also experienced domestic abuse). Unlike Shapiro's examples, however, in *TWD* such an extension of viewer alignment toward zombie characters occurs only in isolated scenes, and the show remains otherwise firmly committed to the sole perspective of its human protagonists.

The aforementioned scenes offer another disruptive moment for the discourse of serialised survival. In order for the zombie to be put to use as a potent, manifold cultural allegory, it has to be perceived as essentially stripped of all remnants of societal belonging. To be powerful metaphors, zombies cannot be intersectional; they can know no gender, no race, no class, no bodily ability or impairment, no sexual orientation. Such a cultural understanding echoes in the first speech Rick delivers to his potential new group: 'There are no n****** anymore. No dumb-as-shit, inbred white-trash fools either. Only dark meat and white meat' (1.2 'Guts'). It is precisely the zombie's non-discriminatory nature that Natasha Patterson finds 'restores pleasure to the female viewer through the zombie's ambivalence toward gender (and genre)' (2008: 110). Zombies 'trouble gender', Pye and O'Sullivan argue, 'because of the contrast between perceived biological sex and their gender performances' (2012: 108). More accurately, zombies complicate an idea of gendered performance as a conscious expression of identity and highlight how gender performances depend on one's surroundings. Even if zombies possess no conscious gendered identity, *TWD* at times employs the bodies of female zombies to effectively depict (male) violence, as the earlier examples illustrate. These zombie bodies carry palimpsestic traces of the women they were before, and because those traces cannot be erased, they disrupt their 'killability' at the hands of resilient human survivors. Yet *TWD* does not undertake explorations of zombies as satisfied, content creatures, because this depiction would complicate the celebration of zombie workouts – just as we so often appear hesitant or unable to imagine convincing alternatives to neoliberal capitalist competition.

Ultimately, it is the refusal to stop that distinguishes successful humans (survivors) from unsuccessful humans (zombies) in depictions of a zombie apocalypse. As Evan Calder Williams pinpoints,

> it's not dying that makes you a zombie. It is *not-dying* that does, already present in you as you fight off the hordes you will one day join. It is the fact that you don't, can't or won't – in the varied inflections of will and non-agency of each option – stay down. (Williams 2010: 90)

As the paradox at the core of *TWD*, no character is safe – regardless of the physical fitness that makes survival a temporal question rather than a strategic issue. However, the franchise dodges the questions suicides raise: what is so great about survival? Why keep going? Why not opt out and become a zombie? One non-fictional, non-serial paratext, the mobile app *Dead Yourself*, is exceptional in this regard. The picture editing program allows users to add wounds, gory special effects, and different levels of decay to their portraits. As dead versions of themselves, viewers suddenly align their point of view not with the surviving human characters, but with the undead zombie hordes. While not explicitly drawing on the survival theme, the app provides a playful approach to survivalism by exploring a 'fun', tongue-in-cheek aspect of survival failure as a gimmicky alternative to other paratextual extensions' investments in zombie literacy, consumerism, or fitness.

Viewers, of course, have increasingly also opted out of the franchise, as their own form of refusing to survive, that is, to watch and engage with *TWD*. Critic Emily Nussbaum's negative review of the show culminated in the question: 'But how many times can your heart break? As the corpses pile up, and the living characters become increasingly incoherent, the deaths are just marks on a to-do list' (2013). Nussbaum made her comment during the show's fourth season, and six years later her rejection appears to be shared by more viewers, as the show's declining ratings illustrate. Frank Kelleter finds many long-running series to be haunted by '[r]ecurrence, properly a condition of survival [which] can [also] foster an excess of self-reference that may turn unhealthy, sickening, mad' (2015: 71). This appears especially true for *TWD*, which made recurrence not just central to its theme of survival, but also a feature of its own ongoing, crossmedia paratext seriality. Interestingly, it is precisely in the moments that the show itself claims are unhealthy, 'weak', or 'sad', such as characters' preference to become zombies over the continued human survival struggle, or the hinting at zombies as more than mere obstacles to be disposed of, that I locate disruptive potentials. These marginal disruptions make visible how the show and its paratexts otherwise encourage viewers to participate in serialised survival as entertainment and preparation for the competition within neoliberal capitalism. Thus, such fringe moments briefly disrupt the serial performance of television authorship and *TWD*'s hierarchy of storytellers, characters, and viewers as mere story consumers: female characters become the authors of their own deaths and upset the franchise's understandings of killing as Kirkman's prerogative, the 'good death', and the prized figure of the neoliberal survivor to be emulated by viewers.

NOTES

1. This contrast is enhanced through the lack of female survivors in the pilot episode. While viewers encounter several male characters, the only female characters are zombies, yet several conversations are *about* women and their supposed irrationality or emotionality (see Chapter 8).
2. Granted, Rick does not have any emotional connections to the zombie he so easily 'dispatches'. Furthermore, Morgan's wife Jenny is visually different from the decaying bodies of 'bicycle girl' and other zombies. With her long, white nightgown, reduced zombie make-up, and her attempts to enter the shelter of her family, Jenny appears less like a zombie and more like a ghost haunting her loved ones. None of the characters directly encounters her, but instead they watch Jenny through devices (a door spyhole, the rifle frame). Through such camera practices, the female African American zombie is set up as a spectacle to be observed and evaluated by the characters and the show's viewers. Rather than having her story told (the story of 'bicycle girl' is explored in the web series *Torn Apart*), Jenny appears solely as a catalyst for Morgan's suffering.

3. Examples of such weapons are Michonne's katana, Daryl's crossbow, Tyreese's hammer, Morgan's aikido stick, and Negan's baseball bat. These weapons place their owners in a superhero comic book tradition, stand in for the characters in paratextual extensions, and are popular merchandise items.
4. Whereas other instalments of the franchise rely heavily on injured or disabled bodies (scars, amputated limbs, lost eyes), through which past plots become physically inscribed in the characters' bodies, it is remarkable how little permanent injury the bodies of the show's survivors suffer despite their ongoing struggle. This media-specific deviation of the show further highlights the distinction between the injured, killable zombie bodies and the intact human bodies.
5. Creed's reading here is informed by Julia Kristeva's notion of the abject. Such a theorisation of the abject relates to the ways *TWD*'s viewers are drawn to identify with the intact/contained bodies and distance themselves from the excessive bodies of the zombies.

Conclusion: Archiving Snapshots

> I know it's been a rough couple of years. Obama, *Empire*, *Hamilton*, . . . *Star Wars* movies where the only white characters are stormtroopers.
>
> Aziz Ansari (Saturday Night Live 42.12)

Media scholar Bonnie Dow opens her book *Prime-Time Feminism* (1996) with an argument about the politics of television – and the role of critique:

> Whether or not television 'reflects' reality outside the tube is beside the point: we watch television and it is therefore part of life. Rather than existing in some autonomous realm outside of political life, media is part of it. What criticism can do is to accentuate the importance of that realization and offer specific arguments for that meaning. (Dow 1996: 5)

Dow's words have aged well and can serve as a backdrop to the work undertaken in this book. However, the political contours of popular culture, and television specifically, have grown sharper in the decades since Dow's publication, so that by now, it is almost commonplace for 'real life' and politics to coincide within television's cultural imagination. The understanding that popular culture is ever more political infiltrates the ways that we consume television and the ways that cultural artefacts present themselves to us. Current television's savvy commercialisation of politics and the pleasures of its viewers becomes even more pronounced when contrasted with the shocking naïvety of cultural artefacts around the time of Dow's writing. For example, in the 1998 pilot episode of *Sex and the City* Samantha approvingly pronounces her friend Carrie's object of desire 'the next Donald Trump. Except he's younger and much better looking' (1.1 'Sex and the City'). A signpost of sexualised, white capitalist power in the late 1990s, two decades later, business mogul and former reality television personality Donald Trump is the forty-fifth president of the United

States. A day after Trump's inauguration, comedian Aziz Ansari hosted an episode of *Saturday Night Live* and humorously sought to come to terms with the country's willingness to endorse an openly racist and misogynistic president. Ansari's opening monologue suggested that many white US-Americans could have been alienated by the diversity and progressivism upheld by commercial popular culture (and represented by Trump's predecessor Barack Obama). These are strange times for cultural observers, times in which reality television is intrinsically connected to the presidency, fictional representations of diversity may motivate voters, and comedy shows offer coverage that is neglected by traditional news outlets bridled by questions of authenticity surrounding 'fake news'. These are times in which Dow's suggestion to 'accentuate the importance of [political television] . . . and offer specific arguments for that meaning' becomes a dazzling task for popular culture criticism. Under the eye of commercial business interests, popular culture constitutes a space within which political positions clash, confront, and feed off one another. In particular, US-American popular culture often understands itself as a player and contributor to social movements, unlike the more distanced position that, for example, German popular culture takes in response to socio-political issues. It is a convenient time to pursue American studies from a transnational perspective, when one can safely observe from afar and rest in supposedly more progressive spaces, although upon closer examination they may be only differently racist, sexist, and classist, albeit in more veiled and 'secure' ways for white middle-class academics.

The speed and urgency with which these gendered and racialised entanglements of US-American popular culture and politics are mushrooming into a vast, conflicting cultural mediascape is challenging for any bystander. Ongoing cultural conversations surrounding intersectional gender shape what we understand as 'America'. At the same time, multiple developments occur and are full of controversies: a reality television persona becomes president and mobilises cultural artefacts to distract from his administration's horrific policies (massive neoliberal privatisation, disenfranchisement, social division, contributions to global warming); a 'woke' feminist comedian is shown to be complicit in the gendered system he criticises;[1] a drag queen does not disrupt mass media's heteronormative structures and frequently calls out the president on prime time television.[2] In light of such practices, the notion that commercial popular culture is always in flux – especially when it comes to gender and race – feels more accurate than ever. Of course, serial, fictional television narratives are rarely quite as obvious in their references to gendered politics as the examples from comedy and reality television mentioned. Even though they may frustrate us just the same, overall, serial television's fictions entice us and incorporate political discourses dear to us in more nuanced ways. Serial television narratives do not as openly aspire to quick laughs as do late night comedy or reality television, yet, through their manifold deployments of viewer practices, they contribute to and draw upon various political conversations just as forcefully.

Again and again, the notions that gender and popular culture are serial, changing, and interactive are mentioned in scholarship. This book thinks through the diverse implications and the ways in which this occurs, in order to develop a practice-focused approach to serial gender. My point of departure was the intersection of two conceptions of seriality, the seriality of television shows and the seriality of gendered identity performance. It is due to the seriality of both gender and popular culture that these shows become promising for the exploration of how we, as a society, tell, read, and enact intersectional identities in series. Because both gender performances and serialised television narratives are 'moving targets' (see Kelleter 2017), any attempt to transfix these ongoing processes in static writing is an inherently risky enterprise. The different terminologies that the nine chapters of this book cultivate help readers approach the vast, shifting dynamics of extensively proliferating materials.

(GENDERED) SERIALITIES

My starting point for exploring the three shows' 'gendered serialities' was to ask about the processes by which serial television develops gendered identities and how these processes rely on different modes of audience feedback. The concept *thinkpiece seriality* referred to the way that *Girls* courts the analytical engagements of viewer-critics. Chapter 1 found crucial aspects of this kind of serialised storytelling to be a lack of focalisation, narrative fragmentation, metatextuality, and a general emphasis on a dynamic of 'showing' rather than 'telling'. These different characteristics of the show aspire to mobilise the activities of serial television criticism as an accompaniment, an engagement referred to as the show's critical sphere. In doing so, the show progresses beyond HBO's previous 'Quality TV': instead of courting controversy through gratuitous depictions of violence, sexuality, and profanity, *Girls* does so through ambiguity, asking viewer-critics to actively interpret the show.

While *Girls* rarely deviates from a temporal impression of 'liveness', *How to Get Away with Murder* offers abundant temporal experimentation to mobilise a very different kind of viewer engagement. Its *looped seriality* is the result not of a critical feedback loop but of a conversational feedback loop between the audience and the show. In Chapter 4, specific viewer practices, such as the internet humour of GIFs and ritualised snack and drink consumption, served as examples of the show's interactive storytelling with social media-using viewers.

Meanwhile, Chapter 7 explored how television authorship is itself developed as an ongoing narrative that seeks to escort and shape viewer practices. Different 'official' textual accompaniments, authorised paratexts, are central sites for establishing such ongoing performances of authorship and communicating preferred readings. In my case study of *TWD*, I described how the show mobilises the comic book series and other instalments of the franchise (especially *Talking Dead* and the comic's letter column) by means of my notion of *paratext seriality*.

These terminological concepts are useful to demonstrate the entanglements of gender with shows' preferred modes of viewer engagement.[3] I suggest that future studies of serial television should identify a show's most dominant mode of viewer engagement as a first step. By asking which viewers a show imagines as its ideal audience, much can be understood about its particular form of gendered storytelling as well as the ways viewers talk back to such audience conceptions. For example, *Girls* caters to critical responses, *Murder* to Twitter responses, and *TWD* literally curates responses through its paratexts. There are poignant differences between the audience segments that these shows imagine as ideal. This imagining is made material through the shows' engagements with these particular groups – and viewers who are neglected in these engagements. *Girls* emphasises social or cultural capital, and it targets a journalistic (and possibly academic) demographic with its mode of address. *Girls* demonstrates that even if television criticism no longer possesses the cultural gatekeeping function of earlier decades, online television writing still mobilises audience tastes. On the opposite end of the spectrum, *Murder* is interested in a different kind of buzz, one that is less analytical and more emotional: responses through tweets. It targets a 'socially progressive' audience and often explicitly addresses viewers of colour who may have felt neglected by the other #TGIT shows. Because *Murder* resembles feminised guilty-pleasure television, it stands in contrast with the *TWD* franchise, which relies on gendered conceptions of fandom and genre enthusiasm to determine its imagined audience as male (and often white), in accordance with its most dominant expressions of authorship. Hence, the question of who a show imagines as its ideal viewer becomes performatively linked to its preferred and gendered modes of audience engagement.

(SERIAL) GENDERS/GENDERINGS

Based on the shows' respective forms of serial storytelling, I asked which kinds of serial genders evolve and how are they are organised within a show. To answer this, I developed three analytical metaphors: the carousel, the (outward) spiral, and the palimpsest. These metaphorical objects allowed me to trace how gendered identities are serially maintained and how they incorporate various intertextual references.

The *carousel* utilises narrative omissions and fragmentations as characters are alternately brought into focus and then removed from sight. It captures how *Girls*'s characters circle around cultural types with no seeming progress. This model relies on the frustrations of (critical) viewers who watch these characters and seek to find meaning by understanding them as representations of larger cultural dynamics. Alternatively, the metaphor of the *outward spiral* thickens cultural meanings. It invites immediate reactions from viewers, who respond not with analytical distance but by reading culturally and socially relevant moments as expressions of their personal lives or of TV history in the making. These moments resonate for viewers and spiral into larger debates with widening ripples. Finally, the metaphor of the *palimpsest* captures the paradox of mobilising (paratextual) artefacts as part of the storytelling while also seeking to overwrite them. Through this model, *TWD* activates its viewers, encouraging them to decipher, notice, and compare such traces. However, not all palimpsestic echoes are intentional: sometimes palimpsestic reinscriptions cause unintentional viewer responses and, consequently, conflicts of authorisation.

Television gendering crucially employs intertextual references to other cultural figures, cultural knowledges, and gendered or racialised stereotypes. This book's models demonstrate the limited utility of a trope- or type-based reading for interpretations of serial storytelling. This is because these types become starting points for popular culture's serial gendering, and hence they should not be accepted as an end to analysis. The concept of carousel gendering demonstrates how *Girls*'s characters run circles around cultural references; for example, the female writer, the slacker, and the 'pretty girl protagonist'. Through spiral gendering, I have explored how *Scandal*'s Olivia Pope and racialised tropes of black femininity become starting points from which *Murder*'s protagonist Annalise evolves in ways that the show's viewers consider culturally meaningful. The model of palimpsest gendering captures how racialised and gendered images shimmer through *TWD*'s characterisation, sometimes intentionally and with acknowledgement, as is the case when Carol instrumentalises the tropes of the 'battered wife' or 'older woman', and in other instances unintentionally, as in the one-sided racialised strength of Michonne or the antagonistic television wife Lori.

Viewers are mobilised to analyse (carousel gendering), be inspired and celebrate (spiral gendering), or remember and compare (palimpsest gendering). The respective chapter subheadings break each model down into a central position that drives its interactive gendering by means of these distinct viewer responses: controversy (Chapter 2's carousel), recognisability (Chapter 5's spiral), and accountability (Chapter 8's palimpsest). They describe how each show unfolds its serial genders, but also how viewers become involved in these gender performances. These concepts have enabled *Gender and Seriality* to go beyond a cultural artefact's intended and accidental audiences, that is, to engage audience-cum-consumer responses. My readings explore the subsumption of radical critique to neoliberal commercialisation and an incredible proliferation of representations of gender in this Age of a Social Media/Reality TV Presidency.

It would be productive to investigate other television characters with the models developed in this book. Future studies of serialised, gendered storytelling may choose similar focal points for deciding which characters are deemed exemplary. In Chapter 2, I was interested in the show's preferred, hegemonic gender identities and investigated how they depend on the contrast with less preferred characters to take on hegemonic status within the show. Here, a combination of sociological gender studies research and television studies scholarship by Raewyn Connell, Mimi Schippers, and Amanda Lotz proved helpful for my readings. In Chapter 5, I had already recognised that the show's protagonist, Annalise, is *Murder*'s preferred gender identity. I proceeded with an in-depth interpretation of the areas in which I found her most resonant for viewers: moments which are expanded for her characterisation and the show's interest in cultural conversations, such as those about black beauty culture or bisexuality. Chapter 8 extended my interest in hierarchies of characters beyond what the show considers its preferred gender identities, asking how viewers agree with or diverge from such conceptions. Palimpsest gendering allowed me to explore viewer responses to, and (para)textual characterisations of, 'fan favourites' in contrast with the most disliked 'worst characters'.

CULTURAL DISCOURSES

The analysis of serial genders and gendered serialities is followed up by a larger interrogation of the different socio-political discourses that these formations allow shows to participate in. The term 'cultural conversation' here helps to capture the shifting, inconsistent positions that serial television occupies in these discourses. At times shows manifest or represent certain ideologies, at other times they incorporate and thus in a way defang or tame radical critiques of ideologies. The capitalistic flexibility to mix and match various ideological positions in the interest of maintaining them is what distinguishes these cultural artefacts as serial.

In my readings, I asked how these cultural conversations enable a series to establish and continue its identity as a show and to position itself within sociopolitical histories. In Chapter 3, *Girls*'s participation in a discourse of universality and specificity prompted a larger analysis of current postfeminism(s) in popular culture. *Girls* participates within a new wave of postfeminist co-optation that absorbs, appropriates, and commercialises feminism in a highly aware, deeply veiled manner. Drawing on the work of media scholar Charlotte Brunsdon, Chapter 3 describes the *ur-feminist impulse* that current metatextual postfeminist media generate in order to solicit the feminist evaluations of their viewer-critics. Chapter 6 dissected *Murder*'s participation in cultural conversations of political progressivism, social activism, and identity politics, a participation necessary for the show's branding of itself as 'political television'. I emphasised that such political television can never be political in and of itself, but may inspire the politics of viewers, from which it then benefits. Unlike the intellectual address of *Girls*'s urfeminist impulse, *Murder*'s politics take the form of affective, emotional routes by addressing social realities that are often neglected within mainstream popular culture (via 'truth-talker' Annalise). By doing so, the show seeks to fill a political vacuum, especially during the times of political crisis felt by so many of its viewers confronted with the Trump administration's politics and involved in the hashtag activism of #BlackLivesMatter.

The Introduction opened with the claim that 'each case study is an intricate example of the commercialised engagement with continued systems of sexism and racism in US-American culture – and Western cultures more generally'. Whether such political aspirations are seen as inconsequential, ambiguous, or just plain 'wrong' in the eyes of many of *Girls*'s viewers (because the show never clearly positions itself and relies on viewer-critics to articulate this engagement), or done 'right' as the tweet celebrations of *Murder*'s viewers demonstrate, they amount to a driving dynamic for these shows to perpetuate themselves in interaction with their viewers. It is striking, then, that *TWD* carefully steers clear of any form of political positioning. Chapter 9 argued that the show does so because it participates in a discourse of serialised survival, which serves as a prerequisite for survival not so much in an actual disaster scenario as in a competitive neoliberal capitalist marketplace. Unlike the other two examples, *TWD* seeks to obscure the workings of sexism and racism that the other shows are so interested in exposing in their respective ways.

It is too simplistic or counterproductive to claim that these three cultural conversations contribute to a master discourse of gender and (serial) popular culture. In fact, any such argument would curtail the detailed readings and specific circumstances that these chapters develop. However, despite their differences, these cultural discourses share a larger socio-economic aspect: the commercialisation of political debates. In all these instances, forms of previously radical critique, thought, and activism are contained so that they effectively lose their political bite. Whether it is the postfeminist marketisation of feminism, the more racially aware 'political television' brand as a variation on (adjusted) colourblindness, or the aestheticisation of the neoliberal zombie workout and related resilience, all of these discussions seek to 'tame' various forms of critical reflection and analysis. In the process, the observations of feminist critics, black feminist thinkers, critical race scholars, and newer Marxist critics become separated from their larger arguments and anchored within popular cultural practices. In other words, through their participation in these cultural discourses, these television narratives water down feminist concerns, deflect demands for racial awareness, and, ultimately, even reimagine neoliberal competition as less pressing, merely 'fun' entertainment. By doing so, potentially disruptive ideas are rendered profitable: through the incorporation of such fragments of tamed critique, cultural artefacts present themselves as political, current, caring, and disinterested in mere commercial concerns, all while perpetuating themselves through precisely such dynamics. *Gender and Seriality* paints a dark picture for femininities, social and ethnic minorities, and people with non-normative gender identities and sexual orientations. This is particularly worrisome because serialised popular culture so effectively and intricately avails itself of representational and political criticisms. This book demonstrates how necessary a sophisticated theoretical-methodological approach to the gendered practices of US-American television is to understand these dynamics, and ultimately how much heavy lifting is required to trace the complex operations of gender and seriality in popular culture.

At this point, I return to the two approaches of seriality studies and gender studies that influenced this book and helped it address issues of capitalism, politics, and gender. Frank Kelleter argues that 'popular series are ideological not so much by means of their narrative content . . . but more by means of their self-adaptive narrative operations and media procedures (which include representational inequities and activist countermeasures)' (2017: 29). While this is generally true, concerning intersectional representations of gender, the interconnections between narrative content and such procedures specifically determine these shows' ideologies via the cultural conversations in which they participate. In other words, television narratives develop their own ideologies or become ideological through serial genders and gendered serialities. The ways in which they do so are so habitual and routinised, so deeply and complexly layered, that they appear mechanical. While Judith Roof's notion of gender regimes is different from my conceptualisation of televisual, ongoing performances, the machine-like function of gender regimes accurately describes the socio-economic tamings that television shows perform through cultural conversations:

> Gender regimes are neither imposed nor chosen, but are constantly produced as a machine: as complex systems that preserve, in one way or another, a culture's own fantasy. In the case of contemporary Western culture, that fantasy is reproduction merged with capitalism. . . . One of the functions of contemporary gender regimes is, thus, to negotiate between the extrabinary, nonreproductive interpretations of identity and difference and the exigencies of a culture obsessed with the fantasmatic profit (and compensation) imagined to come from the preservation of a fantasy of organized and very asymmetrical difference. (Roof 2016: 28)

Overall, this is what distinguishes fictional, serialised television narratives from the popular culture examples at the beginning of this Conclusion. Their intersectional gender performances are so challenging to examine because they form the foundation for a show's cultural conversations and also mobilise these conversations as part of their gendering. Scholars similarly have to analyse the ideological underpinnings of televisual gender politics as ongoing without recapitulating, and returning to surface evaluations of either gendered tropes or of static conceptions of gender. Such readings become part of the practices shows have in mind when they cast their ideal viewers and interactively accumulate structures to accommodate viewer activities. To explore how feminist, racially progressive, or sexist a show is often means providing the kind of engagements that these shows need and want for their continuation.

At the moment that I am finishing this book (January 2020), *Girls* is the only show of the three that has ended, whereas the conclusion of *Murder*'s final, sixth season and the premiere of *TWD*'s eleventh season are several months away. It seems precarious to conclude a project while these shows are still in production, but just like gendered networks, serial dynamics are fluid, with their endpoints attempting to renegotiate, yet never truly changing what has already been narrated. Thus, I end with the knowledge that this book functions as an archive of snapshots. Television narratives will not cease to provide frustrating and empowering, clichéd and original, thought-provoking and normalised portrayals of genders and gender relations. The various ways in which these ongoing portrayals employ viewers for interconnected commercial and gendered continuations are at the core of the cultural meanings Bonnie Dow asks media scholars to pursue. Like gender on television, critical scholarship has to be serial, it has to strategically remember, and it must strategically forget. Unlike snapshots that fade, serial genders and gendered serialities have to shift and change to continue to remain urgent, commercially relevant, and culturally accountable.

NOTES

1. Twelve months after Ansari prominently helped many US-Americans work through a devastating political moment, the comedian became one of the focal points of the #MeToo movement. This Twitter hashtag has become a ubiquitous space for mostly cis- and trans-female voices to draw attention to systemic sexism and sexualised violence. A self-proclaimed supporter of the movement, Ansari stood accused of not respecting a date's boundaries. This accusation is a tragically ironic turn, since Ansari had co-written a semi-sociological dating guide, *Modern Love* (2015), which prizes consent and communication.
2. *Ru Paul's Drag Race* (Logo TV/VH1, 2009–) brings the art of drag queen (and, rarely, drag king) performance as well as questions of sexual orientation, transgender identity, and gender performativity to a larger audience. At the same time, the show is criticised

for 'mainstreaming' aspects of queer culture without its culturally and historically specific context and without situating drag within a larger mainstream that often polices the performers celebrated in the show.
3. Although factors like industrial contexts, temporal storytelling, and genre cannot neatly be mapped onto other examples, a comparable form of paratext seriality operates in *Game of Thrones*, which employs the novel series *A Song of Ice and Fire* as a paratext. Further, enthusiasm for cinematic Mafia narratives determined the authorship and viewership of *The Sopranos* and resulted in similar fan discussions in paratexts, although these were not as stringent as the serialised paratexts which Chapter 7 considered. Because looped seriality depends on simultaneous temporal experimentation and social media interactivity, a slightly similar narrative operation occurs in the series *Big Little Lies* (HBO, 2017–19) and the way it ties in with the current #MeToo movement. Lastly, it would be hard to establish a cultural equivalent of the specific temporality, metatextuality, and notoriety of *Girls*, but, to a lesser degree, similar extratextual conversations accompany shows like *UnREAL* (Hulu, 2015–18) and *The Handmaid's Tale* (Hulu, 2017–).

Bibliography

Ahmed, Sara (2017), *Living a Feminist Life*, Durham, NC: Duke University Press.
Albrecht, Michal Mario (2015), *Masculinity in Contemporary Quality Television*, London: Routledge.
Allrath, Gaby, Marion Gymnich, and Carola Surkamp (2005), 'Introduction: Towards a Narratology of TV Series', in Gaby Allrath and Marion Gymnich (eds), *Narrative Strategies in Television Series*, Basingstoke: Palgrave Macmillan, pp. 1–43.
Anderson, Benedict (1995), *Imagined Communities*, rev. edn, London/New York: Verso Books.
Andriolo, Karin R. (1998), 'Gender and the Cultural Construction of Good and Bad Suicides', *Suicide and Life-Threatening Behaviors*, vol. 28, no. 1, pp. 37–49.
Ang, Ien (1985), *Watching Dallas: Soap Opera and the Melodramatic Imagination*, London: Routledge.
Arthurs, Jane (2007), '*Sex and the City* and Consumer Culture: Remediating Postfeminist Drama', in Horace Newcomb (ed.), *Television: The Critical View*, 7th edn, Oxford: Oxford University Press, pp. 315–31.
Autostraddle Editors (2017), 'QTPOC Roundtable: TV and Movie Characters That Made Us Feel Seen', *Autostraddle*, 7 August, <www.autostraddle.com/qtpoc-roundtable-tv-and-movie-characters-that-made-us-feel-seen-389862> (last accessed 12 July 2018).
Auverset, Lauren A., and Andrew C. Billings (2016), 'Relationships Between Social TV and Enjoyment: A Content Analysis of *The Walking Dead*'s Story Sync Experience', *Social Media & Society*, vol. 2, no. 3, pp. 1–12.
Bailey, Jocelyn L. (2015), '"The Body Police": Lena Dunham, Susan Bordo, and HBO's *Girls*', in Elwood Watson, Jennifer Mitchell, and Marc Edward Shaw (eds), *HBO's Girls and the Awkward Politics of Gender, Race, and Privilege*, Lanham, MD: Lexington Books, pp. 27–41.
Barkman, Ashley (2012), 'Women in a Zombie Apocalypse', in Wayne Yeun (ed.), *'The Walking Dead' and Philosophy: Zombie Apocalypse Now*, Chicago: Carus Publishing, pp. 97–106.
Barry, Angie (2012), 'The Problem with Lori: Feminism and *The Walking Dead*', *Criminal Element*, 2 July, <www.criminalelement.com/blogs/2012/07/the-problem-with-lori-feminism-and-the-walking-dead-angie-barry-thriller-zombies> (last accessed 3 July 2018).

Becker, Ron (2006), *Gay TV and Straight America*, New Brunswick, NJ: Rutgers University Press.
Beirne, Rebecca (2012), 'Introduction: Queer Women on Television Today', in Rebecca Beirne (ed.), *Televising Queer Women: A Reader*, Basingstoke: Palgrave Macmillan, pp. 1–10.
Bell, Katherine (2013), 'Obvie, We're the Ladies!: Postfeminism, Privilege, and HBO's Newest *Girls*', *Feminist Media Studies*, vol. 13, no. 2, pp. 363–6.
Bell, Vikki (ed.) (1999), *Performativity and Belonging*, London: Sage Publications.
Bendix, Regina F. (2013), 'Teilhaben: Zur *Tatort*-Rezeption im sozialen Netzwerk *Facebook*', *kulturEN*, vol. 7, no. 1, pp. 30–44.
Berlant, Lauren (2014), *Cruel Optimism*, Durham, NC: Duke University Press.
Berman, Judy (2017), 'What You Should Read About the "Girls" Series Finale', *The New York Times*, 17 April, <www.nytimes.com/2017/04/17/watching/girls-finale-what-to-read.html> (last accessed 14 July 2018).
Berry, Lorraine (2012), '*The Walking Dead* Has Become a White Patriarchy', *Salon*, 11 November, <www.salon.com/2012/11/11/the_walking_dead_has_become_a_white_patriarchy> (last accessed 3 July 2018).
Bianco, Marcie (2014), 'Hannah's Self-Writing: Satirical Aesthetics, Unfashionable Ethics, and a Poetics of Cruel Optimism', in Betty Kaklamanidou and Margaret Tally (eds), *HBO's Girls: Questions of Gender, Politics, and Millennial Angst*, Newcastle upon Tyne: Cambridge Scholars, pp. 73–90.
Bibel, Sara (2015), 'Sunday Cable Ratings: *The Walking Dead* Wins Night, *Talking Dead*, *Real Housewives of Atlanta*, *Sister Wives*, *Shameless*, *Bar Rescue* & More', *TV by the Numbers*, 3 March, <tvbythenumbers.zap2it.com/sdsdskdh279882992z1/sunday-cable-ratings-the-walking-dead-wins-night-talking-dead-real-housewives-of-atlanta-sister-wives-shameless-bar-rescue-more/369504> (last accessed 14 July 2018).
Birke, Dorothee, and Birte Christ (2013), 'Paratext and Digitized Narrative: Mapping the Field', *Narrative*, vol. 21, no. 1, pp. 65–87.
Bobo, Jacqueline (1995), *Black Women as Cultural Readers*, New York: Columbia University Press.
Bonansinga, Jay (2011), 'A Novelist and a Zombie Walk into a Bar: Translating *The Walking Dead* to Prose', in James Lowder (ed.), *Triumph of 'The Walking Dead': Robert Kirkman's Zombie Epic on Page and Screen*, Dallas: BenBella Books, pp. 54–65.
Bordwell, David (2017), 'Wayward Ways and Roads Not Taken', *David Bordwell's Website On Cinema*, 17 May, <www.davidbordwell.net/blog/2017/05/17/wayward-ways-and-roads-not-taken> (last accessed 14 July 2018).
Bowen, Sesali (2016), *Bitches Be Like . . . : Memes as Black Girl Counter and Disidentification Tools*, MA thesis, Georgia State University.
Bowleg, Lisa (2008), 'When Black + Lesbian + Woman ≠ Black Lesbian Woman: The Methodological Challenges of Qualitative and Quantitative Intersectionality Research', *Sex Roles*, vol. 59, no. 5, pp. 312–25.
Boylorn, Robin M. (2017), 'Beauty Parlor Politics', in Brittney C. Cooper, Susana M. Morris, and Robin M. Boylorn (eds), *The Crunk Feminist Collection*, New York: Feminist Press, pp. 282–4.
Brandl-Risi, Bettina (2012), 'Das Leben des Bildes und die Dauer der Pose: Überlegungen zum Paradox des Tableau Vivant', in Bettina Brandl-Risi, Gabriele Brandstetter, and Stefanie Diekmann (eds), *Hold it! – Zur Pose zwischen Bild und Performance*, Berlin: Theater der Zeit, pp. 52–67.
Brock, André (2012), 'From the Blackhand Side: Twitter as a Cultural Conversation', *Journal of Broadcasting & Electronic Media*, vol. 56, no. 4, pp. 529–49.

Bronfen, Elisabeth (1992), *Over Her Dead Body: Death, Femininity and the Aesthetic*, Manchester: Manchester University Press.
Brunsdon, Charlotte (2005), 'Feminism, Postfeminism, Martha, Martha, and Nigella', *Cinema Journal*, vol. 44, no. 2, pp. 110–16.
Burton, T K (2012), 'Make Sure Your Face is Clean Now, Can't Have No Dirty Dead: Race, Gender, and *The Walking Dead*', *Pajiba*, 8 November, <www.pajiba.com/think_pieces/make-sure-your-face-is-clean-now-cant-have-no-dirty-dead-race-gender-and-the-walking-dead.php> (last accessed 3 July 2018).
Butler, Judith (1988), 'Performative Acts and Gender Constitution: An Essay in Phenomenology and Feminist Theory', *Theatre Journal*, vol. 40, no. 4, pp. 519–31.
Butler, Judith (2008), *Gender Trouble*, New York: Routledge.
Caldwell, John T. (2013), 'Authorship Below-the-Line', in Jonathan Gray and Derek Johnson (eds), *A Companion to Media Authorship*, Hoboken, NJ: John Wiley & Sons, pp. 349–69.
Carroll, Noël (2013), *Minerva's Night Out: Philosophy, Pop Culture, and Moving Pictures*, Hoboken, NJ: John Wiley & Sons.
Carroll, Rebecca (2012), 'White *Girls*, Big City: What HBO's New Show Misses', *The Daily Beast*, 20 April, <www.thedailybeast.com/articles/2012/04/20/white-girls-big-city-what-hbo-s-new-show-misses.html> (last accessed 14 July 2018).
Cauvin, J. L. (2012), 'In Defense of *Girls*', *Huffington Post*, 19 April, <www.huffingtonpost.com/jl-cauvin/girls-hbo_b_1437041.html> (last accessed 14 July 2018).
Chatman, Dayna (2017), 'Black Twitter and the Politics of Viewing *Scandal*', in Jonathan Gray, Cornel Sandvoss, and C. L. Harrington (eds), *Fandom: Identities and Communities in a Mediated World*, New York: New York University Press, pp. 299–314.
Chen, Joyce (2013), 'Howard Stern Calls Lena Dunham "Little Fat Girl," Likens *Girls*' Sex Scenes to "Rape"', *US Weekly*, 12 January, <www.usmagazine.com/celebrity-news/news/howard-stern-calls-lena-dunham-little-fat-girl-likens-girls-sex-scenes-to-rape-2013121> (last accessed 12 May 2018).
Chesaniuk, Marie (2016), 'The Female Slacker', *The Point Magazine*, 28 October, <www.thepointmag.com/2009/criticism/the-female-slacker> (last accessed 12 May 2018).
Choi, Mary (2014), 'I Slept with My Best Friend's Ex: Learning the Hard Way That Violating Girl Code is a Loser's Game', *Cosmopolitan*, 9 March, <www.cosmopolitan.com/sex-love/advice/a5898/lost-friend-after-dating-ex> (last accessed 14 July 2018).
Christian, Aymar Jean (2018), *Open TV: Innovation Beyond Hollywood and the Rise of Web Television*, New York: New York University Press.
Clover, Carol (1992), *Men, Women, and Chainsaws*, Princeton, NJ: Princeton University Press.
Coates, Ta-Nehisi (2012), '*Girls* Through the Veil', *The Atlantic*, 20 April, <www.theatlantic.com/entertainment/archive/2012/04/girls-through-the-veil> (last accessed 12 May 2018).
Coe, Erin (2013), '5 Courtroom Fashion Flops Lawyers Should Avoid', *Law360*, 25 April, <www.law360.com/articles/435333/5-courtroom-fashion-flops-lawyers-should-avoid> (last accessed 12 July 2018).
Coleman, Robin R. Means (2014), 'The Enduring Woman: Race, Revenge, and Self-Determination in *Chloe, Love Is Calling You*', in Norma Jones, Maja Bajac-Carter, and Bob Batchelor (eds), *Heroines of Film and Television: Portrayals in Popular Culture*, Lanham, MD: Rowman & Littlefield, pp. 163–76.
Collins, Patricia Hill (2000), *Black Feminist Thought: Knowledge, Consciousness, and the Politics of Empowerment*, New York: Routledge.
Collins, Patricia Hill (2005), *Black Sexual Politics: African Americans, Gender, and the New Racism*, New York: Routledge.
Connell, R. W. (2016), *Masculinities*, Cambridge: Polity Press.

Creed, Barbara (1995), 'Horror and the Carnivalesque', in Leslie Devereaux and Roger Hillman (eds), *Fields of Vision: Essays in Film Studies, Visual Anthropology, and Photography*, Berkeley, CA: University of California Press, pp. 127–59.

Crenshaw, Kimberlé (1989), 'Demarginalizing the Intersection of Race and Sex: A Black Feminist Critique of Antidiscrimination Doctrine, Feminist Theory, and Antiracist Politics', *University of Chicago Legal Forum*, no. 1, pp. 139–67.

Crenshaw, Kimberlé (1991), 'Mapping the Margins: Intersectionality, Identity Politics, and Violence Against Women of Color', *Stanford Law Review*, vol. 43, no. 6, pp. 1241–99.

Cruz, Eliel (2014), 'The Year in Bisexual Invisibility', *The Advocate*, 30 December, <www.advocate.com/year-review/2014/12/30/year-bisexual-invisibility> (last accessed 12 July 2018).

Daalmans, Serena (2013), '"I'm Busy Trying to Become Who I Am": Self-Entitlement and the City in HBO's *Girls*', *Feminist Media Studies*, vol. 13, no. 2, pp. 359–62.

Daggett, Chelsea (2014), '"Occupy" *Girls*: Millennial Adulthood and the Cracks in HBO's Brand', in Betty Kaklamanidou and Margaret Tally (eds), *HBO's Girls: Questions of Gender, Politics, and Millennial Angst*, Newcastle upon Tyne: Cambridge Scholars, pp. 199–216.

Davies, Madeleine (2013), 'In Defense of Hannah', *Jezebel*, 18 March, <www.jezebel.com/5991050/in-defense-of-hannah> (last accessed 14 July 2018).

Davis, Angela (1998), 'Afro Images: Politics, Fashion, Nostalgia', in Monique Guillory and Richard C. Green (eds), *Soul: Black Power, Politics, and Pleasure*, New York: New York University Press, pp. 23–31.

De Kosnik, Abigail (2011), 'Soaps For Tomorrow: Media Fans Making Online Drama From Celebrity Gossip', in Sam Ford, Abigail De Kosnik, and C. L. Harrington (eds), *The Survival of Soap Opera: Transformations for a New Media Era*, Jackson, MS: University Press of Mississippi, pp. 233–49.

De Kosnik, Abigail (2013), 'One Life to Live: Soap Opera Storytelling', in Ethan Thompson and Jason Mittell (eds), *How To Watch Television*, New York: New York University Press, pp. 355–63.

Dean, Michelle (2012), 'What We Talk About When We Talk About Lena Dunham', *The Nation*, 9 October, <www.thenation.com/article/what-we-talk-about-when-we-talk-about-lena-dunham> (last accessed 12 May 2018).

Dean, Michelle (2013), 'The Internet's Toxic Relationship with HBO's *Girls*', *The Nation*, 28 January, <www.thenation.com/article/internets-toxic-relationship-hbos-girls> (last accessed 12 May 2018).

Dean, Michelle (2014), '*Girls* Whiplash Report: Why, Despite Everything, Lena Dunham's Nudity is Radical', *Flavorwire*, 10 January, <www.flavorwire.com/432925/girls-whiplash-report-why-despite-everything-lena-dunhams-nudity-is-radical> (last accessed 12 May 2018).

DeCarvalho, Lauren J. (2013), 'Hannah and Her Entitled Sisters: (Post)Feminism, (Post)Recession, and *Girls*', *Feminist Media Studies*, vol. 13, no. 2, pp. 367–70.

Dejmanee, Tisha (2016), 'Consumption in the City: The Turn to Interiority in Contemporary Postfeminist Television', *European Journal of Cultural Studies*, vol. 19, no. 2, pp. 119–33.

Denby, David (2007), 'A Fine Romance', *The New Yorker*, 23 June, <www.newyorker.com/magazine/2007/07/23/a-fine-romance> (last accessed 14 July 2018).

DeVega, Chauncey (2012), 'Michonne or Maggie? Race, Gender, and Rape on *The Walking Dead* TV Series', *Daily Kos*, 26 November, <www.dailykos.com/story/2012/11/26/1164790/-Michonne-or-Maggie-Race-Gender-and-Rape-on-The-Walking-Dead-TV-Series> (last accessed 3 July 2018).

Dhaenens, Frederik (2017), 'Reading the Boys of *Girls*', in Meredith Nash and Imelda Whelehan (eds), *Reading Lena Dunham's* Girls: *Feminism, Postfeminism, Authenticity and Gendered Performance in Contemporary Television*, Basingstoke: Palgrave Macmillan, pp. 121–33.

Dow, Bonnie J. (1996), *Prime-Time Feminism: Television, Media Culture, and the Women's Movement Since 1970*, Philadelphia: University of Pennsylvania Press.
Eburne, Jonathan P. (2014), 'Zombie Arts and Letters', in Edward P. Comentale and Aaron Jaffe (eds), *This Year's Work at The Zombie Research Center*, Bloomington: Indiana University Press, pp. 389–415.
Eco, Umberto (1985), 'Innovation and Repetition: Between Modern and Post-Modern Aesthetics', *Daedalus*, vol. 114, no. 4, pp. 161–84.
Edelman, Lee (2004), *No Future: Queer Theory and the Death Drive*, Durham, NC: Duke University Press.
Eppink, Jason (2014), 'A Brief History of the GIF (So Far)', *Journal of Visual Culture*, vol. 13, no. 3, pp. 298–306.
Erigha, Maryann (2014), 'Working *Girls*? Millennials and Creative Careers', in Betty Kaklamanidou and Margaret Tally (eds), *HBO's Girls: Questions of Gender, Politics, and Millennial Angst*, Newcastle upon Tyne: Cambridge Scholars, pp. 144–55.
Erigha, Maryann (2015), 'Shonda Rhimes, *Scandal*, and the Politics of Crossing Over', *The Black Scholar*, vol. 45. no. 1, pp. 10–15.
Etti, Sequoia (2014), 'Oops: What It's Like Sleeping With Your Friend's Ex', *Elite Daily*, <www.elitedaily.com/dating/sleeping-friends-ex-post-production/860260> (last accessed 9 June 2020).
Everett, Anna (2015), 'Scandalicious: *Scandal*, Social Media, and Shonda Rhimes' Auteurist Juggernaut', *The Black Scholar*, vol. 45, no. 1, pp. 34–43.
Ferdinand, Renata (2015), 'Skin Tone and Popular Culture: My Story as a Dark Skinned Black Woman', *The Popular Culture Studies Journal*, vol. 3, no. 1/2, pp. 325–48.
Feuer, Jane (2007), 'HBO and the Concept of Quality TV', in Janet McCabe and Kim Akass (eds), *Quality TV: Contemporary American Television and Beyond*, New York: I.B. Tauris, pp. 145–57.
Florini, Sarah (2014), 'Tweets, Tweeps, and Signifyin': Communication and Cultural Performance on "Black Twitter"', *Television & New Media*, vol. 15, no. 3, pp. 223–37.
Ford, Jessica (2016), 'The "Smart" Body Politics of Lena Dunham's *Girls*', *Feminist Media Studies*, vol. 16, no. 6, pp. 1029–42.
Foster, Audrey Gwendolyn (2014), *Hoarders, Doomsday Preppers, and the Culture of Apocalypse*, Basingstoke: Palgrave Macmillan.
Foucault, Michel (1998), *Aesthetics, Method, and Epistemology*, trans. James D. Fabion, New York: The New Press.
Freeman, Elizabeth (2010), *Time Binds: Queer Temporalities, Queer Histories*, Durham, NC: Duke University Press.
Fuller, Sean, and Catherine Driscoll (2015), 'HBO's *Girls*: Gender, Generation, and Quality Television', *Continuum – Journal of Media & Cultural Studies*, vol. 29, no. 2, pp. 253–62.
Ganz-Blättler, Ursula (2012), 'DSDS als Reality-Serie: Kumulatives Storytelling "on the go"', in Frank Kelleter (ed.), *Populäre Serialität: Narration – Evolution – Distinktion: Zum seriellen Erzählen seit dem 19. Jahrhundert*, Bielefeld: Transcript, pp. 123–41.
Gay, Roxane (2014a), 'Roxane Gay Talks to Lena Dunham About Her New Book, Feminism, and the Benefits of Being Criticized Online', *Vulture*, 2 October, <www.vulture.com/2014/10/roxane-gay-interview-lena-dunham-bad-feminist-not-that-kind-of-girl-books.html> (last accessed 12 May 2018).
Gay, Roxane (2014b), *Bad Feminist*. New York: HarperCollins.
Gay, Roxane (2017), *Hunger: A Memoir of (My) Body*, New York: HarperCollins.
Genette, Gérard (1982), *Palimpsestes. La littérature au second degré*, Paris: Seuil.
Genette, Gérard (1997), *Paratexts: Thresholds of Interpretation*, trans. Jane E. Lewin, Cambridge: Cambridge University Press.

Genz, Stéphanie (2017), '"I have Work . . . I Am Busy . . . Trying to Become Who I Am": Neoliberal *Girls* and Recessionary Postfeminism', in Meredith Nash and Imelda Whelehan (eds), *Reading Lena Dunham's* Girls*: Feminism, Postfeminism, Authenticity and Gendered Performance in Contemporary Television*, Basingstoke: Palgrave Macmillan, pp. 17–30.

Gerhard, Jane (2005), '*Sex and the City:* Carrie Bradshaw's Queer Postfeminism', *Feminist Media Studies*, vol. 5, no. 1, pp. 37–49.

Gill, Rosalind (2007), 'Postfeminist Media Culture: Elements of a Sensibility', *European Journal of Cultural Studies*, vol. 10, no. 2, pp. 147–66.

Gill, Rosalind (2016), 'Post-postfeminism? New Feminist Visibilities in Postfeminist Times', *Feminist Media Studies*, vol. 16, no. 4, pp. 610–30.

Gill, Rosalind (2017), 'Afterword – *Girls*: Notes on Authenticity, Ambivalence and Imperfection', in Meredith Nash and Imelda Whelehan (eds), *Reading Lena Dunham's* Girls*: Feminism, Postfeminism, Authenticity and Gendered Performance in Contemporary Television*, Basingstoke: Palgrave Macmillan, pp. 225–42.

Gill, Rosalind, and Christina Scharff (2011), 'Introduction', in Rosalind Gill and Christina Scharff (eds), *New Femininities: Postfeminism, Neoliberalism and Subjectivity*, Basingstoke: Palgrave Macmillan, pp. 1–17.

GLAAD (2015), *Where Are We On TV Season 2015/2016*, GLAAD Media Institute.

GLAAD (2017), *Where Are We On TV Season 2017/2018*, GLAAD Media Institute.

Gomez, Stephanie L., and Megan D. McFarlane (2017), '"It's (not) handled": Race, Gender, and Refraction in *Scandal*', *Feminist Media Studies*, vol. 17, no. 3, pp. 362–76.

Grant, Ruby, and Meredith Nash (2017), 'From *Sex and the City* to *Girls*: Paving the Way for "Post?Feminism"', in Meredith Nash and Imelda Whelehan (eds), *Reading Lena Dunham's* Girls*: Feminism, Postfeminism, Authenticity and Gendered Performance in Contemporary Television*, Basingstoke: Palgrave Macmillan, pp. 61–74.

Gray, Herman S. (2005), *Cultural Moves: African Americans and the Politics of Representation*, Berkeley, CA: University of California Press.

Gray, Jonathan (2010), *Show Sold Separately: Promos, Spoilers, and Other Media Paratexts*, New York: New York University Press.

Gray, Jonathan (2011), 'The Reviews Are in: TV Critics and the (Pre)Creation of Meaning', in Michael Kackmann, Marnie Binfield, Matthew Thomas Payne, Allison Perlman, and Bryan Sebok (eds), *Flow TV: Television in the Age of Media Convergence*, New York: Routledge, pp. 114–27.

Gray, Jonathan (2013), 'When is the Author?', in Jonathan Gray and Derek Johnson (eds), *A Companion to Media Authorship*, Hoboken, NJ: John Wiley & Sons, pp. 88–111.

Grdešić, Maša (2013), '"I'm Not the Ladies!": Metatextual Commentary in *Girls*', *Feminist Media Studies*, vol. 13, no. 2, pp. 355–8.

Hagedorn, Roger (1988), 'Technology and Economic Exploitation: The Serial as a Form of Narrative Presentation', *Wide Angle*, vol. 10, no. 4, pp. 4–12.

Haglund, David, and Daniel Engber (2013), 'Guys on *Girls*, Season 2: Was That the Worst Episode of *Girls* Ever?', *Slate*, 10 February, <www.slate.com/articles/arts/tv_club/features/2013/girls_season-2/week_5/girls_on_hbo_one_man_s_trash_episode_5_of_season_2_reviewed_by_guys.html> (last accessed 12 May 2018).

Halberstam, Judith (1998), *Female Masculinity*, Durham, NC: Duke University Press.

Halberstam, Judith (2005), *In a Queer Time and Place: Transgender Bodies, Subcultural Lives*, New York: New York University Press.

Hamad, Hannah, and Anthea Taylor (2015), 'Introduction: Feminism and Contemporary Celebrity Culture', *Celebrity Studies*, vol. 6, no. 1, pp. 124–7.

Hamilton, Nikita T. (2014), 'So They Say You Have a Race Problem? You're in Your Twenties, You Have Way More Problems Than That', in Betty Kaklamanidou and Margaret Tally (eds), *HBO's Girls: Questions of Gender, Politics, and Millennial Angst*, Newcastle upon Tyne: Cambridge Scholars, pp. 43–58.

Hämmerling, Christine (2016), *Sonntags 20: 15 Uhr – 'Tatort': Zu sozialen Positionierungen eines Fernsehpublikums*, Göttingen: Universitätsverlag Göttingen.

Hämmerling, Christine, and Mirjam Nast (2017), 'Popular Seriality in Everyday Practice: *Perry Rhodan* and *Tatort*', in Frank Kelleter (ed.), *Media of Serial Narrative*, Columbus: The Ohio State University Press, pp. 248–60.

Haraway, Donna (1988), 'Situated Knowledges: The Science Question in Feminism and the Privilege of Partial Perspective', *Feminist Studies*, vol. 14, no. 3, pp. 575–99.

Harding, Sandra (2009), 'Standpoint Theories: Productively Controversial', *Hypatia*, vol. 24, no. 4, pp. 192–200.

Harrigan, Pat, and Noah Wardrip-Fruin (eds) (2009), *Third Person: Authoring and Exploring Vast Narratives*. Cambridge, MA: MIT Press.

Harrington, Stephen (2014), 'Tweeting About the Telly: Live TV, Audiences, and Social Media', in Katrin Weller, Axel Bruhns, Jean Burgess, Merja Mahrt, and Cornelius Puschmann (eds), *Twitter and Society*, Bern: Peter Lang, pp. 237–47.

Harris, Tamara Winfrey (2015), *The Sisters Are Alright: Changing the Broken Narrative of Black Women in America*, San Francisco: Berrett-Koehler.

Hassler-Forest, Dan (2014), '*The Walking Dead*: Quality Television, Transmedia Serialization and Zombies', in Rob Allen and Thijs van den Berg (eds), *Serialization in Popular Culture*, New York: Routledge, pp. 91–105.

Havas, Julia (2016), *Invocations of Feminism: Cultural Value, Gender, and American Quality Television*, Dissertation, University of East Anglia.

Havas, Julia, and Maria Sulimma (2018), 'Through the Gaps of My Fingers: Genre, Femininity, and Cringe Aesthetics in Dramedy Television', *Television & New Media*, June, <doi.org/10.1177/1527476418777838> (last accessed 14 July 2018).

Hayward, Jennifer (2009), *Consuming Pleasures: Active Audiences and Serial Fictions from Dickens to Soap Opera*, Lexington: University Press of Kentucky.

Hemmings, Clare (2011), *Why Stories Matter: The Political Grammar of Feminist Theory*, Durham, NC: Duke University Press.

Henderson, Maureen J. (2012), 'She's No Seth Rogen in Stilettos: Tearing Down the Slacker Girl Stereotype', *Forbes*, 4 April, <www.forbes.com/sites/jmaureenhenderson/2012/04/04/shes-no-seth-rogen-in-stilettos-tearing-down-the-slacker-girl-stereotype/#2a10148c549e> (last accessed 14 July 2018).

Henry, Astrid (2004), 'Orgasms and Empowerment: *Sex and the City* and Third Wave Feminism', in Kim Akass and Janet McCabe (eds), *Reading 'Sex and the City'*, New York: I.B. Tauris, pp. 65–82.

Herbert, Rosemary (2003), *Whodunit? A Who's Who of Crime & Mystery Writing*, Oxford: Oxford University Press.

Hess, Amanda (2013), 'Was That a Rape Scene in *Girls*?', *Slate*, 11 March, <www.slate.com/blogs/xx_factor/2013/03/11/girls_adam_and_natalia_sexual_assault_and_verbal_consent_on_hbo_s_girls.html> (last accessed 14 July 2018).

Hickethier, Knut (2003), 'Serie', in Hans-Otto Hügel (ed.), *Handbuch Populäre Kultur*, Stuttgart: J.B. Metzler, pp. 397–403.

Hills, Matt (2005), *The Pleasures of Horror*, London: Continuum.

Hoby, Hermione (2012), 'The Slacker is Back – and this Time She's Female', *The Guardian*, 25 March, <www.theguardian.com/culture/2012/mar/25/slacker-back-female-lena-dunham> (last accessed 14 July 2018).

Hochschild, Arlie, and Anne Machung (2012), *The Second Shift: Working Families and the Revolution at Home*, London: Penguin Books.

Hofmann, Viola (2007), 'Das Kostüm der Macht. Das Erscheinungsbild von Politikerinnen und Politikern zwischen Vereinheitlichung und Maskerade', in Gabriele Mentges (ed.), *Uniformierungen in Bewegung: Vestimentäre Praktiken zwischen Vereinheitlichung, Kostümierung und Maskerade*, Münster: Waxmann, pp. 159–70.

Holmes, Anna (2012a), 'White *Girls*', *The New Yorker*, 23 April, <www.newyorker.com/culture/culture-desk/white-girls> (last accessed 14 July 2018).

Holmes, Anna (2012b), 'The Age of Girlfriends', *The New Yorker*, 6 July, <www.newyorker.com/books/page-turner/the-age-of-girlfriends> (last accessed 14 July 2018).

Holmes, Linda (2015), 'Television 2015: Is There Really Too Much TV?' *NPR*, 16 August, <www.npr.org/sections/monkeysee/2015/08/16/432458841/television-2015-is-there-really-too-much-tv> (last accessed 14 July 2018).

Hoo, Fawnia Soo (2015), 'All the Costume Secrets Behind *How to Get Away with Murder*', *Fashionista*, 12 February, <www.fashionista.com/2015/02/how-to-get-away-with-murder-tv-costumes> (last accessed 12 July 2018).

Hope, Clover (2014), 'Objection: A Real Lawyer Fact Checks *How to Get Away with Murder*', *Jezebel*, 10 October, <www.jezebel.com/objection-a-real-lawyer-fact-checks-how-to-get-away-wi-1644750449> (last accessed 12 July 2018).

Horeck, Tanya (2014), *Public Rape: Representing Violation in Fiction and Film*, New York: Routledge.

Householder, April Kalogeropoulos (2015), 'Girls, Grrrls, Girls: Lena Dunham, *Girls* and the Contradictions of the Fourth Wave Feminism', in Adrienne Trier-Bieniek (ed.), *Feminist Theory and Pop Culture*, Boston: Sense, pp. 19–33.

Hu, Jane (2017), 'The *Girls* Finale: Noisy Criticism', *LA Review of Books*, 24 April, <www.lareviewofbooks.org/article/the-girls-finale> (last accessed 14 July 2018).

Huber, Linda (2015), 'Remix Culture and the Reaction Gif', *Gnovis: A Journal of Communication, Culture & Technology*, 25 February, <www.gnovisjournal.org/2015/02/25/remix-culture-the-reaction-gif> (last accessed 12 July 2018).

Hustvedt, Siri (2011), *The Summer without Men*, London: Sceptre.

Hyden, Steven (2017), 'Even if You Never Watched *Girls* it Changed the Way You Talk About Television', *Uproxx*, 9 February, <www.uproxx.com/tv/girls-hbo-thinkpieces-legacy> (last accessed 12 May 2018).

Jackson, Lauren Michele (2017), 'We Need to Talk About Digital Blackface in Reaction GIFs', *Teen Vogue*, 2 August, <www.teenvogue.com/story/digital-blackface-reaction-gifs/amp> (last accessed 12 July 2018).

Jahn-Sudmann, Andreas, and Frank Kelleter (2012), 'Die Dynamik serieller Überbietung: Amerikanische Fernsehserien und das Konzept des Quality-TV', in Frank Kelleter (ed.), *Populäre Serialität: Narration – Evolution – Distinktion: Zum seriellen Erzählen seit dem 19. Jahrhundert*, Bielefeld: Transcript, pp. 205–24.

James, Kendra (2012), 'Dear Lena Dunham: I Exist', *Racialicious*, 19 April, <www.racialicious.com/2012/04/19/dear-lena-dunham-i-exist> (last accessed 14 July 2018).

Jamieson, Kathleen Hall (1995), *Beyond the Double Bind: Women and Leadership*, Oxford: Oxford University Press.

Jenkins, Henry (2013), '*The Walking Dead*: Adapting Comics', in Ethan Thompson and Jason Mittell (eds), *How To Watch Television*, New York: New York University Press, pp. 373–82.

Joseph, Ralina L. (2016), 'Strategically Ambiguous Shonda Rhimes: Respectability Politics of a Black Woman Showrunner', *Souls*, vol. 18, no. 2–4, pp. 302–20.

Jowett, Lorna, and Stacey Abbott (2013), *TV Horror: Investigating the Dark Side of the Small Screen*, New York: I.B. Tauris.

Juzwiak, Rich (2012), 'Tune In, Recap, Drop Out: Why I'll Never Recap a TV Show Again', *gawker*, 22 March, <gawker.com/5895232/tune-in-recap-drop-out-why-ill-never-recap-a-tv-show-again> (last accessed 12 July 2018).

Kaklamanidou, Betty, and Margaret Tally (2014), 'Introduction', in Betty Kaklamanidou and Margaret Talley (eds), *HBO's Girls: Questions of Gender, Politics, and Millennial Angst*, Newcastle upon Tyne: Cambridge Scholars, pp. 1–9.

Kanzler, Katja (2012), 'Of Legal Roulette and Eccentric Clients: Contemporary TV Legal Drama as (Post)Postmodern Public Sphere', in Sebastian. M. Herrmann, Carolin Alice Hofmann, Katja Kanzler, and Frank Usbeck (eds), *Participating Audiences, Imagined Public Spheres: The Cultural Work of Contemporary American(-ized) Narratives*, Leipzig: Leipziger Universitätsverlag, pp. 63–90.

Kanzler, Katja (2015), 'Truth, Justice, and Contingency in *The Good Wife*', in Christoph Ernst and Heike Paul (eds), *Amerikanische Fernsehserien der Gegenwart*, Bielefeld: Transcript, pp. 133–51.

Karlyn, Kathleen Rowe (1995), *The Unruly Woman: Gender and the Genres of Laughter*, Dallas: University of Texas Press.

Kearns, Megan (2013), 'Nothing Can Save *The Walking Dead*'s Sexist Woman Problem', *Bitch Flicks*, 1 May, <www.btchflcks.com/2013/05/nothing-can-save-the-walking-deads-sexist-woman-problem.hml> (last accessed 3 July 2018).

Kelleter, Frank (2011), 'Serienhelden sehen dich an', *Psychologie Heute*, April, pp. 70–5.

Kelleter, Frank (2012), 'Populäre Serialität: Eine Einführung', in Frank Kelleter (ed.), *Populäre Serialität: Narration – Evolution – Distinktion: Zum seriellen Erzählen seit dem 19. Jahrhundert*, Bielefeld: Transcript, pp. 11–46.

Kelleter, Frank (2014), *Serial Agencies: The Wire and Its Readers*, Winchester/Washington: Zero Books.

Kelleter, Frank (2015), '"Whatever Happened, Happened": Serial Character Constellation as Problem and Solution in *Lost*', in Christoph Ernst and Heike Paul (eds), *Amerikanische Fernsehserien der Gegenwart*, Bielefeld: Transcript, pp. 57–87.

Kelleter, Frank (2017), 'Five Ways of Looking at Popular Seriality', in Frank Kelleter (ed.), *Media of Serial Narrative*, Columbus: The Ohio State University Press, pp. 7–34.

Kelleter, Frank, and Kathleen Loock (2017), 'Hollywood Remaking as Second-Order Serialization', in Frank Kelleter (ed.), *Media of Serial Narrative*, Columbus: The Ohio State University Press, pp. 124–47.

Kelleter, Frank, and Daniel Stein (2012), 'Autorisierungspraktiken seriellen Erzählens: Zur Gattungsentwicklung von Superheldencomics', in Frank Kelleter (ed.), *Populäre Serialität: Narration – Evolution – Distinktion: Zum seriellen Erzählen seit dem 19. Jahrhundert*, Bielefeld: Transcript, pp. 259–90.

Kissell, Rick (2015), '*Scandal*, *The Walking Dead* Have the Most Socially Loyal Fans, Nielsen Report Says', *Variety*, 24 August, <www.variety.com/2015/data/news/scandal-the-walking-dead-most-socially-loyal-fans-1201576823> (last accessed 12 July 2018).

Kissling, Elizabeth Arveda (2017), 'All Postfeminist Women Do: Women's Sexual and Reproductive Health in Television Comedy', in Meredith Nash and Imelda Whelehan (eds), *Reading Lena Dunham's Girls: Feminism, Postfeminism, Authenticity and Gendered Performance in Contemporary Television*, Basingstoke: Palgrave Macmillan, pp. 209–23.

Klein, Amanda Ann (2012), 'Reconsidering *Girls*', *The Judgmental Observer*, 19 May, <www.judgmentalobserver.com/2012/05/19/reconsidering-girls> (last accessed 12 May 2018).

Lagerwey, Jorie, Julia Leyda, and Diane Negra (2016), 'Female-Centered TV in an Age of Precarity', *Genders Online Journal*, vol. 1, no. 1, <www.colorado.edu/genders/2016/05/19/female-centered-tv-age-precarity> (last accessed 12 July 2018).

Lehman, Katherine J. (2014), '"All Adventurous Women Do": HBO's *Girls* and the 1960–70s Single Woman', in Betty Kaklamanidou and Margaret Tally (eds), *HBO's Girls: Questions of Gender, Politics, and Millennial Angst*, Newcastle upon Tyne: Cambridge Scholars, pp. 10–29.

Lesniak, Britta (2018), *Epic Television: Music and Sound in 'Ramayan' and 'Mahabharat'*, Dissertation, Georg-August-Universität Göttingen.

Leverette, Marc (2008), 'Cocksucker, Motherfucker, Tits', in Marc Leverette, Brian L. Ott, and Louise Buckley (eds), *It's Not TV: Watching HBO in the Post-Television Era*, New York: Routledge, pp. 123–51.

Levy, Yael (2015), 'Girls Issues: The Feminist Politics of *Girls*' Celebration of the "Trivial"', in Elwood Watson, Jennifer Mitchell, and Marc Edward Shaw (eds), *HBO's Girls and the Awkward Politics of Gender, Race, and Privilege*, Lanham, MD: Lexington Books, pp. 63–70.

Lewis, Melinda M. (2014), '"I Want Somebody to Hang Out with All The Time": Emotional Contradictions, Intimacy and (Dis)Pleasure', in Betty Kaklamanidou and Margaret Tally (eds), *HBO's Girls: Questions of Gender, Politics, and Millennial Angst*, Newcastle upon Tyne: Cambridge Scholars, pp. 172–85.

Leyda, Julia (2018), 'Financial Times: Economic and Industrial Temporalities in Netflix's *Arrested Development*', *Television & New Media*, vol. 19, no. 4, pp. 345–60.

Leyda, Julia, and Diane Negra (2015), 'Introduction: Extreme Weather and Global Media', in Julia Leyda and Diane Negra (eds), *Extreme Weather and Global Media*, New York: Routledge, pp. 1–28.

Lloyd, Christopher (2017), 'Sexual Perversity in New York?', in Meredith Nash and Imelda Whelehan (eds), *Reading Lena Dunham's Girls: Feminism, Postfeminism, Authenticity and Gendered Performance in Contemporary Television*, Basingstoke: Palgrave Macmillan, pp. 197–207.

Loock, Kathleen (2014), 'Introduction: Serial Narratives', in Kathleen Loock (ed.), *Serial Narratives*, special issue of *Literatur in Wissenschaft und Unterricht*, no. 1/2, pp. 5–9.

Loock, Kathleen (2017), 'The Sequel Paradox: Repetition, Innovation, and Hollywood's Hit Film Formula', in Kathleen Loock and Frank Krutnik (eds), *Exploring Film Seriality*, special issue of *Film Studies*, vol. 17, no. 1, pp. 92–110.

Lotz, Amanda D. (2008), 'On Television Criticism: The Pursuit of the Critical Examination of a Popular Art', *Popular Communication*, vol. 6, no. 1, pp. 20–36.

Lotz, Amanda D. (2014), *Cable Guys: Television and Masculinities in the 21st Century*, New York: New York University Press.

Maase, Kaspar (2010), *Was macht Populärkultur politisch?*, Wiesbaden: VS Verlag für Sozialwissenschaften.

McAlone, Nathan (2017), 'HBO's Programming President Says "Think Pieces" are a Good Measure of a Show's Success', *Business Insider*, 13 June, <www.businessinsider.de/hbo-uses-think-pieces-as-a-metric-of-a-new-shows-success-2017-6> (last accessed 14 July 2018).

McCabe, Janet, and Kim Akass (2007), 'Sex, Swearing and Respectability: Courting Controversy, HBO's Original Programming and Producing Quality TV', in Janet McCabe and Kim Akass (eds), *Quality TV: Contemporary American Television and Beyond*, New York: I.B. Tauris, pp. 62–76.

McCann, Hannah (2017), '"A Voice of a Generation": *Girls* and the Problem of Representation', in Meredith Nash and Imelda Whelehan (eds), *Reading Lena Dunham's Girls: Feminism, Postfeminism, Authenticity and Gendered Performance in Contemporary Television*, Basingstoke: Palgrave Macmillan, pp. 91–104.

McDermott, Catherine (2017), 'Genres of Impasse: Postfeminism as a Relation of Cruel Optimism in *Girls*', in Meredith Nash and Imelda Whelehan (eds), *Reading Lena Dunham's Girls: Feminism, Postfeminism, Authenticity and Gendered Performance in Contemporary Television*, Basingstoke: Palgrave Macmillan, pp. 45–59.

McDonald, Jordan (2018), 'Nova, Nola, and Annalise: Queer Black Women and the Arc of Representation', *Bitchmedia*, 3 January, <www.bitchmedia.org/article/nova-nola-annalise-queer-black-women-onscreen> (last accessed 12 July 2018).

McKenna, AJ (2018), 'Sixty-Three Days', in Roxane Gay (ed.), *Not That Bad: Dispatches from Rape Culture*, New York: HarperCollins, pp. 79–88.

McKenzie, Lara, and Laura Dales (2017), 'Choosing Love? Tensions and Transformations of Modern Marriage in *Married at First Sight*', *Continuum – Journal of Media & Cultural Studies*, vol. 31, no. 6, pp. 857–67.

McRobbie, Angela (2009), *The Aftermath of Feminism: Gender, Culture and Social Change*, London: Sage Publications.

Marghitu, Stefania, and Conrad Ng (2013), 'Body Talk: Reconsidering the Post-Feminist Discourse and Critical Reception of Lena Dunham's *Girls*', *Early Career Researchers*, special issue of *Gender Forum: An Internet Journal for Gender Studies*, vol. 45, pp. 108–25.

Martin, Peter (2013), 'The *Girls* Recap for Men: Self-Indulgent Dreaming', *Esquire*, 10 February, <www.esquire.com/blogs/culture/girls-season-2-episode-5-recap> (last accessed 12 May 2018).

Martinez, Brianna (2017), 'Nielsen Social Ratings: October 26, 2017', *Fanfest*, 26 October, <www.fanfest.com/2017/10/27/nielsen-social-ratings-october-26-2017> (last accessed 12 July 2018).

Masters, Kim (2011), '*The Walking Dead*: What Really Happened to Fired Showrunner Frank Darabont', *The Hollywood Reporter*, 10 August, <www.hollywoodreporter.com/news/walking-dead-what-happened-fired-221449> (last accessed 3 July 2018).

Mayer, Ruth (2017), 'In the Nick of Time? Detective Film Serials, Temporality, and Contingency Management, 1919–1926', *The Velvet Light Trap*, no. 79, pp. 21–35.

Miller, Taylor Cole (2017), 'The Fashion of Florrick and FLOTUS: On Feminism, Gender Politics, and "Quality Television"', *Television & New Media*, vol. 18, no. 2, pp. 147–64.

Mills, Brett (2010), 'Being Rob Brydon: Performing the Self in Comedy', *Celebrity Studies*, vol. 1, no. 2, pp. 189–201.

Mittell, Jason (2006), 'Narrative Complexity in Contemporary American Television', *The Velvet Light Trap*, vol. 58, no. 1, pp. 29–40.

Mittell, Jason (2015), *Complex TV: The Poetics of Contemporary Television Storytelling*, New York: New York University Press.

Mizejewski, Linda (2014), *Pretty/Funny: Women Comedians and Body Politics*, Dallas: University of Texas Press.

Modleski, Tania (1991), *Feminism without Women: Culture and Criticism in a Postfeminist Age*, London: Routledge.

Molina-Guzmán, Isabel (2016), '#OscarsSoWhite: How Stuart Hall Explains Why Nothing Changes in Hollywood and Everything is Changing', *Critical Studies in Media Communication*, vol. 33, no. 5, pp. 438–54.

Molloy, Tim (2014), 'Judd Apatow and Lena Dunham Get Mad at Me for Asking Why She's Naked So Much on *Girls*', *The Wrap*, 9 January, <www.thewrap.com/judd-apatow-lena-dunham-get-mad-asking-shes-naked-much-girls> (last accessed 14 July 2018).

Monk-Payton, Brandy (2015), '#LaughingWhileBlack: Gender and the Comedy of Social Media Blackness', *Feminist Media Histories*, vol. 3, no. 2, pp. 15–35.

Mulvey, Laura (1975), 'Visual Pleasure and Narrative Cinema', *Screen*, vol. 16, no. 3, pp. 6–18.

Murray, Rona (2018), 'A Survivor Just Like Us? Lena Dunham and the Politics of Transmedia Authorship and Celebrity Feminism', *Feminist Theory*, vol. 18, no. 3, pp. 245–61.

Nakamura, Lisa (2008), *Digitizing Race: Visual Cultures of the Internet*, Minneapolis: University of Minnesota Press.

Nash, Meredith, and Ruby Grant (2015), 'Twenty-Something *Girls* v. Thirty-Something *Sex and the City* Women', *Feminist Media Studies*, vol. 15, no. 6, pp. 976–91.

Nash, Meredith, and Imelda Whelehan (eds) (2017), *Reading Lena Dunham's* Girls*: Feminism, Postfeminism, Authenticity and Gendered Performance in Contemporary Television*, Basingstoke: Palgrave Macmillan.

Navar-Gill, Annemarie (2018), 'From Strategic Retweets to Group Hangs: Writers' Room Twitter Accounts and the Productive Ecology of TV Social Media Fans', *Television & New Media*, vol. 19, no. 5, pp. 415–30.

Negra, Diane (2009), *What a Girl Wants?: Fantasizing the Reclamation of Self in Postfeminism*, London: Routledge.

Negra, Diane, and Yvonne Tasker (2014), 'Introduction: Gender and Recessionary Culture', in Diane Negra and Yvonne Tasker (eds), *Gendering the Recession: Media and Culture in an Age of Austerity*, Durham, NC: Duke University Press, pp. 1–30.

Nelson, Erika M. (2014), 'Embracing the Awkwardness of AUTEURship in *Girls*', in Betty Kaklamanidou and Margaret Tally (eds), *HBO's* Girls*: Questions of Gender, Politics, and Millennial Angst*, Newcastle upon Tyne: Cambridge Scholars, pp. 91–107.

Newman, Michael Z. (2017), 'In the Gif Space', *FLOW: A Critical Forum on Media and Culture*, 2 October, <www.flowjournal.org/2017/10/in-the-gif-space> (last accessed 12 July 2018).

Newman, Michael Z., and Elana Levine (2011), *Legitimating Television: Media Convergence and Cultural Studies*, London: Routledge.

Nilsen, Sarah, and Sarah E. Turner (eds) (2014), *The Colorblind Screen: Television in Post-Racial America*, New York: New York University Press.

Nussbaum, Emily (2012), 'It's Different for *Girls*', *The New Yorker*, 25 March, <www.nymag.com/arts/tv/features/girls-lena-dunham-2012-4> (last accessed 12 July 2018).

Nussbaum, Emily (2013), 'Utter Rot: The Creeping Disappointment of *The Walking Dead*', *The New Yorker*, 23 December, <www.newyorker.com/magazine/2013/12/23/utter-rot> (last accessed 3 July 2018).

Nygaard, Taylor (2013), 'Girls Just Want to Be "Quality": HBO, Lena Dunham, and *Girls*' Conflicting Brand Identity', *Feminist Media Studies*, vol. 13, no. 2, pp. 370–4.

Obaro, Tomi (2017), '*Girls* Has Gotten Less White, but Not in a Good Way', *Buzzfeed*, 31 March, <www.buzzfeed.com/tomiobaro/on-girls-people-of-color-are-just-here-to-help> (last accessed 12 July 2018).

Ochs, Robyn (2017), 'Bisexual', *Robyn Ochs*, 26 December, <www.robynochs.com/bisexual> (last accessed 14 July 2018).

OED (2018), 'think-piece', *OED Online*, Oxford University Press, June, <www.oed.com/view/Entry/200799?redirectedFrom=think-piece#eid18553589> (last accessed 15 July 2018).

O'Keeffe, Kevin (2014), 'TV's Renaissance for Strong Women is Happening in a Surprising Place', *The Atlantic*, 9 October, <www.theatlantic.com/entertainment/archive/2014/10/how-to-get-away-with-murder-and-the-rise-of-the-new-network-tv-heroine/381021> (last accessed 12 May 2018).

Oltean, Tudor (1993), 'Series and Seriality in Media Culture', *European Journal of Communication*, vol. 8, no. 1, pp. 5–31.

'On Fucking Your Friend's Ex' (2015), *Dear Coquette*, 4 August, <www.dearcoquette.com/on-fucking-your-friends-ex> (last accessed 14 July 2018).

O'Sullivan, Sean (2017), 'The Inevitable, the Surprise, and Serial Television', in Frank Kelleter (ed.), *Media of Serial Narrative*, Columbus: The Ohio State University Press, pp. 204–21.
Pantozzi, Jill (2015), 'We Will No Longer Be Promoting HBO's *Game of Thrones*', *The Mary Sue*, 18 May, <www.themarysue.com/we-will-no-longer-be-promoting-hbos-game-of-thrones> (last accessed 3 July 2018).
Parody, Clare (2011), 'Franchising/Adaptation', *Adaptation*, vol. 4, no. 2, pp. 210–18.
Paskin, Willa (2014), 'The New TV Genre Invented by Shonda Rhimes', *Slate*, 25 September, <www.slate.com/articles/arts/television/2014/09/how_to_get_away_with_murder_review_viola_davis_show_is_the_latest_shonda.html> (last accessed 12 July 2018).
Paskin, Willa (2017), 'The Monstrous Brilliance of *Girls*', *Slate*, 7 February, <www.slate.com/articles/arts/television/2017/02/season_6_of_girls_reviewed_the_end_of_lena_dunham_s_prickly_powerful_series.html> (last accessed 12 July 2018).
Patterson, Natasha (2008), 'Cannibalizing Gender and Genre: A Feminist Re-Vision of George Romero's Zombie Films', in Shawn McIntosh and Marc Leverette (eds), *Zombie Culture: Autopsies of the Living Dead*, Lanham, MD: Scarecrow Press, pp. 101–18.
Penny, Laurie (2017), *Bitch Doctrine: Essays for Dissenting Adults*, London: Bloomsbury.
Perkins, Claire (2014), 'Dancing on My Own: *Girls* and Television of the Body', *Critical Studies of Television*, vol. 9, no. 3, pp. 33–43.
Petersen, Anne Helen (2014), 'Pretty Girl Privilege', *LA Review of Books*, 4 February, <www.lareviewofbooks.org/article/girls-child> (last accessed 14 July 2018).
Petersen, Anne Helen (2017), *Too Fat, Too Slutty, Too Loud: The Rise and Reign of the Unruly Woman*, New York: Plume.
Piwowarski, Allison (2015), 'Your *How to Get Away with Murder* Drinking Game, Because Annalise is Too Intimidating without Alcohol', *Bustle*, 24 September, <www.bustle.com/articles/61248-your-how-to-get-away-with-murder-drinking-game-because-annalise-is-too-intimidating-without-alcohol> (last accessed 12 July 2018).
Platts, Todd K. (2013), 'Locating Zombies in the Sociology of Popular Culture', *Sociology Compass*, vol. 7, no. 7, pp. 547–60.
Platts, Todd K. (2014), '*The Walking Dead*', in Alain Silver and James Ursini (eds), *The Zombie Film: From 'White Zombie' to 'World War Z'*, Lanham, MD: Applause Theatre & Cinema Books, pp. 294–7.
Poe, Edgar Allan (1846), 'The Philosophy of Composition', *Graham's Magazine*, vol. 28, no. 4, April, pp. 163–7.
Polan, Dana (2007), 'Cable Watching: HBO, *The Sopranos*, and Discourses of Distinction', in Sarah Banet-Weiser, Cynthia Chris, and Anthony Freitas (eds), *Cable Visions*, New York: New York University Press, pp. 261–83.
Poniewozik, James (2017), 'Ways *Girls* Changed Television. Or Didn't: Chronicling Think-Piece Culture', *The New York Times*, 2 February, <www.nytimes.com/2017/02/02/arts/television/girls-season-six.html> (last accessed 14 July 2018).
Pramaggiore, Maria (1996), 'Straddling the Screen: Bisexual Spectatorship and Contemporary Narrative Film', in Maria Pramaggiore and Donald E. Hall (eds), *RePresenting Bisexualities: Subjects and Cultures of Fluid Desire*, New York: New York University Press, pp. 272–98.
Prasad, Pritha (2016), 'Beyond Rights as Recognition: Black Twitter and Posthuman Coalitional Possibilities', *Prose Studies*, vol. 38, no. 1, pp. 50–73.
Prince, Richard (2014), 'NY Times TV Critic Defends Angry Black Woman Story', *The Root*, 21 September, <www.theroot.com/blogs/journalisms/2014/09/new_york_times_tv_critic_alessandra_stanley_defends_angr%E2%80%A6> (last accessed 11 May 2016).
Projansky, Sarah (2001), *Watching Rape: Film and Television in Postfeminist Culture*, New York: New York University Press.

Puff, Simone (2015), 'Another *Scandal* in Washington: How a Transgressive, Black Anti-Heroine Makes for New "Quality TV"', in Birgit Däwes, Alexandra Ganser, and Nicole Poppenhangen (eds), *Transgressive Television: Politics and Crime in 21st-Century American TV Series*, Heidelberg: Winter Verlag, pp. 103–25.

Pye, Danee, and Peter Padraic O'Sullivan (2012), 'Dead Man's Party', in Wayne Yeun (ed.), *'The Walking Dead' and Philosophy: Zombie Apocalypse Now*, Chicago: Carus Publishing, pp. 107–16.

Radway, Janice (1984), *Reading the Romance: Women, Patriarchy, and Popular Culture*, Chapel Hill: University of North Carolina Press.

Raftery, Brian (2016), '*Girls* is the Best Show No One's Talking About Right Now', *Wired*, 21 March, <www.wired.com/2016/03/girls-conversation> (last accessed 12 May 2018).

Rahm, Lina (2013), 'Who Will Survive? On Bodies and Boundaries After the Apocalypse', *Gender Forum: An Internet Journal for Gender Studies*, no. 45, pp. 72–83.

Reifenberger, Julia (2013), *Girls with Guns: Rape & Revenge Movies – Radikalfeministische Ermächtigungsfantasien?*, Berlin: Bertz + Fischer.

Roberts, Andrew (2013), 'We Need to Talk About How George A. Romero Hates *The Walking Dead*', *Uproxx*, 14 November, <www.uproxx.com/gammasquad/need-talk-george-romero-hates-walking-dead> (last accessed 3 July 2018).

Robinson, Phoebe (2016), *You Can't Touch My Hair: And Other Things I Still Have to Explain*, New York: Plume.

Rodriguez, Amanda (2013), 'The Women of *The Walking Dead*: A Comparative Analysis of the Comic vs. TV', *Bitch Flicks*, 13 February, <www.btchflcks.com/2013/02/the-women-of-the-walking-dead-a-comparative-analysis-of-the-comic-vs-tv.html> (last accessed 3 July 2018).

Roof, Judith (2016), *What Gender Is, What Gender Does*, Minneapolis: University of Minnesota Press.

Rose, Lacey (2017), 'It's Goodbye *Girls* as Lena Dunham, Cast, Execs Overshare in Show Oral History', *The Hollywood Reporter*, 1 February, <www.hollywoodreporter.com/features/goodbye-girls-as-lena-dunham-cast-execs-overshare-show-oral-history-970777> (last accessed 12 May 2018).

Rosenberg, Alyssa (2012), 'Lena Dunham's Looks, the Misogyny of the "Girls" Backlash, and Staying in Your Assigned Story', *Thinkprogress*, 29 May, <www.thinkprogress.org/alyssa/2012/05/29/491372/lena-dunham-girls> (last accessed 12 May 2018).

Ross, Dalton (2013), '*Sons of Anarchy*: Maggie Siff on "Disturbing" Fan Hostility Toward Tara', *Entertainment Weekly*, 10 December, <www.ew.com/article/2013/12/10/sons-of-anarchy-maggie-siff-tara-fans> (last accessed 3 July 2018).

Roth, LuAnne, and Kate Shoults (2015), '"Three men, and the place is surrounded": Reel Women in the Zombie Apocalypse', in Amy L. Thompson and Antonio S. Thompson (eds), . . . *But If a Zombie Apocalypse Did Occur: Essays on Medical, Military, Governmental, Ethical, Economic and Other Implications*, Jefferson, NC: McFarland, pp. 227–45.

Rowe, Sam (2014), 'Adam from *Girls*: The Archetypal Modern Male?', *The Telegraph*, 20 January, <www.telegraph.co.uk/men/thinking-man/10584290/Adam-from-Girls-the-archetypal-modern-male.html> (last accessed 14 July 2018).

Ruditis, Paul (2011), *'The Walking Dead' Chronicles: The Official Companion Book*, New York: Abrams.

Ruthven, Andrea (2014), 'Zombie Postfeminism', in Edward P. Comentale and Aaron Jaffe (eds), *This Year's Work at The Zombie Research Center*, Bloomington: Indiana University Press, pp. 341–60.

Ryan, Maureen (2017), 'Emmys Review: Sleek, Sincere, but We've Still Got a Long Way to Go', *Variety*, 17 September, <www.variety.com/2017/tv/columns/2017-emmy-awards-review-stephen-colbert-12025 62279> (last accessed 12 July 2018).
Ryan, Michelle K., and S. Alexander Haslam (2005), 'The Glass Cliff: Evidence That Women Are Over-Represented in Precarious Leadership Positions', *British Journal of Management*, vol. 16, no. 2, pp. 81–90.
Saisi, Boké (2014), '(Just White) Girls?: Underrepresentation and Active Audiences in HBO's *Girls*', in Betty Kaklamanidou and Margaret Tally (eds), *HBO's Girls: Questions of Gender, Politics, and Millennial Angst*, Newcastle upon Tyne: Cambridge Scholars, pp. 59–72.
San Filippo, Maria (2013), *The B Word: Bisexuality in Contemporary Film and Television*, Bloomington: Indiana University Press.
San Filippo, Maria (2015), 'Owning Her Abjection: Lena Dunham's Feminist Politics of Embodiment', in Elwood Watson, Jennifer Mitchell, and Marc Edward Shaw (eds), *HBO's Girls and the Awkward Politics of Gender, Race, and Privilege*, Lanham, MD: Lexington Books, pp. 43–61.
San Filippo, Maria (2017), '"Art Porn Provocateurs": Feminist Performances of Embodiment in the Work of Catherine Breillat and Lena Dunham', in Meredith Nash and Imelda Whelehan (eds), *Reading Lena Dunham's Girls: Feminism, Postfeminism, Authenticity and Gendered Performance in Contemporary Television*, Basingstoke: Palgrave Macmillan, pp. 165–80.
Sanders, Judith, and Daniel Lieberfeld (1994), 'Dreaming in Pictures: The Childhood Origins of Buster Keaton's Creativity', *Film Quarterly*, vol. 47, no. 4, pp. 14–28.
Saraiya, Sonia, and Maureen Ryan (2017), 'Variety TV Critics Discuss the Legacy and Impact of *Girls* (Part 1)', *Variety*, 13 April, <www.variety.com/2017/tv/columns/hbo-girls-show-ending-lena-dunham-legacy-1202030241> (last accessed 14 July 2018).
Sartain, Jeffrey A. (2013), 'Days Gone By: Robert Kirkman's Re-envisioned Western, *The Walking Dead*', in Cynthia J. Miller and A. Bowdoin Van Riper (eds), *Undead and the West II: They Just Keep Coming*, Lanham, MD: Scarecrow Press, pp. 249–68.
Sartre, Jean-Paul (1976), *Critique of Dialectical Reason (vol. 1)*, trans. Alan Sheridan-Smith, New York: New Left Books.
Sattar, Atia (2014), 'Zombie Performance', in Edward P. Comentale and Aaron Jaffe (eds), *This Year's Work at The Zombie Research Center*, Bloomington: Indiana University Press, pp. 248–75.
Saxena, Jaya (2017), 'Women Aren't Ruining Food', *Taste*, 30 October, <www.tastecooking.com/women-arent-ruining-food> (last accessed 12 July 2018).
Schippers, Mimi (2007), 'Recovering the Feminine Other: Masculinity, Femininity, and Gender Hegemony', *Theory and Society*, vol. 36, no. 1, pp. 85–102.
Schippers, Mimi (2016), *Beyond Monogamy: Polyamory and the Future of Polyqueer Sexualities*, New York: New York University Press.
Scott, A. O. (2017), 'Ways *Girls* Changed Television. Or Didn't: Sharing a Distinct Voice', *The New York Times*, 2 February, <www.nytimes.com/2017/02/02/arts/television/girls-season-six.html> (last accessed 14 July 2018).
Scott, Suzanne (2012), 'Who's Steering the Mothership? The Role of the Fanboy Auteur in Transmedia Storytelling', in Aaron Delwiche and Jennifer Jacobs Henderson (eds), *The Participatory Cultures Handbook*, London: Routledge, pp. 43–52.
Scott, Suzanne (2014), 'Walking the Talk: Enunciative Fandom and Fan Studies' "Industrial Turn"', conference talk, Annual Meeting of the Society for Cinema and Media Studies, Seattle, WA, 21 March.
Seaton, Wallis (2017), '"Doing Her Best with What She's Got": Authorship, Irony, and Mediating Feminist Identities in Lena Dunham's *Girls*', in Meredith Nash and Imelda

Whelehan (eds), *Reading Lena Dunham's* Girls*: Feminism, Postfeminism, Authenticity and Gendered Performance in Contemporary Television*, Basingstoke: Palgrave Macmillan, pp. 149–62.

Seitz, Matt Zoller (2017), '*Girls* Final Season Was the Show at Its Saddest, and Best', *Vulture*, 17 April, <www.vulture.com/2017/04/girls-review-the-final-season-was-the-show-at-its-best.html> (last accessed 14 July 2018).

Sepinwall, Alan (2015), 'Review: *Girls* – "Triggering"', *Uproxx*, 1 January, <www.uproxx.com/sepinwall/review-girls-triggering-the-dead-zone> (last accessed 14 July 2018).

Sepinwall, Alan (2017), 'Three Things to Know About the Beginning of the End of *Girls*', *Uproxx*, 9 February, <www.uproxx.com/sepinwall/girls-final-season-review-hbo-lena-dunham> (last accessed 14 July 2018).

Shapiro, Stephen (2014), 'Zombie Health Care', in Edward P. Comentale and Aaron Jaffe (eds), *This Year's Work at The Zombie Research Center*, Bloomington: Indiana University Press, pp. 193–226.

Shaw, Marc Edward (2015), 'Falling from Pedestals: Dunham's Cracked *Girls* and Boys', in Elwood Watson, Jennifer Mitchell, and Marc Edward Shaw (eds), *HBO's* Girls *and the Awkward Politics of Gender, Race, and Privilege*, Lanham, MD: Lexington Books, pp. 71–86.

Shepherd, Julianne Escobedo (2012), 'Why I'm Deeply Skeptical of HBO's Super-Hyped Show *Girls*', *Alternet*, 11 April, <www.alternet.org/story/154957/why_i%27m_deeply_skeptical_of hbo%27s_super-hyped_show_%27girls%27> (last accessed 12 May 2018).

Shifman, Limor (2014), *Memes in Digital Culture*, Cambridge, MA: MIT Press.

Slotnick, Stacey (2014), 'If the Color Fits, Wear It: Redefining the Female Lawyer's Uniform', *Huffington Post*, 25 July, <www.huffingtonpost.com/stacy-slotnick/redefining-the-rules-for-_b_5610807.html> (last accessed 12 July 2018).

Smith, Molly C. (2014), 'EW's *Walking Dead* Cover Photographer Reveals How to Kill a Zombie', *Entertainment Weekly*, 2 September, <www.ew.com/article/2014/09/02/ew-walking-dead-cover-zombies> (last accessed 3 July 2018).

Soller, Bettina (2014), 'Fan Fiction and Soap Operas: On the Seriality of Vast Narratives', in Kathleen Loock (ed.), *Serial Narratives*, special issue of *Literatur in Wissenschaft und Unterricht*, no. 1/2, pp. 191–205.

Spigel, Lynn (1992), *Make Room For TV: Television and the Family Ideal in Postwar America*, Chicago: Chicago University Press.

Stack, Steven, and Ira Wasserman (2009), 'Gender and Suicide Risk: The Role of Wound Site', *Suicide and Life-Threatening Behavior*, vol. 39, no. 1, pp. 13–20.

Stahler, Kelsea (2014), 'In Defense of *Girls*' Marnie (Sort Of)', *Bustle*, 11 February, <www.bustle.com/articles/14986-in-defense-of-girls-marnie-sort-of> (last accessed 14 July 2018).

Stanley, Alessandra (2014), 'Wrought in Rhimes's Image', *The New York Times*, 18 September, <www.nytimes.com/2014/09/21/arts/television/viola-davis-plays-shonda-rhimes-latest-tough-heroine.html> (last accessed 12 July 2018).

Stein, Daniel (2013), 'Superhero Comics and the Authorizing Functions of the Comic Book Paratext', in Daniel Stein and Jan-Noël Thon (eds), *From Comic Strips to Graphic Novels: Contributions to the Theory and History of Graphic Narrative*, Berlin: De Gruyter, pp. 155–89.

Stevens, Leslie, and Nicole Maurantonio (2018), 'Black Twitter Asks Rachel: Racial Identity Theft in "Post-Racial" America', *Howard Journal of Communications*, vol. 29, no. 2, pp. 179–95.

Stieger, Kay (2011), 'No Clean Slate: Unshakable Race and Gender Politics in *The Walking Dead*', in James Lowder (ed.), *Triumph of 'The Walking Dead': Robert Kirkman's Zombie Epic on Page and Screen*, Dallas: BenBella Books, pp. 100–14.

Sulimma, Maria (2014a), *Die anderen Ministerpräsidenten: Geschlecht in der printmedialen Berichterstattung über Berufspolitik*, Münster: LIT Verlag.
Sulimma, Maria (2014b), 'Simultaneous Seriality: On the Crossmedia Relationship of Television Narratives', in Kathleen Loock (ed.), *Serial Narratives*, special issue of *Literatur in Wissenschaft und Unterricht*, no. 1/2, pp. 127–43.
Sulimma, Maria (2017), 'Lena Dunham: Cringe Comedy and Body Politics', in Linda Mizejewski and Victoria Sturtevant (eds), *Hysterical!: Women in American Comedy*, Dallas: University of Texas Press, pp. 379–401.
Tally, Margaret J. (2014a), 'Postfeminism, Sexuality, and the Question of Millennial Identity on HBO's *Girls*', in Laura Matton D'Amore (ed.), *Smart Chicks on Screen: Representing Women's Intellect in Film and Television*, Lanham, MD: Rowman & Littlefield, pp. 161–78.
Tally, Margaret J. (2014b), 'Post-Modernity, Emerging Adulthood and the Exploration of Female Friendships on *Girls*', in Betty Kaklamanidou and Margaret Tally (eds), *HBO's Girls: Questions of Gender, Politics, and Millennial Angst*, Newcastle upon Tyne: Cambridge Scholars, pp. 28–42.
Tasker, Yvonne (2008), *Spectacular Bodies: Gender, Genre and the Action Cinema*, London: Routledge.
Tasker, Yvonne, and Diane Negra (2007), 'Introduction: Feminist Politics and Postfeminist Culture', in Yvonne Tasker and Diane Negra (eds), *Interrogating Postfeminism: Gender and the Politics of Popular Culture*, Durham, NC: Duke University Press, pp. 1–25.
Thomas, Deborah J. (2017), '"You Shouldn't be Doing That Because You Haven't Got the Body for It": Comment on Nudity in *Girls*', in Meredith Nash and Imelda Whelehan (eds), *Reading Lena Dunham's* Girls: *Feminism, Postfeminism, Authenticity and Gendered Performance in Contemporary Television*, Basingstoke: Palgrave Macmillan, pp. 181–95.
Thompson, Beverly Yuen (2015), *Covered in Ink: Tattoos, Women, and the Politics of the Body*, New York: New York University Press.
Thompson, Derek (2014), 'Why Nobody Writes About Popular TV Shows', *The Atlantic*, 7 May, <www.theatlantic.com/business/archive/2014/05/why-nobody-writes-about-popular-tv-shows/361> (last accessed 14 July 2018).
Tolentino, Jia (2017), 'On Finally Watching "Girls," a Different and Better Show Than I'd Been Led to Imagine', *The New Yorker*, 13 April, <www.newyorker.com/culture/jia-tolentino/on-finally-watching-girls-a-different-and-better-show-than-id-been-led-to-imagine> (last accessed 14 July 2018).
Tolins, Jackson, and Patrawat Samermit (2016), 'GIFs as Embodied Enactments in Text-Mediated Conversation', *Research on Language and Social Interaction*, vol. 49, no. 2, pp. 75–91.
Turner, Kimberly (2014), 'Queering the Single White Female: *Girls* and the Interrupted Promise of the Twenty-Something', in Betty Kaklamanidou and Margaret Tally (eds), *HBO's* Girls: *Questions of Gender, Politics, and Millennial Angst*, Newcastle upon Tyne: Cambridge Scholars, pp. 156–71.
TV By The Numbers Editors (2015), '*Empire*: Top Nielsen's Twitter TV Ratings for the Week of September 21–27', *TV By The Numbers*, 28 September, <www.tvbythenumbers.zap2it.com/internet/empire-leads-nielsen-twitter-tv-ratings-for-sept-28-oct-4-daily-show-snl-join> (last accessed 12 July 2018).
Upadhyaya, Kayla Kumari (2016), 'Shonda Rhimes' Characters Are Defined by What They Drink', *A.V. Club*, 19 September, <www.avclub.com/shonda-rhimes-characters-are-defined-by-what-they-drin-1798252070> (last accessed 12 July 2018).
Valenti, Lauren (2015), 'The Alicia Florrick Guide to Looking Good in an Uptight Office: Tailoring is Everything', *Marie Claire*, 6 March, <www.marieclaire.com/fashion/news/a13619/corporate-office-style> (last accessed 12 July 2018).

VanDerWerff, Emily (2013), 'What We Talk About When We Talk About *Girls*', *A.V. Club*, 14 March, <www.avclub.com/article/what-we-talk-about-when-we-talk-about-igirlsi-93685> (last accessed 14 July 2018).

Vayo, Lloyd Isaac (2015), 'Marnye on the Ones and Twos: Appropriating Race, Criticizing Class in *Girls*', in Elwood Watson, Jennifer Mitchell, and Marc Edward Shaw (eds), *HBO's Girls and the Awkward Politics of Gender, Race, and Privilege*, Lanham, MD: Lexington Books, pp. 167–82.

Veblen, Thorstein (1899), *The Theory of the Leisure Class: An Economic Study of Institutions*, London: Macmillan.

Villarejo, Amy (2014), *Ethereal Queer: Television, Historicity, Desire*, Durham, NC: Duke University Press.

Wade, Lisa, and Myra Marx Ferree (2015), *Gender: Ideas, Interactions, Institutions*, New York: Norton.

Walsh, Kimberly R., Elfriede Fürsich, and Bonnie S. Jefferson (2008), 'Beauty and the Patriarchal Beast: Gender Role Portrayals in Sitcoms Featuring Mismatched Couples', *Journal of Popular Film and Television*, vol. 36, no. 3, pp. 123–32.

Wanzo, Rebecca (2016), 'Precarious-Girl Comedy: Issa Rae, Lena Dunham, and Abjection Aesthetics', *Camera Obscura*, vol. 31, no. 2, pp. 27–59.

Warhol, Robyn (2003), *Having a Good Cry: Effeminate Feelings and Pop-Culture Forms*, Columbus: The Ohio State University Press.

Warhol, Robyn (2014), 'Binge-Watching: How Netflix Original Programs are Changing Serial Form', in Kathleen Loock (ed.), *Serial Narratives*, special issue of *Literatur in Wissenschaft und Unterricht*, no. 1/2, pp. 145–58.

Warner, Kristen J. (2015a), 'ABC's *Scandal* and Black Women's Fandom', in Elana Levine (ed.), *Cupcakes, Pinterest, and Ladyporn: Feminized Popular Culture in the Early Twenty-First Century*, Champaign: University of Illinois Press, pp. 32–50.

Warner, Kristen J. (2015b), 'If Loving Olitz is Wrong, I Don't Wanna Be Right', *The Black Scholar*, vol. 45, no. 1, pp. 16–20.

Warner, Kristen J. (2017), 'The *Girls* Habit', *LA Review of Books*, 21 February, <www.lareviewofbooks.org/article/the-girls-habit> (last accessed 14 July 2018).

Waters, Melanie (2017), 'Bad Sex and the City? Feminist (Re)Awakenings in HBO's *Girls*', in Meredith Nash and Imelda Whelehan (eds), *Reading Lena Dunham's* Girls: *Feminism, Postfeminism, Authenticity and Gendered Performance in Contemporary Television*, Basingstoke: Palgrave Macmillan, pp. 75–88.

Watson, Elwood (2015), 'Lena Dunham: The Awkward/Ambiguous Politics of White Millennial Feminism', in Elwood Watson, Jennifer Mitchell, and Marc Edward Shaw (eds), *HBO's* Girls *and the Awkward Politics of Gender, Race, and Privilege*, Lanham, MD: Lexington Books, pp. 145–65.

Watson, Elwood, Jennifer Mitchell, and Marc Edward Shaw (eds) (2015), *HBO's* Girls *and the Awkward Politics of Gender, Race, and Privilege*, Lanham, MD: Lexington Books.

Weitz, Rose (2016), 'Feminism, Post-Feminism, and Young Women's Reactions to Lena Dunham's *Girls*', *Gender Issues*, vol. 33, no. 1, pp. 218–34.

Wescott, Alex (2014), *Arrested Development: Neoliberalism and the Rise of the Slacker in the 20th and 21st Century United States*, Dissertation, University of Southern California.

West, Candace, and Don H. Zimmerman (1987), 'Doing Gender', *Gender & Society*, vol. 1, no. 2, pp. 125–51.

West, Candace, and Sarah Fenstermaker (1995), 'Doing Difference', *Gender & Society*, vol. 9, no. 1, pp. 8–37.

Whelehan, Imelda (2010), 'Remaking Feminism: Or Why is Postfeminism so Boring?', *Nordic Journal of English Studies*, vol. 9, no. 3, pp. 155–72.

Whelehan, Imelda (2014), 'Representing Women in Popular Culture', in Mary Evans, Clare Hemmings, Marsha Henry, Hazel Johnstone, Sumi Madhok, Ania Plimien, and Sadie Wearing (eds), *The SAGE Handbook of Feminist Theory*, London: Sage Publications, pp. 232–50.
Whelehan, Imelda (2017), 'Hating Hannah: Or Learning to Love (Post) Feminist Entitlement', in Meredith Nash and Imelda Whelehan (eds), *Reading Lena Dunham's* Girls*: Feminism, Postfeminism, Authenticity and Gendered Performance in Contemporary Television*, Basingstoke: Palgrave Macmillan, pp. 31–44.
Wiele, Lisanna (2019), 'Dead Man Walking: On the Physical and Geographical Manifestations of Sociopolitical Narratives in George Thompson's *City Crimes—or Life in New York and Boston*', in Daniel Stein and Lisanna Wiele (eds), *Nineteenth-Century Serial Narrative in Transnational Perspective, 1830s–1860s: Popular Culture—Serial Culture*, Basingstoke: Palgrave Macmillan, pp. 247–70.
Williams, Apryl, and Vanessa Gonlin (2017), 'I Got All My Sisters with Me (on Black Twitter): Second Screening of *How to Get Away with Murder* as a Discourse on Black Womanhood', *Information, Communication & Society*, vol. 20, no. 7, pp. 984–1004.
Williams, Evan Calder (2010), *Combined and Uneven Apocalypse*, Winchester/Washington: Zero Books.
Williams, Linda (1991), 'Film Bodies: Gender, Genre, and Excess', *Film Quarterly*, vol. 44, no. 4, pp. 2–13.
Witherington, Laura S. (2014), '*Girls*: An Economic Redemption through Production and Labor', in Betty Kaklamanidou and Margaret Tally (eds), *HBO's* Girls*: Questions of Gender, Politics, and Millennial Angst*, Newcastle upon Tyne: Cambridge Scholars, pp. 122–39.
Witherington, Laura S. (2015), 'Reading *Girls*: Diegesis and Distinction', in Elwood Watson, Jennifer Mitchell, and Marc Edward Shaw (eds), *HBO's* Girls *and the Awkward Politics of Gender, Race, and Privilege*, Lanham, MD: Lexington Books, pp. 127–43.
Woods, Faye (2015), 'Girls Talk: Authorship and Authenticity in the Reception of Lena Dunham's *Girls*', *Critical Studies in Television*, vol. 10, no. 2, pp. 37–54.
Wortham, Jenna (2012), 'Where (My) "Girls" at?', *The Hairpin*, 16 April, <www.thehairpin.com/2012/04/where-my-girls-at> (last accessed 14 July 2018).
Yoshino, Kenji (2000), 'The Epistemic Contract of Bisexual Erasure', *Stanford Law*, vol. 52, no. 2, pp. 353–461.
Young, Damon (2014), 'Why the "Unmasking" of Viola Davis on *HTGAWM* is the Blackest Thing We've Seen This Week', *Very Smart Brothas*, 17 October, <www.verysmartbrothas.theroot.com/why-the-unmasking-of-viola-davis-on-htgawm-is-the-bla-1822521794> (last accessed 12 July 2018).
Young, Iris Marion (1994), 'Gender as Seriality: Thinking About Women as a Social Collective', *Signs*, vol. 19, no. 3, pp. 713–38.
Zeisler, Andi (2016), *We Were Feminists Once: From Riot Grrrl to Covergirl, The Buying and Selling of a Political Movement*, New York: Public Affairs.
Zoladz, Lindsay (2017), '*Girls* Was Better Than Its Last Season', *The Ringer*, 17 April, <www.theringer.com/2017/4/17/16044262/girls-season-six-finale-review-307009babcb5> (last accessed 14 July 2018).

Index

Note: page numbers in *italics* refer to illustrations

Abbott, Stacey, 155
ABC, 145 *see also* #TGIT
accountability, 9–10, 18, 141
action heroes, female, 177
Actor-Network-Theory, 16
Ahmed, Sara, 3, 80, 205
Alcott, Louisa May, 57–8
Alias, 177
Allrath, Gaby, 13
Ally McBeal, 116
Anderson, Benedict, 8, 14, 92
Andriolo, Karin, 209
Ansari, Aziz, 215, 216, 223n1
antihero protagonists, 26, 188–9
Apatow, Judd, 27, 51
appointment-based vs. engagement-based model, 92
Arrested Development, 95
asexuality, 183–4
audience engagement *see* looped seriality; political television; spiral gendering and the outward spiral; Twitter
Austin, John, 198
author function, 154
authorship *see* paratext seriality of *The Walking Dead*
auto-referentiality, 15–16 *see also* metatexuality

Barkman, Ashley, 175
Barthes, Roland, 194n1
Bass, Linda, 117–18
beauty norms
    FEMEN and, 83
    Girls and, 54–5, 64, 76
    How to Get Away with Murder and, 120–3
Bechdel, Alison, 67n6
Bechdel Test, reverse, 65
Becker, Ron, 35
Beirne, Rebecca, 132n10
Bell, Katherine, 27
Benioff, David, 158
Berlant, Lauren, 49
Berry, Lorraine, 179
Bianco, Marcie, 84
Big Little Lies, 224n3
Billings, Alexandra, 137–8, 149n5
binge-watching, 97
bisexuality
    in *The Good Wife*, 126, 132n12
    in *Grey's Anatomy*, 125–6
    in *How to Get Away with Murder*, 123–31
    numbers on broadcast television, 132n10
    representation scarcity and cultural invisibility of, 125–6
    triangularity and, 127

blackface, digital, 105–6
#BlackLivesMatter, 92, 146, 148
Black Twitter, 92, 93, 109, 148
Boardwalk Empire, 188
body genres, 78, 103
body politics
   beautiful female corpses, 210
   beauty norms, 54–5, 64, 76, 83, 120–3
   cringe aesthetics and body genres, 78
   fat shaming, 206
   GIFs and, 105–6
   Girls and unruly femininity, 75–9
   How to Get Away with Murder and, 105–6, 112n17
   memes and, 103
   nudity and gaze in *Girls*, 40–4, *43*, 76
   The Walking Dead, resilient bodies, and zombie workouts, 203–7
Bonansinga, Jay, 158
Boondock Saints, The, 183
Bordwell, David, 98
bottle episodes
   about, 45n11
   Girls and, 34–5, 54, 76
Bowen, Sesali, 106
Bowleg, Lisa, 3
Boylorn, Robin M., 122
Breaking Bad, 188
Bridget Jones's Diary, 50, 81
Broad City, 86n1
Brock, André, 92
Bronfen, Elisabeth, 210
Brooks, Max, 198
Brown, Yvette Nicole, 157, 164, 171
Brunsdon, Charlotte, 80–3
Buffy the Vampire Slayer, 177
'bury your gays' trope, 125
Butler, Judith, 10, 11, 17

Callies, Sarah Wayne, 175, 186
camera
   the client shot, 98–100, *99*
   in *Girls*, 32, 40–3, 64, 77
   in *How to Get Away with Murder*, 94, 98, 119, 136, 142
   in *The Walking Dead*, 213n2

carousel gendering
   about, 47–50, 218–19
   cultural-type characterisation and, 48–52
   femininity characterisations in *Girls*, 50–5
   male and female intimacies in *Girls* bathroom scenes, 60–5
   masculinity characterisations in *Girls*, 55–60
Carroll, Noël, 59
Carroll, Rebecca, 73
cause-sumption, 134, 150n8
celebrity fans, 157
celebrity feminism, 69, 75, 80
Centers for Disease Control (CDC), 198
Certeau, Michel de, 194n1
class
   diet and class-belonging, 108, 109
   Girls and, 72, 82
   How to Get Away with Murder and, 94, 108–9, 113, 121, 123, 139–42
   New York apartment depictions and, 63
   Peak TV and, 145
   Sartre on, 8
   slacker figure and, 51
   The Sopranos and, 70
   survivalism and, 202
   The Walking Dead and, 185
client shot, 98–100, *99*
closure
   cinema vs. serial television and, 127
   continuation or renewal vs., 15, 18
   How to Get Away with Murder and, 100, 101
   seriality and ideal of, 7
clothing and black professional femininity, 115–18
Clover, Carol, 172
Coates, Ta-Nehisi, 73
Colbert, Stephen, 146
Coleman, Chad, 167–8
Coleman, Robin Means, 179
Collins, Patricia Hill, 114, 177
colourblindness
   about, 113–14
   How to Get Away with Murder and, 144
   #TGIT and, 121, 122–3
   The Walking Dead and, 179

Connell, Raewyn, 56, 64
connoisseur auteurs, 161, 198
consumerism, zombie-oriented, 200–3
consumption loops, 106–10
controlling images, 114, 126, 177–80
costume, 115–17
Cox, Laverne, 138
Creed, Barbara, 206
Crenshaw, Kimberlé, 3
cringe aesthetics, 78
critical sphere, history of, 28–9
critical sphere and *Girls see* carousel gendering; thinkpiece seriality; universality and specificity discourse
cruel optimism, 49
Cudlitz, Michael, 167
cultural conversations, 220–2
cultural types, characters as, 48–52

Dangerous Liaisons, 120
Darabont, Frank, 158–61, *159*
Davis, Angela, 120
Davis, Viola, 91, 109, 116–17, 119–20, 135
Dawkins, Richard, 102
Dawn of the Dead, 189–90
Dead Yourself app, 212
Dean, Michelle, 71
death, gendered portrayals of, 210 *see also* survivalism discourses, neoliberal
DeCarvalho, Lauren, 58
De Kosnik, Abigail, 96, 131
Denby, David, 66n4
Derrida, Jacques, 194n1
detective fiction genre, 98
DeVega, Chauncey, 171
Dexter, 188
Dhaenens, Frederik, 57
Dickens, Charles, 13
digital blackface, 105–6
diversity paradox, 147
Dow, Bonnie, 81, 215, 223
Downton Abbey, 115
Driscoll, Catherine, 48
Driver, Adam, 44, 59
Dunham, Lena, 26–7, 32, 42–3, 51, 68–9, 71–80, 83–4, 86n8, 153

Eburne, Jonathan, 200
Eco, Umberto, 13, 111n6
Ellis, Sarah Kate, 134

Emmy Awards, 135, 147
Empire, 134
engagement-based vs. appointment-based model, 92
Everett, Anna, 94, 103

family
 Girls and, 39–40
 How to Get Away with Murder and, 131
 parenting theme in *The Walking Dead*, 187
 production family, 205
 Scandal and, 121
 The Walking Dead and, 180, 183–8, 196, 205, 211
fanboy auteurs, 160, 161
fatherhood *see* family
Fear the Walking Dead, 196
feedback loops
 authorised paratexts and, 155
 binge-watching and, 97
 recursivity and, 18
 in seriality studies, 15–16
 The Walking Dead and, 176
FEMEN, 83
femininities
 beautiful female corpses and aestheticisation of death and, 210
 bisexual, in *How to Get Away with Murder*, 123–6
 black professional femininity, visual assemblages of (*How to Get Away with Murder*), 114–23
 the carousel and, 48
 discrimination from masculinity, in *Girls*, 55–6, 63–5
 disliked female characters in *The Walking Dead*, 186–93
 favourite female characters in *The Walking Dead*, 177–81
 Girls characterisations, 36, 41–4, 50–5, 58–9
 hegemonic, 56
 middle-aged, in *The Walking Dead*, 184–6
 pariah femininity, 65
 postfeminism and, 81
 Scandal and, 147
 serial consumption and, 13–14
 striptease and, 41

strong black woman and hypersexual
  black woman stereotypes, 177–80
 unruly, 77–9
 zombie survivalism and, 196
 see also beauty norms
feminism
 celebrity feminism, 69
 cultural analysis, feminist, 3
 femvertising, 82
 identity and politics, conflation of,
  81–2
 killjoy stereotype, 80, 82, 84
 postfeminist marketplace, ur-feminist
  impulse in *Girls*, and, 79–86
 'Quality TV' canon and feminist
  criticism, 26
 second-wave feminist stereotype,
  80, 84
 ur-feminist article as genre, 80–5
 'women's websites', 72
Ferdinand, Renata, 116
Ferree, Myra Marx, 18
Fido, 211
final girl, 172
Fish, Stanley, 92
flashbacks and flash-forwards
 in *How to Get Away with Murder*, 95–6,
  100–1, 113, 127–8
 lack of, in *Girls*, 31, 36
 in *The Walking Dead*, 180
Flavor of Love, 105
Ford, Jessica, 41
forensic fandom, 14, 101
Foucault, Michel, 154
fragmentation
 carousel gendering and, 47, 218–19
 in *Girls*, 30–2, 35, 40, 60
 see also carousel gendering
franchise storytelling, 156
Freeman, Elizabeth, 11–12
Fresh Prince of Bel-Air, The, 105
Friends, 57, 63
FUBU (For Us and By Us), 72
Fuller, Sean, 48

Game of Thrones, 70, 115, 158, 164, 170,
  224n3
Gay, Roxane, 79
'gay best friend' trope, 67n7
gaze, objectifying, 40–4

gender
 defined, 2, 6
 as popular culture, 17
 as serial collective, 8
 in seriality studies, 12–18
 as series, in Young, 7–9
 troubled by zombies, 212
 as work-net of agency, 16–17
 see also carousel gendering; femininities;
  masculinities; palimpsest gendering;
  spiral gendering and the outward
  spiral
gender performances
 about, 6–7
 bodies as sites of, 20n4
 Butler on, 10
 carousel and, 65–6
 cultural texts as orientation points for, 59
 deviations and rule-breaking, 17–18
 gender created through process of, 17
 gender studies and, 2
 as moving targets, 217
 professionalism and, 115
 Ru Paul's Drag Race and, 223n2
 shifting, 1
 unruly femininity and, 77
 West and Zimmerman's 'doing gender'
  and, 9–10
 zombies and, 212
gender regimes, 11, 222
gender studies, 2, 7–12, 222
Genette, Gérard, 155, 194n1
genres and subgenres
 awareness and knowledge of, 44, 160,
  168, 197–202
 detective, 98, 100, 110
 dramedy, 34n75
 gender and, 10, 160
 horror, 78, 103, 155, 158
 hybrids, 155, 164, 204
 melodrama, 94, 155
 mumblecore, 32–4
 rape-revenge, 172–3, 179
 romantic comedy, 66, 94
 soap opera, 14, 96, 107, 131
 zombie, 155–6, 158, 173n3
Genz, Stéphanie, 50
Get Christie Love!, 114
GIFs, 103–6, 144
Gill, Rosalind, 81, 85

Gimple, Scott M., 157–8, *159*, 161–2, 167, 174n8, 198
'girl' as cultural figure, 49–50
Girls
   Berlant's cruel optimism and, 49
   body politics, 75–9
   bottle episodes, 34–5, 54, 76
   carousel gendering and, 47–50, 65–6
   character perspective, cutback of, 32
   characters as cultural types, 48–9
   as critic's show, 28–30
   defence, rhetoric of, 83
   drunken dancing scenes, 77–8, *78*
   ensemble scenes, lack of, 32, *33*
   femininity characterisations, (Hannah and Marnie), 50–5
   feminism interpretive frame and, 68–9
   flood of thinkpieces on, 28
   fragmentation and omission in, 31–2
   How to Get Away with Murder compared to, 110
   intersectionality and, 70–1
   love triangles and decline of female friendships, 36–9
   male and female intimacies in bathroom scenes and contrasting masculinities, 60–5, *62*
   marriage and family, criticism of, 39
   masculinity characterisations (Adam and Ray), 55–60
   'Meeting the Guy while High' scenarios, 36
   metatexuality and, 27–8, 31
   millennial identity and, 27, 69, 71
   mumblecore and, 32–4
   narrative characteristics of thinkpiece seriality, 30–5
   narrative vastness and, 70
   network context of, 5
   plot repetitions, 35–40
   political television and, 147
   'Quality TV' and, 25–6
   racial representations, 71–4
   reality television and, 34
   sexuality, nudity, and gaze, 40–4
   stillness in, 41, 43–4
   temporal experimentation, lack of, 31
   ur-feminist impulse, postfeminist marketplace, and, 79–86
   viewer loving/hating binary, 71
   voice-overs, lack of, 32, 49–50

GLAAD, 134
Gomez, Stephanie, 114
Gonlin, Vanessa, 93, 120
Good Wife, The
   bisexuality in, 126, 132n12
   courtroom performances, 140
   female professionalism and, 115–18, 123
   female visual uniformity in, 132n2
   home vs. professional life in, 102
   judicial system, portrayal of, 138–9, 143, 149n6
Grace and Frankie, 145
Gramsci, Antonio, 56
Gray, Herman, 140, 147
Gray, Jonathan, 154
Grdešić, Maša, 71
Grey's Anatomy, 91, 107, 111n5, 125–6, 146
guilty pleasure, popular culture as, 25, 80, 105, 107, 230

Hagedorn, Roger, 13
hair care and hairstyles
   black female hair salons, 122
   in *How to Get Away with Murder*, 120–3
   in *Scandal*, 115, 121
Halberstam, Jack, 12
Hamad, Hannah, 86n2
Hämmerling, Christine, 14, 92, 107
Handmaid's Tale, The, 224n3
Haraway, Donna, 3
Harding, Sandra, 3
Hardwick, Chris, 156–7, 167, 169, 174n10, 177, 200
Harrigan, Pat, 14
Harris, Tamara Winfrey, 179
Havas, Julia, 118, 140
Hayward, Jennifer, 13
HBO 'Quality TV' campaign and canon, 25–6, 30, 70, 170
HBO's Girls *and the Awkward Politics of Gender, Race, and Privilege* (Mitchell and Shaw), 69
HBO's Girls*: Questions of Gender, Politics, and Millennial Angst* (Kaklamanidou and Talley), 69
hegemonic masculinity and femininity, 56–7, 65
Hemmings, Clare, 80

Her Story, 149n5
Hess, Amanda, 59
Hickethier, Knut, 13
Hills, Matt, 155, 198
hipster racism, 84n9
HIV status and portrayals, 134, 149n1
Hofmann, Viola, 116
Holden, Laurie, *159*, 191
Holmes, Anna, 72
homosexuality
  Annalise as 'not gay' in *How to Get Away with Murder*, 128–9
  'bury your gays' trope, 125
  family and, in *Girls*, 46n13
  'gay best friend' trope, 67n7
  Girls bathroom scenes and, 61, 63
  male gaze in *Girls*, homosexual, 42
  Post-closet TV, 35
  relationship between heterosexual and homosexual masculinity, 65
  see also bisexuality
horror, televisual, 155–6 see also *Walking Dead, The*
House of Cards, 132n3
How to Get Away with Murder
  about, 94
  alcohol and snacks as consumption loops, 106–10
  Annalise's house, 102–3
  Annalise's nicknames, 94
  Annalise's put togetherness and taking off, 118–20
  binge watching and, 97
  bisexuality and love triangle, 123–31
  black professional femininity, visual assemblages of, 114–23
  body politics of, 112n17
  broken legal/judicial system, extralegal violence, and cases of the week, 136–44
  client shot and jury-detective viewing position, 98–100, *99*
  courtroom scenes, 139–42
  crossover double-episode with *Scandal*, 121–2
  endorsement by Melania Trump, 145–7
  flash-forwards, flashbacks, and looped seriality, 95–6, 100–1
  Girls compared to, 110
  GLAAD reports and, 134
  hairstyles and black hair culture, 120–3

HIV-positive Oliver, 134
memes, GIFs, and internet humour, 102–6, *104*
narrative characteristics, 94–7
network context of, 5
outward spiral and, 113, 114
political television and branding, 124, 144–8
post-racial television and, 113–14
social media interactivity and second-screen viewing, 91–3
as television history in the making, 135
TGIT and, 91–2
tweets, number of, 111n3
victims actively involved in narratives, 101
#whodunnit, detective fiction, and, 97–101
Hu, Jane, 30
Huber, Linda, 105
Hunger (Gay), 79
Hurd, Gale Anne, 157, 160, 167
Hustvedt, Siri, 38
Huth, Denise, 160
Hyden, Steven, 29
hyperdrama, 94

identity politics
  Girls, feminism, and, 82
  How to Get Away with Murder and, 135–6, 148
  Peak TV and, 145
  political television and, 134
  Rhimes and, 146
  see also intersectionality; political television
imagined communities, 8, 14, 92, 93
Insecure, 73–4, 86n1
intersectionality, 3, 70–1, 222–3
intertextuality, 5, 9, 48, 158, 199, 202, 218–19 *see also* cultural types, characters as; paratexts
I Spit on Your Grave, 172
iZombie, 211

Jackson, Lauren Michele, 105
Jahn-Sudmann, Andreas, 30, 48
James, Kendra, 72, 74
Jamieson, Kathleen Hall, 115
Janssen, Famke, 123, 132n9
Joseph, Ralina, 146

Jowett, Lorna, 155
judicial/legal system, portrayals of
   The Good Wife, 138–9
   How to Get Away with Murder, 136–44

Kang, Angela, 162, 174n8
Kanzler, Katja, 123, 138–9
Karlyn, Kathleen Rowe, 76, 79
Karpovsky, Alex, 57
Kaufman, Andy, 58–9
Keaton, Buster, 64
Kelleter, Frank, 14–16, 18, 30, 40, 48, 154, 156, 176, 213, 222
Kinney, Emily, 167–8
Kirke, Jemima, 26, 87n8
Kirkman, Robert, 157–72, *159*, 195, 202, 205
Klein, Amanda Ann, 28
Knocked Up, 51
Konner, Jenni, 27
Kristeva, Julia, 214n5

Lagerwey, Jorie, 118
LA Law, 116
Landgraf, John, 44n1
Last House on the Left, The, 172
Latour, Bruno, 16
legal system *see* judicial/legal system, portrayals of
Lehman, Katherine, 36
Lesniak, Britta, 14–15
'Letter Hacks', 162–8, 172, 190–1
Leyda, Julia, 95, 97, 118, 205
Lindelof, Damon, 169
Little Women (Alcott), 57–8, 64
Loock, Kathleen, 14, 30, 176
looped seriality
   alcohol and snacks as consumption loops, 106–10
   Arrested Development and, 95
   binge-watching and, 97
   Eco's loop-series, 111n6
   the loop metaphor, 95
   memes, GIFs, and internet humour, 102–6, *104*
   temporal markers and rippling, 96–7
   Twitter's looped logic, 111n8
   #whodunnit and temporal unreliability, 97–101
   see also Twitter

Lotz, Amanda, 56, 182
love triangles
   in *Girls*, 36–9
   in *How to Get Away with Murder*, 123, 127–31
L Word, The, 133n13

Ma, Roger, 198
Maase, Kaspar, 144–5
McCann, Hannah, 147
McDermott, Catherine, 49
McDonald, CeCe, 137
McDonald, Jordan, 126
McFarlane, Megan, 114
McGorry, Matt, 146
McNutt, Miles, 42
McRobbie, Angela, 81
Mad Men, 115, 170
male gaze, 40–1 *see also* gaze, objectifying
Mamet, Zosia, 26, 87n8
Married at First Sight, 39
Martin, George R. R., 158
Mary Tyler Moore Show, The, 66n2
masculinities
   bachelor pad in *Girls*, 63
   the carousel and, 48, 49
   drinks and, 108
   exaggerated hypermasculinity performance in *Talking Dead*, 167, 175
   female, 55
   Girls bathroom scenes and, 60–5
   Girls characterisations and male girlhood, 55–60
   Hardwick and, 157
   hegemonic, 56–7, 65
   heterosexual and homosexual, relationship between, 65
   law profession in *How to Get Away with Murder* and, 115
   objectifying gaze and, 44
   physicality of actors and, 204
   Post-closet TV and, 35
   'Quality TV' canon and, 26
   rape-revenge, slasher films, and masculinisation/demasculinisation, 172
   reliable, in *Girls*, 53
   showrunners, authority, and, 158

survival assumptions in *The Walking Dead*, 175–6
The Walking Dead characterisations, 182–3, 186, 188
zombie survivalism and, 195–6
Master of None, 86n1, 145
Mayer, Ruth, 100
Mazzara, Glen, 158, *159*, 160–1
Mean Girls, 38
memes
  black, 106
  defined, 102
  How to Get Away with Murder and, 102–3, *104*, 106
metatexuality
  Girls and, 27–8, 31, 35, 77, 84–6
  How to Get Away with Murder and, 97
  thinkpiece seriality and, 30–1
  ur-feminist impulse and, 84
#MeToo movement, 223n1, 224n3
millennial identity, 27, 69, 71
Miller, Taylor Cole, 132n12
Mills, Brett, 75
Misadventures of an Awkward Black Girl, The, 86n4
Mittell, Jason, 14, 101, 153–4, 170, 188
Mizejewski, Linda, 53, 76
Modleski, Tania, 80–1
Mogk, Matt, 197–8, 200, *201*
Molina-Guzmán, Isabel, 147
Monk-Payton, Brandy, 106
Moore, Tony, 173n7
Morgan, Jeffrey Dean, *159*
motherhood *see* family
Mulvey, Laura, 40–1
mumblecore, 32–4
Murray, Rona, 76

Nakamura, Lisa, 106
narrowcasting, progressive, 134–5, 148
Negra, Diane, 55, 118, 205
neoliberalism *see* survivalism discourses, neoliberal
Nicotero, Greg, 157, 158, 162, 167
Night of the Living Dead, 177, 196
Nilsen, Sarah, 179
Nowalk, Peter, 100, 110n1, 132n8
nudity, in *Girls*, 40–4, *43*
Nussbaum, Emily, 68, 71, 72, 74, 165, 213

Obama, Barack, 216
Obama, Michelle, 117
Obaro, Tomi, 74
objects, practico-inert, 8–9
Ochs, Robyn, 126–7
omissions
  carousel gendering and, 47
  in *Girls*, 31–2, 40
  operational aesthetic and, 49, 170–1
Orange Is the New Black, 134, 145, 149n5
O'Sullivan, Peter Padraic, 175, 191, 212
O'Sullivan, Sean, 13
outward spiral *see* spiral gendering and the outward spiral
Oz, 26

palimpsest gendering
  about, 176, 219
  antagonistic wives and incompetent female warriors, 186–93
  strength, gendered and racialised, 177–86
  zombie bodies and, 212
paratexts
  authorised, 155
  concept of, 155
  Davis's Emmy acceptance speech, 135
  How to Get Away with Murder and drinks and snacks as, 107
  Rhimes and, 146
paratext seriality of *The Walking Dead*
  about, 153–5
  'Letter Hacks', 162–8, 172, 190–1
  management of multi-authorship, 156–62
  merchandise and consumerism, 200–3
  online tests and polls, 199–200
  palimpsest gendering and, 176
  recurrence and, 213
  sexualised violence depictions and, 168–73
  Talking Dead, 156–62, *159*, 167, 173n3, 197, 200
  zombie literacy, guidebooks, and survival guides, 197–200
parenting theme in *The Walking Dead*, 187
Parody, Clare, 156
Paskin, Willa, 71–2

Patterson, Natasha, 212
Peak TV, 26, 145
Penny, Laurie, 70, 74
performance, defined, 10 see also gender performances
Perkins, Claire, 76
Petersen, Anne Helen, 52
Platts, Todd, 200
Poe, Edgar Allan, 210
political television
    bisexuality in *How to Get Away with Murder* and, 124
    broken legal/judicial system in *How to Get Away with Murder*, 136–44
    commercial interests and, 145
    commercialisation of political debates, 221–2
    Dow on role of critique and, 215
    GLAAD reports, 134
    politicalness and branding of, 144–8
    progressive narrowcasting, 134–5, 148
    serial vs. reality or comedy television, 216–17
    social movements, trivialisation of, 143
    special episodes, 145
    The Walking Dead and, 200, 208
politics *see specific topics, such as* feminism, racial representation, or universality and specificity discourse
polyamory
    in *Girls*, 33
    in *How to Get Away with Murder*, 127, 131
    in *The Walking Dead*, 180–1, 183
Poniewozik, James, 28
popular culture
    defined, 2, 4
    feminist identity and politics, conflation of, 81–2, 83
    gender as, 17
    gendered and racialised entanglements with politics, 216
    as guilty pleasure, 25, 80, 105, 107, 230
    neoliberal, and radical criticism, 149
    the political and, 144–5
    postfeminist, 85–6
Popular Seriality: Aesthetics and Practice, 4
pornography, 41–4, 59, 84, 103
Post-closet TV, 35

postfeminism
    concept of, 81
    Girls and, 55, 69
    popular culture, postfeminist, 85–6
    ur-feminist impulse in *Girls* and postfeminist marketplace, 79–86
post-racial ideology
    accountability, notion of, 141
    How to Get Away with Murder and, 113–14, 141
    The Walking Dead and, 179, 208
practice-focused approach, 1–2, 217
Pramaggiore, Maria, 127
Prasad, Pritha, 92
Prepper/Survivalist Forum, The, 201
pretty girl privilege, 52, 54–5
professional femininity, black, 114–23
progressive narrowcasting, 134–5, 148
Projansky, Sarah, 169
Pye, Danee, 175, 191, 212

'Quality TV' canon
    demographic of, 45n7
    Girls and, 30
    HBO promotional campaign, 25–6
    intersectionality and, 70
    lack of diversity in, 135
    sexualised violence in, 170
    white cis-male showrunners and, 153
queer commodification, 132n11
queer studies, 11–12

racial representations
    bisexuality and, 125–6
    black professional femininity, visual assemblages of, 114–23
    controlling images of black women, 114, 126, 177–80
    digital blackface, 105–6
    emotionality and, 106
    in *Girls*, 71–4
    hipster racism, 84n9
    the hypersexual black woman, 179
    the 'magical negro', 74, 180
    sexualised violence and, 169–70
    the strong black woman, 177–8
    universality and, 74
    see also Black Twitter; colourblindness; post-racial ideology

Rae, Issa, 73–4
rape-revenge genre, 172–3, 179 *see also* violence, sexualised
Reading Lena Dunham's Girls (Nash and Whelehan), 69
reality television
   GIFs from, 105
   Girls and, 32, 34, 39
   Married at First Sight, 39
   thinkpiece seriality and, 31
   Trump and, 215–16
recurrence, 213
recursivity, 16, 18
Reedus, Norman, *159*, 183
refraction, 114
Reifenberger, Julia, 172
remaking as second-order serialisation, 176
repetition
   binge-watching and, 97
   Butler on, 10
   the carousel and, 65
   gender rule-breaking and, 18
   GIFs and, 105
   How to Get Away with Murder and, 109
   internet humour and, 102
   long-running series and recurrence, 213
   paradox of newness vs., 13
   plot repetitions in *Girls*, 35–40
   as postmodern queer method, 12
   television and, 1
   The Walking Dead and, 155
   see also carousel gendering
Rescue Me, 170
Resident Evil, 203
resilience discourse, 204–5
Rhimes, Shonda, 5, 73, 91, 100, 107, 122, 135, 146, 153
rippling narrative style, 96–7
Robinson, Phoebe, 121
Rodriguez, Amanda, 193
Romero, George A., 158, 190, 198, 200, 208
Roof, Judith, 10–11, 16, 50, 222
Rosenberg, Alyssa, 76
Roth, LuAnne, 203
Ru Paul's Drag Race, 223n2
Ruthven, Andrea, 205
Ryan, Maureen, 72, 147

San Filippo, Maria, 42, 60, 126, 128
Sartain, Jeffrey, 181
Sartre, Jean-Paul, 7–8
Sattar, Atia, 202
Saxena, Jaya, 108
Scandal
   colourblindness and, 114
   crossover double-episode with *How to Get Away with Murder*, 121–2
   food and drink consumption and, 107–9
   hairstyles, 115, 121
   professional femininity and, 118
   refraction and, 114
   representation, recognition, and, 147
   setting, 111n5
   social justice and, 146
   stylistic and narrative features, 94–5
   #TGIT and, 91
   Twitter and, 93, 111n3, 121
Schippers, Mimi, 38, 56, 65
Scott, Suzanne, 156–7, 160, 161
second-screen viewing, 92–3
Seitz, Matt Zoller, 74
self-reflection, authorial, 165–6, *166*, 174n11
Sense8, 149n5
Sepinwall, Alan, 71
serial collectives
   accountability and, 10
   awareness of, 17–18
   gender as, 2, 8
   Young on, 7–9
seriality, in gender studies, 7–12
seriality studies, 12–18, 222
serial narratives, fundamental characteristics of, 12
serial outbidding, 48
serial television see *Girls*; *How to Get Away with Murder*; *Walking Dead, The*
series
   defined, 13
   Sartre on group vs., 7–8
   series/serials binary, 13
   Young on gender as, 7–9
Sex and the City
   apartments in, 63
   culture figure of 'the girl' and, 49
   Girls compared to, 32, 39, 48
   political naïvety of, 215
   postfeminism and, 81

sexposition, 42
sexuality
  asexuality in *The Walking Dead*, 183–4
  Girls and, 40–4
  the hypersexual black woman stereotype, 179–80
  see also bisexuality; homosexuality; polyamory
Shapiro, Stephen, 211
Shifman, Limor, 105
Shoults, Kate, 203
showrunners
  authorship and, 153–4, 158
  female, 27, 45n3, 68, 73, 173n1
  as figure, 153, 173n1
  male, 70
  steward, 161–2, 167, 173n6
  see also Dunham, Lena; paratext seriality of *The Walking Dead*; Rhimes, Shonda
Siff, Maggie, 189
Singleton, IronE, 167
situatedness, 3–4
slacker as cultural figure, 50–2
soap opera genre, 14, 96, 107, 131
social activism *see* political television
Society, Science, Survival: Lessons from AMC's The Walking Dead (online course), 198
Soller, Bettina, 14
Sons of Anarchy, 164, 188–9
Sopranos, The, 26, 70, 170, 224n3
specificity and universality *see* universality and specificity discourse
Spigel, Lynn, 106–7
spiral gendering and the outward spiral
  about, 113–14, 219
  black professional femininity, visual assemblages of, 114–23
  serialised bisexuality and love triangles, 123–31
Stanley, Alessandra, 91
Stein, Daniel, 154, 163
Stern, Howard, 76
Stieger, Kay, 169
strength, gendered and racialised, 177–86
Sugar Hill, 179
Summer Without Men, The (Hustvedt), 38

survivalism discourses, neoliberal
  about, 195–6
  physicality, resilient bodies, and zombie workouts, 203–7
  suicide and alternative narratives of survival failure, 207–13
  survival failure and gender, 196–7
  zombie literacy vs. zombie consumerism, 197–203

tableau staging, 98–9
Talking Dead, 156–62, *159*, 167, 173n3, 197, 200
Tambor, Jeffrey, 149n5
Tasker, Yvonne, 204
Tatort, 107
tattoos, 86n5
Taylor, Anthea, 86n2
temporalities
  Arrested Development and, 95
  Girls, lack of temporal experimentation in, 31
  How to Get Away with Murder and, 95
  queer, 11–12
  The Walking Dead and, 156
  see also flashbacks and flash-forwards; looped seriality
#TGIT (ABC)
  about, 91–2
  black hair and colourblindness, 121–3
  drinks and snacks as consumption loops, 106–10
  interracial relationships in, 133n17
  post-racialism and, 143–4
  sexual orientation and, 125–6
  stylistic and narrative features of, 94–5
thinkpiece seriality
  Girls plot repetitions and, 35–40
  narrative characteristics of, 30–5
  'Quality TV' canon and, 25–6
  sexuality, nudity, and gaze in *Girls* and, 40–4
  thinkpiece, defined, 29
  universality vs. specificity and, 68, 71
Thomas, Deborah, 43
Tiny Furniture (Dunham), 26, 32
Torn Apart, 213n2
trans actors, 149n5
trans characters and representation, 137–8
Transparent, 134, 145, 149n5

Trump, Donald, 215–16
Trump, Melania, 145–7
Turner, Sarah E., 179
Twilight, 52
Twitter
    about, 110n2
    alcohol and snacks as consumption loops, 106–10
    bisexuality in *How to Get Away with Murder* and, 123–5, 128–9
    Black Twitter, 92, 93, 109, 148
    digital blackface, 105–6
    hashtag activism, 148
    #HTGAWM, #DatMurda, and #TGIT, 93
    looped logic of, 111n8
    memes, GIFs, and internet humour, 102–6, *104*
    #MeToo movement, 223n1, 224n3
    number of tweets, 111n3
    Scandal and, 93, 111n3, 121
    second-screen viewing, 92–3
    taking off/reveal in *How to Get Away with Murder* and, 119–20
    TGIT, social media interactivity, and, 91–2
    typical reactions on, 93
    #whodunnit and temporal unreliability, 97–101

universality and specificity discourse
    about, 68
    body politics in *Girls* and, 75–9
    feminist frame for *Girls* and, 68–70
    intersectionality and, 70–1
    millennial identity and, 69, 71
    racial representation in *Girls* and, 71–4
    ur-feminist impulse, postfeminist marketplace, *Girls*, and, 79–86
    vastness and, 70
UnREAL, 224n3
unruly femininity, 77–9
Upadhyaya, Kayla Kumari, 137
ur-feminist article as genre, 80–5
ur-feminist impulse, 79–86

VanDerWerff, Emily, 72
vastness, narrative, 70
Villarejo, Amy, 1, 12

violence, sexualised
    Girls and, 59–60
    in serial television, 170
    'survivor' label and, 208–9
    The Walking Dead and, 168–73, 208–9
voice-overs
    lack of in *Girls*, 32, 49–50
    Zombieland, 206

Wade, Lisa, 18
Walking Dead, The
    author function and, 154
    authorial power to kill, 164–8
    comic book, 154, 156, 163–5, 169–72, 180–1, 187, 190–4
    comic book editors, 174n10
    disliked female characters (Lori, Andrea), 186–93
    fan-favourite characters (Michonne, Carol, Daryl), 177–86
    gender roles, question of, 175–6
    as hybrid horror-melodrama, 155
    kill scores, 203
    'Letter Hacks', 162–8, 172, 190–1
    multi-authorship and *Talking Dead*, 156–62, *159*
    narrative vastness and, 70
    network context of, 5
    physicality of actors and resilient bodies, 203–7
    prepper viewers, 201–2
    props and signature weapons, 171n12, 203, 214n3
    sexualised violence and rape-revenge narrative, 168–73
    suicide and alternative narratives of survival failure, 207–13
    survival failure and gender, 196–7
    temporality and franchise storytelling, 156
    tweets, number of, 111n3
    writer demographics, 174n8
    zombie characters and gender, 211–12
    zombie literacy vs. zombie consumerism, 197–203
Walking Dead Wiki, The, 171
Wardrip-Fruin, Noah, 14
Warhol, Robyn, 13–14, 95, 97
Warm Bodies, 211
Warner, Kristen, 49, 121

warrior women, white, 177
Waters, Melanie, 59
Watson, Elwood, 73
Weiss, D. B., 158
Weitz, Rose, 80
Wescott, Alex, 51
West, Candace, 9–10, 18
What Gender Is, What Gender Does (Roof) *see* Roof, Judith
Whelehan, Imelda, 85
Wiele, Lisanna, 13
wife characters, viewer perceptions of (*The Walking Dead*), 188–9
Williams, Allison, 52, 54, 87n8
Williams, Apryl, 93, 120
Williams, Evan Calder, 212
Williams, Linda, 103

Wire, The, 26, 156
Woods, Faye, 71, 72
work-nets of agency, 16–17, 155
WTF-plot points, 94, 125, 130

Xena: Warrior Princess, 177

Yeun, Steven, 164, 167
Yoshino, Kenji, 126
Young, Iris Marion, 7–9, 18

Zeisler, Andi, 82
Zimmerman, Don H., 9–10, 18
zombie genre, 155–6, 158, 173n3 see also *Walking Dead, The*
Zombieland, 206
Zombie Research Society, 197–8

EU representative:
Easy Access System Europe
Mustamäe tee 50, 10621 Tallinn, Estonia
Gpsr.requests@easproject.com